D1242364

Franz Grillparzer

PLAYS ON CLASSIC THEMES

Also translated by Samuel Solomon

The Complete Plays of Jean Racine

Pierre Corneille: Seven Plays

Franz Grillparzer

by M. M. Daffinger

PHOTO: COURTESY OF AUSTRIAN NATIONAL LIBRARY

RANDOM HOUSE · *New York*

Franz Grillparzer

PLAYS *on* CLASSIC THEMES

Translated into English Verse

and with a

Biographical Appreciation and Notes by

SAMUEL SOLOMON

9 8 7 6 5 4 3 2

Library of Congress Catalog Card Number: 72-85607

Manufactured in the United States of America
by H. Wolff Book Manufacturing Co.

Book design by Mary M. Ahern

FIRST PRINTING

To
my daughter,
Celia

CONTENTS

The titles of the plays in the original are: *Sappho*, *Das Goldene Vliess: I Der Gastfreund, II Die Argonauten, III Medea,* and *Des Meeres und der Liebe Wellen.*

FOREWORD

"For about a generation now, Franz Grillparzer has won a secure place in the gallery of world literature. He is incontestably regarded as one of the greatest dramatic poets of all times and nations. He has become a classic. He has conquered the schools, even abroad. He has been translated into many languages. In French, Italian, English, Swedish, there are good books on his life and his works. In America, as in Europe, he is the subject of the most zealous, devoted research. His fame continues to spread."

Thus August Sauer wrote in Vienna, in December 1909—thirty-seven years after Grillparzer's death—in the opening paragraph of his Introduction to Volume I of the standard critical forty-three volumed (Vienna 1909–1948) edition of Franz Grillparzer's collective works of which he, together with Reinhold Backmann, were the chief editors.

If such was the estimation of his devoted, posthumous editor, his contemporary classic, the renowned Byron—acclaimed by Goethe himself as a prince of poets—was sufficiently carried away after reading Grillparzer's *Sappho* to prognosticate a little rashly in his diary (January 12, 1821) that posterity would now have to learn to pronounce the author's "devil of a name," a name of which Grillparzer himself, with his hypersensitive ear, was so ashamed, that he refused to have it displayed on the playbills even of *Sappho!*

If, after the lapse of a century and a half, Byron's prognostication has hardly yet been realized, August Sauer's estimation has in one respect at least proved valid. For while it was within fifteen years of the publication of Sauer's pronouncement that the present translator, as a schoolboy at Clifton, was first introduced to Grillparzer—*Sappho,* of course, for which ever since he has retained a soft spot—it was more than a generation later, indeed as recently as May 1967, on a visit to his school as a very old boy, that he found the boys in the upper German class studying Grillparzer's *Des Meeres und der Liebe Wellen.*

Ever since my schooldays I have desired to make Grillparzer —certainly the greatest Austrian dramatist, and one of the greatest truly *dramatic* poets of the German tongue—better known; and if this volume goes only a little way in the English-speaking world in furthering Byron's prognostication, I shall feel my labors amply rewarded.

In a single volume of selected plays for a non-German public, the choice of Grillparzer's five Grecian plays seemed, out of his dramatic corpus of some fifteen plays, almost self-indicated, for not only are the plays in this volume among Grillparzer's finest —and they certainly contain the greatest of his feminine creations, all smitten with the fever of love, in which, like Racine, he is preeminent—but also they have a more universal appeal than his other plays. While in Germany, and particularly in Austria, his historical tragedies are most highly regarded—especially *König Ottokars Glück und Ende* and the posthumously performed *Ein Bruderzwist in Habsburg*—it is inevitable that when performed abroad their merits, firmly based at home on German, and even more on Austrian dynastic patriotism, are diminished and their defects enhanced by that very circumstance. As for instance, while Shakespeare's *Richard II,* with John of Gaunt's:

> This royal throne of kings, this sceptred isle,
> This precious stone set in the silver sea

can never fail to move a British audience, and to film over some of the defects in that play, it is likely to have less appeal abroad.

In translating Grillparzer, I have more or less strictly followed the meter adopted by Grillparzer—normally the iambic pentameter of ten or eleven syllables, with occasional lines of twelve syllables or less than ten with which Grillparzer sometimes varies the general flow with considerable dramatic effect. On very rare occasions a rhyme appears, almost accidentally, like some exotic seasoning, there being about a dozen rhymes altogether in the five plays in this volume, as in the original. Only in the free rhythms that Grillparzer has adopted in *The Golden Fleece* to distinguish the speech of the barbarian Colchians from the Greeks have I decided not to be slavishly free, but at liberty to adopt free rhythms that seemed to me more natural in English.

For my work in this volume I have relied on three editions of Grillparzer, generally referred to in the footnotes for the sake of brevity as the Vienna, Berlin and Munich editions.

The Vienna edition is, of course, the forty-three volumed standard critical edition of Franz Grillparzer's collective works, *Sämtliche Werke,* commissioned by the City of Vienna—custodian of the Grillparzer archives—and edited by August Sauer and Reinhold Backmann (published by Anton Schroll & Co., Vienna).

Sappho appears in Volume I, edited by August Sauer, 1909. *Das Goldene Vliess, The Golden Fleece* trilogy, appears in Volume II, edited by Reinhold Backmann, 1913, and *Des Meeres und der Liebe Wellen, The Waves of Sea and Love,* appears in Volume IV, edited by Reinhold Backmann, 1925.

The Berlin edition is the three-volumed edition of Franz Grillparzer's *Dramatic Masterworks* (*Dramatische Meisterwerke*) which, curiously enough, omits *Libussa* and *Ein Bruderzwist in Habsburg* on the ground they were seldom performed, in favor of the unfinished *Esther,* because of its famous love scene—published by the Deutsche Bibliothek in Berlin (the editor's Introduction (Felix Rosenberg) is dated 1923). The text of this edition relies on the editions published in Grillparzer's lifetime, rather than on the manuscripts preferred by the Vienna edition, of which, at the time of the Deutsche Bibliothek in Berlin edition, only Volumes I and II were already out.

In their slight but not altogether negligible divergence, I have sometimes followed the one and sometimes the other, generally indicating my preference in footnotes. Only in *The Argonauts* there is no divergence. Grillparzer's refusal to allow a collective edition of his works in his lifetime is the cause of these discrepancies.

The Munich edition is the recent four-volumed, Carl Hanser edition of Franz Grillparzer's collective works—*Sämtliche Werke,* edited by Peter Frank and Karl Pörnbacher; Volume I, 1960, Volume II, 1961, Volume III, 1964 and Volume IV, 1965. Its text follows faithfully the standard Vienna edition.

All translations of French and German poets, as well as translations from Grillparzer's other works found in the footnotes and other parts of this text, are my own versions.*

I should like to express my thanks to Dr. Gisela Lord, of Westfield College, University of London, for her valuable assistance in clearing up doubtful points in the German.

SAMUEL SOLOMON

London, September 5, 1968.

* The quotations of Racine are taken from *The Complete Plays of Jean Racine* (Random House, New York, and Weidenfeld & Nicolson, London); Corneille is quoted from *Piere Corneille: Seven Plays* (Random House, New York).

INTRODUCTION

A Biographical Appreciation

Franz Serafikus Grillparzer was born in Vienna on January 15, 1791, the same month that Wolfgang Amadeus Mozart had been born thirty-five years before, and the same year that Mozart was to die in Vienna, eleven months later. It would seem that the Fates, about to cut short the life of Austria's greatest musical dramatist, relented a little to compensate her with the birth of her greatest literary dramatist.* It was not altogether unconnected. For in the musical salon of Grillparzer's maternal grandfather, Christoph Sonnleithner, a dean of the Viennese Law Faculty, not only Mozart, but Haydn too, were frequent visitors. Indeed, so fond of music were the Sonnleithners that the house of Christoph's son, Ignaz, was to be graced by the first performance of many of Schubert's immortal songs.

It was thus at the cultural hub of Europe, in a city which was the creative center of an outpouring of music such as the world has never seen—Haydn, Mozart, Beethoven, Schubert—in a city it was Napoleon's aim to crush and which, on his final defeat, became the political cynosure of Europe, with the Congress of Vienna presided over by Metternich (whom Grillparzer in old age grew increasingly to resemble!), that Franz Grillparzer, "the German Shakespeare, a greater dramatist than others of his tongue"† was born and lived and died.

His father, Wenzl Grillparzer, of sturdy peasant stock, was a lawyer; strict, conservative and reserved, his word was his bond—a feature not without influence on the subject matter of

* Grillparzer's father recorded the birth in his wife's prayer book: "Today my son Franz was born, may God make him prosper to our joy and to our country's honor."

† Douglas Yates, *Franz Grillparzer,* Vol. I, p. 3 (Basil Blackwell, Oxford, 1946).

Grillparzer's comedy, *Weh dem, der Lügt* (*Woe to the Liar*), his last completed play to be performed in his lifetime just as it had inspired Grillparzer's second completed play, the one-act *Die Schreibfeder* (*The Pen;* 1807–09), for which—although it was never publicly performed and was not published till the Cotta (Stuttgart) edition of his collective works in 1887—Grillparzer nevertheless had a soft spot.*

The Napoleonic Wars had impoverished Dr. Wenzl Grillparzer, never very affluent, and the French occupation of Austria had aggravated in his patriotic heart the ravages of illness, to which he succumbed on November 10, 1809, leaving his eldest son, Franz, now barely nineteen years of age, to care for his widow and his three younger sons.

Grillparzer's mother, Anna Franziska Sonnleithner, was nervous, unmethodical and untidy. Imaginative and passionately fond of music, she tried to instruct Franz in it, inflicting on him through her lessons, as he himself states, "the torture of my boyhood!"

At the age of six, Franz was sent to a private school, where he made little progress except that his love of reading continued his course in self-education. When he was eight, he received private tuition till his father, in 1800, succeeded in bribing the entrance examiner to admit him to the second year's class at the Gymnasium. For four years he made indifferent progress, since he had never been adequately grounded in the elements of any nonliterary subject, but he managed nonetheless to secure a certificate admitting him to a sort of finishing course at the University of Vienna.

At the University, Grillparzer's literary talents came to light, and much encouraged by his friends, in particular Georg Altmütter, whose admiration and stimulus gave Grillparzer that self-confidence which his shy and self-mistrustful temperament greatly needed, he went on to compose a number of works, all of which have remained fragments except four: *Die Unglücklichen Liebhaber,* a one-act skit on his professors, written at the age of fifteen (1806); *Die Schreibfeder* (1807–09); the inordinately long, five-act verse tragedy, *Blanka von Kastilien* (1808–09), influ-

*Tagebuch 12 and 21 (1808).
Tagebuch (diary) will hereafter be abbreviated Tgb.

enced by Schiller's *Don Carlos,* first performed only a few years ago, a century and a half later, on September 26, 1958, at the Wiener Volkstheater;* and the one-act rhyming comedy, *Wer Ist Schuldig? (Who Is Guilty?)* 1811. The last three were first published in the Cotta (Stuttgart) edition of 1887. The first had to await the "historical critical" Vienna edition of 1909–1948 to see the light of publication.

At the University, Grillparzer, doubtless to please his father, who frowned on his literary endeavors, studied law and succeeded in securing his university certificate, though he never practiced law. His father's outward harshness, despite his secret partiality for his "favorite" eldest son, a harshness that had persisted even on his deathbed, when he turned his back on the weeping Franz, saying that his affection was now "too late," left a permanent scar on the sensitive poet, and, combined with his horror at the instability inherited from his mother, was to warp him for the rest of his life, to rob him of domestic happiness, and was doubtless also responsible for that blind spot in his mental and moral attitude that was to prove fatal in his dealings with the opposite sex, marring at times even his greatest work.**

Forced, by his father's death, to earn his living in his penultimate year at the University, he secured part-time occupation as tutor to two young gentlemen, who paid him liberally enough to allow him to support not only himself, but also part of his dependent family. In 1812, with the end of his studies, he accepted a position as law tutor to the nephew of the Count von Seilern, whose gluttony was later to be caricatured in *Weh dem, der Lügt.* But most valuable to Grillparzer was his access to the count's library, where Shakespeare's works, in the original, and in Schlegel's excellent translations,*** were first included in his avid reading. This was further stimulated by his employment in February 1813 as unpaid apprentice in the Vienna *Hofbibliothek*

*The manuscript had been rejected by the Burgtheater in 1810, with damaging results to Grillparzer's self-confidence.

**On the other hand, it was also his father's tenacity, which Franz inherited, that stood him in good stead, and despite thoughts of suicide when in acute depression, ensured his survival to a ripe old age.

***Grillparzer's previous knowledge of Shakespeare had been imbibed through Eschenburg's inadequate prose versions.

(Court Library) where, with Calderon, the great Spanish writers "swam into his ken." In the summer he accompanied the Seilern family to their country estates; there, in autumn, he fell seriously ill. The disease was diagnosed as contagious, and he was abandoned by them in a local quack's cottage. He reappeared in Vienna, and the subsequent cure under his mother's and family doctor's loving care was deemed miraculous.

Upon recovery, Grillparzer continued teaching for a livelihood, together with his unpaid occupation at the Court Library, which greatly furthered his general education and gave him that wide knowledge of the great achievements of many foreign cultures that, combined with his psychological perception, was to make him one of the best critical minds of his age.

At the end of 1813, he entered the Civil Service. In various capacities he served, not very happily, till in 1832 he attained the position of Archive Director of the Court Chamber. In 1856, at the age of sixty-five, he retired on pension from the Civil Service.

Although a thoroughly loyal servant of the Crown, Grillparzer's independence of spirit—the birthright of every poet—accorded ill with the cramped atmosphere of Metternich's repressive Austria; and Grillparzer's lofty idea of the poet's vocation, which he fancied entitled him to privileges outside the common run, was not calculated to endear him to his colleagues and seniors in the Civil Service. He found time to continue to read extensively, and added the Greek classics to his foreign "conquests." Provoked by Schlegel's translations of Calderon, he attempted to improve on him, and painstakingly translated half of the first act of *La Vida es Sueño* (*Life Is a Dream*), following the rhyming meter of the original. This exercise, by one of those twists of fate which Grillparzer loved casually to illustrate in his plays, was to be the means that was to lead to his first success.

In June 1816, Josef Schreyvogel's translation of Calderon's *La Vida es Sueño* was performed at the Hofburgtheater, where he was director (*Hoftheatersekretär*). Hebenstreit, an adversary of Schreyvogel, took advantage of a publication of Grillparzer's version side by side with Schreyvogel's, in the *Wiener Modezeitung,* to denigrate the latter's dramatic ability. Grillparzer had not been consulted, and when Schreyvogel informed the poet how mortified he was that a son of his former friend should have treated him so shabbily, Grillparzer was able to explain his innocence. This led to a most fruitful relation between the two men, beginning with their first meeting in June 1816, and lasting till the death of the older man in 1832.* It was Schreyvogel, who, hearing from Grillparzer his dramatic ideas (i.e., the outlines of *Die Ahnfrau*), encouraged him to proceed, saying, "The play is ready, all you need to do is to write it down." But Grillparzer, with his usual self-mistrust, now convinced he was no dramatist, continued to shilly-shally, and made no progress till August, when Schreyvogel mentioned that he himself had once been in a similar fix with Goethe, who had assured him that all one had to do to begin was to "blow in one's hand."

This exhortation of the great Goethe galvanized Grillparzer's sleeping spirits and set his dramatic genius in motion; and he promptly began to compose the first lines of the play which was soon to be completed. *Die Ahnfrau,* written in trochaic rhymed verse and extensively revised under Schreyvogel's guidance, was first performed on January 31, 1817, at the Theater an der Wien, and was a huge popular success, carrying Grillparzer's fame beyond Austria, into Germany. His name, about which he was so sensitive, he had taken pains to suppress on the playbills! In Grillparzer's lifetime the play was performed eighty-one times at the Burgtheater. Although it has lost its appeal for modern audiences, it is a powerful blood-and-thunder thriller with the guilty ancestral ghost hovering over her breed till they are blotted out in expiation.

In reaction against hostile criticism of *Die Ahnfrau,* Grillparzer, now determined to show he could write a tragedy in the best classical manner, composed *Sappho*. This, written within a month and performed in 1818, is his first acknowledged masterpiece, carrying his fame far beyond the bounds of the German lands with translations in Italian, English and French, following soon after publication, in 1819, 1820 and 1821 respectively.

*Grillparzer, in his autobiography (1853), speaks most warmly of Schreyvogel's "fatherly" treatment of him. The autobiography ends with the performance of *Des Meeres und der Liebe Wellen.*

In May 1818, as a result of the success of *Sappho,* Grillparzer was, with Schreyvogel's backing, appointed by Count Stadion, the Finance Minister, as dramatic poet to the Hofburgtheater for five years.

But meanwhile tragedy had already overtaken Grillparzer's personal life and brought him, like his heroine, from the poetic heights "where Aganippe roars" down

> ". . . into the suffocating valley,
> Where misery reigns and faithlessness and crime."
> (*Sappho, Vs. 944–45*)

In November 1817, his youngest brother, Adolph, aged seventeen, had drowned himself in the Danube, leaving a remorseful note with the ominous sentence: "If Franz should ever marry and have children, he should warn them that they should not resemble me."

Meanwhile, Grillparzer had become emotionally entangled with his cousin's wife, Charlotte von Paumgartten, and was guilty of the "faithlessness" toward his cousin Ferdinand of which his heroine, Sappho, complained. This had led to the "misery," based on self-reproach accentuated by the fact that in the interest of his art, as he saw it, he was determined to hold himself detached, and was therefore unable to give Charlotte as much as he took from her. He was using her as the prototype for his next heroine, Medea—he himself had been a prototype for both Sappho and Phaon—and he was resolved to extricate himself from her at the first suitable opportunity. His journey to Italy for several months in 1819, after his mother's suicide in a fit of religious mania, was as much an escape from Charlotte as a measure of recovery from the terrible blow* his mother's hanging had dealt him.

His labors with *The Golden Fleece* have been discussed at some length in the Translator's Note to that play, and need not be reiterated here. Suffice it to say that when *The Golden Fleece* —and especially *Medea,* the last play of the trilogy—was per-

* Grillparzer, fifteen years later, refers to his mother as "the guardian angel" of his life. (Autobiographical Fragment, 1834–35.)

formed at the Hoftheater in March 1821, Grillparzer had reached the summit of his tragic art.*

But with his artistic triumph came the breach with Charlotte, who had inspired it, and several years later on her deathbed—she died on September 16, 1827—she accused Grillparzer of being responsible for her decline. Grillparzer, with his usual honesty, records in his diary on the day of her death, "I have forsaken, ill-treated her. I have perhaps contributed to her death."

He was indeed *"un homme fatal,"* not that he was at all Don Juanesque. On the contrary, he even considered himself repugnant to look at. This, however, is not borne out by his likeness in his younger days and there is ample testimony from both sexes to his charm. Indeed, a young girl, Marie Piquot, appears literally to have pined and died of unrequited love for him—a circumstance that only came to Grillparzer's knowledge after her death. (Tgb. 1109, dated May 5, 1822.) It would seem that with all his perspicacity into the hearts of his women characters he kept his knowledge for his plays. In real life, due to his innate diffidence, he seems to have missed the obvious.

In the case of the great passion of his life, Marie von Smolenitz, the "heavenly beauty" who was the inspiration behind so many of his heroines—Erny, Hero, Rahel—and his ideal love in the sense that her beauty represented to him its own integrity unstained by any act of hers, he failed to realize from her "Hero" glance at him at the theatre, when she was in his rival Daffinger's company—the glance he sums up perfectly as, "One, two, three brief and everlasting moments"—that it was he, Grillparzer, whom she preferred. But plagued by his heredity and by the knowledge that he was seventeen years her senior, he did not dare to propose to her, and let the glib Daffinger, who was one

*Some German critics, like Walter Naumann (*Grillparzer, das Dichterische Werk,* W. Kohlhammer, Stuttgart, p. 14), and even Douglas Yates—otherwise so discerning—seem not to have appreciated the full greatness of *Medea,* which, however, continues to gain warm adherents in support of Schreyvogel's just contemporary estimation of its dramatic excellence. Its wider popularity, of course, is inevitably compromised by the grimness of the theme.

year *his* senior, bear off the prize. He did dare propose to the woman who remained faithful to him to the end, Katherina Fröhlich, whose letters evince the warmest affection for him, but he did not dare to marry her; although in 1849 he did, as a lodger, take up permanent residence with her and her sister till he died on January 21, 1872, leaving her his literary estate. She died seven years later, having in the meanwhile arranged for the publication of the first collective edition of his works in twenty volumes by Cotta (Stuttgart), edited by August Sauer.

Grillparzer's courtship of Kathi Fröhlich coincided with the happy time when he was composing the first of his great historical tragedies, *König Ottokars Glück und Ende.* The subject had interested him as early as 1818 when he wrote his verses, *Rudolf Und Ottokar,* covering the subject matter of the first act of the play.

The Golden Fleece had put the subject out of his mind, but the death of Napoleon in May 1821 brought once more before him the parallel between the fate of Napoleon and of Ottokar, both of whose fortunes took a downward turn after their second marriage in search of offspring to found a dynasty. After extensive studies of the sources, which give the play its richness in local color, Grillparzer eagerly took up the task of actual composition and wrote the play in a few weeks, during February and March 1823. But the censors sat on it for over a year, and if the empress did not happen to read the manuscript and warmly approve of the play, it would doubtless have remained in limbo for many more years.

The first performance, on February 19, 1825, was a spectacular success, but hostile criticisms were not wanting (the censors took care to suppress the favorable ones!), and the cloud of official stupidity continued to hang not only over this play, but also his next play, based on Hungarian history. This, *Ein Treuer Diener Seines Herrn,* was completed in December 1826. But Grillparzer did not hand it to the theatre till a year later, after Marie von Smolenitz had married his rival, Daffinger. For in this play too, as in *Ottokar,* the triangular relationship in which Grillparzer was personally involved was portrayed. The characterization of Erny, the wife of the hero, Bancbanus, "the loyal servant" of the Crown is, as is usual with Grillparzer's heroines, superb, and had she been the protagonist, the play, with her suicide to maintain her integrity, may have been an unqualified success. But as her husband is the protagonist, a protagonist who like Ottokar, turns, for reasons of State it would seem, a blind eye on a rival's advances to his wife—in the case of Ottokar, advances made blatantly in public—an air of unreality creeps in, as with so many of Grillparzer's men, and compromises the protagonist's essential hold on the sympathy of the audience. In the case of Ottokar, the author's evident partiality for Rudolf von Habsburg—the founder of the reigning Austrian dynasty—in the latter half of the play further compromises our interest in the protagonist and lessens the impact of the tragedy.

The Emperor himself graced three of the first performances of *Ein Treuer Diener Seines Herrn*—the premiere was received with enormous applause on February 28, 1828—but so brittle was his empire and so stupid his bureacracy, that he took fright at the seditious possibilities of this most loyal of plays and offered to buy up all the author's rights in order to suppress it! Although Grillparzer did not sell, he too, like his beloved Mozart before him, felt tempted to leave Austria to escape such lack of appreciation, not to say persecution, dating from his unfortunate poem *Campo Vaccino,* 1819, on which emperor and pope alike had frowned. But so great was his devotion to his fatherland that, except for brief journeys abroad, he never left.

His journeys began with the Italian tour of 1819—which had inspired the peccant *Campo Vaccino*—and included three to Germany in 1826, when he visited Goethe in Weimar, and again in 1836 and 1847; to France and England in 1836 when he met Heine in Paris; to Turkey and Greece in 1843. Visiting Sestos, the scene of the last play in this volume, on Monday, September 25, 1843, he imagined Aphrodite's Temple as it may have stood on a hillock by the seashore, studded with ruins, and living once more through all the emotions that had fashioned his masterpiece, with the sea the brightest of blues, he records in his diary, "I count today as one of the pleasantest of my life."

It is unnecessary to dwell further here on *Des Meeres und der Liebe Wellen,* first performed in 1831—as the Translator's Note to the play deals with it at some length. Once more its lack of immediate success disproportionately discouraged the author who, however, was clear-sighted enough to admit that his handling of the fourth act was partly responsible. But the deep emotion that he infused into his Hero's grief in the fifth act should have impressed his first audience, already enthusiastic over the first three acts, had the part been at all convincingly played.

Another disappointing outcome for the poet was the eventual performance of *Melusina,* his romantic opera, in Berlin in 1833, set by Conradin Kreutzer instead of Ludwig van Beethoven.

In 1823, when Grillparzer, with *Die Ahnfrau, Sappho, Medea* behind him and *Ottokar* completed, was the acknowledged leading dramatic poet of Austria, and when the success of Weber's romantic operas, held inferior by both Beethoven and Grillparzer, was considerable, Beethoven was induced to approach Grillparzer for a libretto, doubtless in order to achieve what it was thought would be the greatest opera of the age.

Beethoven's commission reached Grillparzer through Count Moriz Dietrichstein, the head of both the Court theatres (the Opera and the Burgtheater) and Grillparzer, without consulting Beethoven about the subject—Beethoven did not seem to mind—composed *Melusina* within a fortnight (March 15 to 23, 1823).* Beethoven apparently was sufficiently satisfied with the work to wish promptly to enter into a formal contract with Grillparzer. He had demurred to the opera's beginning with a huntsmen's chorus *à la* Weber and was pleased at Grillparzer's readiness to delete it. But although the composer more than once assured the poet of his intention to proceed, the work still remained unset on Beethoven's death. This negative outcome should not have surprised those who were aware of the agonies Beethoven—not unlike Grillparzer with his *Golden Fleece*—had experienced in bringing to fruition his sole opera, *Fidelio.* His genius had never been partial to opera, and still less in the last years of his life was it possible for him to descend to the human bondage of words, when his great spirit was already soaring among the sublime regions of the *Cavatina* in his B-flat major quartet (opus 130).

The personal relations between Grillparzer and Beethoven are

*He had been interested in the subject since 1817, the year he wrote *Sappho,* and *Melusina* has the same basic theme, the conflict between domestic happiness and artistic isolation.

of the greatest interest. Grillparzer tells us in 1844, in his *Erinnerungen an Beethoven* (*Recollections of Beethoven*), how as a boy of thirteen or fourteen he first saw Beethoven, twenty-one years his senior, along with Cherubini and the virtuoso Abbé Vogler, in his uncle Joseph Sonnleithner's musical salon. On one occasion when Beethoven was their neighbor in Heiligenstadt near Vienna, in the same house divided by a passage, his mother had stood in the passage at their door, rapt at the great man's piano playing, when suddenly Beethoven's door opened and he caught her listening. Such was his indignation that his piano lay untouched for the rest of their stay in Heiligenstadt, despite the earnest pleas of Grillparzer's mother, conveyed to him through his servant, that their door on the common passage would henceforth remain locked!

Even more illuminating a sidelight into Beethoven's gauche, naïve, but intensely warm character is offered by Grillparzer's account of their penultimate meeting, in Hetzendorf, where Beethoven had invited Grillparzer to see him, doubtless to make amends for his remissness with *Melusina.* Grillparzer was most cordially received and while Beethoven placed one bottle of wine before his own plate and that of Anton Schindler,* he placed no less than three before Grillparzer's. He further insisted on accompanying Grillparzer back in the public coach to the town, and when he took his leave of him at the city's gates, Grillparzer noticed he had left behind a little paper packet on his seat. When he called after Beethoven, Beethoven shook his head, laughed loudly and ran off in the opposite direction. On opening the packet Grillparzer found the exact fare for the journey. He accepted this sheepish gesture of atonement in the spirit it was meant, and laughingly paid the presented fare to the coachman!

In March 1827 when Beethoven lay dying, Grillparzer was approached by Schindler this time to compose his funeral oration. He was shocked at the commission, as he had not known of Beethoven's grave condition. He was halfway through the task when Schindler came once more to announce Beethoven's death (March 26). Grillparzer, who "truly loved Beethoven," burst into tears and felt he could no longer finish the composition in the mood he had previously envisaged. The oration was duly

* Schindler's biography of Beethoven appeared in 1840.

pronounced by the actor Anschütz at the cemetery gates, to which the mourners were relegated by the inclement weather and the irate ecclesiastical authorities at the graveside. Some months later Grillparzer was asked once more to compose the oration, on the occasion of the unveiling of Beethoven's tombstone, and in noble words he set the final seal on their relationship: "Rare are the moments of divine inspiration in this spiritually impoverished age. Sanctify yourselves! He who lies here was divinely inspired. Striving for the One, caring for the One, suffering for the One, devoting his all to the One, thus this man went on his life's way. He knew no wife, nor child; hardly any joy, few pleasures. If an eye vexed him, he tore it out and strode on, on, on to his goal. If we still have some sense of the whole in this riven age, let us muster by his grave."*

Grillparzer's last completed play† to be acclaimed in his lifetime was the dramatic fairytale in four acts, *Der Traum ein Leben* (*Dreaming Is Living*), in trochaic verse, first performed on October 4, 1834, with an ovation for the absent author. The first act had been composed as far back as 1817, after the completion of *Sappho,* but other labors did not allow him to take up the work again till 1826. Once more Grillparzer's old complaint of coming to a firm halt in midcomposition, which he suffered in *The Golden Fleece* and in *The Waves of Sea and Love,* gripped him in the last act of this play and prompted his oft-quoted declaration, "If one of my works is to succeed it must stand before me right from the beginning with the clearest inevitability" (Tgb. 1698, 1829). Drawing its subject matter from Voltaire's *Le Blanc et le Noir* and *Zadig,* and Calderon's *La Vida Es Sueño,* Grillparzer infused into the play his own imaginative charm in addition to the attractions of the Vienna

*There is a personal poignancy in this tribute of Grillparzer (uttered after Marie's marriage to Daffinger), who realized that Beethoven had achieved in his art through the sacrifice of domestic happiness what he, torn between art and domestic happiness, had failed to achieve in either.

†Although the later *Esther* was performed repeatedly in the last years of Grillparzer's life (the first performance was on March 29, 1869, in the old opera house in aid of needy students of the Vienna Academy of Commerce, followed by twenty performances at the Burgtheater), it has remained a fragment.

popular theatre—snakes, witches, princes and princesses. It was a favorite in Grillparzer's lifetime (with seventy-eight performances at the Burgtheater), and has many warm admirers today, some comparing it with Shakespeare's *A Midsummer Night's Dream.*

Grillparzer's last completed play to be performed in his lifetime was his sole full-length comedy, *Weh dem, der Lügt* (*Woe to the Liar*), in five acts of blank verse. Based on an account in Gregor of Tours' *Historia Francorum* (*History of the Franks*) of a young kitchen-hand who had rescued the Bishop of Chalons' nephew from "barbarian" captivity in the Rhineland, while strictly adhering to the bishop's injunction never to tell a lie, and in the process had won the "barbarian" count's charming daughter, Edrita, it is a delightful play showing Grillparzer's genuius in a lighter vein, of which Naukleros, in *The Waves of Sea and Love,* had already given us hints. This was the time when Grillparzer was attracted by Heloise Hoechner, supposedly the model for Edrita, and the inspiration for one of Grillparzer's most moving poems, "Entsagung" ("Resignation"—1836), where the poet, parting from her and overwhelmed by his emotions at the grave of Abélard and Héloïse in Paris, renounces his hopes both of fame and the joys of life which he had so long sacrificed for fame.

The first performance of *Weh dem, der Lügt* took place on March 6, 1838. Far from being amused, the aristocratic audience was furious. It was bad enough that the Germans should appear as "barbarians" compared with the Franks, but that Galomir, the son of the count of the Rhineland, should be portrayed as an idiot, was too much for the aristocracy of Vienna, who left the theatre, loudly slamming the doors of their boxes. After only four performances, the play—one of the more often performed of Grillparzer's plays today—closed. Grillparzer, like Racine after the reception of *Phèdre,* was now sick at heart of the theatre and its volatile public, and withdrew from the professional stage. Although he was to complete three more tragedies, these were firmly shut in his desk till his death.

The first of these is *Libussa.* As early as 1818, his researches into Ottokar had led Grillparzer to the Bohemian Libussa, and in 1822 he had noted the dramatic possibilities, but the first act was not completed till 1827 and the play, with which Grillparzer, despite its admirers, was fundamentally dissatisfied, was not resumed before 1831. Progress was very intermittent on a play, the heart of which the author deemed "dead," and it was not completel till 1847. The performance of the completed play after Grillparzer's death (the first act had been performed in aid of a charity in 1840) took place in January 1874, but met with little success, closing after six performances.

The next tragedy, *Ein Bruderzwist in Habsburg,* had interested Grillparzer many years earlier when he was contemplating a cycle of Austrian historical plays. In 1824 appear the first notes on the play, and a year later the outlines of Acts I and II. Composition began in 1828; the first act was finished in the autumn of that year, and the second act taken up.

But once more Grillparzer's old dread of inadequate inspiration seized him and halted the work. The play was not completed till 1848. Grillparzer remained dissatisfied and ordered in his will (December 7, 1848) that both *Libussa* and *Ein Bruderzwist* be destroyed.*

Yet the play is widely regarded in Austria as Grillparzer's masterpiece; and if outside Austria the history of the beginning of the end of the Habsburg dynasty is of less absorbing interest, the identification of the old Emperor Rudolf's disillusionment with Grillparzer's own disillusionment still gives the play a lyrical charm, similar to the fascination afforded by Corneille's like identification with Surenas, the hero of his last play, *Suréna,* and Shakespeare's identification with Prospero in *The Tempest.*

The first productions of *Ein Bruderzwist in Habsburg* in 1872 at two theatres in Vienna, the first performance on September 24, at the Stadttheater, followed by the first performance at the Burgtheater on the twenty-eighth, were both enthusiastically received, and by 1875 there were altogether twenty-nine performances.

As early as 1816, on reading Mariana's *History of Spain*—also one source of Corneille's *Le Cid*—Grillparzer noted in his diary (Tgb. 152) the theme of his last play, *Die Jüdin von Toledo* (*The Jewess of Toledo*). In 1824 he sketched the first

* He did not destroy them himself, perhaps hoping for fresh inspiration to revise them to his satisfaction.

outlines of the play and composed the opening lines in the Spanish trochaic meter, making notes on Lope de Vega's drama on the same theme. But steady composition was not taken up till 1839, after he had withdrawn from the professional theatre; the play, for the most part in iambic pentameter, was not finished before the summer of 1851 and extensively revised in the same decade. The first performance took place in Prague on November 21, 1872, followed by seven performances at the Burgtheater from January 21, the anniversary of Grillparzer's death, to March 6, 1873.

Although he wrote no more plays, Grillparzer continued to compose epigram after epigram in which his internal frustrations were expressed. Outwardly, he was the reigning prince of letters, not only of Austria but Germany, and kings and emperors showered congratulations and honors on him on the occasion of his seventy-fifth and eightieth birthdays. But the canker in his heart remained.

Almost a century now after Grillparzer's death, his fame as a dramatist, which in August Sauer's estimation, sixty years ago, had ranked him as "one of the greatest dramatic poets of all times and nations," remains assured. A recent television broadcast in Germany of *König Ottokars Glück und Ende* (*King Ottocar's Fortune and Fall*) received widespread acclaim, proving that Grillparzer's dramatic genius can pass the intimate test of the mass media.

Although as a lyric poet Grillparzer cannot compare with his great contemporaries Goethe, Heine or Hölderlin, not to mention more modern lyricists like Rilke, as a dramatic poet he stands unsurpassed by any in the German language and can now, with the lapse of time, look Goethe and Schiller squarely in the face, even though in 1826 on his visit to Weimar he evaded, panic-stricken, an invitation by the great Goethe to a tête-à-tête dinner! For although the transcendant poetic genius of Goethe puts Part I of *Faust,* as a literary creation, above anything that Grillparzer achieved, in purely dramatic terms Goethe is perhaps less convincing than Grillparzer the playwright at his best. As regards Schiller, perhaps *Wallenstein's Tod* (*Wallenstein's Death*) and possibly *Maria Stuart* can still compare with Grillparzer's best, but plays like *Don Carlos* and *Die Jungfrau von*

Orleans (*The Maid of Orleans*), rapturously received in their day, are found dramatically unconvincing by modern audiences. Of the other great German dramatic poets, perhaps Kleist alone has something of the intensity of Grillparzer at his greatest.

To achieve his dramatic ends, Grillparzer uses his verse medium most flexibly and with considerable, sometimes consummate, art. Much of the criticism of Grillparzer's dramatic verse is misplaced. His critics sometimes mistake for faults what, dramatically speaking, are virtues—the language, sometimes deliberately informal or vulgar, placed in the mouths of lesser characters such as Eucharis in *Sappho,* Aeetes in *The Golden Fleece,* or Menander (Hero's father) in *The Waves of Sea and Love,* serve but to underline their characters. Yet there is no denying, the blind spot that besets Grillparzer in viewing some of his male characters also occasionally creeps into his verse. He is overfond of simile, a figure of speech calculated to hold up the dramatic action, and although many of his similes are beautiful and dramatically apt, such as:

> It is the very magic power of love
> That it ennobles all that feels its breath,
> Just like the sun, whose golden rays divine
> Turn even the thunderclouds themselves to gold.
> (*Sappho, Vs. 355–58*)

some like Phaon's:

> When all my longings' winter caterpillars
> Play round me now like golden butterflies.
> (*Sappho, Vs. 493–94*)

may well be spared, not to mention the more elaborate comparison of Melitta—the charming maiden with the quiet mind—to a snail! (*Sappho,* Vs. 761–68.)

He is also overfond of the antithetic play of words, a dramatic defect shared by Goethe and Schiller which, although it makes one admire the cleverness of the poet constructing it, often detracts from the credibility of the character uttering it.

He is very partial also to chiasmus, but as he sometimes achieves the most dramatic effects with this, we need not cavil at an occasional excess. As an illustration of his highly successful use of chiasmus we may perhaps quote here a few lines from a passage that appears more fully in the Translator's Note to *The Waves of Sea and Love.* When Leander in the third act presses Hero to let him come again soon to see her, he expresses the intensity of his impatience thus:

> For should the sea not gulp me,
> I'll die of care, of anguish and of pain.
> Say: day after tomorrow, say in three days,
> Ah, next week say!

This shifting of his third "say" from the beginning of the sentence to the end makes his plea emotionally irresistible, as evinced by Hero's famous reply, "Then come again tomorrow."

In the Translator's Note to *Sappho,* some of Grillparzer's stylistic affinities with Racine,* that supreme master of dramatic style, are discussed. Apart from the interrogation and irony even more extensively used in *Medea* than in *Sappho,* Grillparzer shares with Racine the dramatically impressive use of ellipsis. Thus, once more, to take an example from a passage cited in the Translator's Note to *The Waves of Sea and Love,* when the High Priest in the fifth act, in order to hush up the scandal, tells Hero:

> May eternal silence bury what has happened.

Hero bursts out elliptically and dramatically most effectively:

> I, bury all my bliss and all my ruin
> And criminally join with criminals?
> I'll shout it out aloud through the wide world . . .

But above all Grillparzer, as a true Sonnleithner, most sensitive to music,† is like Racine, a very great artist in employing the sound of words—which, like Racine, too, he would love to

* Grillparzer had the highest regard for Racine, whom he considered as great a creative artist as has ever lived—"Racine, *ein so grosser Dichter als je einer gelebt hat.*" (Tgb. 3384, 1838.)

† Grillparzer describes in his diary how he would vibrate to a single musical note, like some untouched violin to the strings of a violin that was being plucked. (Tgb. 273, 1817). This was the year of *Sappho*—his heroine being summoned to the Gods by the breeze arousing the strings of her lyre.

recite aloud*—to the maximum dramatic effect. Sauer, in his Introduction to Volume I of the standard Vienna Edition, states categorically: "Grillparzer is the most musical poet that German literature knows," and preludes this by the passage: "If, till his advent, Music had reigned supreme among the Arts in Austria, Grillparzer wrested the wreath from her brow; further, in the rhythm and harmony of his dramatic verse, poesy melted with music into an indissoluble union."

Although no non-German should presume to enter too boldly into the battle of the German critical giants over the respective musical merits of the masters of German dramatic verse, there is much evidence than can be cited in support of Sauer. Three examples must suffice, one each from *Sappho, The Golden Fleece* and *The Waves of Sea and Love.*

In *Sappho,* when Phaon, confused in his emotions but already awakening to the charm of the virginal Melitta, views in experienced Sappho's company the evening falling on the seascape, he describes the scene thus, where alliteration, assonance and onomatopoeia combine to paint an exquisite picture:

> Es ist so schön hier, o, so himmlisch schön.
> Mit weichen Flügeln senkt der Sommerabend
> Sich hold ermattet auf die stille Flur,
> Die See steigt liebedürstend auf und nieder,
> Den Herrn des Tages braütlich zu empfangen,
> Der schön dem Westen zu die Rosse lenkt,
> Ein leiser Hauch spielt in den schlanken Pappeln,
> Die, kosend mit den jungfraülichen Säulen,
> Der Liebe leisen Gruss herüberlispeln!
> Zu sagen scheinen: Seht, wir lieben! Ahmt uns nach!
> (*Act III, Sc. i, Vs. 878–87*)

(A perfect passage except perhaps for the last line where the last three words seem discordant, not indeed because of the two extra syllables which add flexibility, but because the vowel sounds of "Ahmt" and "nach," although in assonance with "sagen," still seem to offer too sharp a contrast to the rest.)

> Here is such beauty, ah, such heavenly beauty!
> The summer evening sinks with delicate wings
> In sweet exhaustion on the quiet meadows;

* (Tgb. 96 Saturday, June 30, 1810.)

Love-thirstily the sea breathes up and down,
A bride to welcome on her breast her lord,
Who turns his steeds already to the west;
A gentle breeze plays in the slender poplars,
That softly dallying with the virgin pillars,
Breathe gently, greeting us, the dreams* of love
And seem to whisper: "See, we love! Then you too love!"

In *Medea,* the tormented Medea contemplates the murder of her children and breaks out in an agonizing lament worthy to be set beside Racine's Phèdre's famous apostrophes to Venus, and her sister, Ariadne, in Act I, Scene iii of *Phèdre:*

Dann leer das ganze Haus und ausgestorben,
Verwüstung brütend in den öden Mauern,
Nichts lebend als Erinnerung und Schmerz.
(*Act IV, Vs. 1816–18*)

Then void the entire house—all, all destroyed—
With ruin brooding over barren walls,
Nothing alive but memory and pain.

Note how the ellipsis in the first line and the internal rhyme of "Haus," "aus," plus the following assonance of "*Mau*ern," combined with the unbearable moan of the contorted vowels in "Verw*ü*stung," "br*ü*tend"—"*ö*den" in the second line, make the climactic last word "Schmerz" (pain) almost superfluous!

For the last example of this dramatic use of sound we may examine some lines from a passage cited in the Translator's Note to *The Waves of Sea and Love* as testimony of Grillparzer's deft use of the Leda-and-Swan leitmotiv to illustrate Hero's erotic feelings. When Hero, exhausted by her amorous vigils of the previous night and by the day's fatigues, is awaiting Leander's second visit, half asleep with the rising wind caressing her fevered limbs, she expresses herself thus:

Wie süss, wie wohl!—Komm Wind der Nacht,
Und kühle mir das Aug, die heissen Wangen!
Kommst du doch übers Meer, von ihm.

* "Dreams" is inserted in English to maintain the assonance and to approach, even if only from a distance, the supreme beauty of: *Der Liebe leisen Gruss herüberlispeln!*

Und, o, dein Rauschen und der Blätter Lispeln,
Wie Worte klingt es mir: von ihm wir, ihm, von ihm.
(*Act IV, Vs. 1807–11*)

How pleasant it is! Night wind, come
And cool my eyes and brow and burning cheeks!
You come across the sea from him.
And, oh, your rustling and the whispering leaves
Sing in my ears: "we are from him, him, him, from him."

Here the concertina effect of the lines—shortening and lengthening, with the fall and rise of the wind—add to the music of the words to lull Hero to her fatal sleep, while with the reiteration of "ihm" (him) and the repeated assonance in "i" (to which the Vienna "ü" also approximates), Hero pours out her love for Leander in accents that drift down to us through the ages.

A supreme artist in the dramatic use of verbal music, Grillparzer was also a considerable artist in the plastic representation of his characters and scenes. This quality, already marked in *Ottokar* and *Ein Treuer Diener,* is especially apparent in *The Waves of Sea and Love,* where the finished picture is built up with innumerable deft touches to present an artistic whole. It is for this reason that Grillparzer is so elaborate in his stage directions. He visualizes, with its comings and goings, its groupings and solitary stances, the whole scene so clearly, that he wants it performed just as he sees it, and although some of his directions seem unnecessary, we must perhaps thank his meticulous care for the almost sculptural beauty to which the great threnody of the fifth act of *The Waves of Sea and Love** rises.

Grillparzer is rarely master of the superb phrase, often characteristic of the great poets and of which Shakespeare, with his "golden hand," is perhaps the supreme example. But he is constantly master of the superb sentence. A felicitous example is when Sappho savagely abuses Melitta, whom she suspects of having stolen Phaon's love from her. When Melitta bursts out crying at Sappho's cruelty, Sappho scolds on—"Do not weep," she says:

* Grillparzer's tragedies have something of the pictorial quality of El Greco's famous painting of the "Death of Count Orgaz, in Toledo" —not an inappropriate affinity for one who was such a lover of both Greece and Spain.

Tears are the holy privilege of pain!
(*Sappho, V. 1109*)

Innumerable and even more striking examples of Grillparzer's felicity of language will be found in many of the passages cited in the three Translator's notes in the volume and the point, therefore, need not be labored here.

Great as he was as a creative artist, Grillparzer was no less great as a critic of penetrating insight and sound judgment. His imaginary conversations, set in Elysium, between Frederick the Great and Lessing will repay careful study. Fluent in seven languages—ancient Greek and Latin, French, Spanish, English and Italian—including of course, his mastery of German, he had direct access to the greatest minds that had fashioned the dramatic and literary heritage of Europe. Of the ancients, Euripides,* Plato and, in the creation of his great Medea, Apollonius Rhodius seem to have influenced him most. Of the moderns, above all Calderon, Lope de Vega, Shakespeare and, more subtly, Racine, with whom he shares the palm of connoisseur *par excellence* of the feminine heart. Although in his earlier work the influence of Goethe and Schiller is evident, he was, as his diaries attest, soon able to assess that they had little to teach him in the dramatic, as distinct from the purely literary, field. And, with the test of time, he is increasingly regarded as at least their equal in the hierarchy of German dramatic poets.

*Heinrich Laube relates in his *Reisenovellen,* 1836, how Grillparzer in August 1833, had championed Racine and Euripides against the attacks of the Schlegels. Laube rightly notes the affinity of Grillparzer's dramatic intensity with that of Euripides and Racine, but wrongly dubs it "rhetoric of emotion."

Grillparzer shows a due regard for French classical tragedy, rare in German authors of his day, still influenced by Lessing's strictures and Lessing's presumptuous claim that he could improve on any tragedy of the great Corneille! (Tgb. 4045, 1850.) Twelve years later (Tgb. 4312, 1862) Grillparzer, as an old man, wisely noted that the French classical dramatists, in imitating the simplicity of the Greeks, omitted to observe that the chorus, the music and dance automatically added complexity in Greek tragedies. He should, however, have further noted that this is precisely what Racine did do in his last two plays, *Esther* and *Athalie,* where, especially in *Athalie,* there is spectacular splendor at the end—not unlike Grillparzer's own splendid spectacles to bring down the curtain.

Franz Grillparzer's Completed Plays

*Die Unglücklichen Liebhaber** (1806) (*The Unlucky Lovers*)	First Published Standard Vienna Edition (HKA 11,3)
Die Schreibfeder (1807–09) (*The Pen*)	First Published 1887
Blanka von Kastilien (1808–09) (*Blanche of Castille*)	First Published 1887 First Performed 1958
Wer Ist Schuldig? (1811) (*Who Is Guilty?*)	First Published 1887
Die Ahnfrau (*The Ancestress*)	First Performed 1817
Sappho	First Performed 1818
Das Goldene Vliess (*The Golden Fleece*) 1 *Der Gastfreund* (*The Guest*) 2 *Die Argonauten* (*The Argonauts*) 3 *Medea*	First Performed 1821
König Ottokars Glück und Ende (*King Ottocar's Fortune and Fall*)	First Performed 1825
Ein Treuer diener Seines Herrn (*A Faithful Servant of his Master*)	First Performed 1828
*Melusina***	First Performance of Opera 1833

* This, Grillparzer's first completed play, written at the age of fifteen, is a one-act prose comedy caricaturing his professors. His friend Mailler passed as the "tragic" author, while Grillparzer was the student expert in 'comedy." With *Blanka von Kastilien,* the long five-act tragedy in verse, the tragic Grillparzer had "arrived" at eighteen, although not yet on the stage. For public performance he had to wait till *Die Ahnfrau.*

** The text had been completed by Grillparzer for Beethoven in 1823. But Beethoven never set it, the music eventually being composed by Kreutzer.

Des Meeres und der Liebe Wellen (*The Waves of Sea and Love*)	First Performed	1831
Der Traum Ein Leben (*Dreaming Is Living*)	First Performed	1834
Weh dem, der Lügt (*Woe to the Liar*)	First Performed	1838
Libussa	First Performed	1874
Ein Bruderzwist in Habsburg (*Fraternal Discord among the Hapsburgs*)	First Performed	1872
Die Jüdin von Toledo (*The Jewess of Toledo*)	First Performed	1872
*Esther****	First Performed	1868

*** Although a fragment, *Esther* is included here, as unlike Grillparzer's numerous youthful fragments, it not only has considerable merit, but was actually performed in Grillparzer's lifetime twenty times at the Burgtheater. All Grillparzer's works, except *Melusina* (Berlin) and *Die Jüdin von Toledo* (Prague), were first performed in Vienna.

Franz Grillparzer

PLAYS ON CLASSIC THEMES

SAPPHO

TRANSLATOR'S NOTE

The sensational popular success of *Die Ahnfrau,* Grillparzer's first play to be professionally performed (1817), left the highbrow critics cold, and could not satisfy the maturing Grillparzer, who was now determined to show them that he could achieve dramatic impact without the assistance of "robbers, ghosts and such-like 'pop' effects." In search of a simple theme, he was thus in a receptive frame of mind when, on Sunday, June 29, 1817, an acquaintance, Dr. Joël, whom he casually met while strolling in the Prater, suggested that he write a libretto for the composer Weigl on the subject of Sappho. Not interested in a libretto, Grillparzer immediately replied that the subject was suitable for tragedy—this was the legendary or historic tale of the unrequited love of Sappho for Phaon, and her leap to her death in the sea from the Leucan cliff. Leaving Dr. Joël somewhat abruptly, Grillparzer strolled on and on in the Prater shaping the plot in his mind, and, returning home late, he promptly wrote it down. The next day he went to the Hofbibliothek (Court Library), and, perusing the scanty remnants of Sappho's work, translated at once the ode which becomes her closing monologue in Act I, Scene vi of the play. From July 1 to 25, with a break on the nineteenth because of a toothache, he systematically composed and wrote out daily the first manuscript of the play.

To this heated composition we owe the classical unity and perfection of form of *Sappho,* as well as its romantic enthusiasm. We need not pay too much attention to Grillparzer's apparent concession to carping criticism—admitting a dichotomy between the Sappho of the earlier and later acts.*

* See Grillparzer's otherwise convincing reply to Adolf Müllner's letter of February 14, 1818, criticizing the first two acts.

Sappho was eventually performed on April 21, 1818, at the Hofburgtheater, with Sophie Schröder, Germany's leading tragedienne, in the title rôle. It was one of the great parts of her career, as she felt deeply the pangs of her heroine, since she herself had been involved since 1816, at the age of thirty-five, in a liaison with Morris Daffinger, the painter who was nine years her junior—the man who later was to rival Grillparzer in the affections of Marie von Smolenitz, Grillparzer's elusive "ideal" love, whom Daffinger married.

The play was an immediate success, and spread Grillparzer's fame for the first time beyond the borders of the German lands. Despite its not very important defects, it has lost little of its appeal in the century and a half that has elapsed, and with its youthful freshness has greater dramatic impact than its German dramatic models, whether Zacharias Werner's *Wanda,* or Goethe's maturer *Iphigenie* and *Tasso,** however much greater these Goethe plays may be regarded as literary as distinct from dramatic achievements. *Sappho* was the play selected for gala performance on January 15, 1871, in celebration of Grillparzer's eightieth birthday. During its author's lifetime it was performed sixty-six times at the Burgtheater.

The background influences shaping *Sappho* are numerous—Wieland's novels of classical antiquity, *Agathon* and *Aristipp,* and perhaps most important, his *Menander and Glycerion,* which Sauer has called an "inverted Sappho tragedy," because Glycerion, like Phaon with Sappho, mistakes as love her boundless admiration for the genius of Menander, the comic playwright, only to be disabused at closer quarters. More recent was the influence of Madame de Staël's *Corinne,* which Grillparzer had read only the previous year and which must have left a powerful impression on his mind, as there are many parallels between the story of her fictive English-Italian poetic heroine, the glory of modern Rome, and that of Grillparzer's historic heroine, the glory of ancient Greece. So much for the influence of novels. Of

*Grillparzer, the very year he wrote *Sappho,* shows a critical acumen that is remarkable at a time when Goethe was adulated. "Goethe," he wrote (Tgb. 225, 1817) "is infinitely great as a *poet* in whatever he touches, but as a *dramatic* poet he seems to me quite unimportant."

dramatists, the influence of the Greek tragedians, of Goethe's *Iphigenie* and above all *Tasso,* the favorite Goethe reading of Grillparzer in his adolescence, and of Zacharias Werner's *Wanda,* is to be expected from a novice out to make his name in the field of classical German drama. More interesting is the clear evidence of the influence of Racine, with the happiest dramatic results. For although compared to the stark simplicity of *Bérénice,* Racine's most "romantic" play, *Sappho* with its "rose," its "kiss," its "dagger," its chase on the high seas, is complexity itself, Grillparzer yet had the sound sense, even if subconsciously, to apply in his art some of the dramatic principles of which Racine—whom Grillparzer held in the highest esteem*—had proved himself a master.

Apart from the musicality of his verse, which Grillparzer at his best shares with Racine, and of which perhaps the finest example is in this play (Phaon's description of the caressing poplars, Act III, Scene i, Vs. 878–87), we find in this very scene Racine's psychological insight also, first paralleled by Grillparzer. In Act III, Scene vii of Racine's *Bajazet,* Roxana, like Sappho, has stumbled on the truth that Bajazet—who, like Phaon with Sappho, is supposed to love her—in fact loves Athalida, the woman on whom she reposes her trust (as Sappho with Melitta). She seeks to clutch at consolation for a self-deluding moment in similar terms as Sappho, who muses:

> Yet am I not a fool to rack myself
> And to bewail what perhaps does not exist?
> Who knows what fleeting, rasable impression,
> What insubstantial fancy drew him to her,
> A whim, dissolving swift as swift it sprang,
> Deserving neither forethought nor reproach?
> What bids me seek the measure of his feelings
> In this, my deeply agitated breast?
>
> (*Vs. 803–10*)

Again in her fine monologue in the very next scene, like Racine's great Mithridates who upbraids his fiancée Monima

*"Racine, as great a poet as has ever lived . . ." (Tgb. 3384, 1838).

for spurning him, when he had selected her, a humble girl, as his bride, preferring her to scores of royal princesses, Sappho in accents worthy of Racine utters perhaps her greatest speech:

How can I longer doubt? Clear it is, clear!
Yes, she's the one who sways his perjured heart,
She hovers in his mind devoid of shame,
In *her* apparel are his dreams enveloped,
Insinuating on the recreant's couch.
What, Sappho spurned, in favor of her slave?
Spurned? Who? In heaven's name! And spurned by whom?
Am I no longer then the very Sappho
Who saw so many monarchs at her feet,
And, playing fondly with their proferred crowns,
First saw and heard the proud men, then dismissed them?

* * *

O fool! Why did I come down from the heights
The laurel crowns, where Aganippe roars,
And Muses' chorus consort with star-music,
Down here into the suffocating valley,
Where misery reigns and faithlessness and crime?

* * *

I will see her, this paragon of beauty,
Who glories in such triumph over Sappho.
What am I to believe? Is memory false,
That, when I question it, brings to my senses
A silly child with imbecilic features?
With eyes forever turned toward the ground,
With lips that mouth the simperings of a child,
With empty bosom whose poor surgings only
The love of play and fear of punishment
Can sometimes rouse out of their hollow calm?
Or are my eyes alone blind to that charm
That draws him with such power into her presence?

(*Vs. 928–74*)

More important than the casual parallels between Sappho and Racine's Roxana and Mithridates are interrogation and irony, two essential features of Racine's dramatic style that infuse the Grillparzer passages quoted above—and highlight their dramatic splendor. In *Medea,* Grillparzer was to go even further and parallel Racine's psychological profundity with its peculiar, characteristic insights. But to another feature of Racine's dramatic practice, the scene or scenes of "moral recognition" in his tragedies, Grillparzer poses, and best of all in *Sappho,* his scene of moral vindication. In Racine's tragedies, a character or characters, generally the protagonists, recognize their errors toward the end of the play and make moral restitution, even toward their enemies, with telling pathos and dramatic effect. Likewise in all Grillparzer's Grecian tragedies, his heroine—Sappho, Medea, Hero—is vindicated, but with this important difference —it is not the protagonists who confess and seek absolution, but a minor, indeed humbler character, loyal in service, who upholds the cause of the injured heroine against her adversaries, wresting her absolution from the audience. The persecuted Hero, in the last act of *The Waves of Sea and Love,* is defended by her serving companion, Ianthe, against her callous persecution by her uncle, the offended High Priest. More eloquently, in the last act of *Medea,* Gora, Medea's nurse, stoutly champions her against the violent attacks of Jason and King Creon, to their faces. Most splendid of all, in *Sappho*—and indeed worthy to be set beside Emilia's inspired tirades against the supine Othello and her villainous husband, Iago, in the last act of Shakespeare's *Othello*—is the slave, Rhamnes' passionate defense of his mistress in the last act of the play against the blind onslaughts of the somewhat callow Phaon.*

Rhamnes, a very well-observed character, as so many of Grillparzer's minor characters of both sexes are, in sharp contrast to the obtuseness of so many of his "anti-heroic" heroes, not only wins us over to himself—our liking for him, the faithful

* It is interesting to contrast that while Grillparzer's moral vindications were made by servants—not surprising in the author of *Ein Treuer Diener Seines Herrn* (*A Faithful Servant of His Master*), Racine's "moral recognitions" were made by kings and queens and princes and princesses. Indeed, in his Preface to *Phèdre,* Racine argues that moral obliquity is more likely in the nurse, Oenone—contrast Medea's nurse, Gora—than in the royal Phèdre. Evidently royal savoir-faire had improved in Racine's day, for we find in Euripides that it was Phaedra herself, and not her old nurse, who falsely and indelibly accused Hippolytus of raping her, in a letter to her husband, before she hanged herself.

old retainer is, indeed, never in jeopardy—but wins us over completely to Sappho, whose melodramatic daggers, banishments and postures were in danger of alienating our sympathy. Above all Rhamnes' remorseless fury against the beaten Phaon succeeds miraculously in winning back our sympathy for Phaon himself, who, unlike Jason in *The Golden Fleece,* does show that he is not almost wholly insensitive. When Phaon, in his bravado—like Leander in the bravado of his despair violently proclaiming his love to Hero in Act II of *The Waves of Sea and Love*—fulminates to Rhamnes against Sappho:

> Even if the earth before me here split open,
> The sea in thunder crashed, to swallow me,
> Could she in dread conspiracy unite
> Against me all great Nature's mighty forces,
> I'd cling to my belovèd, mock her anger,
> Despising her and all her menaces!
>
> (*Vs. 1806–11*)

Rhamnes explodes. It is the word "despising" applied to his mistress, Sappho, "the gem of Hellas," that causes the dramatic detonation:

> Despise? You, Sappho? Who then, pray, are you,
> That you dare put your word into the scales
> In which humanity weighs its elect?
> Presume to speak, where Greece has long since spoken?
>
> * * *
>
> You deem a gem opaque, because your eye is?
> That she did love you, that she should have raised
> Up to her from the dust the thankless viper
> That lacerates her heart with venomous tooth
>
> * * *
>
> This is the single blemish in her life
> And even envy cannot brand her else—
> Be silent! . . . Even this defiance on which
> You prop yourself against her is not yours!
> How could you have presumed—you abject creature,
> You playboy, the obscurest of the obscure—
> To mouth complaints against the gem of Hellas?
>
> (*Vs. 1812–30*)

When Phaon concedes he would not challenge her poetic fame, Rhamnes, who has correctly read the despair in Sappho's eyes, explodes again:

> You would not? Fine, indeed! As if you could!
>
> * * *
>
> In far-off times, among far foreign men,
> When our decaying bodies are long crumbled
> And when our graves are no more to be found,
> Shall Sappho's song resound from human lips
> And her name still live—and shall still live yours,
> Yes, yours! Boast of the immortality
> Your wickedness against her wins for you!
> In foreign-lands, to coming generations
> When many centuries as yet unborn,
> Have been engulfed within the tomb of time,
> Shall every mouth continually proclaim:
> She who first sang this song, her name was Sappho,
> And Phaon is his name, who murdered her!
>
> (*Vs. 1834–50*)

When Melitta and Phaon in their discomfiture interrupt, Rhamnes brushes them aside:

> You would not challenge her poetic fame!
> And what fame else of hers do you then challenge?
> Dare you have any doubts about her heart,
> You who must thank her heart for what you are?
>
> * * *
>
> Question that quivering creature at your side,
> Accomplice rather of your deed than guilt,
> How she has found our mistress treating her?
>
> (*Vs. 1853–68*)

And in a final spurt of fury he pulverizes Phaon with:

> Where will you flee?
> There is no refuge for you on this earth;
>
> * * *
>
> Your reputation shall precede your steps
> And cry aloud in every human ear:

"Here Sappho's murderer comes! The gods' foe comes!"
And you shall wander outlawed through the land
With her, whom you gave ruin for protection.

* * *

And when you flee, the dread Eumenides,
The dark, avenging messengers from Hell,
Tossing their serpent tresses around your head,
Shall hiss forever "Sappho" in your ears,
Until the grave you dug has swallowed you!

(*Vs. 1875–92*)

Even more successful is Grillparzer's creation of the fictive Melitta, as Sappho's rival for Phaon's love. Her introduction may indeed have been a "cabbie's conception," *"Fiakeridee,"* of "pairing like with like," as her author disparagingly observed—but then if we are to exclude the eternal triangle, with disparate elements, on that score, a good deal of the great literature in the world, including Racine's *Phèdre* and *Bajazet,* would be lost!

Nor is Melitta a mere "silly girl" (*albernes Mädel*), as Grillparzer doubtless in an unconsidered moment also declared to Zimmermann.* On the contrary, Melitta, as her name implies, is his sweetest and perhaps his most delightful creation, worthy to be set beside Shakespeare's most attractive heroines. She may not be able to soar with Sappho to the heights "where Aganippe roars," but she is equally incapable of descending with her to the "suffocating valley" where Phaon's violent abuse of Sappho as "hypocritic Circe" seems not entirely undeserved.

Like Rosalind or Juliet she falls in love (even if unconsciously)† at first sight, as she sees Phaon approach on the chariot with Sappho—"so tall and splendid" like "Apollo with his lyre," although unlike Orlando or Romeo, Phaon, still under the fascination of Sappho, scarcely notices her slave. When Eucharis teases her for having spilt the wine at the banquet,

*Noted by Professor Robert Zimmermann on January 6, 1866.

†It is true that Grillparzer in his letter to Müllner (February–March 1818) designates Phaon's kiss as Cupid's first shaft, but Melitta is clearly involved from the beginning as her nostalgic monologue further emphasizes. His attention rightly riveted on Sappho, Grillparzer was perhaps not fully aware of his artistic success with Melitta.

where she has already been teased by Sappho when wine-tasting before serving Phaon, she cannot suppress her tears.

"Dear me, even a little tear appears!" observes Eucharis (V. 544). Left alone for a moment, Melitta, in a monologue suffused by the deep nostalgia of a young girl snatched from her parents and sold to slavery at the age of two or three, gives vent to her longing for love rather than "only pity" that has been her lot hitherto; and in her loneliness begs the gods for release:

> Dear Gods, who have so often heard my prayers,
>
> * * *
>
> O lend me now once more a gracious ear!
> Ah, lead me gently back to my own kindred,
> That I might cool my sorrow-fevered brow
> Upon a soft and sympathetic breast,
> Ah, lead me to my kindred, or else bear me
> Aloft to you! . . . to you! . . . to you!
> (*Vs. 581–89*)

When she finds that Phaon, who has overheard her, returns her love, she is naturally overjoyed, but not unmindful of her obligations to Sappho, though at first as an individual of character (not a "silly girl") she refuses to obey Sappho's harsh command to surrender the rose that Phaon pinned on her breast. When Sappho in her anguish, having discovered their love, reminds her how she had rescued her from the slavers, and asks if she still remembers "that far-off day," thirteen years before, when Sappho herself, "a girlish creature," * had locked Melitta "with warm affection on her maiden breast," Melitta bursts out in true gratitude: "Oh, could I ever, ever not remember?" (V. 1060.) She is honest as well as grateful, for she admits to Phaon that she had provoked her mistress to draw the dagger:

> The blame is mine;
> I spoke, as was not seemly for a slave.
> (*Vs. 1127–28*)

* This indicates that Sappho was barely thirty when the play opens, just as Mellita was barely sixteen (V. 1041). We may presume Phaon to be in his twenties, though there is no exact chronology pinning his age.

Sappho's anguish causes her, unlike Phaon, genuine distress.

> Am I to see her, whom I love, in pain?
> (*V. 1181*)

she cries, but Phaon tries to take her away. When Sappho is about to break down and calls to her, Melitta falls on her knees in equal anguish:

> Yes, Sappho, yes, I, I! Here, take this rose!
> Take it, O take my life! Where is your dagger?
> (*Vs. 1185–86*)

After her elopement with Phaon and their recapture, she strives to win Sappho's forgiveness, ignoring Phaon's furious expostulations. To his:

> You shall not supplicate! She knows neither
> Your worth, nor hers; else she would on her knees
> Before you, guilt to innocence, pay homage!
> Come here to me, come here!
> (*Vs. 1756–59*)

She replies:

> No, let me kneel,
> As well befits a child before its mother;
> If she deem right to punish, let her punish;
> I will not fret at all against her will.
> (*Vs. 1759–62*)

* * *

Then turning to Sappho she pleads:

> Here will I kneel until a gentle look,
> A kindly word, proclaims to me my pardon.
> How often I have lain here, in this spot
> And ever stood up smilingly once more;
> She will not this time send me off in tears!
> Dear lady, please look down upon your child!
> (*Vs. 1769–74*)

When Sappho remains silent and Phaon accuses her of being "cold and dumb," Melitta with better insight retorts:

> She is not cold, and though her mouth is silent
> I feel her heart is speaking to my heart.

Be judge, O Sappho, between me and him!
Bid me go with him, and with him I'll go,
Bid me renounce him—mighty gods—all! . . . all!
(*Vs. 1776–80*)

When Sappho, pricked by Phaon's plea: "Consider what you do and who you are!" leaves deep in thought to meditate her end, Melitta in misapprehension exclaims:

Alas! she flees, rejecting me, her child.
(*V. 1785*)

Phaon's attempts to console her leave her disconsolate:

I cannot live if she has sentenced me,
Her eye to me has ever been my mirror,
In which I tested all my acts and feelings;
It shows me now my own deformity.
What she must suffer, our offended lady.
(*Vs. 1788–92*)

When Phaon continues in his ungenerous temper to accuse Sappho of jealous pride, Melitta, grateful to the end, avers:

If she seem proud, she still was kind to me,
If often strict, the sharp exterior hid
A sweet and gracious sustenance for me still.
Alas! That I could ever have forgotten!
(*Vs. 1795–98*)

We are therefore perhaps not wrong to imagine that if it was Phaon's intellectual appeals that spurred Sappho to resolve her problem, it was Melitta's true sympathy that moved her to her end in reconcilement, and won her blessing on the young couple.

Phaon is not a memorable creation, but rather an interesting one, being like all his Grecian heroes, and indeed like the old Emperor Rudolf in *Ein Bruderzwist in Habsburg,* a reflection of Grillparzer himself. Phaon's intoxicated admiration for Sappho's poetry, which spurred him and his horses to Olympia at such breakneck speed that his "stretched horses on the way fell dead," characterizes Grillparzer's intoxicated admiration for Goethe's *Tasso,* which drew him headlong on the poetic path of fame.

Whatever Phaon's rustic status in the legend, in the play he springs "from the noblest stock" (V. 72), and is highly cultivated, both in the athletic and artistic fields; he speaks like a poet—when he is not shouting at Sappho or boasting about his prowess—and Grillparzer has put into the mouth of Phaon, his personal representative, as it were, some of the most beautiful lines in the play. Abashed when he first comes into the presence of the "crown of women" at Olympia, he keeps his eyes on the ground before Sappho, like Leander before Hero, but once he realizes his power over her, it does not take him long to stride forth as Sappho's equal and—when in a moment of jealous aberration she descends to a murderous gesture—to browbeat her as her superior. It is only at the end of the play that his better nature—which he, unlike Jason, does have beneath his brash exterior—reasserts itself and moves him to appeal to Sappho in terms that spark the elevated denouement of the tragedy.

In fairness, Phaon was never in love with Sappho the woman, whom he had not even seen, when he was already in love with Sappho the poetess, and it is clear from Sappho's own words that, like Bajazet with Roxana in Racine's *Bajazet,* his amorous responses never satisfied Sappho's ardent expectations. When one of her passionate declarations to him:

> Only one thing I cannot bear to lose—
> You, Phaon, you, your friendship and your love.
> Therefore, belovèd, carefully consider!
> You do not yet know the infinitude
> That surges ever up and down my breast.
> Oh let me never, dearest, never suffer
> That I should lay my full heart on your own
> To find it empty!

merely elicits the response "Noble lady!" she cries out in disappointment:

> Not so!
> Cannot your heart urge you to sweeter names?
> (*Vs. 123–131*)

When she heaps her kindnesses and hospitality on him, he is discomfited and bursts out:

> Sappho!
> How can I ever pay back so much kindness?

My mounting debt is almost choking me
(*Vs. 298–300*)

He is confused about his true feelings, ardent admiration for the poetess and great lady, veiling his lack of ardor for the woman, so that he longs, away from the bustle, to know himself:

And see in clear and calm *deliberation,*
How quite to be what I desire to be!
(*Vs. 317–18*)

When brought back with Melitta to Sappho's presence to receive sentence for their attempted escape, Phaon appeals to Sappho's better nature, recalling his rapt admiration for her:

Soft as her song was her transfigured spirit,
* * *
And her whole being was melody to me.
* * *
Ah! Do not turn from me your downcast eyes!
Look at me! Let me gaze into your face,
That I may know if you are still the same,
If these the lips that softly touched my mouth,
If these the eyes that smiled at me so gently,
If, Sappho, you are she, you, Sappho?
(*Vs. 1697–1708*)

And when Sappho, shrinking with grief, cries, "Alas!" and to his appeal:

Act like a goddess! Bless us, Sappho, bless!
(*V. 1721*)

calls Phaon a "Deceiver!" he goes on to explain his feelings clearly and to strike deep chords in her soul:

No, in truth, I am not one!
When I swore love to you, it was no sham;
I loved you as one may, perhaps, love gods,
As one loves what is good and beautiful.
Let Sappho consort with the lofty ones;
One may not with impunity descend
From the gods' feast to mortal company.

The arm in which the golden lyre rests
Is dedicated, may not touch what's earthly.
(*Vs. 1722–30*)

Then when Melitta kneels before Sappho, Phaon too kneels before her and finally exhorts her:

To mortals love, and reverence to the Gods,
Give us what's ours, and take from us what's yours!
Consider what you do and who you are!
(*Vs. 1782–84*)

and at last succeeds in quickening Sappho's dazed spirit to take its final, gracious resolution on earth.

Sappho herself is a much more complex character, whom her creator has fashioned with remarkable skill. While with Böttiger,* we may deplore her somewhat melodramatic descent to the dagger in Act III from the "heights of humankind," Grillparzer has cunningly prepared us from the beginning to expect the gold of her temperament as an artist to be alloyed with her almost shrewish violence as a woman. Nor is this admixture out of character. Indeed, the very authority she exercised as the "gem of Hellas" and the sovereign lady of Lesbos would tend to make her impatient of any questioning of that authority, let alone of insubordination in a slave—who was at the same time her successful rival in love! Thus, in Act I, Grillparzer deftly depicts her annoyed at Rhamnes' understandable surprise when she introduces the newly arrived Phaon to him as his master. "Who questions here?" she snaps, followed by her intense, "What do you mean?" (Vs. 302–03) This is a particularly subtle stroke, as not only does it portray her impatience at Rhamnes' questioning, but also her self-questioning, for she must have detected in the surprise of Rhamnes, her old, faithful slave, his doubts as to the wisdom of her choice, doubts she must have secretly shared when she reflected that Phaon was just a handsome youth, younger than herself, who had been drawn to her in advance only by his passionate love of her art.

Grillparzer is at his happiest in depicting Sappho as a born poetess: "You're weeping love!" she exclaims on her entrance, as she greets the tears of joy of the islanders at her homecoming

* See the footnote to V. 1123.

(V. 65).* She explains to the islanders much to Phaon's embarrassment, her choice of him as her partner:

> Ah yes, my friends! You may as well know this,
> I love him. On his dear head fell my choice!
> With his superb endowments he was destined
> To draw me down with sweet compulsive force
> From the high cloudy peaks of poetry
> Into the fair and flowery vales of life:
> (*Vs. 87–92*)

When alone with Phaon she explains her hitherto vain search for a permanent love in haunting, almost prophetic terms:

> I've felt the fangs of falsehood and the sting
> Of base ingratitude, and in this breast
> The pangs of friendship frustrate—and of love.
> Yes, I have learnt to lose and do without!
> (*Vs. 119–122*)

She recognizes the difficulty of harnessing high artistic ambition to the yoke of domestic bliss (a favorite theme of Grillparzer, for which, like Sappho, he had to pay dearly):

> It's not for nothing that the Muses' chorus
> Have picked the laurel as a mark of grace;
> Cold, fruitless, scentless, it fatigues the head
> As recompense for many a sacrifice.
> A harsh wind haunts the heights of humankind
> And the poor artist is forever forced
> To beg a little from life's overflow!
> (*Vs. 271–77*)

But she hopes that in Phaon she has at last found the answer to her problem:

> Let us endeavor then, my dearest friend,
> To wind *both* garlands round our eager brows,
> To quaff life from the dizzy cup of art
> And art from out the gentle hand of life.
> (*Vs. 280–83*)

* I have followed the Vienna Edition which has, clearly, the poetically powerful transitive "Ihr weinet Liebe!" rather than the Berlin and Munich editions, whose comma after "weinet" is confusing.

So set is she on her dream of happiness with Phaon whom she, because of his admiration for her art, fancies the ideal partner, that she mistakes most ironically the smitten Melitta's silence as lack of appreciation of Phaon's qualities and snaps out at her, "Indeed, I feel I hate you! Go!" (V. 329.) But basically, with her high intelligence, she is unsure of Phaon and is tormented by her insecurity as the older and more mature partner. Nostalgically she confides her fears to Melitta:

> Poor that I am, what can I offer him?
> He stands there in the fullness of his youth
> Adorned with all the finest flowers of life.
>
> * * *
>
> And I! O Gods and Goddesses of Heaven,
> O give me back again the golden past!
> Wipe out the furrowed trace within my heart
> Of former sufferings and of former pleasures;
>
> * * *
>
> O let me go back once more to the time
> When I, still shy, with rounded girlish cheeks
> And unfamiliar stirrings in my breast,
> Looked at the wakening world with wakening spirit;
> When only dreams—no torturing experience—
> Inspired the golden playing of my lyre,
> When love was still a magic land to me,
> An unknown, strange and wondrous magic land!
>
> (*Vs. 370–92*)

But encouraged by Melitta's praise of her fame, she takes heart and declares hopefully:

> Let him not scoff at fame who once has won it,
> It is no empty echo, meaningless;
> Its fingers are endowed with power divine!
> Once more I breathe. Then I am not so poor.
> Against his wealth I may set equal wealth—
>
> (*Vs. 416–20*)

With her feeling of insecurity and her intense desire for a permanent companion, it is not surprising that Sappho should be unhinged by jealousy when she stumbles on Phaon kissing Melitta and, later, on his telltale dream:

How close he held her! How his arm embraced her!
And then how, yielding softly to her urge,
Upon his mouth she— Stop! I will not think of it!
The very thought kills me a thousand times! *
(*Vs. 799–802*)

In her first confrontation with Melitta after this, her jealousy erupts at the least occasion. When she asks Melitta her age and Melitta replies, "I believe I'm sixteen," she snaps, "No! you're lying!" (V. 1041) adding, "you're barely fifteen," as though a few months would put her safely beyond Phaon's reach!

The sight of Melitta decked out in her finery maddens her:

Go! Other clothes!
This gaudy show offends my eyes— Away!
Melitta, simple, always simply walked,
So many veils suggest there's something veiled.
(*Vs. 1084–87*)

And so in erratic, emotional progress, powerfully depicted by Grillparzer, she arrives at demanding the rose that Phaon has given Melitta, and through this demand touches Melitta's resistance and with it the climax of the play, leading inevitably to the denouement as required by the rules of classical tragedy, closely observed in the play.

In his portrayal of Sappho's character Grillparzer has put in many cunning strokes to round off the picture and to retain our sympathy for his heroine, despite the displeasing actions to which she is driven by her jealousy. When in trying to excuse to herself Phaon's conduct she seeks to distinguish a man's love from a woman's, she gives us a clear insight into the depth of her own feelings, in words exemplified later by Hero's conduct in Act IV of *The Waves of Sea and Love*.

* Grillparzer did not need to draw on his predecessors in depicting jealousy. He has himself told us how violently subject he was to this passion. See the revealing entry in his diary, when he was under 18 years of age (Tgb. 17, about 19th July 1808) which explains also why he was to be so unfortunate in his relations with women, incapable as he was of meeting their love with equal love.

He does not know the deep primeval glow
That love engenders in a woman's breast;
How all her being, thinking and desiring
Turns single-minded round this single point.
(*Vs. 825–28*)

Sadly she muses that her dream to combine the divine vocation of her art with domestic bliss is proving vain:

Let him whom gods have chosen for their own
Not consort with the citizens of earth;
The portion of mankind and the immortals
Can never mingle in the selfsame cup.
(*Vs. 948–51*)

Most moving is her weariness and distress in her opening monologue in Act IV, with the first clear hint of her approaching suicide:

And lonely, as a stranger straying late,
My weeping voice goes wandering through the night.

Whoever like the birds might fall asleep,
Only much longer, never to awaken,
Forever wrapped in deeper, sweeter slumber,
Where everything—the very pulse-beat—sleeps,
No ray of dawn awakes to fresh despairs,
No thankless man—Stop! Do not stir the snake.
(*Vs. 1199–1206*)

She prays for divine assistance, recognizing the dark depths of which she is capable, depths that do not exclude her possible Lesbian attachment to Melitta, of which there are many hints in the play, so subtly and with such masterly ambivalence has Grillparzer woven the tangled threads of her emotions.*

Dear Gods, protect me! Save me from myself:
The sinister spirits of my inmost being
Awake and shake their dungeon's iron bars!
(*Vs. 1219–21*)

* It is unnecessary to overstress this aspect here. But quite a thesis could be made of this theme.

Lost in her agony of spirit, she is impervious to the presence of Rhamnes, whom she has summoned, and who asks for her orders. When eventually she becomes aware of him, she is clearly ashamed of her plan to banish Melitta, divinely-inspired though she claims it to be. When hesitatingly she brings herself to tell him that he is to take Melitta to Chios and hand her over to the custody of a friend there, her essential decency breaks through her anger and makes her withdraw her instruction that Melitta be held strictly:

> Tell him to keep her till I send for her,
> And strictly—no, not strictly should he treat her,
> She is indeed chastened enough.
>
> (*Vs. 1325–28*)

Again when she hears that Melitta has been accidentally injured by an oar blow meant for Phaon, she winces not only out of genuine concern for Melitta, but also out of shame at the violent lengths to which her conduct has led.

All this Grillparzer achieves by one of his happier stage directions*—"Sappho hides her eyes with her hand" after the countryman's lines describing the overtaking of Phaon's boat. (Vs. 1583–85.) It is this combination of shame with anguish which ensures that Sappho is never in real danger of losing our sympathy, and lends her something of the stature of Racine's incomparable Phèdre.

Her frenzy, when she learns the young lovers have escaped, leaving her forlorn, is shattering:

> Down to the beach! Man everyone his skiff
> And follow, swift as wind, the traitors' track!
> Remember, I await you here in torment
> And every moment until you return
> Will jab a hundred daggers in my heart.
> Who brings them to me, who gives me the joy
> Of jabbing with my flaming eyes his eyes,
> Of asking him: "What have I done to you,
> (*Bursting into tears*)

* Grillparzer, like some later dramatists, carried his predilection for stage directions to excess, as for instance in *The Waves of Sea and Love,* where not a few seem superfluous.

That you should kill me?" . . . No, revenge alone!
Who brings them to me shall have all my gold,
My life—away! On the wings of the winds, away!
(*Vs. 1523–33*)

She is emotionally at the end of her tether, consumed as she is with rage, anguish and humiliation at being compelled to harbor passions unworthy of her divine vocation; and as she staggers, and is saved from falling by Eucharis, the fourth act ends with her cry, superb in its stark despair:

O, let me fall! Why are you holding me?

This simple line, a subtle testimony to Grillparzer's art, clearly indicates that the climax of emotion has been reached in Sappho's soul, that the harsher passions of rage and revenge are already receding, leaving in possession anguish and humiliation out of which self-knowledge and ultimate serenity will arise. Phaon's harshness toward Sappho in the earlier scenes of the fifth act, before he is fully brought to his senses by Rhamnes, serves but to chasten her further and to reinforce in her this process of self-knowledge, by illuminating for her the depths to which she might indeed have sunk had her nobler nature not reasserted itself in time.

To Phaon's accusations and taunts:

With what right
Dare you detain me here, in scandalous bondage,
Me, a free man, whom none owns but himself?
Look at these here! Did you not send them forth
With most improper weapons? Did you not? Speak!
So dumb! The poetess's sweet lips dumb?

She merely murmurs: "This is too much!" When he relentlessly continues his abuse:

I see your cheek is glowing—
All reddened by the hot flames of your rage—

(Purblind as usual, Phaon mistakes humiliation for rage)

Good, throw your mask away, be what you are,
And rave, and murder, hypocrite Circe!

Recognizing in Phaon's distorted mirror the dreadful image of what she might indeed have become if she had not overcome her baser passions, she repeats:

> This is too much,

but adds significantly

> Rise, heart, and arm yourself!
>
> (*Vs. 1655–66*)

When Phaon in his turn is chastened by Sappho's softening, and kneeling pleads with her to be true to herself:

> To mortals love, and reverence to the gods;
> Give us what's ours, and take from us what's yours!
> Consider what you do and who you are!

Sappho, as already indicated, is deeply stirred and withdraws for self-communion which the kneeling pair mistakenly believe to be a gesture of rejection. Alone with her thoughts, Sappho hears the vibration of the strings of her lyre, touched by the sea breeze, as a divine call, pointing to her the way out. She returns to the others serenely and gravely to dispose of her earthly obligations. When Phaon seeks to approach her she warns:

> Do not touch me!
> I am devoted to the gods!
>
> (*Vs. 1956–7*)

When he persists, she insists:

> I looked for you and I have found myself!
>
> (*V. 1960*)

She takes her leave of the others, and stepping forward offers her final prayer to the gods:

> Let me accomplish as I have begun,
> Spare me the bloody torment of this struggle.
> I feel myself too weak to fight on longer,
> Grant to me victory, spare me from the fight!
>
> (*Vs. 2012–15*)

Now, inspired, as she feels her prayer answered, she turns to Phaon and Melitta and kisses them, and walking to the edge of the cliff, stretches out her hands in blessing over the couple, repeating Phaon's line that had struck the basic chord in her soul and given her back to her higher self:

> To mortals love, and reverence to the gods!
> Enjoy what flowers you may, and think of me!
> Thus I repay the last debt of my life,
> Bless them, great Gods, and bear me up to you!
> (*Vs. 2025–28*)

Thus saying, she throws herself over the cliff and finds release in the measureless sea.

With *Sappho,* Grillparzer had at last arrived. The critics were impressed. In Germany Goethe voiced his praise. Abroad Byron was enthusiastic. Grillparzer's niche in the gallery of the immortals was assured.

S. S.

SAPPHO*

A Tragedy In Five Acts

* *Sappho* was first performed at the Hofburgtheater, Vienna (commonly also referred to as the Burgtheater or the Hoftheater), on April 21, 1818. It was first published by J. B. Wallishausser, in 1819.

To
Carl August West*
is dedicated this,
his second dramatic endeavor,
as a mark
of
gratitude and friendship

The Author

* Carl August West was the nom de plume of Josef Schreyvogel, the director of the Hofburgtheater, who was instrumental in launching Grillparzer on his career as a professional dramatist, who stimulated and nursed to triumph at his theater *Die Ahnfrau*, Grillparzer's first performed play, and after the triumph of *Sappho*, contracted Grillparzer as professional dramatist to Vienna's Hofburgtheater (May 1, 1818).

CHARACTERS

SAPPHO	
PHAON	
EUCHARIS } MELITTA }	*Sappho's serving girls*
RHAMNES	*Slave*
A COUNTRYMAN	
SERVANTS,	*female and male, and country folk*

ACT I

The curtain opens on a landscape. In the background is the sea, whose flat shore rises on the left to rocky heights. An altar of Aphrodite stands just by the shore. On the right foreground is seen the entrance to a grotto overgrown with bushes and ivy; further back is the end of a pillared passage with steps leading to SAPPHO'*s dwelling. On the left side of the foreground a tall rosebush stands behind a grassy bank.*

SCENE I

A sound of cymbals and flutes is heard with confused shouts of acclamation in the distance. RHAMNES *rushes in.*

RHAMNES

Up! Up from slothful sleep! She's almost here!
Too bad, only our *wishes*[1] should have wings,
While the foot limps, with heart all animated.
Come out, you lazy maidens. Will you dally?
He who calls youth swift-footed does not know you.

(EUCHARIS, MELITTA *and other female attendants come out of the pillared passage)*

MELITTA

Why are you scolding? Here we are!

RHAMNES

She's coming.

[1] This italicizing of individual words, unusual today, is common in Grillparzer.

MELITTA

Who? . . . Gods!

RHAMNES

Why, Sappho's coming!

ISLANDERS *(From within)*

Hail, Sappho, hail!

RHAMNES

Indeed, hail, Sappho, hail! You splendid people.

MELITTA

But what's the meaning?

RHAMNES

Now, by all the gods!
How strange your question sounds, you silly girl! *10*
She's come home from Olympia[2] with the wreath,
Decked with the laurel wreath of victory.
Before the whole of Greece assembled there,
In eager witness of the noble strife,
She won the prize for poetry and song.
For this the people rush to her, rejoicing,
Despatching to the clouds her happy name
On the broad wings of their triumphant shouts!
To think *this* hand it was and *this* my mouth
That taught her first the lyre's enchanting speech, *20*
And how to fetter songs' unruly flow
With the sweet discipline of harmony!

ISLANDERS *(From within)*

Hail, Sappho! Sappho, hail!

RHAMNES *(To the maidens)*

Come now, rejoice.
You see the wreath?

[2] At Olympia (Elis) the famous athletic contests were held every four years beginning 776 B.C. Poetic contests took place at the Pythic games in Delphi.

MELITTA

Sappho alone I see!
Let's go to greet her.

RHAMNES

Wait a moment, wait!
What will your meager plaudits mean to her?
She is accustomed to much nobler praise!
Rather make sure all's ready in the house.
A servant's service honors best his master.

MELITTA

Do you see by her side? . . .

RHAMNES

What?

MELITTA

Do you see? *30*
With her another form, so tall and splendid,
As they depict Apollo with his lyre
And with his bow—

RHAMNES

I see, but off with you!

MELITTA

And only now you called us!

RHAMNES

Called you, yes!
You were to know the mistress was approaching,
You were to know your duty to rejoice,
But to rejoice only inside the house.
A *man* may greet his love with cries of joy,
A *wife* loves quietly, working for his comfort.

MELITTA

Let us but—

RHAMNES

No, no, no, away! Away! (*He drives the* *40*

maidens off) Now let her come! No silly noisiness
Shall now disturb her festive harmony!

SCENE II

SAPPHO, *richly clad, enters on a chariot drawn by white horses with a golden lyre in her hand and the wreath of victory on her head. Beside her stands* PHAON, *simply dressed. The vehicle is surrounded by wildly cheering people.*

ISLANDERS *(Entering)*

Hail, Sappho, hail!

RHAMNES *(Mingling with them)*

Hail, Sappho! Dearest lady!

SAPPHO

Thanks, friends, dear countrymen, my thanks!
For your sakes I take pleasure in this wreath
That crowns the *citizen* but irks the *poet;*
Only in your midst do I call it mine!
Here, where the earliest plans and dreams of youth,
Where the beginners' hesitations, strivings,
And where accomplishment's ecstatic frenzy 50
Confronted suddenly my reeling soul;
Here, where the cypresses breathe out to me
Soft, ghostly greetings from my parents' graves,
Here, where so many, cut off young, repose,
Who once took pleasure in my tries, my triumphs,
Here, in the midst of you who know and love me,
I feel at last this wreath is without taint
And I may deem its arrogance adornment! [3]

[3] In this speech there are echoes of Goethe's *Tasso,* over which the young Grillparzer was enthusiastic. When in Italy in 1819, Grillparzer visited Tasso's grave. He also translated into German (1808) the first ten stanzas of Tasso's epic masterpiece, *Gerusalemme Liberata* (*Jerusalem Liberated*).

AN ISLANDER

Oh happy we, who may call you our own!
Have you not heard her modest speech, my friends? *60*
More than all Greece, her words have glorified her.

RHAMNES *(Pressing forward)*

My warmest, warmest greetings, splendid lady!

SAPPHO

(Dismounting from the chariot and greeting those about her affectionately)

My faithful Rhamnes, greetings—you, Artander,
You also here in spite of your old age?
Callisto—Rhodope!—You're weeping love!
The eye can throb as truly as the heart,
For your tears, my tears—see! Come, spare me now!

AN ISLANDER

Be welcome home upon your ancient soil,
Welcome among your own rejoicing people!

SAPPHO

You shall not greet your citizen in vain, *70*
As thanks I bring you a new citizen—
Here Phaon. From the noblest stock he springs,
And proudly may take place among the noblest.
Although the years may call him still a youth,
By word and deed he's proved himself a man.
If ever you should need the warrior's sword,
The orator's bold lips, the poet's mouth,
A friend's wise counsel, or a strong right arm,[4]
Then call to him and you need seek no further!

PHAON

Sappho, you're mocking me, a simple youth! *80*

[4] Compare Ophelia speaking of Hamlet (Act III, Scene i):

The courtier's, soldier's, scholar's, eye, tongue, sword;
Th' expectancy and rose of the fair state,
The glass of fashion and the mould of form

How could I possibly have earned such praise?
Who thinks so highly of one so untested?

SAPPHO

Who sees you blush because I'm saying it!

PHAON

I can, in shame, but wonder and keep silent.

SAPPHO

You but assure to you what you would shun;
Why, silence is the very twin of merit.
Ah yes, my friends! You may as well know this,
I love him. On his dear head fell my choice!
With his superb endowments he was destined
To draw me down with sweet compulsive force *90*
From the high cloudy peaks of poetry
Into the fair and flowery vales of life;
And by his side I now intend to lead
A simple, quiet, pastoral life among you,
Gladly exchanging laurel wreath for myrtle,[5]
And in sole praise of quiet, homely joys
Awakening the strings of this, my lyre.
Whom, hitherto, you've honored and admired,
My friends, you now shall learn to love, *to love!*

ISLANDERS

Praise to you, splendid lady! Sappho, hail! *100*

SAPPHO

Enough, my friends. I give you all my thanks.
Follow my servant, he will escort you,
That you may crown with food and drink and dances
The festive happiness of our reunion—
Your sister's home-returning to her kin.
Good-bye! *(To the countrymen who greet her)* You too —and you—all—every one!

*(*RHAMNES *goes off with the* ISLANDERS*)*

[5] Symbol of love and marriage.

SCENE III

SAPPHO, PHAON

SAPPHO

You see, my friend, your Sappho lives like this!
For kindness thanks, and friendliness for love,
This ever was my lot in life's exchange;
I was content and shall be more than happy 110
If you too give me half what you'll receive,
If you do not consider this excessive.
Yes, I have learnt to lose and do without!
When I was but a child my parents died;
And leaving scars upon my faithful heart,
My brothers and my sisters in their turn,
Part through their own fault, part the whim of fate,
Have now already crossed the Acheron.[6]
I've felt the fangs of falsehood and the sting
Of base ingratitude, and in this breast 120
The pangs of friendship frustrate—and of love.
Yes, I have learnt to lose and do without!
Only one thing I could not bear to lose—
You, Phaon, you, your friendship and your love.
Therefore, belovèd, test yourself!
You do not yet know the infinitude
That surges ever up and down my breast.
Oh let me never, dearest, never suffer
That I should lay my full heart on your own
To find it empty!

PHAON

Noble lady!

[6] The river Styx across which Charon transported the shades of the dead.

SAPPHO

Not so! *130*
Cannot your heart urge you to sweeter names?

PHAON

I hardly know what I am doing, saying.
Plucked from my quiet life's obscurity
And drawn magnetic to the ray of light,
Set high aloft upon an airy peak
To which the noblest vainly strive to attain,
My spirit faints with unexpected joy;
And in this bliss I cannot find myself.
I seem to see the woods and shores rush past,
The blue hills and the lowly hamlets vanish, *140*
And I can hardly reassure myself
That everything stands firm and only I
Am dizzily borne away upon the happy waves!

SAPPHO

You flatter prettily, yet, love, you flatter!

PHAON

And are you then indeed the lofty lady,
Whom reputation raises to the stars
With acclamation from the farthest shore
Of Pelop's isle to where the Thracian mountains
Stand rugged on the joyous Hellas border,
On every isle that, far from men and land, *150*
Kronos's[7] hand hurled in the sea of Greece,
In Asia's prosperous coasts of dazzling sun;
Yes, everywhere where a Greek mouth may but
Serenely sing or speak the tongue divine?
And if you are indeed that lofty lady,
How could your gracious eye fall on a youth,
Obscure and nameless, without reputation,
Who boasts no greater worth than this—your lyre,
Esteemed alone because *your* hand has touched it.

[7] Kronos was the leader of the twelve Titan brothers, sons of Heaven and Earth, and was father of Zeus.

SAPPHO

A plague upon the wretched, tuneless lyre! 160
Will it, when touched, hum its own mistress' praise?

PHAON

Ever since I could think and my weak hand
Tried childishly to test the lyre's strings,
It was your lofty form that stood before me!
When in the happy circle of my home
We sat around our parents' humble hearth,
And when Theano, my belovèd sister,
Used to bring down the scroll from the black shelf
To sing to us a song by you, by Sappho:
How all the noisy youth fell dumb at once, 170
How all the maidens huddled close together
In order not to lose one golden word!
And when indeed she sang; the passionate song
Of Aphrodite and her handsome youth,
The measured moan of lonely, sleepless nights,
The dalliance with Andromeda and Attis, [8]
How tensely each one listened, quick to accuse
His very breathing—heightened by the swell
Of ecstasy—of rowdy interruption.
Then would Theano lay her dreamy head 180
Right back upon her chair, and looking round
The spacious twilight of the hut, would ask,
"How do you think our lofty lady looks?
I think I see her, and by all the gods,
Would recognize her from a thousand women!"
Then would the fetters fall from all our tongues
And each would torture his imagination,
In order to adorn you with fresh charms.

[8] Objects of the poetess' passion in one of her songs. The name Attis has some special significance, being that of the god of vegetation, the castrate spouse of the goddess Cybele, and the patron divinity of eunuchs. Andromeda, the daughter of the Ethiopian King Cepheus and of Cassiopeia, was condemned, due to her mother's misdeed, to exposure to a monster on an island, whence she was freed by Perseus.

One gave you Pallas' eyes,[9] one Hera's arm,[10]
One Aphrodite's charm-embroidered girdle;[11] *190*
But I would silently arise and wander
Into the lonely realm of holy night.
There, to the pulse beats of sweet sleeping Nature,
Encompassed by her mighty magic spell,
There I would stand and stretch my arms toward you;
And when a wisp of snow from the fleecy clouds,
The zephyr's balmy breath, the mountain fragrance,
The silver-pale reflections of the moon,
All merged in one, was wafted o'er my brows,
Then you were mine; then I would feel your presence, *200*
And Sappho's features floated in the clouds!

SAPPHO

You lend me grace from your rich fantasy.
Woe, if you ever took back what you lent!

PHAON

And when my father sent me to Olympia
To take part in the open chariot race,
And everywhere upon my way I heard
That Sappho's lyre would there compete, would win
The laurel crown in the poetic challenge,
Then my heart swelled with indescribable yearning,
And my stretched horses on the way fell dead, *210*
Before Olympia's rooftops came in sight.
I entered it. The chariot's thrilling race,
The wrestler's art, the discus' happy throw,
All failed to move my far, foreboding mind;
I did not even ask who won the prize—
The finest, highest palm was mine already.
I was to see her, her, the crown of women!

[9] Pallas-Athene, goddess of wisdom, with radiant eyes, was the presiding deity of Athens.

[10] Hera, wife of Zeus and goddess of wedlock, was noted for the whiteness of her arms.

[11] Aphrodite, goddess of love, wore a girdle with magical properties. (See Homer's *Iliad* 14, V. 215.)

Then dawned the day of the poetic challenge.
Alcaeus sang, Anacreon, in vain!
They could not loose the bonds that bound my spirit. 220
But hark! A murmuring breaks through the people,
The crowd divides—it happened at long last!
Holding a golden lyre in her hand,
A woman walked through the admiring throng:
Her garment, white as innocence, flowed down
In graceful folds upon her hidden ankles,
A flood that over flowery hillocks flows.
The hem proclaimed green palms and laurel branches,
Depicting delicately fame and peace,
The poet's need and ultimate reward. 230
Like rosy morning clouds around the sun,
A purple mantle flowed about her shoulders,
And through the black night of her raven locks
There shone the moon of her bright diadem,
The flashing high mark of authority.
My soul cried: She's the one! And it was you.[12]
Before I put in words my premonition,
The people's thousand-voicèd shouts of joy
Gave confirmation to my sweet surmise.
How you then sang, how you then triumphed, how, 240
Adorned then with achievement's lofty crown,
In the enthusiasm of victory,
You let your lyre slip, while I rush forward
And, overcome by your victorious glance,
The bashful youth stands dumb and shamefaced there,
Better than I, all this you know, great lady,
Than I, who half awake still ask myself
How much of this took place, and how much I have
dreamt!

SAPPHO

I know well how you stood in silent shyness,
Your whole life seemed to beam forth from your eyes alone,

[12] Compare Premislaus in Grillparzer's *Libussa:*

And all my being cried out: She's the one!
(Act IV, V. 1587)

That, very rarely raised above the ground,[13] 250
Sufficed to bear clear witness to your unquenched fire.
I bade you follow, and you followed me,
Sunk deep in wonder and uncertainty.

PHAON

But who'd have thought that Hellas's first lady
Would deign to look on Hellas's last youth.

SAPPHO

You are unfair to fate and to yourself!
Do not despise the golden gifts of the gods,
That they bestow at birth, on cheek and brow
And limb, on heart and breast, upon the child 260
Whom they have destined to a happy life.
They are sure staves to which existence may
Attach its tender, easily broken threads.
The body's beauty is a noble blessing,
And joy of living is a precious prize;
A hero's courage, and an emperor's strength,
Determination, joy in that which *is,*
With fantasy as fit, a gracious servant,
All these adorn the rough paths of our lives,
Where *living* is indeed the highest aim of life! 270
It's not for nothing that the Muses' chorus
Have picked the laurel as a mark of grace,
Cold, fruitless, scentless, it fatigues the head
As recompense for many a sacrifice.
A harsh wind haunts the heights of humankind
And the poor artist is forever forced

(Stretching out her arms to PHAON*)*

To beg a little from life's overflow!

PHAON

What can you say, most gracious enchantress,
That would not pass as true because you say it?

[13] Like Leander in Act I of *The Waves of Sea and Love.*

SAPPHO

Let us endeavor then, my dearest friend, 280
To wind *both* garlands round our eager brows,
To quaff life from the dizzy cup of art
And art from out the gentle hand of life.
Behold this countryside that in its charm
And quiet seems belonging part to earth
And partly to the fields caressed by Lethe;[14]
Within these grottoes and these shrubs of roses,
And in the friendly shadow of these columns,
Here let us taste, united—like the immortals,
Who neither hunger nor satiety know, 290
But only the eternal flow of pleasure—
The joys and beauty of a happy life.
Whatever's mine is also yours. Only when you
Make use of it will its possession please me.
Then look around you, you are in your house!
I'll show you to the servants as their master.
Their mistress' example will teach them how to serve.
Come out, you maidens, slaves, come hither!

PHAON

Sappho!
How can I ever pay back so much kindness?
My mounting debt is almost choking me. 300

SCENE IV

(EUCHARIS, MELITTA, RHAMNES, MEN-SERVANTS AND MAID-SERVANTS *with the above)*

RHAMNES

You called, my lady!

[14] A river in Hades, the water of which, if drunk, caused forgetfulness of the past.

SAPPHO

Yes, I did; come nearer!
Behold your master here!

RHAMNES

(Astonished, half aloud) Master?

SAPPHO

Who questions here?
(Intense) What do you mean?

RHAMNES

(Withdrawing) Nothing!

SAPPHO

Then do not question!
You here behold your master. All his wishes
Are all commands for you, the same as mine.
He who is disobedient, woe to him,
Whom even one cloud on his master's brow
Should charge with having broken my command!
Lapses against myself I may forget,
Who ruffles *him* will wake my instant anger. *310*
And now, my friend, I pray, look to your comfort;
The journey's load upon your brow lies hard.
Let them provide high hospitality,
Enjoy in friendship Sappho's earliest gift!

PHAON

Oh could I only change my earlier life,
Casting it quite aside, just like my clothes
And see, in clear and calm *deliberation,*
How quite to be what I desire to be!
Then fare you well. It will not be for long.

SAPPHO

I shall await you. You, Melitta, stay! *320*

(Exeunt PHAON *and the others)*

SCENE V

SAPPHO, MELITTA

SAPPHO

(Looking long in the direction of PHAON*)*

Well now, Melitta?

MELITTA

What's my mistress' will?

SAPPHO

Does warm blood then flow only in *my* veins,
While dripping ice is lodged in others' hearts?
They saw him and they listened to his voice;
This selfsame air that played upon his brow
Has fanned her empty, almost lifeless breast.
Most hollow sounds her "What's my mistress' will?" then,
The very first words wrung out from their lips!
Indeed, I almost hate you! Go!

*(*MELITTA *silently turns to go)*

SAPPHO

(Who has meanwhile sunk down upon the grassy bank)
Melitta!
And could you utter nothing else at all 330
That might have sought to please me, dearest child?
And yet you saw him, did you then observe
Nothing worth seeing and commenting on?
Where were your eyes, my girl?

(Seizing her by the hand and drawing her to her knees)

MELITTA

You will remember what you've often told us,

That it is not becoming for young women
To spend their eyes in strangers' company.

SAPPHO

So, you poor thing, you lowered your pretty eyes?
(*Kisses her*) So that was it. The lesson was meant for
Your elders only who are less composed; 340
And girls may yet do what young women may not.

(Looking at her closely)

But let me see! How very much you've changed
Since I left here, I hardly recognize you.
By so much taller and—*(Kisses her again)* You sweetest creature!
You were quite right. The lesson was for you too! *(Rising)*
Why are you still so silent and so shy?
You were not so before. What makes you draw back?
It's not your mistress Sappho standing here,
Sappho your friend, Melitta, speaks to you!
Pride, thirst for fame, and anger's venomed sting, 350
And what unlovely else was in your friend—
Have not, I tell you, come back home with her;
I've drowned all that in the bosom of the waves
During my homeward voyage by his side.
It is the very magic power of love
That it ennobles all that feels its breath,
Just like the sun, whose golden rays divine
Turn even the thunderclouds themselves to gold.
If I have ever with impetuous speech,
If ever with a sharp word wounded you, 360
Then pardon me! We will in future live
With him, like sisters intimate and twin,
Distinguished only by his love for one.
Oh I will yet be good, both meek and good!

MELITTA

Are you not good now and were you not always?

SAPPHO

Yes, good, as one calls good what is not bad!

Should that suffice for such a great reward?
You think he will feel happy here, Melitta?

MELITTA

Who could feel otherwise, when you are near!

SAPPHO

Poor that I am, what can I offer him? 370
He stands there in the fullness of his youth,
Adorned with all the finest flowers of life.
The fresh-awakened spirit, with glad wonder
Examining the sum of its own powers,
Spreads forth its wings and aims its eagle eye
In keen desire at all the highest goals.
Whatever's fine and great and high and worthy
Is his! The world belongs to him who's strong!
And I! O Gods and Goddesses of Heaven,
O give me back again the golden past! 380
Wipe out the furrowed trace within my heart
Of former sufferings and of former pleasures;
Whatever I have felt, said, done and suffered
Wipe out, O, even from remembrance, wipe!
O let me go back once more to the time
When I, still shy, with rounded girlish cheeks,
And unfamiliar stirrings in my breast,
Looked at the wakening world with wakening spirit;
When only dreams—no torturing experience—
Inspired the golden playing of my lyre, 390
When love was still a magic land to me,
An unknown, strange and wondrous magic land!

(Leaning on MELITTA*'s breast)*

MELITTA

What is the matter? Are you ill, my mistress?

SAPPHO

There stand I on the brink of the abyss
That yawns devouring between him and me;
I see the golden land that beckons me.

My eye may reach it, ah, but not my foot! [15]
Woe to the man, lured from a quiet home
By the vain shadows of proud name and fame!
He sails a torn, tempestuous sea *400*
Upon a fragile craft. There no tree grows,
Nor sprouts a seed, nor flourishes a flower;
But all around the gray infinitude.
Only from far he sees the sunny coast
And, mingled with the waters' hollow roar,
The voice of his belovèd calls to him.
If he decides at long last to return
And seeks the light-forsaken fields of home,
He finds that spring is past, no flower remains

(Taking off her wreath and regarding it sadly)

And only withered leaves around him rustle![16] *410*

MELITTA

The glorious wreath! How such high fame must please!
By thousands coveted and not attained!

SAPPHO

By thousands coveted and not attained!
Not so, Melitta? Not so, dearest maiden?
By thousands coveted and *not* attained!

(Replacing the wreath)

Let him not scoff at fame who once has won it,
It is no empty echo, meaningless;
Its fingers are endowed with power divine!
Once more I breathe. Then I am not so poor.
Against his wealth I may set equal wealth— *420*
Against this wreath the present offers me,
The blossoms of the past and of the future!

[15] Like Moses and the Promised Land.

[16] A very poignant and prophetic confession of Grillparzer himself, who was to feel later that his sacrifice of domestic joys to his artistic ambition had not been worthwhile.

You look amazed and fail to understand me?
Ah, happy you! Learn never to understand!

MELITTA

You're angry?

SAPPHO

No, dear child, no, not at all!
Go to the others now, and come and tell me
When your new master wishes to receive me.

(*Exit* MELITTA)

SCENE VI

SAPPHO *(Alone)*

She lays her brow on her hands, sunk in thought, then she sits down on the grassy bank and takes up her lyre, accompanying the following with individual chords.

SAPPHO

Golden-thronèd Aphrodite; [17]
Wile-spinning daughter of Zeus,
Burden not with care and sorrow, *430*
Goddess sublime, my throbbing heart!

But come to me, if ever thou found'st pleasing
The strains of my lyre,
To whose music thou often wouldst listen,
Forsaking thy father's golden house.

Thou didst prepare the shimmering chariot
And thy blithe pair of sparrows
Gaily spreading their darkling wings
Bore thee down from heaven to earth.

[17] Grillparzer translated these verses from one of Sappho's own poems.

And thou camest; divine Aphrodite, 440
With thy immortal smiling eyes,
Didst thou ever ask, what tortured thy suppliant,
Why her cry for succor was uttered?

What her dreaming heart desired,
Whom her trembling breast longed softly
To entangle in the net of love;
"Who is it, Sappho, who troubles thee?

If now he flee thee, soon he will follow thee;
Despising gifts, yet he himself will give them,
If he loves thee not, soon, soon he shall love thee, 450
Faithfully following thy every beckoning!"

Come also now and shed the grief
That weighs my heavy bosom down,
Help me to wrest, for what I am wrestling,
Be my companion in the strife of love!

(She leans back her head, exhausted)

Curtain

ACT II

Open countryside as in the previous act

SCENE I

PHAON *enters*

PHAON

How pleasant! Here it's quiet. No loud feasting,
Nor clash of cymbals, nor the sound of flutes,
Nor noisy movement of unbridled joy
Reaches me here beneath the gracious trees,
That whispering softly, as though loath to jar, *460*
Invite me now to solitary reflection.[18]

How everything within my soul has changed
Since I forsook my parents' quiet roof
And turned my horses toward Olympia.
In calm deliberation I was able
To follow with keen eyes and to untangle
The subtle threads of complicated feelings,
Till, clearly recognized, each lay apart;
But now, like an oppressive summer night
That sweetly suffocates, there brooding lies *470*
A heavy cloud over my sleeping senses,
Through which the distant lightning of my thoughts,
Flashes, now here, now there and now

[18] Both Wieland's Agathon and Schiller's Maid of Orleans similarly flee from a festive din in search of self-knowledge.

Not anywhere, in torturing confusion—
The past is hidden from me by a veil;
I hardly now remember yesterday,
Or in the present moment that just past.
I ask myself: Are you indeed the same
Who stood beside her in Olympia?
Beside her in the thrill of victory? 480
Was it *your* name that the delirious throng,
Coupled with hers, shouted aloud to heaven?
Though all says "yes" to me, I scarce believe it!
What sort of wretched creature then is man,
When what, as hope, awakened all his senses,
Plunges them, in fulfillment, to sound sleep.
When I had not yet seen nor known her, only
Fancy had drawn her ill-resembling picture,
Seen through gray mist and still indefinite,
Then it seemed easy for her single glance, 490
For one kind word, to offer up my life;
And now when she is mine, belongs to me,
When all my longings' winter caterpillars
Play round me now like golden butterflies,
I still stand asking, thinking, hesitating!

Alas! I'll be forgetting quite myself
And her and parents—O my parents!
Must I now, only now, remember you!
How could I leave you so long without news?
Perhaps you mourn my death, or else perhaps 500
The mouth of rumor has already whispered
That I, your son, whom you sent not to love
But to take part in high Olympia's challenge,
In Sappho's arms—

Who dares to slander her?
The glory of her sex, the crown of women!
And if the spit of envy did besmirch her,
I'd champion her against an accusing world!
And even my father, if he but once sees her,
Would put aside the former prejudice

The sight of forward, zither-strumming women 510
Used to imprint repugnant in his breast.
(Sunk in thought) What's that? The noisy crowd is coming.
How tiresome! I'll escape! Where? Ah—here!

(He enters the grotto)

SCENE II

Enter EUCHARIS, MELITTA, *Slave girls with flowers and garlands.*

EUCHARIS *(Noisily)*

Come on, you maidens, bring more flowers here!
Flowers in great quantities! Adorn the house
And courtyard, hall, doors, columns and thresholds.
Yes, even adorn the flowerbeds fresh with flowers.
Add spice to seasoning, in celebration
Today of our mistress's feast of love.

MAIDENS *(Showing her their flowers)*

Here see!

(They begin to hang garlands and chains of flowers on the columns and trees)

EUCHARIS

Well done! Well done! Melitta, you? 520
Where have you kept your flowers?

MELITTA

(Looking at her empty hands) I—my flowers?

EUCHARIS

Yes, you! Ah, look at her, the dreaming girl!
Do you alone come here with empty hands?

MELITTA

I mean to fetch—

EUCHARIS

She means to fetch, she says,

And does not budge. She means—and fetches nothing.
You little hypocrite, come now, confess,
What's worrying you? What passed today at table,
That the mistress should so often glance at you,
A secret knowing smile upon her face,
And then her glances teasingly would lower! *530*
Each time she did, I saw you hotly blush
And, trembling in embarrassing confusion,
Forget to serve, as you are well accustomed:
And when she called you to present and taste
The great cup of the handsome stranger and
You shyly put the brim between your lips,
She suddenly exclaimed—"Down with your eyes!"
When woe, half the contents of the great cup
You promptly spilt upon the polished floor.
Why, Sappho laughed herself. What means all this? *540*
Come on, confess. Denial will not help!

MELITTA

Oh, let me be!

EUCHARIS

Not likely, child, no mercy!
Head up and everything first clean confessed!
Dear me! Even a little tear appears—
Contrary puss! I shall not push you further,
But do not cry. If you repeat such conduct,
Then I'll be just as hard— Do not cry!
What, girls, are there no flowers left? Come on then,
Let's find some fresh ones! Come, you may sit there,
Here are more roses, help us wind a wreath! *550*
Be quick, my child. Cry no more, do you hear?

(Exeunt with the girls)

SCENE III

MELITTA *(alone)* [19]

She sits on the grassy bank and begins to twine a wreath. After a while she shakes her head sadly and sets down beside her what she has begun.

MELITTA

It is no use—alas! My head is bursting
And in my breast my heart is beating fast!
Here I must sit, forlorn and all forsaken,
Far from my parents' hearth in a foreign land,
With slavish fetters pressing on my hands
That I stretch longingly toward my kin.
Alas! I sit forlorn and all forsaken
And no one cares to hear or notice me!
With tears I see around me, friends and relatives *560*
Embracing as do relatives and friends;
Here no heart beats in sympathy with me,
And all my relatives live far from here.
I gaze at the children romping round their father,
Kissing his grave brow, his belovèd locks;
My father lives beyond the distant seas,
Where nor his daughter's kiss nor voice can reach;
They treat me here as though I were beloved,
And neither is there lack of gentle words;
And yet it is not love but only pity, *570*
That even to the slave grants kindly words;
The mouth, one moment full of flattering speech,
May soon be filled with scorn and bitter mock.

[19] This monologue recalls Iphigenia's opening monologue in Goethe's *Iphigenie auf Tauris,* but Melitta's anguish is keener and therefore dramatically, as distinct from literarily, more effective.

Ah *they* may love and hate, do what they will,
And what the heart feels, may the lips express,
Purple and gold and jewels all adorn them
And every eye in admiration turns;
The slave girl's place is by the humblest hearth,
No eye regards her there, and no tongue questions;
For her no glance, no thought and no desire! 580

Dear gods, who have so often heard my prayers,
And have with bounteous hand sent me fulfillment,
When I entreated you with pious heart,
O lend me now once more a gracious ear!
Ah, lead me gently back to my own kindred,
That I might cool my sorrow-fevered brow
Upon a soft and sympathetic breast,
Ah, lead me to my kindred, or else bear me
Aloft to you! . . . to you! . . . to you! [20]

SCENE IV

PHAON, MELITTA

PHAON, *who has appeared during the foregoing monologue at the entrance of the grotto, but has retired listening, now comes forward and from behind places his hand on* MELITTA*'s shoulder.*

PHAON

So young and yet so melancholy, maiden?

MELITTA *(Shrinking back)*

Ah! 590

[20] Compare Grillparzer's youthful tragedy *Blanka von Kastilien* (written in 1808 and 1809 but not performed till September 26, 1958, when it was staged at the Volkstheater in Vienna), where Fedriko addresses his dead father's portrait in similar terms:

> Ah save me from my doubts, or, Father, bear me
> Aloft to you! . . . to you! . . . to you!
> (Act IV, Scene iii Vs. 3338–39)

PHAON

I have just heard you praying to the gods
For the breast of a friend. Here is a friend.
And equal pain unites like equal blood,
And those who mourn are everywhere related.
I also feel the absence of dear parents
And am nostalgic drawn towards my home.
Come, let's exchange! So that the grief of one
May turn to balm to soothe the other's breast.
You hold your tongue. Why this mistrust, dear maiden?
Look up at me! I do not mean to harm you. *600*

(He raises her head up by the chin)

Aha! So *you* are the little wine-taster
Who pledged the polished floor and not the guest!
For that you're shy! Cheer up! The accident
Delighted both your mistress and myself.

(MELITTA *has somewhat flinched at the last words; raises her eyes and looks at him, then stands up and turns to go)*

My child, I did not mean to be offensive,
Can gentle eyes like yours have such grave looks?
You must explain. I will not let you go!
I noticed you already at the banquet;
Through all the wild and dizzy revel shone
The tender sweetness of your virgin quiet. *610*
Who are you? And what keeps you in this place?
You did not sit at table, you were serving,
The slaves in their familiarity
Seemed to address you as their *peer*—

MELITTA

I am.

(She turns away and is about to go)

PHAON *(Detaining her)*

Stay!

MELITTA

What do you want of the slave, my lord?
Let her seek out some slave-girl's breast and . . .

(Tears choke her voice)

Bear me aloft to you, to you, dear gods!

PHAON *(Touching her)*

You're deeply moved, you tremble. Calm yourself!
The fetters of a slave bind but his *hands*.
The mind decides who's free and who is slave. 620
Console yourself. Sappho is good and gentle;
A word from me and she'll restore you to
Your kindred and your father without ransom.

*(*MELITTA *shakes her head silently)*

Believe me, she will do it. Or perhaps
The passionate longing for your fatherland
That seized you now has quickly disappeared?

MELITTA

Ah, tell me first, *where* is my fatherland?

PHAON

You do not know it?

MELITTA

I was snatched away
In tender childhood from its firm protection.
My memory at present but remembers 630
Its blossoms and its valleys, not its name.
I fancy it lay somewhere to the Orient,
For everything was bright and radiant there.

PHAON

Then it is far from here?

MELITTA

Oh, very far!
I was surrounded there by other foliage
And by the fragrance of quite other flowers.

In bluer skies there twinkled fairer stars,[21]
And good and friendly men were dwelling there.
I lived there in the midst of many children,
And ah! an old man with white silver hair, *640*
I called him Father, used to fondle me;
And then another man, so handsome, gracious,
With brownish hair and eyes, almost like—you—

PHAON

You hold your tongue? The man?

MELITTA

He too—

PHAON

Fondled you,
Not so?

(Seizing her hand)

MELITTA *(Softly)*

I was a child.

PHAON

I well believe it!
A sweet and charming, uninhibited child!

(Leaving her hand)

Go on!

MELITTA

So every day passed smoothly by,
Till one night I was wakened by wild cries
Resounding loud from all sides in my ears.
The nurse approached, they quickly took me up *650*
And carried me into the raging night.
There all around I saw the huts in flames
And men who fought, and men who fled and fell.
Now came a savage, who laid hands on me,

[21] Compare Mignon's song in Goethe's *Wilheim Meister:*

> Knowest thou the land where the pale lemon blows,
> In leafy gloom the golden orange glows
> A gentle wind the deep-blue heaven fans?

And all was tumult, lamentations, groans;
When I came to, it was upon a ship
That glided through the dark waves, arrow-swift.
I saw yet other maidens, children, weeping,
But ever smaller grew our wretched number
The further we were parted from our land. *660*
For many days and nights we voyaged on,
It seemed like months. At last I was alone
Of all the captives with the savage men.
And then we came in sight of Lesbos' shores,
Then I was disembarked. Then Sappho saw me
And offered gold and made Melitta hers.

PHAON

And was your lot so hard in Sappho's hands?

MELITTA

Ah no! She treated me most kindly, gently;
She dried my tears and looked well after me
And full of love she educated me; *670*
For even if she's sometimes quick and bitter,
Yet Sappho's good, she's truly kind and good.

PHAON

And yet you cannot quite forget your home?

MELITTA

Alas! I did forget it all too soon!
In dance and play and in domestic duties
I seldom thought of loved ones left behind.
Yet sometimes, when oppressed by pain and sorrow,
A yearning glides into my anguished heart,
And then remembrance with its sad-sweet hand
Unveils its far and radiant, blossoming gold. *680*
And so today, I felt forlorn, distressed,
And every lightly spoken word fell wounding,
As though the fibers of my flesh were touched.
But now I feel much better and am merry!

VOICES WITHIN

Melitta!

PHAON

Listen. They are calling.

MELITTA

I must go.

(She gathers up the unfinished wreath and flowers)

PHAON

What have you here?

MELITTA

Why, flowers!

PHAON

Flowers? For whom?

MELITTA

For you—for you and Sappho.

PHAON

Stay!

MELITTA

They call.

PHAON

You must not leave me with such gloomy looks!
Show me your flowers!

MELITTA

Here they are!

PHAON *(Picking out a rose)*

Take this rose!

(He pins it on her breast)

Let it remind you of this hallowed hour, *690*
Remind you that not only in your homeland,
But also in remote lands you have—friends.

*(*MELITTA, *having started at his touch, stands now motionless with agitated breast, both hands hanging down, her head*

and eyes lowered. Phaon has withdrawn a few steps and observes her from a distance)

VOICES WITHIN

Melitta!

MELITTA

Did you call me?

PHAON

Not I. The house.

MELITTA *(Picking up the wreaths that have fallen from her)*
I'm coming!

PHAON

What, so miserly, Melitta?
Did not my gift deserve some recompense?

MELITTA

A gift from me? What can a slave girl have?

PHAON

Gold is the gift of vanity, crude pride.
The gift of friendship and of love is flowers.
Here you have flowers—

MELITTA *(Throwing away the flowers)*

What, these wretched flowers
That those untutored maidens there have plucked, 700
That are intended for— No, never!

PHAON

What then?

MELITTA

How they have plundered all the bushes here!
I find no trace here of a single flower.

(Looking up at the rosebush)

I see a rose there hanging on that branch,
But it is much too high. I cannot reach it.

PHAON

I will help you.

MELITTA

Ah no, indeed.

PHAON

Why not?

So easily I will not yield my claim.

MELITTA *(Mounting the grassy bank)*

Come on then! I shall bend the branch.

PHAON

All right!

MELITTA

(Standing on tiptoe, bending the branch, at the extremity of which the rose is hanging)

Can you reach it?

PHAON

(Who is observing MELITTA, *without paying attention to the rose)*

Not yet.

MELITTA

Then now—alas,

I'm slipping, falling!

PHAON

No, I'll hold you.

(The branch escapes her hand, and swiftly snaps back, she trembles and sinks into PHAON*'s arms, which he extends to receive her)*

MELITTA

Leave me! *710*

PHAON *(Holding her to him)*

Melitta!

MELITTA

Let me go! Alas!

PHAON

Melitta!

(He imprints a kiss quickly on her lips)

SCENE V

SAPPHO, *simply dressed, without wreath or lyre. The above.*

SAPPHO *(Entering)*

You let me seek you, friend? What do I see?

MELITTA

The mistress! Listen!

PHAON

What's that? Sappho here?

(He lets her go. A pause)

SAPPHO

Melitta!

MELITTA

My lady!

SAPPHO

What are you seeking here?

MELITTA

I was seeking flowers.

SAPPHO

And not without success!

MELITTA

That rose there—

SAPPHO

It is burning on your lips.

MELITTA

It hung so high.

SAPPHO

Perhaps not high enough!

Go!

MELITTA

Shall I first—

SAPPHO

Just go, I tell you, go!

(*Exit* MELITTA)

SCENE VI

SAPPHO, PHAON

SAPPHO *(After a pause)*

Phaon!

PHAON

Sappho.

SAPPHO

You arose

And left the table early. You were missed. 720

PHAON

I do not care for drink, nor noisy revels.

SAPPHO

Not *noisy*. That sounds almost a reproach.

PHAON

How?

SAPPHO

As though perhaps I had done wrong in letting

My welcome-feast become so brash and boisterous?

PHAON

I did not mean it thus.

SAPPHO

A heart that's full
Seeks often the full din of noisy revel
In order, unobserved, to beat in quiet,
In rapture, mid the general cheer and tumult.

PHAON

Of course.

SAPPHO

I also had to thank our neighbors
For all the love and goodness they have shown. *730*
Such thanks are paid in wine, as you well know.
No tiresome feasting will in future mar
The quiet, that you love no more than I.

PHAON

I thank you.

SAPPHO

You are going?

PHAON

Should I stay?

SAPPHO

You may decide yourself to go or stay.

PHAON

You're angry?

SAPPHO *(Moved)*

Phaon!

PHAON

Do you want something?

SAPPHO

Nothing. . .
Just one thing *(With self-control)* I saw you jesting with Melitta.

PHAON

Melitta! . . . Who? . . . Ah yes, quite right. Go on!

SAPPHO

She is a sweet child.

PHAON

So it seems, indeed!

SAPPHO

The one I love most of my servant girls, 740
Yes, of my *children,* I might almost say,
For I have always loved them as my children.
If I have not yet sundered their slave-fetters,
It's only, since a sweeter tie's denied
By Nature, that the parentless and homeless
Should not forego, before the time is ripe,
A teacher's eye, a mother's tender care.
This is my constant practice. In the circle
Of Mytilene's most highly thought-of women
Are many who in glad remembrance call 750
Themselves the handiwork of Sappho's former days.

PHAON

Good! Very good!

SAPPHO

Of all the maidens, whom
The sport of fortune ever brought to me,
None was more dear to me than she, Melitta,
The charming maiden with the quiet mind.
Though not intelligent, of moderate gifts,
And useless in the practice of the arts,
Yet out of all she was the most beloved,
Thanks to her unassuming, modest ways,
Her deep and lovable sincerity, 760
That, slowly, like the quiet garden snail
That is at once the dwelling and the inmate,
Is ever ready, at the slightest sound
Affrightened, to withdraw into itself

And feeling all around with soft antennae
Dares, only hesitant, touch what is strange,
Yet firmly clings to what it once has grasped
And only dying lets go what it holds.

PHAON

Good! Very good, indeed.

SAPPHO

I did not wish—
My dear friend, pardon me! I did not wish *770*
That any inconsiderate fleeting jest
Should ever in her heart awake desires,
That unfulfilled, with bitter sting would rankle.
I want to shelter her from the experience
Of self-consuming longing unappeased,
The gnawing torments of a love that's spurned.
My friend—

PHAON

What are you saying?

SAPPHO

You are not listening!

PHAON

I'm listening: love torments.

SAPPHO

It does indeed!
My friend, you are not in the mood. Let us
Some other time discuss this matter further. *780*

PHAON

All right. Some other time!

SAPPHO

For now, farewell!
This hour I always used to dedicate
To the Muses in that quiet grotto there.
And even if I cannot hope to find

The Muses there today, I will find quiet
And I'm in need of it. Meanwhile, farewell!

PHAON

So you are going!

SAPPHO

Did you want—

PHAON

Farewell!

SAPPHO *(Turning away quickly)*

Farewell!

(She goes off into the cave)

SCENE VII

PHAON *alone, after gazing awhile straight in front of him.*

And have you really—*(Looking round)* She has gone! [22]
I am confused, my heavy head is spinning.

(Looking at the grassy bank)

Here she sat, here, the sweet exquisite child. *(Sits)* 790
Then here will I lay down my head to rest!

(He lays his head, exhausted, in his hands)

Curtain

[22] After this line, the Berlin edition has an extra line:

Then what has happened here? I hardly know.

This is wanting in the Vienna and Munich editions, which I have adhered to.

ACT III

Countryside, as in the former acts

SCENE I

PHAON *lies sleeping on the grassy bank.* SAPPHO *emerges from the grotto.*

SAPPHO

It is in vain! My thoughts swarm far and wide
Returning in stark emptiness to me.
Whatever I now do, wherever turn,
Before my burning brow in garish hues,
Still rampant rears that execrated image,
That I would fain escape, were it beyond,
Far, far beyond the dark bounds of this earth.
How close he held her! How his arm embraced her!
And then how, yielding softly to her urge, *800*
Upon his mouth she—Stop! I will not think of it!
The very thought kills me a thousand times!

Yet am I not a fool to rack myself
And to bewail what perhaps does not exist?
Who knows what fleeting, rasable impression,
What insubstantial fancy drew him to her,
A whim, dissolving swift as swift it sprang,
Requiring neither forethought nor reproach? [23]

[23] Compare Roxana's monologue in Racine's *Bajazet,* Act III, Scene vii Vs. 1075–77:

What bids me seek the measure of his feelings
In this, my deeply agitated breast? 810

Who knows what love, what life is, man and woman,
Does not weigh man's love against woman's passion.
Most fickle is man's fitful disposition,
Subservient to life, most fickle life.
He free bestrides the broad way of existence
Encompassed by the rosy dawn of hope,
With strength and courage, as with shield and sword,
Accoutred for the laureled fields of fame.
He deems the spirit's quiet world too narrow,
The external draws his wild and restless strivings; 820
And should he find love, he may bend perhaps
To pick the pleasing floweret from the ground,
Look at it, take his pleasure, and then stick it
With other trophies coldly in his helmet.
He does not know the deep primeval glow
That love engenders in a woman's breast;
How all her being, thinking and desiring
Turns single-minded round this single point,
How all her wishes, like emergent fledglings
That flutter timorous round their mother's nest, 830
In fearful anguish timidly protect
This love, at once their cradle and their grave;
Like some rare jewel hangs her whole existence
Is room enough for other things than love,
He loves; however, in his ample bosom
Around the neck of her awakened love!
And many matters, wanton to a woman,
Will he permit himself in jest and sport.
He deems it his prerogative to snatch
A kiss wherever the occasion offers; 840
Ah, sad it is to be so, but it is so!

(Turning around and catching sight of PHAON*)*

Yet it may be, perhaps, too quick to fret,
I make too much of just a passing cloud,
Imputing to his love a fleeting whim.

See someone lies, beneath the rose tree's shadow—
Yes, it is he, the fascinating traitor!
He sleeps; repose and calm serenity
Are on his forehead gently now encamped.
Only the holy sleep of innocence
Breathes thus, only the carefree breast thus heaves.
Yes, dearest, I will hearken to your slumber,
However bad the tidings when you wake.
Forgive, belovèd, if in the first moment *850*
I have offended you with vain suspicion,
If I imagined sordid falsehood could
Find any entrance in so pure a temple!
He smiles—his lips appear to part—
It seems some name is hovering in his breath,
Wake up; pronounce awake your Sappho's name,
She is embracing you. Wake up!

(She kisses him on the brow)

PHAON

(Awakes, stretches out his arms and utters with half-shut eyes)

Melitta!

SAPPHO

(Starting back)

Ha!

PHAON

Ah! Who has wakened me? Who, envious, scared
The visions of my sweet dreams from my brow?
You, Sappho? Greetings to you! I knew well *860*
That something gracious stood beside me, since
So gracious too was the image of my dream.
You look so sad! What irks you? I am gay!
What weighed my breast down with anxiety
Has almost, as by miracle, dissolved,
All anguish spent, I once again breathe free;
And like the poor wretch, plunged precipitate
Into the dark dominion of the sea,

Where terror reigns and dull and gnawing dread,
When borne aloft upon the ocean's arm *870*
Into the sunlight's gold serenity,
The air's sweet kiss, the joyous voice of sound,
That all at once impinge upon his senses:
So stand I, drunk with joy, most happy, blessed
And, overwhelmed by all this bliss, could wish
To have more senses or to feel less pleasure.

SAPPHO *(To herself)*

Melitta!

PHAON

Be, belovèd, gay and happy!
Here is such beauty, ah such heavenly beauty!
The summer evening sinks with delicate wings
In sweet exhaustion on the quiet meadows; *880*
Love-thirstily the sea breathes up and down,
A bride to welcome on her breast her lord,[24]
Who turns his steeds already to the west;
A gentle breeze plays in the slender poplars,
That softly dallying with the virgin pillars
Breathe gently, greeting us, the dreams of love
And seem to whisper: "See, we love! Then you too love!"

SAPPHO *(To herself)*

I almost feel my breast deceived afresh,
But no! Too deeply have I plumbed his heart!

PHAON

My dizzy feverishness, that held me fast *890*
So very long, is of a sudden vanished,
And, Sappho, please believe me, I was never
So near to you, so truly near as now.
Come, let's be gay, dear Sappho, gay and happy!
But tell me, Sappho, what do you think of dreams?

[24] Apollo, the sun god, with his chariot driven daily across the sky from east to west.

SAPPHO

They lie and I detest all liars!

PHAON

Listen!
I have just had, as I now lay asleep,
A very marvelous, peculiar dream.[25]
I found myself transplanted to Olympia,
Exactly as the time I saw you first *900*
Contending in the merry challenge there.
I stood surrounded by the cheering throngs
Amidst the din of chariots and of challenge.
Sudden a lyre's note and all was mute;
You it was, singing of love's golden joys,
And I was shaken to my very depths;
I rush toward you—but then, just imagine!
I suddenly no longer recognize you,
She still stood there, the figure that I knew,
The purple mantle streamed from her round shoulders, *910*
The lyre in her white hand still resounded;
Only the features change, kaleidoscopic,
Like mists enveloping the mountains blue,
The laurel wreath, it suddenly had vanished,
The gravity, vanished from the lofty brow;
The lips that even now divinely sang,
Were smiling with an earthly-pleasing smile,
The features that were lifted from Athene,
Are transformed to the countenance of a child.[26]
In short, she's you and is not you, appearing *920*
Sometimes to be Sappho, sometimes—

[25] Agathon, the hero of *Agathon,* Wieland's novel of classical antiquity which exercised a great influence over Grillparzer in his earlier classical plays, has a similar dream about Danae (Sappho) and Psyche (Melitta).

[26] Similarly in Madame de Staël's *Corinne,* which has many parallels with *Sappho,* Oswald, the young hero, dreams of Lucile, Corinne's younger sister, who drives Corinne from his thoughts. It is interesting to note that Sappho refers to Melitta not only in maternal terms, but as a sister.

SAPPHO *(Shrieking)*

Melitta!

PHAON

You almost frightened me! And pray, who told
You, it was she? I hardly knew myself!
You are upset and I—

(SAPPHO bidding him with her hand to keep away)

What? Must I go?
But one thing further, Sappho, let me tell you—

(SAPPHO bidding him once more)

You will not hear? I am to go? I'm going!

(He exits)

SCENE II

SAPPHO *alone*

SAPPHO *(After a pause)*

The bow has twanged;

(Beating her hands together over her breast)

The arrow lodges here!—
How can I longer doubt? Clear it is, clear!
Yes, *she's* the one who sways his perjured heart,
She hovers in his mind devoid of shame, 930
In *her* apparel are his dreams enveloped,
Insinuating on the recreant's couch.
What, Sappho spurned, in favor of her slave?
Spurned? Who? In heaven's name! And spurned by whom?
Am I no longer then the very Sappho,
Who saw so many monarchs at her feet,
And, playing fondly with their proffered crowns,
First saw and heard the proud men, then dismissed them;[27]

[27] Compare Racine's Mithridates, similarly rejected by his affianced Monima:

Remember Ephesus—how I adored you,

The very Sappho, whom the whole of Greece
Acclaimed with shouts of joy its rarest jewel? 940
O fool! Why did I come down from the heights
The laurel crowns, where Aganippe[28] roars,
And Muses' chorus consort with star-music,[29]
Down here into the suffocating valley,
Where misery reigns and faithlessness and crime?
My place was there aloft, there with the clouds,
Here is no room for me, except the grave.
Let him whom gods have chosen for their own
Not consort with the citizens of earth;
The portion of mankind and the immortals 950
Can never mingle in the selfsame cup.
You must make choice of one of these two worlds,
And when *once* chosen, there is no retreat;
One single bite of glory's golden fruit—
Like Proserpine's few pomegranate seeds—[30]
Bears you forever to the quiet shades,
And no more to the living you belong,
However kindly life may beam at you,
May fill your ears with sweet and flattering sounds,
Enticing you as friendship and as love! 960

Preferring you to scores of royal daughters,
Spurning, for your sake, all those powerful allies.
What crowds of kingdoms I placed at your feet!
(Act IV, Scene iv, Vs. 1295–98)

[28] Aganippe, a stream on Mount Helicon in Boeotia, frequented by the Muses.

[29] The music of the spheres, which, according to Pythagoras, was made by the stars in their courses—immortalized by Shakespeare in *The Merchant of Venice* (Act V, Scene i):

There's not the smallest orb which thou behold'st
But in his motion like an angel sings
Still quiring to the young-ey'd cherubins.

[30] Proserpine (Persephone) was the abducted consort of Pluto, King of Hades. At the request of her mother, Demeter, her father (Zeus) permitted her return to earth, provided she had taken no nourishment in Hades. But as she had eaten a few pomegranate seeds there, she had to spend part of every year in Hades.

Ah stop, unhappy you! You would pluck roses,
And thorns instead you press into your breast!

I will see her, this paragon of beauty,
Who glories in such triumph over Sappho.
What am I to believe? Is memory false,
That, when I question it, brings to my senses
A silly child with imbecilic features?
With eyes, forever turned toward the ground,
With lips, that mouth the simperings of a child,
With empty bosom, whose poor surgings only *970*
The love of play and fear of punishment
Can sometimes rouse out of their hollow calm?
Or are my eyes alone blind to that charm,
That draws him with such power into her presence?
Melitta! Yes, I will see her! Melitta!

SCENE III

EUCHARIS, SAPPHO

EUCHARIS

My lady, did you call?

SAPPHO

I called Melitta.
Where is she?

EUCHARIS

Where? I fancy in her room.

SAPPHO

Would she be left alone? What is she doing?

EUCHARIS

I do not know. But strange her manner's been,
And all day long her conduct most peculiar. *980*
This morning she was constantly in tears,
Yet even now I met her looking merry,

Weighed down beneath her linen and her towels,
As she went down toward the crystal stream
That flows inviting through the myrtle wood.

SAPPHO

She glories in her victory! Continue!

EUCHARIS

I, curious to learn what she was after,
Stole after her into the quiet wood;
There I found her—

SAPPHO

With him?

EUCHARIS

With whom?

SAPPHO

Continue!

EUCHARIS

I found her standing in the crystal water, *990*
Her garments on the bank lay scattered round,
And robe tucked high—no listener she suspected—
Scooping up water in her little hands,
She washed, carefully scrubbing arms and face,
That in the gleam of sunlight through the leaves,
Through her persistence and the violent manner
In which the sweet thing swiftly rubbed herself,
Glowed like a fire with a purple flame!
As she stood there, Diana[31] might have taken
Her for her nymph, indeed one of her youngest— *1000*

SAPPHO

I wished to hear her story, not her praise!

EUCHARIS

When the long chore of bathing was accomplished,
And face and breast and cheek were duly dried,

[31] Diana, the Greek goddess Artemis, virgin goddess of the chase, accompanied by nymphs, divinities of natural beauty.

She went back, singing gaily, to the house.
So lost in thought, preoccupied was she,
That she ignored the leaves I threw at her
Out of the thicket, meant to startle her.
Arriving here, she went into her room,
Shut herself in, I don't know what she's up to;
I only hear her rummaging in the cupboards, *1010*
Singing a merry melody the while.

SAPPHO

She *sings,* and Sappho—No! I do *not* weep!
Bring her to me!

EUCHARIS

Melitta?

SAPPHO

Yes, whom else?
Melitta! Ah, a sweet, soft-sounding name!
An ear-bewitching, most endearing name! [32]
Melitta—Sappho—Go, bring her to me!

(Exit EUCHARIS*)*

SCENE IV

SAPPHO *alone. She sits on the grassy bank and supports her head in her hand; a pause.*

SAPPHO

I cannot! Ah! . . . in vain I call on pride,
In place of pride, only love answers me!

(She sinks back into her previous posture)

[32] Melitta (Melissa) signifies bee and honey. Grillparzer, with his sensitive ear, was much taken with the euphony of names, and had an almost pathological horror of his own surname, which for some time he refused to allow to appear on the playbills of his plays!

SCENE V

MELITTA, SAPPHO

MELITTA

(Enters, simply but carefully dressed, roses at her breast and in her hair. She remains standing at the entrance, but comes nearer as SAPPHO *does not stir)*

Here I am.

SAPPHO *(Turning around suddenly and recoiling)*

Ah! By heaven, she is fair!

(Casts her face, covered in both hands, on the grassy bank—a pause)

MELITTA

You called for me?

SAPPHO

How she has decked herself, 1020
The faithless girl, to please her paramour!
I find it hard to hold my inner anger!
What feast decks you so festively today?

MELITTA

A feast?

SAPPHO

Then why this finery? These flowers?

MELITTA

Have you not often scolded me because
I rarely wear the clothes you shower on me,
Forever sparing them, like some old miser,
For other times, for other joyous days?
I thought of that today, and since today

Indeed is also such a joyous day *1030*
I went inside and decked myself a little.

SAPPHO

A joyous day? I do not know this, why?

MELITTA

Why? . . . Well, because you have returned to us,
Because—I know not quite, but I am gay.

SAPPHO

What, minx!

MELITTA

What are you saying?

SAPPHO *(Composing herself)*

Come, Melitta.
Come, let us now talk calmly to each other—
How old are you?

MELITTA

You are aware yourself,
How dismal fortune rudely interrupted
My childhood years; no mother counted them
Year after year in close exactitude, *1040*
But I believe I'm sixteen.

SAPPHO

No! You're lying.

MELITTA

I?

SAPPHO

You do not speak the truth!

MELITTA

My lady, always!

SAPPHO

You're barely fifteen.

MELITTA

It may well be so.

SAPPHO

So young in years and in deceit so ripe
Already? No, that cannot be, Nature
Does not so badly contradict herself!
Impossible! I'll not believe it!—Melitta,
Do you remember, thirteen years ago,
The very day, when you were brought to me?
You had been torn away by savage men, 1050
You wept and sobbed aloud in shrill lament;
I showed my pity for the homeless child,
Moved by her supplication, paid the price,
And locked you, I myself a girlish creature,
With warm affection on my maiden breast.
They wished to take you off, you would not yield,
Clinging with both your hands around my neck,
Till sleep, the comforter, soft loosened them,
Do you remember still that far-off day?

MELITTA

Oh, could I ever, ever not remember? 1060

SAPPHO

When soon thereafter, with its poisonous breath,
The fever gripped you in its serpent coils,
Who was it who kept vigil night on night,
Making her head a pillow for your head,
And self-forgetting, struggled hard with death,
To snatch from him the well-belovèd prey,
And snatched it from him, in rack and anguish snatched?

MELITTA

O, Sappho, you! Ah, what do I possess,
That I do not owe you, not owe your goodness?

SAPPHO

No, no, come here, into my arms, come here! 1070
I knew it well, you cannot cast me down,

With forethought, willfully, not cast me down!
Come, let our hearts harmonious beat together,
With eye on eye in sisterly affection,
Our words be mingled with our confluent breaths,
So that the ear beguiled, the breast attuned,
By unison of feeling sweetly lulled,
In every murmur of the magic mingling
May recognize itself, but not its word.

MELITTA

O, Sappho!

SAPPHO

Yes, I was mistaken. No? *1080*

MELITTA

In what?

SAPPHO

How could you? No, you cannot! No!

MELITTA

My mistress, what?

SAPPHO

You could! I tell you, go!
And first of all put these vain clothes aside,
I cannot see you thus . . . go! Other clothes!
This gaudy show offends my eyes. Away!
Melitta, simple, always simply walked,
So many veils suggest there's something veiled.
Go! Other clothes, I say to you! Then go!
Where are you going? Stay! Look in my eyes!
Why are you staring down? Are you afraid of *1090*
Your mistress' eye? You are not quite so dull!
The moment Phaon—What! I see you're blushing?
Traitress! You have betrayed your very self!
Do you deny it? Not your treacherous tongue,
I'll heed the witness of your glowing cheeks,
The wild reflection of the wanton flames
That burn deep in your hypocritic breast.

Ah! wretched girl! So that was why today
Your conduct at the banquet was so strange!
What I mistook as sign of awkward shyness, *1100*
Was but the cunning wanton's careful trap,
That, spiderlike, planned to ensnare her prey?
So young and yet so shifty, so exquisite
And mould and poison in your wicked heart?
Do not stand dumb there! Do you want for words?
Does not your tongue, that stings, know how to hiss? [33]
Answer!

MELITTA

I do not know what you are meaning.

SAPPHO

Indeed! Poor child! What, tears? Come, do not weep!
Tears are the holy privilege of pain!
Speak out with words! They have been long profaned, *1110*
Do not use innocence's silent speech!
So finely decked, all dressed up like a bride!
Off with those flowers! Off, they scarce avail
To hide the hideous serpent lurking there![34]
Down with the roses!

(MELITTA *takes off her wreath in silence)*

Give this wreath to me,
I will preserve it in remembrance of you,
And should its leaves fall prematurely withered,
Your loyalty I'll think of, and my luck.
Why are you leaving that rose on your breast?
Come, take it off!

(MELITTA *draws back)*

Doubtless, a pledge of love? *1120*
Off with it!

[33] Compare *Medea* (V. 1117) in a similar situation.

[34] The image of a serpent lurking beneath flowers is very frequent in Wieland.

MELITTA *(Clasping both her arms over her breast and thereby hiding the rose)*

Never!

SAPPHO

Useless, all your bristling.
The rose!

MELITTA *(Her hands pressed firmly on her breast, fleeing from her)*

Ah, take my life!

SAPPHO

You treacherous snake!
I too can bite! *(Drawing a dagger)*[35] Give me the rose!

MELITTA

O, Gods!
Protect me now, you high, almighty gods!

SCENE VI

Enter PHAON. *The above.*

PHAON

Who called here? You, Melitta?
Down with the dagger!

(A pause)

What's happening? Sappho, you?

SAPPHO

Why not ask her!

[35] This drawing of a dagger upon a slave girl was criticized, even before the first performance, by K. A. Böttiger in his letter of February 26, 1818, to Grillparzer, as—although in keeping with Sappho's passionate uncontrol—more in consonance with the spirit of the violent North than of classical Greece.

PHAON

Melitta, could you have— . . .

MELITTA

The blame is mine;
I spoke, as was not seemly for a slave.

SAPPHO

You shall not charge yourself with a false blame.
Too heavy lies on you the true, already. 1130
Poor me, if ever I required your kindness.

(With authoritative tone)

I asked her for the rose upon her breast,
And she disdained obedience!

PHAON

Did she do so?
By all the gods! She was quite right to do so,
And no one shall deprive her of the flower!
Myself, I gave it her in memory
Of a fair moment, as a little token
That sympathy for undeserved misfortune
Is not extinguished in all human breasts;
As a small drop of honey in the cup 1140
That alien arrogance presses to her lips;
As warrant of my innermost conviction,
That woman's finest gem's a quiet mind,
And that the happy wreath of innocence
Is dearer than the laurel crowns of fame.
She's weeping! Do not weep, my sweet Melitta!
Did you include her tears too in the price
You paid to the slave-dealer when you bought her?
Yours is her body, come and murder her,
But you shall not extort from her a tear! 1150
Do you look at me with your gentle eyes,
Extracting pity for the pitiless?
You do not know her, do not know proud Sappho!
See there—a dagger glinting in her hand

And two more daggers lying deeply hidden
Beneath her lowered lids![36]

(Seizing the dagger which has slipped from SAPPHO'S *hands)*

Give me the blade! I now intend to wear it
Here on my warm, my fond deluded breast,
And if a memory of the days gone by
Should ever brush my soul with sweet-sad thoughts, *1160*
One glance upon this blade shall cure me quick!

SAPPHO *(Staring at him)*

Phaon!

PHAON

Oh, pay no heed to her sweet tone,
It will entice you only to her dagger!
It has allured me also. Long ago,
Before I saw her, she had thrown round me
Her noose of song from far; with subtle art
She drew me to her with her golden toils,
And if I struggled, closer still and closer
Her subtle magic circles coiled round me.
When I beheld her, my excited senses *1170*
Were in the grip of frenzy; hypnotized,
I threw myself, a slave, at her proud feet;
The sight of *you* first gave me back myself,
Trembling, I saw myself in Circe's[37] house
And felt my neck beneath the yoke already!
But I was not yet free, she had herself,
Herself she had to break her magic spell.

[36] Compare Medea's description of the bolts in Jason's flashing eyes in *The Argonauts* (Act II, v. 562).

[37] Circe, the sister of Aeetes, Medea's father, was a powerful sorceress who through her magic turned men into beasts. See Homer's *Odyssey,* where she turns Odysseus' (Ulysses') men into swine. In calling Sappho, with her poetic vocation aspiring to the gods, "hypocritic Circe" (Act V, Scene iii, V. 1665), Phaon could not have been more consciously cruel nor more unconsciously kind.

SAPPHO *(Still staring fixedly at him)*

Phaon!

PHAON

Pay no heed! Do not look at her,
Her eye is no less deadly than her hand.

MELITTA

She's weeping!

PHAON

Go! Weeping, she weaves fresh spells. *1180*

MELITTA

Am I to see her, whom I love, in pain?

PHAON

She moves me also, therefore quickly go,
Before she throws once more her noose around you!

(He leads her away)

MELITTA

I cannot. Sappho!

SAPPHO *(In a breaking voice)*

Do you call, Melitta?

MELITTA *(Turning round and clasping her knees)*

Yes, Sappho, yes, I, I! Here, take this rose!
Take it, O take my life! Where is your dagger?

PHAON

(Rushing up, snatching the rose from both their hands, and lifting MELITTA *up)*

Yours it is, *yours!* No god shall rob you of it!

(Taking MELITTA *off)*

Come! Quick out of her sight! Let's go!

(He exits with MELITTA*)*

SAPPHO

(With outstretched arms, in a voice that dies away) Phaon!

Curtain

ACT IV

Open countryside as in the previous acts. Moonlight.

SCENE I

SAPPHO *comes, sunk in deep thought. She stops. After a pause.*

SAPPHO

Am I still here? Is *anything* still here?
Did not this widespread universe crash, crumbling 1190
In that dread, dire, devastating moment?
The darkness that sits brooding all around me
Is but the night and not the murky grave!
I've often heard it said a monstrous grief
Can kill—Alas! it is not so!
All round me quiet reigns, the breeze is silent,
And muted are the merry notes of life;
The leaves, all motionless, emit no sound,
And lonely, as a stranger straying late,

My weeping voice goes wandering through the night. 1200
Whoever like the birds might fall asleep,
Only much longer, never to awaken,
Forever wrapped in deeper, sweeter slumber,
Where everything—the very pulse-beat—sleeps,
No ray of dawn awakes to fresh despairs,
No thankless man— Stop! Do not stir the snake!

(With muffled voice)

Most horrible a crime indeed is murder,

And robbery and fraud and all the rest,
The swollen heads of that empoisoned Hydra,[38]
That, by the burning lake of chaos born, 1210
Infects the whole world with her pestilent breath;
Most horrible and shameful, poisonous crimes!
But I know one, against whose black example
The others all appear, all—lily-white;
Ingratitude is its name! It does alone
What all the others only singly do;
It lies, it robs, deceives, and swears false oaths,
Betrays and kills— Ingratitude! Ingratitude!

Dear Gods, protect me! Save me from myself!
The sinister spirits of my inmost being 1220
Awake and shake their dungeon's iron bars!

From Fortune, him alone I had entreated,
From every living mortal him alone;
I wished to place him on the peak of men,
Raised high above the rest of humankind,
And bear him on the wings of fame beyond
The grave and death and dark mortality
Into the radiant future's far horizons.
I wished to wind as wreath about his head
My talents, powers, essence and my name, 1230
Wanting a kind word as my sole reward,
And he—O righteous gods, are you still living?

(As though struck by a sudden thought)

Indeed, you live! From you has come the thought
That flashes now insistent in my soul.
Let me grasp you, swift messenger divine,
And learn the fleeting message of your lips!
You say Melitta is to go to Chios,[39]
To Chios, separated from the traitor,

[38] Hydra, a many-headed monster, slain by Hercules, as one of the Labors with which he was charged.
[39] Chios, one of the Aegean islands.

To turn her wayward heart to penitence,
With love pangs paying for her criminal love? *1240*
Then be it so! Rhamnes! Yes, be it so!
My thanks, O you immortals, for this sign!
I haste to execute!

SCENE II

RHAMNES, SAPPHO

RHAMNES

Your orders, mistress?

SAPPHO

She is my work, what would she be without me!
And to the sculptor, who denies the right
To destroy that which he himself created?
Destroy! Can I? Alas! Her destiny
Lies far beyond the reach of my weak hand!
If, in his love, he dreams of her in Chios,
Is she not happier at her slavish hearth *1250*
Than I in golden mansions void of love?
For one's belovèd it's so sweet to suffer,
And hopes and memories resemble roses,
Sprung from the *same* stock as reality,
Only without a thorn! Then banish me
Far in the ocean's unknown distances
To some small rock, that, rising steep and bare,
Greets as its neighbors but the clouds and waves,
Rough sundered from the primrose path of life!
Wipe out, but wipe out from my memory's pages *1260*
With gentle hand the hours that have just passed;
Leave to me but my faith in Phaon's love,
And I will praise my fate and gladly dwell
In solitude, indeed no solitude:
At every thorn that scratched my naked foot,
In every torment I would tell myself:

"Oh, if he knew!" and, "Now he thinks of you!
To rescue you, what would he not give!" Ah,
And balm would healing flow in every wound.

RHAMNES

Have you not called for me, my gracious lady? *1270*

SAPPHO

Phaon! Phaon! What have I done to you?
Serene I stood in my poetic pastures,
Playing alone upon my golden lyre;
I gazed down on the little joys of earth,
And all her sufferings did not reach to me.
Not hour by hour, but gracious flower by flower,
Woven into the poem's happy wreath,
I told the flow of ever-moving time.
What to my song I gave, it gave me back,
Eternal youth crowned me with evergreen. *1280*
Then comes the boor and with his insolent hands
He tears the golden veil away from me
And drags me down into the desert wastes
Where not a footstep, not a path is seen;
And now when he's the one and only thing
Shining before me in the wilderness,
He draws his hand from me, ah, and escapes!

RHAMNES

O mistress, should you linger so in the dark,
In the damp breath of night, of the sea air?

SAPPHO

Do you know a vice worse than ingratitude? *1290*

RHAMNES

Not I

SAPPHO

More poisonous?

RHAMNES

No, indeed not.

SAPPHO

A more accursèd or more punishable?

RHAMNES

In truth it's rightly charged with every curse!

SAPPHO

Not so? Not so? The other vices all
Are tigers, lions, wolves, hyenas all,
Ingratitude is the snake. Not so? The snake!
So fair, so smooth, so bright, so venomous! Oh!

RHAMNES

Come in with me, inside you will feel better,
For you the house is carefully adorned
And Phaon waits for you within the porch. *1300*

SAPPHO

What? Phaon's waiting for me?

RHAMNES

Yes, my lady,
I saw him, lost in thought, walk up and down;
He now stood still, spoke softly to himself,
Went to the window, peering through the night.

SAPPHO

He's waiting for me? Did he tell you this?
Waiting for *me,* Sappho?

RHAMNES

No, not quite that,
And yet I saw him stand expectant, listening,
And whom should he await but you?

SAPPHO

Whom? Whom?
He's not awaiting me—yet waits in vain!
Rhamnes!

RHAMNES

My lady.

SAPPHO

As you know, in Chios *1310*
There dwells a close friend, from my father's time.

RHAMNES

This I know.

SAPPHO

From its mooring quick untie
The boat that tosses in the neighboring bay,
For you must leave, this very night, for Chios.

RHAMNES

Alone?

SAPPHO

No.

(A pause)

RHAMNES

Who is to accompany me?

SAPPHO

What are you saying?

RHAMNES

Who's to go with me?

SAPPHO

(Leading him to the other side of the stage) Come!

Be silent and discreet, do you hear me?
Go to Melitta's chamber and command her
To come here; say that Sappho's calling her.
Tread softly, so that *he* knows nothing.

RHAMNES

Who? *1320*

SAPPHO

Who? Phaon—If she comes—

(Pausing)

RHAMNES

What then?

SAPPHO

Then bring
Her, be it gently, or be it with force,
But noiselessly, into the unfastened boat,
And promptly set out with all haste for Chios!

RHAMNES

And there?

SAPPHO

There make her over to my friend—
Tell him to keep her, till I send for her,
And strictly—no, not strictly should he treat her,
She is indeed chastened enough. Do you hear?

RHAMNES

I hasten.

SAPPHO

Do not tarry!

RHAMNES

Farewell, Sappho!
By morning we shall be quite far from here. *1330*
You will be satisfied with your true servant.

(He exits)

SCENE III

SAPPHO *alone*

SAPPHO

He's gone! And yet—No! Ah, a tiresome thing
Is habit, chaining one even to what one hates!

(Sunk in thought)

Listen—steps—no, it was the wind. How timidly
My heart is pounding in my stormy breast!
Now voices—ha, she's here—so readily,
Without suspecting for the last time she . . .
Away! I will not see her, will not—cannot!

(She goes quickly off)

SCENE IV

MELITTA, RHAMNES

MELITTA

Did you not say our mistress would be here?
She is not here.

RHAMNES

(Looking around in embarrassment) Not here?

Indeed, she's not. *1340*
She was here even now! So come with me!

MELITTA

Where?

RHAMNES

She has gone down to the shore perhaps,
Wandering in the direction of the bay.

MELITTA

She never goes there.

RHAMNES

But perhaps today.

MELITTA

And why today then?

RHAMNES

Why? Ah well perhaps

Because (*To himself*) . . . Why did she choose me for this task?
I cannot look at her. What shall I tell her?

MELITTA

You are so strange. You turn yourself away,
And dare not back the words you speak to me
With frank and open eyes. What is the matter, *1350*
That you should now become so scared and anxious?
Tell me where Sappho is that I may near her;
And if you do not know, let go.

RHAMNES

Stop there!
You may not go!

MELITTA

Why?

RHAMNES

You must come with me!

MELITTA

Where?

RHAMNES

To . . . Come only to the neighboring bay.
You will soon see.

MELITTA

O gods! What does this mean?

RHAMNES

Come, little girl! It will soon be past midnight.
Time presses. Let's away!

MELITTA

What's your intention?
Must I away—away? To far-off shores?

RHAMNES

Compose yourself, my child! To far-off shores? *1360*
What are you thinking? Is Chios then so far?

MELITTA

To Chios? Never.

RHAMNES

You will have to, child!
It is the mistress' orders.

MELITTA

Sappho's orders?
Away, to her!

RHAMNES

You cannot.

MELITTA

To her feet![40]
Let her hear and judge me.

RHAMNES

No, you may not budge!

MELITTA

What, Rhamnes, you?

RHAMNES

Ah, I can do no other!
I was commanded thus, and I obey.

MELITTA

Let me entreat you!

RHAMNES

Ah, what is the use,
Even if the tears are glistening in my eyes,
It has to be! Therefore, my child, away! *1370*

[40] Compare Bertha (König Ottokar's *Glück und Ende*), rushing to supplicate the queen upon Zawisch's lewd jest that the king intended to marry her!

To her, to her! . . . to die beneath her feet!
(Act I, V. 121)

MELITTA

Here let me fall upon my knees! Relent!
Is there then no one who will hear and save me?

RHAMNES

In vain! You'll wake up all the house. Come, now!

MELITTA

No, never. Is there none to pity me?

SCENE V

Enter PHAON. *The above.*

PHAON

That is Melitta's voice! What, insolent rogue!
You dare to lay your dastard hand on her?

(RHAMNES *lets* MELITTA *go)*

I see my premonition did not cheat me,
When I caught sight of you with furtive glance
Stealing, like wolf, into her innocent presence.
Yet, savage wolf, you have miscalculated; *1380*
The shepherd guards, and doom approaches *you!*

RHAMNES

Sir, I'm but carrying out my lady's orders.

PHAON

What, Sappho's orders? *She,* commanded you?
O Sappho! Sappho! Now I recognize you,
Only alas too late! But why too late?
There is still time for me to shake the bonds
From me and her: and, by heaven, I will do it!
You all-too-willing tool of another's evil!
Why . . . Melitta, you look pale, you're trembling?

MELITTA

O, I am very well!

PHAON

Slave, thank the gods, *1390*
That not the smallest stone has scratched her foot.
By heaven! You should have had to pay to me
A mortal groan for every tear she shed!
You seem exhausted, come then, lean on me,
You will find nowhere such a sure support.
Look at her, scoundrel! And you meant to injure
This gracious creature, Heaven's very image!

RHAMNES

Not injure!

PHAON

What else?

RHAMNES

Only—pardon me;
What I intended, I cannot accomplish.
Then let me go.

PHAON

By all the gods, you shall not! *1400*
I wish to plumb the depths of all your evil!
What did you intend?

RHAMNES

She had to go.

PHAON

Where to?

RHAMNES

To—but that is my lady's secret, sir.

PHAON

You will not tell me?

RHAMNES

She has locked it here,
And in her servant's heart it's firm preserved.

PHAON

Then let this dagger open it. Thanks, Sappho!
Yourself, you gave me arms against yourself!

(Drawing the dagger)

Do not prevaricate: you see me poised
To prize open the firmly-locked-up chest.

MELITTA

O spare him, please! I was to go to Chios. *1410*

PHAON

To Chios?

MELITTA

Yes, a friend of Sappho lives there,
Doubtless he was to keep Melitta for her.

PHAON

How, over the sea?

MELITTA

A boat there in the bay.

PHAON

A boat?

MELITTA

So he said, is it not so, Father?

RHAMNES

Ungrateful wretch, do not dare call me "Father."
You are betraying our mistress brazenly.

PHAON

A boat?

MELITTA *(To* RHAMNES*)*

What have I done that you should scold me?
Did he not ask?

PHAON

A boat! So be it! The sign,
I accept it! It comes from you, kind gods!
Too late I grasp your faithful admonition! *1420*
She is the one, or none else in this world,
Who carries in her breast the second half
Of that which yearning beats within my breast.[41]
You yourselves point the way. Then I will take it!
Melitta, yes, you are to go to Chios!
But not alone! With me, at my true side.

MELITTA

With him!

PHAON

Forsake this hostile, savage shore
Where hate and envy and the Gorgon head [42]
Of thirst for vengeance circumscribe your paths,
And where your foe lays deadly snares for you. *1430*
Come, there's the boat, and here is strength and courage
For your protection, were't against a world!

(He takes hold of her)

MELITTA *(Nervously to* RHAMNES*)*

Rhamnes!

RHAMNES

Consider, sir!

[41] Compare Jason in *The Argonauts* (Act III, Vs. 1208–15), where this idea is further developed, and see the discourse of Aristophanes in Plato's *Symposium,* where the myth of the androgynous being split in two is described. This theme constantly recurs in Wieland's classical novels.

[42] Medusa, the Gorgon, was a frightful monster whose gaze petrified any who looked on her—also referred to (by Socrates in a jest) in Plato's *Symposium.* She was slain by Perseus, who carried off her head as trophy. In this speech Phaon shows himself, the typical, somewhat vainglorious, hero of Grillparzer's Grecian plays, who in his self-centeredness remains insensitive to the anguish of the woman he is taunting.

PHAON

Consider you,
What you intended, that you're in my hand!

RHAMNES

Sir, she is Sappho's.

PHAON

Liar! She is mine!

(To MELITTA*)*

Come, follow.

RHAMNES

The inhabitants of this island
All honor Sappho as a sovereign lady,
Are ever ready at the first appeal
Firm to defend with arms their Sappho's threshold.
One word from me and hundreds will arise— *1440*

PHAON

You're right to warn me, I had forgotten almost
In whose house I am, where. You'll go with us!

RHAMNES

I, sir?

PHAON

Yes, you! But only to the beach.
I do not envy Sappho such a servant!
When we are safe, you may return at leisure,
Recount all that has happened and—Enough,
You'll follow!

RHAMNES

No, never!

PHAON

I have, I fancy,
The means with me to force obedience!

RHAMNES *(Turning toward the house)*

Violence!

PHAON *(Barring his way and approaching him with the dagger)*

Then breathe your last, if you yourself insist!
A small price for this pure girl's safety is 1450
The loss of an accursèd rascal!

MELITTA

Stop!

PHAON

If he obeys!

RHAMNES *(Who has withdrawn to the opposite side)*

O woe, woe, woe to age
When brawn and muscle no more match the will!

PHAON

Now, maiden, come!

MELITTA

Where to?

PHAON

On board, away!

MELITTA *(Hastening from him into the foreground)*

Dear gods! Shall I?

PHAON

Away, the distance stretches
With promise of protection in its arm.
There far away beyond the old, gray sea
Dwells rest, security and love!
O follow me! Beneath a spreading lime tree
That shades in peace my parents' peaceful home 1460
Stands, dearest, the arched temple of our bliss

(Seizing her)

What, you are trembling? Tremble, gracious bride,
Your bridegroom's arm holds you in close embrace!
Come with me! And if not, by all the gods!
On these hands I will bear you off from here
On, on unto to the farthest ends of earth!

MELITTA

Oh, Phaon!

PHAON

Come, the friendly stars are shining;
The sea is rising while the zephyrs stir,
And Amphitrite ever favors love.[43]

(To RHAMNES*)*

Lead the way!

RHAMNES

Sir!

PHAON

Your life's at stake, I say! *1470*

(Exeunt all)

SCENE VI

A pause—then EUCHARIS *appears on the steps*

EUCHARIS

Rhamnes!

(She descends)

I fancied that I heard his voice!
No, there is no one here. I was deceived—
An evil spirit seems to reign, embroiling,
Throughout her house, since Sappho's come back home.

[43] Amphitrite, the consort of Poseidon, god of the sea, and the patron goddess of seafarers.

The anxious inmates flee from one another,
With sorrow and suspicion on their brows.
I sought Melitta and her bed was empty.
Our mistress wanders lonely through the night,
Here Rhamnes' voice, and he himself not here.
Would it were morning! Listen—

RHAMNES *(From afar)*

Help me! Help! *1480*

EUCHARIS

Someone's calling.

RHAMNES *(Nearer)*

Here.

EUCHARIS

Ha, Rhamnes!

RHAMNES *(Near)*

Sappho's slaves!

EUCHARIS

He is quite breathless. What's the matter, Rhamnes?

SCENE VII

Enter RHAMNES, *quickly.* EUCHARIS

RHAMNES

Up, up from slothful sleep! Come here, my friends!
Follow the fugitives! Help!

EUCHARIS

Please explain!

RHAMNES

No questions now! Call Sappho and the servants!

EUCHARIS

Why?

RHAMNES

There's no time for words, I tell you, go!
And see the whole house, wake and haste and save!

EUCHARIS

What may this mean?

(Ascending the steps)

RHAMNES

I can no more! The traitors!
Do not exult! The just gods of the sea
Will haste to avenge so abominable a deed! *1490*

(Several servants gradually enter)

Quick, run down to the valley, wake the people,
Sound loud the alarum summoning all to help,
O, do not ask, away! Sound loud the gongs!

(Exeunt servants)

SCENE VIII

Enter SAPPHO

SAPPHO

What sound of terror jars the quiet night,
Usurping sorrow's place, that scares off sleep?
Besides me, who has cause here for complaint?

RHAMNES

I, O, my lady!

SAPPHO

Rhamnes, you still here?
And where is she?

RHAMNES

Melitta?

SAPPHO

Of course!

RHAMNES

Gone!

SAPPHO

She gone, and you still here?

RHAMNES

She's run off with—

SAPPHO

Stop!

RHAMNES

Off with Phaon!

SAPPHO

No!

RHAMNES

Alas! It is so. *1500*
He overpowered the weakness of my age,
And in the very boat arranged for me,
He leads his prey, this moment, through the waves.

SAPPHO

You lie!

RHAMNES

O would I did lie, just this once!

SAPPHO

Eternal gods, where was your thunder rusting?
Have you then torments but for *Sappho's* heart?
Is the ear of vengeance deaf, and limp its arm?
Flash down upon them your avenging ray,
O flash it down upon the traitors' skulls!
Crush them to dust, as you are crushing me! *1510*
In vain! No lightning cracks the quiet air,
The amorous breezes murmur in the leaves,

And in its broad, embracing arms the sea
Bears, tossing from the beach, the boat of love!
No help from Heaven! Then, Sappho, help yourself!

(The stage has gradually been crowded with slaves bearing torches and with country folk)

Ah, here they are! Thanks, faithful people, thanks!
You mortals, give me what the gods deny!
Come on, my good friends all, avenge your Sappho!
If ever I was dear to you, now show it!

(Mingling among them)

You, Myron, often swore, you too, Terpander— *1520*
Lychas, do you recall that song—and Pheres—
And you, Xenarchos—all my friends, all, all!
Down to the beach! Man everyone his skiff
And follow, swift as wind, the traitors' track!
Remember, I await you here in torment
And every moment until you return
Will jab a hundred daggers in my heart.
Who brings them to me, who gives me the joy
Of jabbing with my flaming eyes his eyes,
Of asking him: "What have I done to you, *1530*

(Bursting into tears)

That you should kill me?"—No, revenge alone!
Who brings them to me shall have all my gold,
My life—away! On the wings of the winds, away!

A COUNTRYMAN

Only with him will we return!

SAPPHO *(To those going off)*

I thank you.

My life is now committed to your hands.
Let my sharp need lend wings to every foot,
And let my vengeance fortify your arms.
Make haste, make haste, by all the gods, make haste!

(Exeunt servants and country folk. Laying her hands over her breast)

They've gone! Now I feel well. Now I will rest.

EUCHARIS

You tremble!

RHAMNES

Woe, you stagger!—Sappho!

EUCHARIS *(Catching the swaying* SAPPHO *in her arms)*

Gods! *1540*

SAPPHO *(In* EUCHARIS' *arms)*

O, let me fall! Why are you holding me?

Curtain

ACT V

Countryside as in the previous acts. Dawn

SCENE I

SAPPHO *sits, half lying on the grassy bank, staring motionless in front of her. At some distance stands* EUCHARIS; *further back several slave girls.* RHAMNES *enters.*

EUCHARIS *(Finger on mouth)*[44]

Quiet, quiet!

RHAMNES

Is she asleep?

EUCHARIS

Her eyes are open,
The body is awake, her spirit sleeps!
For three hours now, she lies thus, motionless.[45]

RHAMNES

You ought to take her back into—

EUCHARIS

I tried to,
Only, she will not go. No news?

[44] Compare similar stage direction at the end of Act IV of König Ottokar's *Glück und Ende.*
[45] Compare Medea at the beginning of Act IV (*Medea*).

RHAMNES

No news,
But sea and clouds as far as eye can see,
There's not the slightest trace of any ship.

SAPPHO *(Starting up)*

Ship? Where?

RHAMNES

My lady, we've seen nothing yet.

SAPPHO *(Sinking back)*

Not yet! Not yet!

RHAMNES

The morning air is cool, *1550*
Allow us to support you back to your—

*(*SAPPHO *shakes her head in refusal)*

My lady, be persuaded. Come with me!

*(*SAPPHO *shakes her head once more.* RHAMNES *draws back)*

As you wish. My heart is stabbed at sight of her!

EUCHARIS

Oh look! Why are they crowding there?

RHAMNES

Let's see!
They're flocking to the shore. They must be coming!

SAPPHO *(Springing up)*

Ha!

(During the following SAPPHO *stands in an anxiously listening posture, leaning back)*

EUCHARIS

Go there upon the rocks and keep a look out,
Perhaps you will catch sight of them.

RHAMNES

I'll look.

(He mounts an eminence by the shore)

EUCHARIS

Be quick, be quick! What do you see?

RHAMNES

Thank the gods!

They're coming!

SAPPHO

Ah!

RHAMNES

The wooded spit of land,

That on the left juts far into the waves, *1560*

Hid from me until now the welcome sight.

A host of little ships are swarming criss-cross

With beating oars, all racing to the beach.

EUCHARIS

What of the fugitives? Are they among them?

RHAMNES

The sun is dazzling me. I can't distinguish!

But wait! A boat already nears the shore,

Sent on ahead to bring the joyful news—

It now lies to. That shepherd from the valley—

He waves his staff. They have been caught for certain!

Come here, my friend, come here—he comes to us. *1570*

(Descending)

EUCHARIS

My mistress, pray be calm, pray be composed!

SCENE II

Enter a COUNTRYMAN. *The above*

A COUNTRYMAN

Greetings to Sappho!

EUCHARIS

Is he captured?

A COUNTRYMAN

Yes.

RHAMNES

Where?

EUCHARIS

How?

A COUNTRYMAN

They had a generous lead on us
And he knows how to row. I almost thought
At one time we should never catch them up.
Eventually, on the high seas we spied
His boat, then all at once gave rapid chase!
Soon he is overtaken, quick surrounded.
We order him to turn, but he refuses,
And with his left hand holding fast his maiden, *1580*
He brandishes his bare blade in his right—
Do you want anything, great lady?

(SAPPHO *indicates to him to continue)*

Well,
He menaces us with his brandished blade
Until one of our oarblows, aimed at him,
Alights upon the little maiden's brow.

*(*SAPPHO *hides her eyes with her hand)*

She falls, he takes her in his arms, while we,
Profiting from the moment, quick on board
Seize him and bring him back with us to you.
They are already landing. Do you see them?
The little girl still staggers, dizzy.

SAPPHO

Stop, *1590*

Not here!

RHAMNES

Then where else? They've already come.

SAPPHO

Who'll save me from his glances! O my maidens!
Thou, Aphrodite, deign to guard thy handmaid! [46]

(She hastens to the background and embraces the altar; her maids stand in a circle around her)

SCENE III

Enter PHAON, *leading* MELITTA. COUNTRYMEN. SAPPHO, *with her servants, in the background.*

PHAON

Beware, let no one dare to touch this maiden!
Defenseless I am not, although disarmed.
My fist will be a club for her protection,
And each one of my limbs become an arm.
Come here, Melitta, here, and do not tremble!
As long as I draw breath, you'll not be harmed!
You monsters, could you lacerate her head, *1600*
Her pure and innocent head, and yet be men?
So cruel could I only deem a woman;

[46] Sappho was a votary of Aphrodite, the goddess of love, whom she praised in her songs. (See Act I, Scene vi.)

A weak, infuriated, cowardly woman!
You, man, you struck at her, I recognize you;
Away with you, lest I forestall the high
Avenging gods and cheat them of their prey!
How are you feeling?

MELITTA

Well.

PHAON

Your look belies you!
This trembling and this pallor loud betray
The first lie that your lovely lips have uttered.
Do not attempt to moderate my fury, *1610*
You merely fan the flames to flare afresh.
Come, sit down here upon this grassy seat,
Here, where your gentle, clear, celestial eyes
Looked for the first time radiantly at me
And, like the golden morning-beams of day,
Released me from the dismal bonds of sleep
Into which that enchantress' singing lulled me;
Here, where sweet love began its gracious work,
On this spot, let it also be accomplished!
Speak, where is Sappho?

MELITTA

Phaon, do not call her! *1620*

PHAON

Be calm, Melitta! Am I not a free man?
Who gave to her the right to bar my steps?
Thank heaven, in Greece there still are courts of justice!
With terror shall the haughty woman learn this.
Away, to Sappho!

A COUNTRYMAN

Stay here!

PHAON

Who dare stop me?

A COUNTRYMAN

All of us here.

PHAON

I am a free man.

A COUNTRYMAN

You were, but now, are due for punishment.

PHAON

Punishment? Why?

A COUNTRYMAN

The abduction of a slave
Calls on the law for vengeance on your head.

PHAON

Let Sappho ask a ransom for her slave, *1630*
And I will pay it, were it Croesus' treasures.[47]

A COUNTRYMAN

It is for her to ask, not you to offer.

PHAON

Are you so tame, that you should lend your men's hands
So docilely to serve a woman's vengeance,
With slave obedience to the whims of love?
Then stand by me, I'm victim of injustice!

A COUNTRYMAN

Just or unjust, Sappho will decide that.

PHAON

Do you say this, old man, and do not blush?
Who then is Sappho, that you heed her tongue
As the determinant in the scale of right? *1640*
Is she the ruler in this land?

[47] This, of course, is an anachronism, as Croesus flourished after Sappho was dead. He was the last King of Lydia (in the sixth century, B.C.), reputed to be the richest man in the world. This is also a typical example of the hyperbole that disfigures so many of Grillparzer's heroes.

A COUNTRYMAN

She is;
Yet not because she rules, because we serve her.

PHAON

So she has spun her spell around you all?
I will yet see how far her magic reaches.

(Going toward the house)

To her!

A COUNTRYMAN

Get back!

PHAON

In vain you threaten me.
I must see her— Sappho, reveal yourself!
Where are you? Or are you afraid to face me?
Ha, I see her servants ranged about the altar!
She too is there! You shan't escape! Come here!

(He breaks through the crowd. At the same time the circle of slave girls opens. SAPPHO *lies, utterly exhausted, on the steps of the altar)*

A COUNTRYMAN

You dare approach, you thoughtless, insolent boy? 1650

PHAON

What business have you on the steps of the gods?
They do not hear the wicked's prayers—stand up!

(He seizes her. At his touch, SAPPHO *starts up and hastens with rapid steps, without looking at him, into the foreground. Following her)*

Would you escape? You must account to me!
You may well tremble, it's high time to tremble!
Are you aware of what you've done? With what right
Dare you detain me here, in scandalous bondage,
Me, a free man, whom none owns but himself?
Look at these here! Did you not send them forth

With most improper weapons? Did you not? Speak! *1660*[48]
So dumb! The poetess's sweet lips dumb?

SAPPHO

This is too much!

PHAON

I see your cheek is glowing—
All reddened by the hot flames of your rage—
Good, throw your mask away, be what you are,
And rave, and murder, hypocritic Circe!

SAPPHO

This is too much! Rise, heart, and arm yourself!

PHAON

Then answer me! Did you not send them forth?

SAPPHO *(To* RHAMNES*)*

Go then, and bring my slave girl back to me,
I bade pursuit of her alone, none else.

PHAON

Get back, I say! Let no one dare to near her! *1670*
Demand your ransom! I am not a rich man,
But friends and parents will contribute gladly
To free my happiness from your avarice.

SAPPHO *(Still turning away)*

I want no gold, but what is mine. She stays.

PHAON

She does not stay, by all the gods, she does not!
Yourself, you forfeited your right to her
That time you aimed your dagger at her breast;
You bought her services and not her life.
Do you believe I'll leave her in your hands?
I tell you, name your ransom and release her. *1680*

[48] Really 1659, as in the English version one line of the original has been contracted without loss of accuracy, but 1660 has been put to maintain uniformity of numbering with the original.

SAPPHO *(To* RHAMNES*)*

Accomplish what I ordered you!

PHAON

Stand back!
You will be touching death if you dare touch her!
What, has your heart become so quite inhuman,
That it is moved no more by human pain?
Then smash your lyre in pieces, poisonous snake,
And never open more your lips in song!
You've forfeited the Muse's golden gifts,
So desecrate no more the name of Art!
It is the blossom from the leaves of life,
Child of the purest urge, that, high aloft, *1690*
Raises its fragrant head in the blue air
Toward the eternal stars, whose shape it bears:
Like poisonous hemlock you made use of this
To ruin in your rage your enemies!
How different, in earlier, fairer days,
I, purblind fool, depicted Sappho once!
Soft, as her song, was her transfigured spirit,
Her heart, supreme perfection, like her songs;
The very harmony her lips poured forth
Was cradled in her gently heaving breast *1700*
And her whole being was melody to me.
Who has transformed you then with magic stroke?
Ah! Do not turn from me your downcast eyes!
Look at me! Let me gaze into your face,
That I may know if you are still the same,
If these the lips that softly touched my mouth,
If these the eyes that smiled at me so gently,
If, Sappho, you are she, you, Sappho?

(He takes hold of her arm and turns her toward him. She looks up, her eyes meet his)

SAPPHO *(Shrinking with grief)*

Ah!

PHAON

You are indeed she, that was Sappho's voice.
May the swift winds dissolve what I have uttered! *1710*
It must not take root in our opening hearts.
Oh, everything is bright before my eyes,
And like the sun after a thunderstorm,
Out of the present clouds—now fully spent—
Shines forth the past in all its pristine splendor.
I bid thee welcome, memory of fair days!
You are once more to me what you once were,
In my far homeland, ere I had beheld you—
The same divine imprint, that I, mistaken,
So long regarded as a human face— *1720*
Act like a goddess! Bless us, Sappho, bless!

SAPPHO

Deceiver!

PHAON

No, in truth, I am not one!
When I swore love to you, it was no sham;
I loved you as one may, perhaps, love gods,
As one loves what is good and beautiful.
Let Sappho consort with the lofty ones;
One may not with impunity descend
From the gods' feast to mortal company.
The arm, in which the golden lyre rested,
Is dedicated, may not touch what's earthly. *1730*

SAPPHO *(Turning away, to herself)*

Then cast the golden lyre to the sea-floor,
If its possession's bought at such a price.

PHAON

I staggered, in a dull intoxication,
At sharp odds with myself and with the world;
It was in vain I conjured up the feelings,
That I believed asleep, but were not there;
You stood before my gaze a baffling vision
To which and from which unseen forces drove me.

You were—too *base,* my anger thought—too *lofty,* 1740[49]
Deliberation tells me, for my love;
And only *equals* fittingly unite.
Then I saw *her* and all the deep springs of
My inmost being shot up to high heaven,
Whose jet until that moment had been stopped.
Come here, my sweet Melitta, come to her!
Ah, do not fear, for she is kind and gentle.
Unveil the shining crystal of your eyes
That she might gaze into your guileless soul,
Gladly acknowledging your spotlessness! 1750

MELITTA *(Approaching shyly)*

My mistress—

SAPPHO *(Keeping her at arms' length)*

Do not near me.

MELITTA

Ah, she's angry!

PHAON

Can she indeed be what I feared to think?
Come here, my sweet Melitta, come beside me!
You shall not supplicate her! In my presence
I will not let her haughtiness insult you,
You shall not supplicate! She knows neither
Your worth, nor hers; else she would on her knees
Before you, guilt to innocence, pay homage!
Come here to me! Come here!

MELITTA

No, let me kneel,
As well befits a child before its mother, 1760
If she deem right to punish, let her punish;
I will not fret at all against her will.

[49] To maintain uniformity with the original—1740—one line being contracted in the version.

PHAON

Not to her only, you belong to me,
And such humility abases me!
We still have means to force her yield to us
What she so peevishly denies our prayers.

MELITTA

Oh, were it so, only her gift could please me!
The greatest bliss, if forced, I'd find a burden.
Here will I kneel until a gentle look,
A kindly word, proclaims to me my pardon. *1770*
How often I have lain here, in this spot
And ever stood up smilingly once more;
She will not this time send me off in tears!
Dear lady, please look down upon your child!

*(*SAPPHO *stands, putting her face on* EUCHARIS' *shoulder)*

PHAON

How can you hear her and stay cold and dumb?

MELITTA

She is not cold, and though her mouth is silent,
I feel her heart is speaking to my heart.
Be judge, O Sappho, between me and him!
Bid me go with him, and with him I'll go,
Bid me renounce him—mighty gods!—all!—all! *1780*
You're trembling! Sappho, do you not hear me?

PHAON

(Embracing MELITTA, *and at the same time kneeling beside her)*

To mortals love, and reverence to the Gods;
Give us what's ours, and take from us what's yours!
Consider what you do and who you are!

*(*SAPPHO *starts up at the last words and gazes fixedly at the kneeling couple, then turns quickly away and goes)*

MELITTA

Alas! She flees, rejecting me, her child.

(Exit SAPPHO, EUCHARIS, *and servant girls follow)*

SCENE IV

The scene is the above, without SAPPHO *and* EUCHARIS

PHAON

Stand up, dear child, and do not beg of mortals,
The gods remain to us and our own selves!

MELITTA

I cannot live, if she has sentenced me,
Her eye to me has ever been my mirror
In which I tested all my acts and feelings; *1790*
It shows me now my own deformity.
What she must suffer, our offended lady!

PHAON

You lend to her your feelings; for in her
Proud breast quite other waves are swelling high!

MELITTA

If she seem proud, she still was kind to me,
If often strict, the sharp exterior hid
A sweet and gracious sustenance for me still.
Alas, that I could ever have forgotten!

RHAMNES

Indeed alas, you ever could forget!

PHAON

Why are you trembling, if you think her gentle? *1800*

RHAMNES

On leaving, she was angry; and her anger
Is boundless like her love. So woe to you!

PHAON

What can she threaten?

RHAMNES

Death to the fleeing slave.

PHAON

Who says?

RHAMNES

It is the country's penal law.

PHAON

I shall protect her!

RHAMNES

You? And who'll protect *you?*

PHAON

Even if the earth before me here split open,
The sea in thunder crashed, to swallow me,
Could she in dread conspiracy unite
Against me all great Nature's mighty forces,
I'd cling to my belovèd, mock her anger, *1810*
Despising her and all her menaces!

RHAMNES

Despise? You Sappho? Who then, pray, are you,
That you dare put your word into the scales
In which humanity weighs its elect?
Presume to speak, where Greece has long since spoken?
You purblind, wanton fool, you think her worthless
Because you have no measure for her worth?
You deem a gem opaque, because your eye is?
That she did love you, that she should have raised
Up to her from the dust the thankless viper *1820*
That lacerates her heart with venomous tooth;
That she should squander all her wealth on you,
In no sense worthy to esteem such treasures,
This is the single blemish in her life
And even envy cannot brand her else—
Be silent! Even this defiance on which
You prop yourself against her is not yours!
How could you have presumed—you abject creature—

You playboy, the obscurest of the obscure,
To mouth complaints against the gem of Hellas? *1830*
That she did look on you, gave you the pride
With which you now presume to humble her.

PHAON

I would not challenge her poetic fame—

RHAMNES

You would not? Fine, indeed! As if you could!
High, where the stars are, she has carved her name
That shall shine on and on in diamond letters,
And only with the stars shall be extinguished!
In far-off times, among far, foreign men,
When our decaying bodies are long crumbled,
And when our graves are no more to be found, *1840*
Shall Sappho's song resound from human lips
And her name still live—and shall still live yours,
Yes, yours! Boast of the immortality
Your wickedness against her wins for you.
In foreign lands, to coming generations,
When many centuries as yet unborn,
Have been engulfed within the tomb of time,
Shall every mouth continually proclaim:
She who first sang this song, her name was Sappho,
And Phaon is his name, who murdered her! *1850*

MELITTA

O, Phaon!

PHAON

Quiet!

RHAMNES

You poor comforter!
Do you bid quiet with unquiet voice?
Let her perceive her crime and let her shudder;
Let Sappho not lack that revenge at least!
You would not challenge her poetic fame!
And what fame else of hers do you then challenge?

Dare you have any doubts about her heart,
You who must thank her heart for what you are?
Look all around you here! There is not one
Whom she has not befriended, who himself, *1860*
In house and field, in wealth and through his kindred
Does not bear rich trace of her gentleness;
Not one, whose proud heart does not faster beat,
When he proclaims he comes from Mytilene
And calls himself a countryman of Sappho.
Question that quivering creature at your side,
Accomplice, rather of your deed than guilt,
How she has found our mistress treating her?
What could a slave have had to offer you?
If she has pleased you, it was Sappho's spirit, *1870*
Was Sappho's generous, maternal spirit
That moved you in the words of her, she fashioned.
You may well rub your brow! Try as you may,
You never can erase the memory!
And what will you now do? Where will you flee?
There is no refuge for you on this earth;
In every mortal's reverential breast
Rises a foe to him who's Beauty's foe.
Your reputation shall precede your steps
And cry aloud in every human ear: *1880*
"Here Sappho's murderer comes! The gods' foe comes!"
And you shall wander outlawed through the land
With her, whom you gave ruin for protection.
No Greek shall open his hospitable door,
No god shall grant you entrance in his temple,
You will flee trembling from the sacred altar
When the priest bids the unholy man depart,[50]
And when you flee, the dread Eumenides,[51]
The dark, avenging messengers from Hell,

[50] In antiquity it was customary, before a sacred ceremony began, for the priest to ask the ceremonially impure to leave.

[51] The Eumenides (euphemistically "the kindly ones") were the daughters of Persephone and Hades, and were the executioners of divine retribution on miscreants.

Tossing their serpent tresses around your head, *1890*
Shall hiss forever "Sappho" in your ears,
Until the grave you dug has swallowed you!

MELITTA

Stop! Stop! Please stop!

PHAON

Will you then make me mad?

RHAMNES

You were mad when you spurned the lofty Sappho!
Now feast upon the fruit yourself have planted!

MELITTA

Let's go with her!

PHAON

Who'll save me from this pain?

SCENE V

Enter EUCHARIS. *The above*

EUCHARIS

What, Rhamnes, you still here? Come quickly!

RHAMNES

Where?

EUCHARIS

To Sappho.

RHAMNES

What? . . .

EUCHARIS

I fear she is unwell.

RHAMNES

May heaven forbid!

EUCHARIS

I followed her from far
Up to the great porch; from my hiding place 1900
I closely watched her every move and gesture.
Leaning against the pillars, there she stood
Gazing down into the measureless sea,
That dashed in foam against the rocky shores.
Speechless and motionless, she stood up there
With staring eyes and cheeks unearthly pale,
A marble statue mid the marble statues.
But now and then she stirs, lays hand on flowers,
On gold and jewels, what her arm may reach,
And tosses all into the roaring sea, 1910
Following their dive with yearning in her eyes.
I was about to near her, when a sound
Rang through the hall convulsing all her being.
Her lyre it was, there hanging on a column,
In whose sweet strings the sea breeze loudly sang.
Drawing deep breaths she glances up and shrinks
Back, as at the touch of some higher power.
Her eyes now riveted upon the lyre,
Her lifeless features suddenly revive
And a peculiar smile plays round her mouth. 1920
At last her lips, till now shut tight, reopen,
And words of terrible import resound
From Sappho's mouth, yet not the words of Sappho.
"Are you, friend, calling me?" she says, "Reminding
Me? Friend upon the wall, I understand you!
You are reminding me of former days!
Thanks!" How she reached the wall and how the lyre
Hanging high up, I cannot say, for quick
As lightning it appeared to flash past me.
When I now look, she holds the instrument, 1930
Pressing it tight upon her stormy breast
That audibly drew breath and gave out breath.
Then round her head she twines her laurel wreath,
Olympia's victory wreath, still hanging there
By the house altar, and around her shoulders
She throws her purple mantle, all aglow

Whoever for the first time saw her now,
Standing upon the altar's lofty steps,
Her lyre in her hand, her heavenward gaze,
And all her radiant form, of heaven breathing, *1940*
Transfiguration beaming all around her,
Would have saluted her as some great goddess
And bent in prayer his supplicating knee.
Yet motionless and silent as she was,
I felt myself a prey to dread and terror,
Her death-in-life gaze filled my heart with horror,
And so I hastened—

RHAMNES

And left her— To her!
But see! Is it not she? Yes, she herself!

SCENE VI

SAPPHO, *richly clad, as in the first act, her purple mantle round her shoulders, her laurels on her head, her golden lyre in her hand, appears, surrounded by her servant girls, upon the steps of the pillared passage, and descends gravely and ceremoniously. A long pause . . .*

MELITTA

O, Sappho, O my mistress!

SAPPHO *(Serene and grave)*

What would you?

MELITTA

At last the blindfold round my eyes has fallen! *1950*
O let me once again become your slave,
That which belongs to you, possess and pardon!

SAPPHO *(As before)*

Do you believe Sappho so ill-endowed
That she may need a present from your hands?
That which belongs to me already is mine!

PHAON

O listen, Sappho! listen!

SAPPHO

Do not touch me!
I am devoted to the gods!

PHAON

If ever,
Sappho, you looked on me with gracious eyes—

SAPPHO

You speak of matters that are long since past.
I looked for you and I have found myself! *1960*
You could not grasp my heart, so go your way!
On firmer ground I now must base my hope.

PHAON

Ah, do you hate me then?

SAPPHO

To love, to hate!
Is there no third between? You were once dear
To me and still are and shall ever be,
Like some companion of a happy voyage
Whom fortune's whim, for a short crossing, leads
Into our boat, till, destination reached,
Each wanders off upon his separate way,
And only sometimes from the alien distance *1970*
Recalls the memory of the dear companion—

(Her voice breaks down)

PHAON *(Moved)*

O Sappho!

SAPPHO

Hush! Let us now part in peace!

(To the others)

You, who have seen your Sappho weak, forgive!

I mean to reconcile you with her weakness,
Only when bent, the bow displays its power![52]

(Pointing to the altar in the background)

Ignite the flame on Aphrodite's altar,
So that it brightly flares to greet the dawn! *(It happens)*
And now, retire, all, leave me alone,
Alone to take my counsel of my kin!

RHAMNES

She wishes it, let us obey, come, all! *1980*

(They withdraw)

SAPPHO *(Stepping forward)*

Sublime and holy Gods!
You have adorned me with your bounteous blessings! [53]
In my hand you bestowed your bow of song,
Bestowed your quiverful of poesy,
A heart to feel, a mind to comprehend,
And power to fashion what I have conceived.
You have adorned me with your bounteous blessings!
I give you thanks!

You have with victory crowned my humble head
And broadcast far and wide in distant lands *1990*
My poet's fame, seed for eternity!
My golden song pours forth from foreign tongues,
And only with the earth shall Sappho perish.
I give you thanks!

You deigned to grant the poetess to sip
From the delicious, wreathèd cup of life!
Sip only, not to drink.

[52] Compare *Medea* (Act III, Vs. 1335–39).

[53] Compare the opening lines of Faust's monologue in the Forest and Cave scene, Part I of Goethe's *Faust:*

> Spirit sublime! you've given me, given me all
> I asked of you.

Oh, see! Obedient to your lofty call,
I put aside the wreathed, delicious chalice
And do not drink! 2000

I have accomplished what you have commanded,
Therefore do not deny my last reward!
Those who belong to you are spared the weakness,
The asp of illness does not creep on them,
In their full strength, full blossom of their being,
You bear them swift aloft to your abodes—
Grant me a like fate, worthy of a crown!

Oh, do not let your priestess Sappho be
The target of your enemies' disdain,
A sport for fools, who fancy they are wise. 2010
You crushed the flowers, then also crush the stalk!
Let me accomplish as I have begun,
Spare me the bloody torment of this struggle.
I feel myself too weak to fight on longer,
Grant to me victory, spare me from the fight!
(Inspired) The flame is flaring and the sun mounts high,
I feel my prayer is answered! Thanks, great Gods!
You, Phaon, you, Melitta, come to me!

(Kissing PHAON *on the brow)*

A friend from far-off worlds is kissing you

(Embracing MELITTA*)*

This is the kiss a mother sends who's dead! 2020
Away! There at the altar of love's goddess
See love's dark lot fulfilled.

(Hastens to the altar)

RHAMNES

What does she plan? Her being is transfigured,
The radiance of the immortals shines round her!

SAPPHO

(Walking to an eminence overhanging the shore and stretching her hands out over the couple)

To mortals love, and reverence to the Gods! [54]
Enjoy what flowers you may, and think of me!
Thus I repay the last debt of my life,
Bless them, great Gods, and bear me up to you!

(Throws herself from the cliff into the sea)

PHAON

Stop! Sappho, stop!

MELITTA

Alas! She crashes, dies!

PHAON *(Preoccupied with* MELITTA*)*

Quick, help! To the shore! Save! Help! *2030*

(Some rush off)

RHAMNES *(Who has gone up to the cliff)*

Save her, great Gods! If once she strikes that crag
There, it's all up, she will be dashed to pieces!
Bear her beyond to safety! Woe! It's happened!

PHAON

Why stand there shrieking? Save her, quick, the boat!

RHAMNES *(Coming down)*

Stop! It is now too late! Grant her the grave,
That she, disdaining this false world, has chosen
Within the holy waters of the sea!

PHAON

Dead?

RHAMNES

Dead.

[54] A significant repetition of Phaon's pregnant words (V. 1782).

PHAON

Impossible! Ah, no!

RHAMNES

It is so—
The laurels all are withered, mute the lyre!
Her dwelling-place was not upon this earth. 2040

(With raised arms)

Home to her kindred she has now returned.[55]

Curtain

THE END

[55] A climactic embellishment of V. 105.

THE GOLDEN FLEECE

TRANSLATOR'S NOTE

The Golden Fleece, a trilogy in ten acts—*The Guest* (one act), *The Argonauts* (four acts) and *Medea* (five acts)—is Grillparzer's most ambitious work and, because of his triumphant success in depicting his heroine Medea, is, despite its defects (more marked in the earlier plays), probably his greatest. Reinhold Backmann, editor of the trilogy in the standard Vienna Edition (Volume Two, 1913) sums it up thus:

> What Grillparzer aimed at was titanic. And titanic too is what was achieved finally, after many tribulations, even though the execution in many respects fell below the aim and, under the pressure of circumstances, had to fall below it. If one examines the details, his progress since *Sappho* is extraordinary. Still greater, moreover, is the broad canvas, brought to life with powerful strokes of light and shade. This is perhaps the very greatest that Grillparzer ever fashioned.

Joseph Schreyvogel's contemporary opinion, recorded in his diary on November 8 and 9, 1820, shortly after the manuscript was received by him, can hardly be bettered in its just appreciation—except perhaps for insufficient regard to the great tension foreshadowing *Medea* in much of the third act of *The Argonauts:*

> 8 November. I have now received from Grillparzer his finished *Golden Fleece.* The third and fourth acts of *The Argonauts* are bad, the earlier good for the most part, and the first half of *Medea* excellent.
>
> 9 November. The whole of *Medea* is more or less a masterpiece, and also the rest does not fall much below.*

*It would seem that on second thought the merits of the third

But if Grillparzer finally achieved success, the process of creation was most painful, and there was more than once a distinct danger of this masterpiece remaining a fragment, like so many other dramatic ruins of Grillparzer before *Die Ahnfrau,* and like his later *Esther,* which, long left untouched, still remained a fragment when he died decades later. That *The Golden Fleece* was rescued from this fate we may chiefly ascribe to the obstinacy inherited from his dead father, to which Grillparzer refers, which prevailed over the dreadful trauma caused by his mother's suicide in the middle of his labors; to the inspiration of his guilty love affair with Charlotte von Paumgartten, his cousin's wife; and lastly but by no means least to the clear even if unconscious influence of Apollonius Rhodius' *Argonautica*—where in Book III Medea's love for Jason first blazes—and Racine's *Phèdre.* The other literary influences, such as Shakespeare's *Macbeth* in the supernatural parts of the trilogy, Calderon's *Three Greatest Wonders* and Ovid's *Metamorphoses* and *Heroides,* especially in the earlier plays, and Euripides' and Seneca's *Medea* in the last play, however important, are essentially peripheral and do not materially affect Grillparzer's chief glory in the trilogy, namely the characterization of Medea herself. In fashioning his Medea, Grillparzer owes something to Corneille's *Médée,* especially in the earlier plays, where he depicts his heroine proud of her will power, only to make all the more potent his debt to Appolonius Rhodius* and Racine, who had already portrayed in a masterly manner the uncontrollable passion of sexual love, that terrible fever, as La Rochefoucauld records in his *Maximes* (72), which, "if one judges it by most of its effects, resembles hatred rather than affection."

Grillparzer was interested in the subject of Medea even before his *Sappho* had been performed. He had been provoked by a perusal of Schlegel's *Lectures* (Vorlesungen) to read Eurip-

---

act of *The Argonauts,* and the very end of the Fourth Act, became more apparent to him.

* Grillparzer translated twenty lines of *The Argonautica* of Apollonius Rhodius, as recorded in his copy of the book purchased at Naples on May 23, 1819. He was, of course, already familiar with the work.

ides' *Medea* for himself, and records in his diary in 1817 (Tgb. 274):

> "If I, as I should well like, were to write a tragedy *Medea,* I should try to motivate Medea's hatred against her children on their attachment to their kinder father."

At the turn of the year he was further stimulated by the performance in Vienna of Gotter's melodrama and Cherubini's opera *Medea.* Indeed, Cherubini's barbarian heroine was so frightful that, on her entrance, her gentle Greek rival Dirce (Creusa) promptly swooned with terror! Grillparzer was doubtless impressed by this ludicrous feature, and perhaps it is to this that we owe the softening of Medea's barbarism—so prominent in all the ancient accounts, not excluding Euripides—and so essential to mitigate, if Medea was to be a tragic heroine in the eyes of modern audiences. This process of civilizing went so far that whatever Grillparzer's original intentions, to point the contrast between barbarism and civilization—apparent in his relegating the barbarous Colchians to free verse, while the Greeks were endowed with the dignity of the iambic pentameter —the finished work was to show the Greek men—Jason, Milo, Creon—mouthing lofty sentiments and behaving like barbarians, and the Colchian women—Peritta, Gora, Medea (her monstrous revenge, rooted in the legend, always excepted)—upholding the standards of civilized conduct.

Grillparzer's original intention to write a single tragedy on Medea's revenge, like Euripides, Seneca and Corneille before him, soon gave way to the more ambitious project of the trilogy. In June 1818 while on a visit to Baden, near Vienna, with his mother, Grillparzer studied Benjamin Hederich's *Mythological Lexicon.* With further preparatory reading which had clearly included Calderon's *Three Greatest Wonders* and the Orphic *Argonaut* epic in Voss' German version and Valerius Flaccus' Latin adaptation of the legend, and further hesitations causing almost a nervous breakdown, followed by recovery at Bad Gastein, he composed *The Guest* in one week (September 29 to October 5, 1818). After more reading, the first act of *The Argonauts* was begun on October 20, 1818, and again finished in a week. Once more at a loss for inspiration, Grillparzer now read Apollonius Rhodius' *Argonautica,* with what revolutionary effect is clear from the second act of *The Argonauts,* where the somewhat adolescent conception of Jason's erupting on Medea in her tower as a god in Act I, inspired by Ovid, is turned into the full knowledge of her utter conquest by sexual passion for a man whom, against her will, she is compelled to love. With the key to this tragic passion now firmly in his grasp, the second act of *The Argonauts,* begun on October 27, was completed, and the third act begun on November 3.

Grillparzer at first found it difficult to portray convincingly the surrender to Jason's advances of Medea, who had scoffed at Peritta's passion, and the work came to a standstill. It was just a year since the suicide of his younger brother, who had drowned himself in the Danube, leaving a note begging forgiveness of his mother and Franz, whom he "had lied to and deceived." Before he could recover from the melancholy of this anniversary, coinciding with the temporary halt of his own inspiration, his mother committed suicide by hanging on the night of January 23, 1819. All thought of further composition was now at an end, and it was not till after his return from his Italian journey of several months, armed with his copy of Apollonius Rhodius, that he was able to complete *The Argonauts.*

Grillparzer began *Medea* in November, but owing to his brush with the police over his poem "The Ruins of Campo Vaccino in Rome," it was not till December that the first act was completed. The second act was begun on December 21, the third on the twenty-seventh, the fourth act on January 17, 1820, and the fifth on January 25, the giant trilogy being completed on January 27, 1820.

After reading the manuscript, Schreyvogel returned it to him, suggesting he let it lie for a while before revising it. Grillparzer did this during the summer, and on November 8, 1820, he handed the revised manuscript of his trilogy to the Burgtheater. Schreyvogel's enthusiasm, as we have seen, was considerable, and he left the entire casting to the author. The trilogy was performed on March 26 and 27, 1821, with much success, and was published the following year. During Grillparzer's lifetime the first two plays ran only nine times at the Burgtheater; *Medea,* thirty-seven times. This to some extent is in accordance with their respective merits.

The Guest (*Der Gastfreund*) is a well-written prologue, with its theme of the murder of Phrixus who bore the Golden Fleece to Colchis from Apollo's Temple in Delphi, impelled thereto by a dream or vision. The supernatural element in the trilogy enters straightaway, and persists as in the Greek legend till the destruction of Creusa and the burning down of her father's palace at the end of *Medea.* This is perhaps the least-convincing element to a modern audience, carried to pantomime lengths, reminiscent of Mozart's *Magic Flute,* in the cavern scene in Act IV of *The Argonauts,* with the serpent or dragon guarding the Golden Fleece. Another unsatisfactory feature in *The Argonauts* is the clashing and counter-clashing of the armed Colchians and Greeks, with much sparring and shouting, but apparently not a drop of blood. Such scenes are essentially destructive of tragic illusion, more worthy of the cinema, with its broad perspectives, than the crowded stage . . . indeed, *The Golden Fleece* should make a memorable film.

But *The Argonauts* is redeemed by the revolutionary nature of Medea's passion for Jason that changes her from an adolescent, fond of running races in *The Guest,* into a woman of tremendous tragic force. The last play, *Medea,* has dramatic tensions of Racinian proportions, and is perhaps the greatest drama in the German language. For this, one must be eternally grateful to Charlotte von Paumgartten, Grillparzer's "tragic Muse," who not only was his prototype for Medea, but also constantly encouraged him to finish the work. Grillparzer's moving tribute to Charlotte, under the guise of "Desdemona," deserves to be quoted in full:

*Dedication to Desdemona**

> "You, from whom I am separated by a dominant necessity † but whose worth I acknowledge and shall continue to acknowledge, as long as a heart beats in my

* This, of course, could not be published without scandal in the 1822 edition of the trilogy, the only one in Grillparzer's lifetime.

† The necessity to renounce life for art. See Grillparzer's poem "Der Bann" ("The Proscription"), 1819.

> breast and power to remember lingers in my brain, may these pages be sacred to you; for they must also mean more to you than to anybody else. Firstly, because they were written by him who highly esteems and loves you unto death. Secondly, because you yourself have participated in the work, through the share of the burden you took from the author, who only in your company could find repose and consolation in his most painful frustrations over this unholy Fleece; because you have prayed for its success; because you have mingled your tears with mine; because you have rejoiced in my joy."

His indirect tribute to Charlotte in verse is equally memorable —his poem "Die Tragische Muse" ("The Tragic Muse"), composed before the completion of *Medea,* when weary with the thought of having convincingly to portray as a tragic heroine a child-murderess, he begs to be released from the task; but the tragic Muse takes her wreath from her fragrant hair and places it on his Medea's head. Overcome, the poet bids his Muse go ahead, for he would surely follow. It is thus clear that Grillparzer had a fair notion of the greatness of his portrayal of Medea, worthy to bear the crown of the Muse of tragedy.

Let us examine a little more closely how Grillparzer has achieved a Medea who excels Euripides' powerful creation and is worthy to be set beside Racine's great tragic heroines.

In the first play *The Guest*—she and Gora, her nurse, are the only characters who appear in all three plays—Medea is represented as a self-willed, independent girl of high spirits, but with a touch of conscience. She is appalled at her father's (Aeetes) murder of the stranger, Phrixus, and his coveting the Golden Fleece. Grillparzer is most careful to represent her as sympathetically as possible. Thus while at Aeetes' repeated orders she lends her medicinal art, inherited with her magic from her mother, Hecate, to drug the drinks of the Greeks, and her considerable charm to relieve Phrixus of his sword, the moment she is charged by Phrixus with having trapped him into defenselessness, she snatches a sword from a Colchian warrior to hand to him. With occult insight, she plainly foretells her father the doom he has brought on his house and on her by his crime. She foresees the Eumenides with their serpent tresses:

Coiling around me;
Me, you, us all!
Despair for you!
For you, for us!
Despair, despair!
(*Vs. 518–22*)

Now sunk in melancholy, a changed Medea is found in the first act of *The Argonauts,* withdrawn from her father's house and shut up with her maidens in a remote tower:

. . . brooding incantations
And brewing potions all day long;
But when it's night . . .
(*Vs. 8–10*)

going forth "like a ghost" and roaming abroad "weeping and moaning." She learns of the arrival of the Greeks, out to revenge Phrixus' murder and take back the Golden Fleece, but when Jason enters her tower at night and wounds her, she mistakes him for the divine Heimdar, and his kiss as the summons of the god of death. She is brought to her senses the next morning by the wise Gora, and when the full force of what has happened to her strikes her, she, like Racine's Phèdre, who had "pined and withered, drowned in burning tears," melts into tears at the unbearable ignominy of being compelled to love against her will. Grillparzer has cunningly struck this soft note of melting into tears on repeated occasions in the last two plays of the trilogy, as a sort of leitmotiv, similar to the Leda-and-Swan theme to denote eroticism in *The Waves of Sea and Love.* Thus for the first time on stage, Medea weeps on Peritta's shoulder—*herself* now smitten with the same passion which she had previously scornfully dismissed in Peritta. Again after confessing her love for Jason to her father, and beseeching him to protect her from it, she takes her leave of him, throwing herself "sobbing loudly into his arms." * When in Act III of *The Argonauts,* Jason, on his knees, declares his passion, he exclaims:

* It is an ironic reflection that, had not the storm washed away the bridges on the circuitous route leading to Medea's retreat, she might never have seen Jason again and her tragedy might thus have been averted. Similarly in *The Waves of Sea and Love,* had Hero

> You're weeping! All in vain, I know no pity!
> (*V. 1264*)

brutally emphasizing her helplessness.

When she turns a deaf ear to all Jason's pleas and he returns her to her father's arms, making an eloquent speech taking a final leave of her, Aeetes finds her weeping on his shoulder. Again when, at the end of *The Argonauts,* her brother Absyrtus with his Colchians comes up to her and the Greeks and asks her if it is true that she wishes to go off with the foreign men:

> Forsaking our dear country, hearth and home,
> Our father, and, Medea, me,
> Me too, who loves you so, my poor, dear sister.
> (*Vs. 1694–96*)

she throws herself round his neck and breaks down in tears.

Finally in Act II of *Medea,* mortified by her husband, Jason's humiliation of her in Creusa's presence, she lets the lyre fall from her hand and weeps, only to reap—on Creusa's expostulation at Jason's cruelty—further insults from him:

> Leave her alone. You do not understand.
>
> * * *
>
> Had you but seen her in the dragon's den,
> How she rose raging, rivalling the monster,
>
> * * *
>
> Your bosom would be steeled against her tears.
> (*Vs. 909–17*)

The fever of love that has afflicted Medea, holding her helpless in its grip, is depicted by Grillparzer with masterly strokes. To escape from it Medea begs her father not to attempt accommodation with the Greeks, but to send them:

> packing, packing from your land.
> Let their swift ship bear them away to safety,

---

seen Leander but a few moments earlier, before she had taken her vow of chastity, there might have been no tragedy, and certainly no play! Such "twists of fate" are not infrequent in real life, and Grillparzer seems to have relished the irony.

Or death to all of them—to all!
(*Vs. 961–63*)

When her father questions her sincerity, she clearly explains her situation:

When I see him, my senses swim
With dull fear creeping over head and heart,
And I'm no more the one I am.
Drive him away, pursue him, kill him!
Yes, if he will not fall back, kill him, Father!
I'll gaze upon him dead, with tears I'll gaze,
But not on him alive.
(*Vs. 1041–47*)

In her predicament, death to her seems kind. Once safe from Jason, she will return faithfully to her father and look after him in his old age:

Until death comes, the kindly god,
And gently soothing, fingertips on lips,
Upon his dusty, mossy pillow,
Lulls thoughts to sleep and all desires to rest.
(*Vs. 996–99*)

Jason's power over her she recognizes as baleful. She intuitively gauges the nature of his "love."

O sweet name
For an accursèd thing!
(*Vs. 1035–36*)

When at the end of the third act of *The Argonauts* she, despite her desperate entreaties, fails to dissuade him from venturing forth to seize the Fleece, which she has plainly recognized as "disaster's emblem," she determines loyally to accompany him in his danger:

You shall not die alone,
One house, one body and one ruin . . . one!
(*Vs. 1464–65*)

When Jason, touched by her sincerity, approaches to caress her she bitterly withdraws:

Leave out caresses,
I know what they are worth!
(*Vs. 1466–67*)

In Act IV of *The Argonauts,* when Jason is about to enter the dragon's den and she fears she may never see him alive again, her desperate love bursts out, and falling round his neck, she cries:

Jason! . . . I kiss you thus, and thus, and thus, and thus!
Go to your grave and leave room too for me!
(*Vs. 1532–33*)

But when the door opens and the first sight of the serpent makes Jason quail, Medea winces at his weakness and now—in the moral infirmity of her "lord and master"—recognizes her Eumenides:

The serpent makes you quake? You serpent!
Who've coiled round me, ensnaring me,
Who's ruined me and murdered me!
Look, look at it, the monster,
And go and die!
(*Vs. 1541–45*)

Finally Jason enters and the doors shut behind him, cutting him off; Medea in desperate shame and anguish prays to the gods:

Look down on us, you heavenly beings,
But no, no, do not look down
On the guilty daughter,
The spouse of the guilty girl!
Ah, keep your help and spare me from your vengeance!
Let no divine eye see,
Let dark night cover
Our deeds and us!
Jason, are you alive? Answer me!

* * *

He does not speak, is dead—dead!
My bridegroom, have you fallen? Leave room,
Room for your bride!
(*Vs. 1563–76*)

The nature of Jason's love for Medea is quite different. While it may not be as frankly commercial as Corneille's Jason's love*

*Corneille's Jason in the opening scene of *Médée* blandly admits:

I am not of the common run of lovers:
I adjust my love to the furtherance of my interests.

(and we must remember Grillparzer put a good deal of himself into his Jason), it was clearly subservient to his ambition, just as Grillparzer's love for Charlotte was. The shallower Jason's love, the more charming he appeared to be. On his first encounter with Medea, when he surprises her at her incantations and, believing her a witch, wounds her in the dark, only to be astounded at her beauty when the lamp eventually illumines her, he is "divinely" fascinating with his glib tongue:

> Come, raise your eyes and look me in the face,
> That I might see the enigma of your ways
> Illumined in the noonday of your glance.
>
> * * *
>
> You're sighing! Speak! Come, let your words resound,
> Entrust them to the air as messengers,
> Else my mouth shall induce them from your lips!
>
> (*Vs. 457–66*)

Although he is not very deeply involved with Medea—to his friend Milo's question: "So you're in love with her?" He replies: "In love?"—yet he is determined to win her, "and like a high adventure drives his love."

In the famous wooing scene in Act III of *The Argonauts,* which gave Grillparzer so many headaches, he prosecutes his love like a veritable Petruchio! He literally wrestles with Medea's resistance:

> I long to know the measure of your toughness—
>
> (*V. 1227*)

Medea falls on her knee, crying "Alas!" Jason triumphantly exclaims:

> You see? Yourself you wanted this,
> So recognize your lord and master now!
>
> (*Vs. 1228–29*)

In the dragon's cave, when Medea threatens to kill herself if he will not turn back from the fatal Fleece, he replies:

> I may lament you, but cannot turn back.
>
> (*V. 1503*)

Although Jason is physically courageous, this is less an heroic resolve than insensitivity to the feelings of the woman who loves him, as his later conduct in Corinth shows. Indeed, although he boasts to Absyrtus in the final scene of *The Argonauts:*

> I do not want your blood. In silence go!
> My arm is used to fighting against dragons,
> And not with fools like you!
>
> (*Vs. 1717–18*)

there is precious little fighting in his encounter with the dragon guarding the Fleece, the monster having been drugged to impotence by Medea's potion!

This sort of vainglorious language—a recurring defect in Grillparzer's style—is common among the Argonauts. Milo, who as their elder statesman ought to have known better, assails Gora with his boorish arrogance:

> If we take all these animals to Greece,
> I fear we shall be crushed to death by crowds
> Coming to see the sights!
>
> (*Vs. 1650–52*)

. . . a jest in very dubious taste for a civilized Greek, and all the more deplorable as Gora has just shown her dignity as a human being by taking to task the Greek soldier who had contemptuously referred to Medea as "the Colchian woman":

> Colchian woman?
> What, slave! She is Medea,
> The daughter of the Colchian king.
>
> (*Vs. 1627–29*)

With both Greek and Colchian bristling at each other with affronted dignity, and with Jason's love, as it was, there was small hope of a happy outcome to Medea's union with Jason, and this, Aeetes, her father, clearly saw, when instead of a blessing he parted from her with a curse which was to echo in her heart to the end of her days.

> You have deceived, betrayed me;
> Stay! You shall no more cross my threshold!
> You shall be cast out, like the beast of the wilderness,
> Shall die in foreign parts, forsaken and alone.
> Follow your paramour back to his homeland,

And share his bed, his wanderings, his disgrace!
Live in a foreign land, a foreigner,
Disdained, despised, discarded and distraught!
Himself, for whom you give up father and fatherland,
He shall despise you and himself discard you,
When passion is all spent, and all desire stilled:
Then you shall stand and wring your hands,
And stretch them toward your fatherland,
Sundered from it by wide, raging seas,
Whose murmuring waves shall bear to you your father's
curse.

(*Vs. 1364–78*)

Thus in despair, Medea, accompanied by Gora, sails away with Jason and his Greeks from the land of her fathers, where her brother Absyrtus has just thrown himself to drown in the sea rather than remain a captive in Greek hands, and Aeetes, distraught at the sight, begs to be placed in the grave beside his son.

Four years later, on landing in Greece with Jason and their two sons, Medea promptly experiences, in their hostile reception by the Greeks, the beginning of the fulfillment of her father's curse. Driven out within a month from Iolcos, Jason's native city, upon the mysterious death of King Pelias, Jason's uncle, the unhappy family seek refuge in Corinth where Jason had been a welcome guest at the palace in former days. As mark of her earnestness to make a fresh start and identify herself with her husband's people, Medea (in the opening scene of *Medea*) buries all the implements of her magic art, frowned upon by the Greeks, and with them the Golden Fleece. Gora, already aware of Jason's weakness in being unable to face up to the hostility of his people to his misalliance, rebukes Medea for not wishing to listen to her warnings:

You want me hold my tongue?
Let her who's guilty hold her tongue, not I!
If from my fatherland you've dragged me here
To slavery, in your false lover's wake,
Where I, my free arms chained, pour out my sighs
Through all the wretched, wakeful, lonely nights,

* * *

A butt to ridicule, a prey to scorn,
Suffering from lack of everything but pain,

Then you shall have to hear me if I speak.
(*Vs. 57–67*)

When Medea, with a brave front, tries to elude her questioning about Jason's changed attitude, Gora retorts:

You would elude me? Oh, you shan't escape!

* * *

Weep your misfortune and I'll comfort you,
Only you must not monstrously pretend,
Denying still the justice of the gods,
When you deny your pain, their punishment.
(*Vs. 89–96*)

As Medea persists in prevaricating, Gora breaks out savagely:

Is he the same still? What, you tremble? Tremble!
He shrinks and runs from you, he shuns you, hates you;
As you your kindred, so he now betrays!
(*Vs. 106–8*)

And the same forthrightness and fearlessness Gora was to show to the end when under arrest in the fifth act, upon Medea's monstrous revenge, she turns the table on her accusers, King Creon and Jason:

Wring, wring your hands! Yes, wring them for yourselves!
(To the KING*)*
Why did your child covet another's bed?
(To JASON*)*
Why did you steal her, if you did not love?

* * *

You two have only reaped what was your due!
Now you shall no more mock the Colchian woman.
I do not wish to linger on the earth;
Two children dead, the third now most abhorrent!
Lead me away and kill me if you will:
Some faith in life beyond now stirs within,
That I have seen requital follow sin.
(*Vs. 2251–62*)

Relations between Gora and Jason had of course never been cordial. Gora saw clearly Jason's combined ruthlessness and weakness and resented his debasement of her proud Medea. But Grillparzer once more, with his blind spot where his heroes were concerned, makes Jason needlessly boorish. He snaps at Gora:

> I'm itching for my sword; go while there's time!
> I've often had a strong desire to test
> Whether your brow's as hard as it appears.
> (*Vs. 200–2*)

This streak of ruthlessness was an essential trait in his love for Medea. Like Racine's Nero, who "loved the very tears he caused to flow" in the eyes of the woman who fascinated him, Jason confesses to Creon about Medea:

> Her deeds alone, her words would tell me nothing.
> Then madness also whirled within my senses;
> Her silence all the more excited me:
> (*Vs. 463–65*)

and goes on to describe in memorable terms the sinister nature of their love:

> Through her I won the enigmatic Fleece.
> She led me to that horror-haunted cavern,
> Where I victorious won it from the dragon.
> Since then, each time I gaze into her eyes,
> I see within their depths the serpent gleaming,
> And shuddering grant her title of my wife.
> (*Vs. 470–75*)

His cruelty to Medea in Creusa's presence has already been noted, but when faced with the test of common misfortune upon their proscription by the Amphictyonies,* not only does his brittle courage break, to make him seek retreat "behind Creusa's skirts," but his tenuous bond with Medea snaps as he publicly rages at her:

* Grillparzer later felt that he had perhaps been mistaken in introducing the Amphictyonies as in Seneca, but as this precipitates one of the most dramatic scenes in the play, perhaps he was once more being unduly critical. The Amphictyonies was the council of states in charge of the administration of Apollo's Temple at Delphi, armed also with judicial powers.

To me your nature from the first was hateful,
And I have cursed the very day I saw you,
And pity only held me to your side:
But now at last, forever I renounce you
And curse you as the whole world curses you.
(*Vs. 1100a–1104*)

It is clear that their attachment, based on mutual desire and not on mutual understanding, left them fundamentally estranged, as Gora and Aeetes had noted from the beginning and as Medea herself was bitterly to realize in the end when she tells Jason—with the ghosts of their dead children between them:

Were you not still a stranger to my breast
As you have ever been, you'd see the pain,
That, seething endless like a surging sea,
Swallows the several ruins of my grief
And drags them, hid in horrid desolation,
Into the vortex of the infinite.
(*Vs. 2318–23*)

Like Racine's Phèdre, a granddaughter of the sun-god (the legend had attributed the paternity of Aeetes to Helios, the sun, just as it did of Pasiphaë, Phèdre's mother), Medea had warm blood in her veins. Quick to respond to kindness, the moment Creusa begs her pardon for having offended her, she thaws:

How sweet the sound! Who spoke that gentle word?
They often have offended me most deeply;
But no one stayed to ask if I were hurt!
(*Vs. 370–72*)

Like Racine's Phèdre too, she is well aware and thoroughly ashamed of the dark force that has dragged her down to be the reject of Jason and of Greece, as she goes on to tell Creusa:

You stare at me? And shudder now at me?
There was a time I would myself have shuddered,
Had I conceived a creature now like me!
(*Vs. 396–98*)

In her insecurity she views wistfully Creusa's security, not only her outer security because of her royal position (a position she herself had once enjoyed in Colchis: "I was, like you, born daughter of a king," she reiterates), but also her inner security, such as she, Medea, with her psychic and occult powers, in disharmony with her Amazonian attributes—love of the chase and skill at arms—had never enjoyed:

> You are, I see, of gentle, winsome ways,
> So self-secure, so much at one with self.
> To me the Gods denied that happiness;
> (*Vs. 408–10*)

So when the terrible fever of love (such as La Rochefoucauld describes) struck her at sight of Jason, she realized at once she was doomed, just as Racine's Phèdre realized at first sight of Hippolytus:

> Je le vis, je rougis, je palis à sa vue.
> (I saw, I blushed, I paled at sight of him.)
> (*Phèdre, V. 273*)

Medea explains her plight to Creusa:

> Thus he stood, shining in his strength and beauty,
> A hero, god, enticing me, enticing,
> Till he seduced his victim and destroyed her,
> Then cast her off and no one raised her up.
> (*Vs. 624–27*)

When Creusa demurs at Medea's assessment of Jason, Medea retorts savagely:

> You do not know him, but I know too well!
> And when I call to mind what has befallen,
> I think I laughingly could see him die.
> (*Vs. 638–40*)

As Creusa shows her impatience at Medea's "hard and unforgiving heart," Medea thaws once more and begs her, at least, not also to cast her off. As Creusa relents with:

> Now you are gentle, yet were full of hate!
> (*V. 659*)

Medea sums up her situation with:

> The hate for me, for Jason only love!
> (*V. 660*)

To retain her husband's love she begs Creusa to impart to her something of her own feminine charm:

> The strength, that was my pride from earliest childhood,
> Has shown itself as weakness in my struggle:
> Oh, teach to me the strength that springs from weakness.
> (*Vs. 685–87*)

But when her attempted exercise of this feminine charm imparted by Creusa (the singing to Jason of his favorite boyhood song) fails to arrest Jason from his selfish course of flirting with Creusa and humiliating her, Medea, in Creusa's presence, Medea's dangerous strength flares up and she snaps in two the lyre that Jason would have Creusa play.

When Jason in Act II, upon their proscription by the Amphictyonies, snaps even more resoundingly their marital bond and publicly humiliates Medea, thus further fulfilling her father's curse:

> Away with you to the wilderness, your cradle,
> To the bloodstained folk you love and you resemble!
> But first return to me what you have taken:
> Give Jason back to me, you criminal!
> (*Vs. 1051–54*)

Medea, in desperate shame and rage, retorts in language where Grillparzer's dramatic intensity rises to the greatest heights:

> You call me criminal? Alas, I am one!
> What crimes have I committed and for whom?
> Let these pursue me with their poisonous hate,
> Drive me away and kill me, they have cause,
> For I am an abhorrent, abject creature,
> My own abyss, my own abomination;
> The whole world may abjure me, *you* must not!
> You not, the sole cause, root of all the horror, you!
> (*Vs. 1063–70*)

In the fourth act, brooding over the terrible scene at the end of the third act, where after rejection by her father and husband Medea is subjected to the unbearable agony of being rejected by both her children—a supreme dramatic touch motivating her dreadful revenge more acceptably than any previous dramatist of *Medea*—Grillparzer's Medea in her despair darkly reflects:

If crime is sometimes father of misfortune,
Misfortune far more often fathers crime!
What matters living then?
I would my father had murdered me,
When I was little yet,
As now had nothing suffered,
Had nothing thought—as now!
(*Vs. 1795–1801*)

where the double chiasmus, a favorite figure of speech in Grillparzer, combined with the free verse, is used to superb dramatic effect.

Her despair is turned to horror when she thinks of the occult power with which she has been cursed, and to what abysses it has led her, and in a great passage where this horror, combined with Grillparzer's deep psychological insight, equals Racine's, Medea expresses her agony:

But deep within my inmost soul I shudder,
When I think on it and the bloody Fleece.
I feel my father and my brother's ghosts
Brood over it, and will not let it go.
Do you not know how on the ground he lay,
My gray-haired father, weeping for his son
And cursing me, his daughter? At this, Jason
In hideous triumph held the Fleece on high;
I then swore vengeance, vengeance on the traitor,
Who first my kindred killed and now kills me.*
Had I my bloody box,† I'd execute it,
Only I dare not bring it back;
For were I in the emblem's golden glitter
To see my father's features stare at me,
Believe me, I'd go mad!
(*Vs. 1882–96*)

*With Medea's realization that even before she had given herself to Jason on the voyage from Colchis to Greece, she had subconsciously hated him already for compelling her to love him against her will and to forsake her kith and kin out of desire for him, Grillparzer's psychological insight is revealed at its profoundest.

†The chest containing all her magic implements and the Fleece, which she buries in the opening scene of *Medea*.

In the raw state of her emotions, the least provocation totally unnerves her. When her children automatically follow the slave girl who has brought them to her on Creon's order for her to take her leave of them before her departure from Corinth, and to her question her son explains:

> Our father ordered us to follow her:
> (*V. 2032*)

Medea's blazing resentment against Jason is turned on their son:

> When I consider how my very flesh,
> The child whom I have carried in my womb,
> Whom I have nurtured on this very breast,
> How my own self stands up against myself,
> Then fury flashes searing through my soul
> And bloody thoughts rear up in rampant terror—
> (*Vs. 2034–39*)

Grillparzer's mastery of his art almost everywhere in this play is seen in the smallest details. Thus when Medea waves the children off stage in order that the terrible murder should not take place in the sight of the audience, this gesture is not some empty theatrical trick, but springs from the bottom of her agonized heart, for with her infanticidal thoughts she cannot bear her sons' sleeping beside her:

> How could you think of sleeping here beside me?
> Go there within, there inside you may rest!
> (*Vs. 2123–24*)

When the terrible catastrophe has brought all down in ruin, from the ashes of her fatal love for Jason—"the root of all the horror"—rises, phoenix-like, her own moral regeneration, for all passion now spent, she resumes her former independence of spirit, no longer adolescent, but mellowed by the most tragic experiences that any woman could suffer. Too mature now to take the escape route of suicide:

> Medea's hand may not dispatch Medea.
> (*Vs. 2351*)

she determines at the end of the trilogy, in token of reconcilement, to submit her fate to the judgment of the priests of Apollo at Delphi, where the Golden Fleece, stolen from its sanctity at the beginning, to pilot ambition, would be restored within its sacred portals to harmlessness. The Fleece, she in sad consolation reminds the shattered Jason, was the emblem:

> . . . for which you strove,
> That seemed your laurel crown and happiness!
> What is earth's happiness?—A shadow!
> What is earth's laurel crown?—A dream!
> Poor you, who have of shadows only dreamed!
> (*Vs. 2364–68*)

And on a note that sums up Grillparzer's personal pessimism, this great tragedy ends with Medea's parting exhortation to Jason, like herself, to bear and atone.

S. S.

THE GOLDEN FLEECE

---

*A Poetic Drama in Three Parts**

* First performed at the Hofburgtheater in Vienna on March 1821; the first two plays of the trilogy were performed on March 26, with *Medea* being done on March 27. *The Golden Fleece* was first published by J. B. Wallishausser in 1822.

I

THE GUEST

A Tragedy In One Act

CHARACTERS

AEETES	*King of Colchis**
MEDEA	*His daughter*
GORA	MEDEA*'s nurse*
PERITTA	*One of* MEDEA*'s maidens*
PHRIXUS	
MEDEA'S MAIDENS	
GREEKS	PHRIXUS' *men*
COLCHIANS	

* Colchis is the region at the eastern end of the Euxine (Black Sea) south of the Caucasus, its chief river being the Phasis. In Roman times it became part of Mithridates' realm.

Colchis. Wild landscape of rocks and trees, with the sea in the background. On the shore an altar built of unhewn stones on which stands the gigantic image of a nude man with a beard, who bears a club in his right hand and a ram's pelt on his shoulders. Left, by the center wings, the entrance of a house with steps and rough pillars. It is daybreak. MEDEA, GORA, PERRITTA SUITE OF MAIDENS. *At the rise of the curtain* MEDEA *stands in the foreground with a bow in her hand in the posture of one who has just shot an arrow. On the steps of the altar lies a roe pierced with an arrow.*[1]

MAIDENS

(Who had been standing at a distance, rushing to the altar)

The sacrifice is bleeding!

MEDEA *(In her posture above)*

Hit?

MAIDEN

Right in the heart.

MEDEA *(Handing over the bow)*

That's a good omen. Let us hurry then!
One of you hasten and pronounce the prayer.

[1] This may be interpreted as a symbol of Medea's own tragic fate in the trilogy—piercing Jason with the arrow of love and its deadly consequences, which she herself was instrumental in launching or, more immediately, of Phrixus' fate in this play.

GORA *(Going to the altar)*

Darimba,[2] mighty goddess,
Preserver of mortals, destroyer of mortals!
Who giv'st us wine, and the corn of the field,
Giv'st the refreshing gift of the hunt,
Giv'st the blood of our mortal foe;
Darimba, the chaste, the virginal
Daughter of Heaven, *10*
Hear me!

CHORUS

Darimba! mighty goddess!
Darimba! Darimba!

GORA

Behold! I've killed a roe for thee
Speeding the arrow from the strong bow,
It's thine; may't please thee to accept its blood!
Bless the fields and the teeming woods,
Make us do right and triumph in battle,
Make us love the well-disposed,
And hate him who hates us! *20*
Make us strong and rich, Darimba;
Mighty goddess!

CHORUS

Darimba! Darimba!

GORA

At the altar the twitching sacrifice is still,
So may thy enemies be stilled, Darimba,
Thy enemies and ours!
It is Medea, Aeetes' daughter,
The royal child of Colchis' ruler,
Who's calling to you in your high abode.
Hear me, O hear me, *30*
And fulfil my prayer!

[2] The local version of Artemis or Diana, virgin goddess of the hunt.

CHORUS *(Striking cymbals and tympans)*

Darimba! Darimba!
Mighty goddess!
Eriho! Yeho!

MEDEA

And now enough! The sacrifice is done,
And the preliminaries over.
Then take your bows and arrows, free the hounds,
And let the green woods echo far and wide
The resonant din of the tumultuous chase!
The sun is mounting. Away! Away! *40*
And she who's swiftest and who's lithesomest
Shall be queen of the day—
You here, Peritta? Did I not tell you
To keep away from me and go? Then go!

PERITTA *(Kneeling)*

Medea!

MEDEA

Do not kneel! You must not kneel!
D'you hear? In your place I would shake with shame;
So tame, so craven! It is not your loss
That pains me, but that I must now despise you,
You I once loved.

PERITTA

Ah, if you only knew!

MEDEA

What then? Did you not steal away from the chase *50*
And go to the shepherd of Tergen Dale?
Did you not? Say no, false, ungrateful wretch!
Did you not promise you would be mine, mine,
And no man's? Say, did you not promise this?

PERITTA

Ah, when I promised, did I then know—

MEDEA

Silence!
What's there to know but that you promised me!
I am the royal daughter of Aeetes,
And what I do is right, since I have done it;
And yet, false wretch! If I had promised you
To hack my hand away from my right arm, *60*
I'd do it, yes, I'd do it, since I promised.

PERITTA

It swept me speechless, senseless, quite away,
And not of my own free will, no—

MEDEA

Just listen
She did not will, but did it! Off, what nonsense
How could it ever happen
If you did not *will?* What I do, I will,
And what I will—well, sometimes I *don't* do! [3]
Then go, go to your shepherd's musty hut,
And squat in smoke and filthy exhalations
And grow your cabbage on a tiny plot. *70*
My garden is the free and boundless earth,
My house the pure blue pillars of the sky;
There I will stand erect with my free breast,
Meeting the mountains' free and bracing breezes
And with contempt I will look down at you.[4]
Halloo! To the woods, girls, to the woods, away!

[3] Right from the beginning Grillparzer endows his Medea with a touch of conscience that makes her far more sympathetic than Euripides' heroine, driven solely by her wounded *amour propre* to the most monstrous deeds. On the other hand, Euripides' Jason is perhaps less repugnant than Grillparzer's, with his nauseating self-pity!

[4] Compare Heine's poem prefixed to the "Harzreise"—his brilliant account of a tour in the Harz mountains undertaken in 1824:

On the mountains I will climb,
Where the homely cottage stands,

(As she is about to make her exit, enter a COLCHIAN *from the opposite side of the stage)*

COLCHIAN

Hear me, princess!

MEDEA

What? Who is calling me?

COLCHIAN

A ship with strangers has but now put in.

MEDEA

Then tell my father, do not bother me!

COLCHIAN

Where is he?

MEDEA

In the house.

COLCHIAN

I'll hurry.

MEDEA

Do! *80*

(Exit the MESSENGER *into the house)*

Ah, how these strangers disarrange our hunt!
I see their ship is anchored in the bay
That serves our hunt as its assembling place.
Well, never mind! Bring out the long spears here,
And should one dare approach, he'll pay with blood.
Bring only spears! But softly, do you hear!
For should my father see, he might forbid.
Come . . . Do you see the boundary mark of stones

Where the breezes blow in freedom
And the free breast free expands.

* * *

On the mountains I will climb
And laughingly look down at you.

Up there? Let's see which one will reach it first.
Get ready! Back! No overstepping! Back! *90*
Who wins will have the first shot in the chase.
Get ready then, and when I give the signal,
Then speed, from bow like arrow; steady now!
Steady . . . Go!

(Enter AEETES *meanwhile from the house with the* MESSENGER, *who exits immediately)*

AEETES

Medea!

MEDEA *(Turning around but without leaving her place)*

Father!

AEETES

Going where?

MEDEA

The woods.

AEETES

Stay now.

MEDEA

But why?

AEETES

You must, I wish it.

MEDEA

So you're afraid those strangers . . . ?

AEETES

Then you know?

(Coming nearer, beneath his breath)

Men, landed
From distant shores,
Bringing gold, bringing treasures,
Rich spoils. *100*

MEDEA

For whom?

AEETES

For us, should we but wish.

MEDEA

Us?

AEETES

They're strangers, enemies
Come to waste our land.

MEDEA

Then go and kill them!

AEETES

They're numerous and well-equipped,
Most cunning, these strange men,
They could easily kill *us*.

MEDEA

Then let them go.

AEETES

Never!
They must—

MEDEA

Do as you will;
But let me go a'hunting.

AEETES

Stay, I say! *110*

MEDEA

To do what?

AEETES

Help, advise me!

MEDEA

I?

AEETES

You're wise, you're strong.
You your mother taught
From herbs, from stones,
To prepare brews
That numb the will
And fetter power;
You conjure spirits
And hail the moon.
Help me, my dear child! *120*

MEDEA

Am I your dear child?
Usually you hardly heed me,
When I want something, you do *not*
And scold me and repulse me;
But when you need me,
You flatter me with smooth words,
Calling me, Medea, your dear child.

AEETES

Forget, Medea, what took place before,
You also are not always as you should be.
Stand now by me and help me! *130*

MEDEA

To what end?

AEETES

Only listen, my dear girl!
All the strangers' gold and all their treasures—
Right? You smile?

MEDEA

I?

AEETES

Yes, all that heap of gold,
Those gems of every color, the fine robes,
How they would rich adorn my little girl!

MEDEA

Enough of that!

AEETES

You little rascal, see,
I know your heart is panting for those jewels.

MEDEA

Father, come to the point.

AEETES

I—
Tell the girls there to go.

MEDEA

Why?

AEETES

I insist.

MEDEA

They are to go to hunt with me.

AEETES

No hunt today! *140*

MEDEA

No hunt?

AEETES

No hunt, I say, no hunt!

MEDEA

You praise me first, and—

AEETES

Now be good, my child!
Come here. Nearer! Here, nearer! Good!
You are a clever girl and I can trust you.
I—

MEDEA

Well?

AEETES

Why are you staring at my face?

MEDEA

I'm listening, Father—

AEETES

Oh, I know you well!
Will you command your father, willful girl?
I am the one who says what's good, what's not.
And you *obey*. Out of my sight, you jade!
You are not worthy—off, I tell you, off! [5] *150*

(MEDEA *is about to go)*

Stay! If you'd only try to understand—
I know you can, only you do not want to—
Then be it so, stay shut out from my counsel,
And be a slave, since slave you wish to be.

(Warlike music is heard in the distance)

What's that? Alas! They've caught us unprepared!
Foolish girl, do you see?
Those you wished to spare, they'll kill us now;
The strangers marching here in full procession!
Ah, we are lost! To arms! To arms!

(Reenter the MESSENGER*)*

MESSENGER

My lord, the leader of the strangers— *160*

AEETES

What does he want? My crown? My life?
I still have heart, I still have power,
And still the blood is boiling in my veins,
To barter death for death!

[5] This verse is omitted in the Hanser Edition, based on the Vienna Edition. I have followed the Berlin Edition, as a girl of Medea's high spirits would not immediately appear to comply.

MESSENGER

He begs an audience.

AEETES

Begs?

MESSENGER

To speak to you in friendship,
And come to peaceful terms.

AEETES

Begs? And with force in hand,
With us unarmed and he with arms,
And begs? . . . The fool! *170*

MESSENGER

He means to come into your house
Sit at your table,
Eat of your bread,
And privately tell you
What led him here.

AEETES

Let him come, let him come.
If he but two hours keeps the peace,
Later I'll fear him no more.
Tell him to approach,
But without shield or spear, *180*
Only his sword at side,
He and his companions.
Thereafter go and summon all my men
Throughout the country around,
Bid them come armed, fully accoutred
With shield and armor, lance and sword,
And hide in the adjacent woods
Until I beckon, call them. Go!

(Exit the MESSENGER*)*

I mean to laugh at you, weak fool!
But you, Medea, be of service to me! *190*

There is a brew, as I know you prepare,
That can deprive the senses of their functions
With soft insinuating stupors
And make their master slave of deepest slumber.
Then go and fetch me here some of that brew.

MEDEA

To what end?

AEETES

Go, I say, and fetch it here!
Come back with it. I mean to curb their pride.

(Exit MEDEA*)*

AEETES *(turning to the altar in the background)*

Peronto, god of my fathers!
Let my meditations prosper,
And faithful I will share with you 200
What we win from our foes.

(Warlike music. Armed Greeks march in, with green branches in their hands. PHRIXUS *brings up the rear, also holding a green branch in his left hand, and in his right bearing a golden ram's pelt in the shape of a banner on his lance. Armed* COLCHIANS *enter from the other side. The music ceases. As* PHRIXUS *passes the altar in the background with its erect image, he stops as though riveted by amazement and then speaks)*

PHRIXUS

Can I believe my eyes? The very one!
Then hail! Let me salute you, friendly image
That through the stormy waves and baleful nights
Has led me all this way to these far shores,
Where Safety and serene Tranquility
Smile at me with their simple childlike eyes.
Before your altar thankfully I plant
This emblem you bestowed on me as pledge
Of my salvation in that graceless hour:[6] 210

[6] This refers to Phrixus' fleeing with the Fleece from Apollo's Temple at Delphi.

It's this that's brought me into fortune's haven,
Lighting my dark way like the pilot star.
So prayerfully I bend a pious knee
To you who were a god to me in deed,
Though not to me in name, who am a stranger!

(He kneels)

AETEES *(In the foreground)*

What's this?
He bends his knees to my ancestral god!
Would he rob me of his favor? [7]
Be mindful of my many sacrifices,
And hear him not, Peronto, 220
Ah, do not hear the stranger!

PHRIXUS *(Rising)*

My gratitude's sweet duty is accomplished.
Then lead me to your king! Where is he now?

(The COLCHIANS *make way on both sides silently and with deference.* PHRIXUS, *seeing the king, goes toward him)*

In you I doubtless greet this country's lord?

AEETES

I am the Colchians' prince!

PHRIXUS

My salutations!
A heavenly power has led me to your kingdom,
So honor in me my protecting god.
Is that man holding sway upon the altar
The likeness of a mortal who once lived?
Or do you worship him as an immortal? 230

AEETES

He is Peronto, the Colchians' god.

[7] This verse also is omitted in the Hanser Edition and the Vienna Edition.

PHRIXUS

Peronto! Sounds harsh to a stranger's ear,
But most harmonious to one he saved.
If you revere this god as your protector,
Then please embrace a brother in your arms,
For sons of the *one* father must be brothers.

AEETES *(Evading the embrace)*

He, your protector?

PHRIXUS

Yes, you must hear further.
But let me first present my offering.

(He goes to the altar and plants his banner in the ground in front of it. Enter MEDEA *with a goblet)*

MEDEA *(Aloud)*

Here, Father, is the potion!

AEETES *(Pulling her violently aside. Softly)*

Silence, fool!
Have you no eyes?

MEDEA

What?

AEETES

Give the slave the goblet 240
And hold your tongue!

MEDEA

Who is the man?

AEETES

The stranger's leader, silence!

PHRIXUS *(Coming back from the altar)*

Now I am free to enter your good house.
But who is this exquisite, glowing creature,
That like the silver lining of the storm cloud
Clings closely to your royal warrior form?

Her rosy, rosy lips and radiant cheeks
Appear to promise graciousness and love,
Though, contradicted by her frowning eyes,
That beaming lightning like some baleful comet,
Flash brilliant from the pitch-black of her hair. *250*
Half Charis[8] and half Maenad,[9] there she stands,
Sparked by the sacred fire of her god.
Who are you, lovely maiden?

AEETES

Speak, Medea!

MEDEA *(Drily)*

I am Medea, daughter of this king.

PHRIXUS

Indeed, at once a daughter and a queen!
I greet you as a shining augury
Of a future that is still veiled to us.
Ah, smile, sweet maiden, on my coming here!
Perhaps—who knows?—whether or not your father,
From whom I've sought but refuge and protection, *260*
Might give me more, ah, much more, dear Medea! [10]

AEETES

Now tell me, stranger, what is your desire?

PHRIXUS

Then listen, pray, to what has brought me here,
What I have lost, my lord, and what I seek.
Born of Greek parents in the lovely land
Of Hellas, I'm a Greek of purest blood.

[8] Greek goddess of grace or charm, hence "charisma" and "charismatic."

[9] One of the raving women accompanying Dionysius (Bacchus), the god of wine, and of religious ecstasy or hysteria (see Euripides' *Bacchae*).

[10] Phrixus, in Calderon's *Three Greatest Wonders,* also enthuses over Medea's beauty, and describes his adventures.

There's none alive who boasts a loftier line,
A nobler breed, in Hellas than myself;
For I can call the gods of Greece my forbears,[11]
And my forefather rules the universe. *270*

MEDEA *(Turning aside)*

I'm going, Father—

AEETES

Hold your tongue, remain!

PHRIXUS

My house is thus descended from the gods.
And yet my father, heedless of our fame
And of the rights and fortunes of his children,
In second marriage chose a vulgar woman,
Who, envious of the offspring of his first
And pervious to reproach, since she herself
Was conscious of deserving men's reproach,
Stirred up my father's anger against me.
Discord increased, and he sent bailiffs out *280*
To seize his son, perhaps to murder him.
And so I left my father's house and fled
To foreign parts to seek domestic bliss.
My wanderings brought me to the Delphian city,
Where, seeking help and counsel from the god,
I entered Phoebus' rich and far-famed house.[12]
I stood there in the temple's porticos,
With statues, sacrificial gifts around,
Resplendent in the radiant sunset's rays.
Exhausted by the sights and by the journey, *290*
I shut my eyes, relaxed my weary limbs:
Succumbing to the urge, I fell asleep.
I dreamt I found myself in the same temple

[11] His forbears included minor gods and demi-gods going back to Prometheus, antagonist of Zeus.

[12] The temple of Phoebus Apollo at Delphi was one of the most renowned in ancient Greece, where it was customary for kings and commoners alike to consult the Oracle before embarking on any enterprise.

In which I slept, only awake, alone,
And praying to the god for counsel. Sudden,
A bright light flared around me, and a man
In naked might, a club in his right hand,
With long hair and a beard and a ram's pelt
Around his powerful shoulders, stood before me,
And, graciously inviting, smiled at me, *300*
"With this take victory and revenge," he said,
Unloosening the rich fleece from his shoulders
And handing it to me; trembling I woke.
And look! Illumined by the morning sun
I saw in front of me a shimmering niche:
In it, artistically hewn from marble,
Stood that same man who'd just appeared to me
With beard and hair and pelt as I had dreamt.

AEETES *(Pointing to the statue in the background)*

This one?

PHRIXUS

As like to him as I am to myself.
And thus he stood in godlike power and grace, *310*
Resembling Heracles, although not he;
And on the statue's pedestal, inscribed,
The name "Colchis" stood clearly out in gold.
But I interpreted the god's advice,
And taking what he offered me in riddle,
I—being alone—unloosed the golden gem
From off the statue's neck and rushed away.
I found my father's bailiffs by the gates—
They fell back, cowed by the god's golden banner;
The priests bowed low, and all the people knelt, *320*
And bearing it before me on my lance,
I reached the sea through a thousand enemies.
I here embarked, raising the Fleece aloft
As golden pennon on my storm-wracked mast,
And though the waters foamed, and thunders growled
And wind and waves and hell itself conspired
To doom me shipwrecked to a watery grave,

No hair of mine was hurt;[13] and sound of limb
I landed here upon this sheltering shore,
That no Greek foot has trodden before me. *330*
And now my humble prayer's addressed to you:
Allow me and my men into your land,
If not, myself I'll seize my hearth and home,
Relying on the aid of the high gods, who,
Through this, have pledged me *victory and revenge!*
. . . You're silent?

AEETES

What then would you have me say?

PHRIXUS

Will you grant me an hospitable roof?

AEETES

Enter, should it seem good to you; there's plenty
To eat and drink: so take and eat your fill!

PHRIXUS

Is this the way a host receives his guest? *340*

AEETES

I take you as you would present yourself.
He who demands a gift in guise of war
Must not expect it from the hand of peace.

PHRIXUS

I've laid aside my shield, also my spear.

AEETES

You think your sword sufficient against us,
But do just as you will.

(Softly to MEDEA*)*

Demand his sword.

[13] Unfortunately, Hero's veil, that Leander similarly made into a pennon to serve as a talisman while swimming across the Hellespont, could not save him from drowning (see Act IV, Vs. 1653–57 of *The Waves of Sea and Love*).

PHRIXUS

One thing more! I am bringing many jewels
And precious vessels I would keep secure;
You'll grant them the protection of your house?

AEETES

Do as you will.

(To MEDEA*)*

Demand his sword, I say! *350*

PHRIXUS

Well then, companions! Bring here what we've brought,
Saved from the cruel shipwreck of my fortune,
Into the sure circumference of these walls,
Foundation stone of a new, firmer fortune.

AEETES *(To* MEDEA*)*

The stranger's sword!

MEDEA

But why?

AEETES

His sword, I say!

MEDEA *(To* PHRIXUS*)*

Give me your sword!

PHRIXUS

What was that, pretty child?

AEETES

In the girl's eyes your sword appears forbidding,
With us a man at peace does not go armed.
It must be heavy too.

PHRIXUS *(To* MEDEA*)*

You care for me? *(*MEDEA *turns away)*
Do not be angry! See, I can't refuse you. *360*

(He gives her the sword)

To heaven I shall entrust myself, to you!
Where you are, there is peace. Here, take my sword,
And now into your house, my noble host!

AEETES

You go, I'll follow soon.

PHRIXUS

And you, Medea?
Let me see you too at the merry table!
Come, friends, and share my cheer, as once my peril.

(He exits with his companions. MEDEA *sits down on a rocky seat in the foreground and toys with her bow that she has picked up from the ground.* AEETES *stands on the other side of the foreground and watches* PHRIXUS' *servants, who carry gold and rich vessels into the house. A long pause)*

AEETES

Medea!

MEDEA

Father!

AEETES

What do *you* think?

MEDEA

Nothing!

AEETES

Of the stranger, I mean.

MEDEA

How he speaks and speaks!
I am repelled!

AEETES *(Quickly taking her up)*

Quite so, speaks and dissembles
And is a miscreant, 370
A blasphemer, a temple-robber!
I'll kill him!

MEDEA

Father!

AEETES

Yes, I will!
Is he to decamp with all the wealth
He's robbed, yes, robbed from heaven?
Did he himself not tell how in the temple
He plucked the Fleece from the god's shoulder,
From the Thunderer, Peronto,
The shield of Colchis:
Peronto, I will slaughter him for you!
You'll be avenged, avenged! *380*

MEDEA

What, will you kill the stranger and your guest?

AEETES

Guest?
Have I invited him to my house?
Tendered him bread and salt upon his entrance
And bid him sit upon my chair?
I did not offer hospitality,
Himself he *took* it; he shall pay, the fool!

MEDEA

Father, Peronto will avenge his murder! [14]

AEETES

Peronto *commands* it.
Has not the sinner sinned against him? *390*
Outraged his likeness in the Delphian city?
Has not the angry god himself led him here
That I might punish, might avenge
The god's disgrace and mine?
The fleece there on the glittering spear,
Robe of the god, the Colchians' sanctuary,
Shall any foreign criminal desecrate it?
It's mine, mine! The god sends it to me,

[14] A prophetic intimation.

And *victory and revenge,* bound to this pledge,
May they become our portion! 400
Keep carrying in the precious goods!
You're bringing me some harvest!
Come, not a word! So that he may not miss us;
Revenge shall be both dangerless and full!
Come, I say, come!

(Exeunt both into the house. Enter a COLCHIAN CAPTAIN *with* ARMED MEN*)*

CAPTAIN

We were directed here, what must we do?

(A COLCHIAN *from the house)*

COLCHIAN

Ho there!

CAPTAIN

Here we are!

COLCHIAN

Softly!

CAPTAIN

Speak, what is it?

COLCHIAN

Split up to right and left, and if a stranger—
But hush now! One approaches! Come, hear what follows.

(Exeunt all)

PHRIXUS *(Coming out of the house with anxious steps)*

Great gods! What does this mean? I fear the worst. 410
These grim barbarians growl among themselves
And look upon us with their mocking smiles;
They go, they come, they nod, they leer,
And my companions, one after another,
Slump down in brutish sleep; whether fatigue
Or some accursèd sleeping draught or other
Lulls them, I do not know. O righteous Gods!

Have you led me to my destruction here?
One way alone is left: flight to my ship.
There I shall muster all those who remained, 420
And come back here to save them—what's that?—listen!

(The clash of swords and muffled voices in the house)

They're fighting, killing, woe is me! Too late!
Flight only's left; quick, ere the murderers come!

(About to go—and warriors with spears held forth enter to bar his way)

COLCHIAN

Stand back!

PHRIXUS

I am betrayed! Here!

(From all sides ARMED MEN *with lances lowered bar his way)*

ARMED MEN

Stand back, there!

PHRIXUS

No use, it's all up! Friends, I'll follow you!

(Hastening to the altar)

Well then, O lofty one who led me here,
If you're a god, preserve your protégé.

(Enter AEETES *from the house with drawn sword,* MEDEA *behind him, with their followers)*

AEETES

Where is he?

MEDEA

Father, listen!

AEETES

Where, the stranger?
Ha, by the altar. What're you seeking there?

PHRIXUS

I seek protection!

AEETES

Against whom? Come into the house. 430

PHRIXUS

I will stand here and will embrace this altar,
I trust the Gods; to think I trusted you!

MEDEA

O, Father, listen to me.

PHRIXUS

You too, snake?
Were you so full of beauty and allure,
But to decoy me to the snare of death?
My heart was drawn to you in confidence,
I placed my sword, my last guard, in your hands,
And you betray me?

MEDEA

I have not betrayed you!
If you gave me your sword, here, take another
And defend your life.

(She has snatched a sword from one of those standing by and tenders it to him)

AEETES *(Snatching the sword from her)*

You fool! 440
Off, from the altar!

PHRIXUS

I'll stay!

AEETES

Tear him off!

PHRIXUS *(As some men advance toward him)*

Ah well! must I then die? Then be it so!
But I shall not fall unavenged, unheard.

(He plucks the banner with the Golden Fleece from the earth and comes with it into the foreground)

You, unknown Power, that have led me here,
Bestowing this as pledge of my salvation,
And promising me *victory and revenge;*
To you on high I call, so hear me now!
If through my own fault *victory* I have lost
By putting my own head in the traitor's noose,
And blindly trusting fate, instead of myself, *450*
Then let, I beg, at least *revenge* prevail
And keep the second half of your great promise.

AEETES

Why are you dallying?

PHRIXUS

Aeetes!

AEETES

What now?

PHRIXUS

I am your guest and you're betraying me?

AEETES

My guest? My enemy!
What were you after, stranger, in my land? Temple-robber!
Did I swear hospitality? Invite you to my house?
I promised nothing, you fool!
Destroyed by your own fault!

PHRIXUS

Would you seek thus to palliate your crime? *460*
O do not triumph! Come here.

AEETES

To what purpose?

PHRIXUS

Behold this banner here, my last estate.

You've robbed from me all my most precious treasures,
This one alone remains.

AEETES *(Grabbing at it)*

Remains? For how long?

PHRIXUS

Get back! Look at it, it's my last estate.
On parting with it I shall part with life.
Do you desire it?

AEETES

Yes!

PHRIXUS

Do you desire it?

AEETES *(Stretching out his hand)*

Give it me!

PHRIXUS

Take it, the guest's estate, you noble host,
See, I entrust it to you. Keep it for me!

(With raised voice)

And if you do not give it back, unharmed, *470*
Not give it back to me, to unharmed me,
Then may the Gods' almighty thunder-curse,
That crashes on the faithless, crash on you.
Now I'm at ease. Revenge, revenge, revenge!
He has my estate; preserve it faithfully!

AEETES

Ah! take it back!

PHRIXUS

Not even for your kingdom!
You have my estate, I've entrusted it to you,
Preserve the estate entrusted faithfully!

AEETES *(Pressing the Fleece on him)*

Take it back!

PHRIXUS *(Eluding him)*

You have my estate, preserve it faithfully!
Or else revenge, revenge, revenge!

AEETES *(Chasing him across the stage, and pressing the banner on him)*

Take it, I say! *480*

PHRIXUS *(Eluding)*

I will not take it. Preserve it faithfully!

(Addressing the statue of the god)

You see? He has it, I've entrusted it!
And should he not return it, may you smite him!

AEETES

Take it back!

PHRIXUS *(At the altar)*

No, no!

AEETES

Take it!

PHRIXUS

You preserve it.

AEETES

Take it!

PHRIXUS

Never!

AEETES

Then take this!

(He thrusts his sword into PHRIXUS' *breast)*

MEDEA

Father, stop!

PHRIXUS *(Sinking down)*

It's too late!

MEDEA

What have you done?

PHRIXUS *(To the statue above)*

D'you see, d'you see?

His guest he murders, taking his estate!
You who protect the holy head of guest,[15]
Great god, avenge me! Curse the faithless man!
No friend for him, and no child and no brother, 490
No merry meal and no refreshing drink;
May what he loves the most prove his destruction!
And may this Fleece, he holds now in his hand,
Look down upon the death of all his children!
He has destroyed the man who was his guest.
And keeps back—the estate entrusted him—
Revenge! Revenge! . . .

(He dies. There is a long pause)

MEDEA

Father!

AEETES *(Shrinking back)*

What?

MEDEA

What have you done?

AEETES *(Wanting to press the Fleece on the dead man)*

Take it back!

[15] Peronto the Thunderer (V. 377) was evidently meant to represent the Colchian Zeus, since Zeus was also the guardian of the guest (see *Medea,* end of Act I). Yet in Aeetes' eyes he was not averse to the human sacrifice of strangers for which legendary Colchis, like Tauris, was notorious (V. 379), and resembled rather the Mars depicted by Calderon than Zeus. This vagueness is doubtless due to Grillparzer's change of plan, of which there are still traces in the first two plays of the trilogy, e.g., in *The Argonauts,* a mention of "cave" (V. 256) and of "rocky seat" in the stage direction, second scene of Act I.

MEDEA

No more he'll take it. He is dead!

AEETES

Dead—

MEDEA

Father, what have you done?
Destroyed your guest! *500*
Woe to you, woe to us all— Ha!
From the mists of the underworld it rises up—
Three heads, heads bathed in blood,
Serpents for hair,
Flames for eyes,
Those mocking eyes!
Higher! Higher! They keep on rising!
With skeleton arms, with torch in hand,
Torches! Daggers!
Listen! They open their withered lips, *510*
They mutter, they sing
In croaking chorus:
We guard the oath,
We execute the curse!
Cursèd be he, who slew the guest!
Cursèd be he, a thousand times accursèd!
They are coming, coming nearer,
They are coiling around me; [16]
Me, you, us all!
Despair for you!

AEETES

Medea! *520*

MEDEA

For you, for us!
Despair, despair!

[16] The serpent tresses of the Eumenides with which Rhamnes had threatened Phaon in *Sappho,* and a pregnant premonition of the sinister doom in store for Medea and her family.

(She flees)

AEETES *(Stretching his arms after her)*

Medea! Medea!

THE END

II

THE ARGONAUTS

A Tragedy In Four Acts

CHARACTERS

AEETES	*King of Colchis*
MEDEA ABSYRTUS	*His children*
GORA	MEDEA'*s nurse*
PERITTA	*One of her playmates*
JASON	
MILO	*His friend*
MAIDENS *of* MEDEA	
ARGONAUTS	
COLCHIANS	

ACT I

Colchis—wild landscape of rocks and trees. In the background a half-ruined tower from the top story of which a dim light glimmers.[1] *Further back the view of the sea. Dark night.*

ABSYRTUS *(Behind the scenes)*

The light is shining there. Father, come here.
I'll clear your way. Mind this stone here and this!
Good.

(Enters, hacking the bushes on all sides with his sword)

Out of the way, you useless baggage!
Father, my sword has cleared the way!

(Enter AEETES *with his helmet on, completely muffled in a dark mantle)*

Father, we are now at the spot!
There the tower, where my sister dwells.
Do you not see the light of her cell?
She stays there, brooding incantations
And brewing potions all day long;
But when it's night she goes forth like a ghost *10*
And roams abroad, weeping and moaning.

*(*AEETES *makes an impatient gesture)*

Yes, Father, weeping—so the shepherd told me

[1] Compare Hero's tower in *The Waves of Sea and Love* (already mentioned in Musaeus), from which a bright light shone to guide Leander across the Hellespont.

Who lives in the dale below—wringing her hands,
So he tells me, it was a piteous sight!
Father, why does she brood, behave like this?

(AEETES *walks pensively up and down)*

You do not answer? Father, what is wrong?
Sad and troubled is your temper.
Father, you cannot be afraid of the strangers?

AEETES

Afraid, boy?

ABSYRTUS

Well, *worried,* father!
But neither be afraid nor worried! 20
Have we not weapons, strength and arms?
Are not the strangers but a handful?
I wish they were ten times as many!
Just let them come, we'll chase them back
Pell-mell to their dismal land,
Where there is neither forest, nor mountain,
Nor shine of moon, nor beam of *sun*
That daily, weary of its wandering way,
Sinks down to rest in our sea.[2]
Just let them come, I'll give them fitting welcome, 30
It's not in vain you made me skilled at arms,
Neither in vain gave me this lightning sword
And spear and helmet with the waving crest,
You, arms; and the high gods, courage!
Let's leave my sister with her magic spells,
And now join battle, sword against sword!

AEETES

Feeble worm!

ABSYRTUS

I am your son!
That time, when you struck Phrixus down—

[2] Precisely the description of Colchis by the Greeks. But Absyrtus evidently has no personal experience of Hellas!

AEETES

Silence!

ABSYRTUS

That's just why they are coming
Here to Colchis, those foreign fellows; 40
They fancy they'll avenge his death
And rob our treasure, the radiant Fleece.

AEETES

Silence, boy!

ABSYRTUS

Why are you frightened, Father?
Fast in the firm protection of the cave
It gleams, the golden treasure safe.

AEETES *(Tearing the mantle from his face and seizing his sword)*

Ah, must I kill you, you chattering fool?

ABSYRTUS

What's the matter with you?

AEETES

Silence! Look to that bush!

ABSYRTUS

Why?

AEETES

Something's rustling there
And moving. We are overheard.

ABSYRTUS *(Going to the bushes and striking at the trees)*

Ho there! Come forth! . . . There's not a stir. 50

*(*AEETES *slumps down on a piece of rock in the foreground.* ABSYRTUS *returns)*

It's nothing, Father, no one's listening.

AEETES *(Springing up and seizing him fiercely)*
I tell you, if you love your life
Speak no more of that!

ABSYRTUS
Of what?

AEETES
I tell you: bury it in your breast,
It's not some boyish bauble, boy!
But all here silent! None to welcome me;
Good, as befits the haunts of the perverse girl.

ABSYRTUS
A light is flickering high up in the tower.
She must be sitting there, brooding, imagining.

AEETES
Call her, she must come out!

ABSYRTUS
Good, Father. *60*

(He goes toward the tower)

Come down, you wanderer of the night,
With your long vigils by the lonely lamp!
Absyrtus is calling you, your father's son!

(Pause)

Father, she does not come.

AEETES
She must! Call louder!

ABSYRTUS *(Banging on the door)*
Hullo! The king is here; Come out, you!

MEDEA's *voice (From the tower)*
Alas!

ABSYRTUS
Father!

AEETES

What?

ABSYRTUS *(Returning)*

Did you not hear?
The tower cried "alas!" Was that my sister's cry?

AEETES

Whose else? Be off, a plague upon your folly!
Now I will call, and she will have to hear!

(Going to the tower)

Medea!

MEDEA *(In the tower)*

Who's calling?

AEETES

Your father and your king! 70
Come down!

MEDEA

What for?

AEETES

Come down, I say!

MEDEA

O let me be!

AEETES

Do not delay. You rouse my anger.
Come down this instant!

MEDEA

I'm coming!

(AEETES muffles himself and slumps down once more on his rocky seat)

ABSYRTUS

How mournful, Father, is my sister's voice.
What's troubling her? I'm grieved for her—

You too are, since you keep a painful silence.
The poor girl!

(Holding him)

Father, are you asleep?

AEETES *(Springing up)*

Foolish children are their father's curse!
You and she, *you* are killing me,
Not my foes. *80*

ABSYRTUS

Hush, listen. The bolt is rattling. She's coming, she's here!

*(*MEDEA*, in a dark red robe, embroidered on the seam with golden emblems, wearing on her head a black trailing veil fastened to a bandeau, likewise embroidered with emblems, emerges from the tower with a torch in her hand)*

MEDEA

What do you want, sire?

ABSYRTUS

Is that my sister, Father?
How greatly she is changed, and ah! how pale!

AEETES *(To* ABSYRTUS*)*

Be silent!

(To MEDEA*)*

Come nearer, nearer, but first
Put out your torch, it's dazzling me!

MEDEA *(Extinguishing the torch against the ground)*

The light is out, and it is night, my lord! [3]

AEETES

Come now: but first tell me who gave you leave
To flee the shelter of your father's house
And here, denying obedience, to defy

[3] Another of the symbolic lines to which Grillparzer is partial.

My orders and my summons, in the bosom 90
Of but this wilderness and your wild ways?

MEDEA

D'you ask, indeed?

AEETES

I ask.

MEDEA

Shall I speak?

AEETES

Speak!

MEDEA

Then listen, if you can; take umbrage, if you dare.
Could I be dumb, forever dumb!
I find your house abhorrent,
Your presence makes me shudder.
When you destroyed the stranger,
The guest, the gods protected,
And robbed his estate,
You threw into your house a spark 100
That glows and glows and will not be extinguished.
Even should you pour on it forever
The entire water of the holy spring,
The multitudinous streams and rivers
And all the mighty ocean measureless.[4]
Murder is a foolish marksman
That shoots his arrow into a dark thicket,
Greedy for game and spoils;
And what he took to be his prey,
The joyous game of the chase, 110
He finds it was his child, his flesh and blood,

[4] Compare Aeschylus' *Choephori* (end of first chorus), also Shakespeare's *Macbeth* (Act II, Scene ii):

> No; this my hand will rather
> The multitudinous seas incarnadine,
> Making the green one red.

In search of berries mid the rustling leaves.
Doomed man! What have you done?
Fire spurts from you
To sear the pillars of your house
That, crashing, caves in,
Burying us—

AEETES

Harbinger of doom, what do you know?

MEDEA

In the hour of terror,
When the dread deed was done, *120*
Ah, then my eyes were opened,
And I saw them, saw the unspeakable
Ghosts of revenge
Spider like,
Horrible, terrible,
They crept here in their monstrous ugliness
Spinning their webs, their gleaming webs,
Once, twice, a thousand times
Round their ruined domain.
You fancy you are free, and you are captive; *130*
No man, no god, may loose the bonds
In which an evil deed ensnares itself.
Woe to you! Woe to us all!

AEETES

Why peddle dreams to me for solid facts?
Go, frighten those of your ilk,
Fool, not me!
Have you enquired of the signs, the stars?

MEDEA

You think, I could, I had the power to do so?
A hundred times I've gazed up
To read the shimmering signs *140*
In the nocturnal sky,
And a hundred times
I lowered my eyes

Struck by terror, unenlightened.
I seemed to see against the black of heaven
An open book in which a thousand times
Murder was written and *revenge*
In adamantine letters.[5]
Oh, do not question those eternal stars,
Nor any auguries of silent nature, *150*
Nor in the temple any voice divine:
Heed quivering in the stream the wandering stars,
That shyly twinkle at you through dark brows
The auguries your deeds have stamped on you,
The voice divine that speaks in your own heart;
They'll fashion better oracles,
Much surer than my feeble art,
From what is and has been to what shall be.

ABSYRTUS

Father is silent. Sister, you're so strange.
Once you were quick and merry, full of spirit; *160*
It seems to me that since I saw you last
You have grown three times older!

MEDEA

Grief also like the years can pile on age,
And he, dear brother, who can *forestall* time,
Comes quicker to the goal.

ABSYRTUS

You know already then
About those strangers, who—

MEDEA

What strangers?

AEETES

Stop!
I told you to be silent; silence then!
Medea, let's be sensible and speak

[5] Compare Rhamnes in *Sappho* (Act V, Scene iv), speaking of the poetess's fame. (Vs. 1835–37.)

About the present, from what now is present
And not regard the present from the past. *170*
Then know: strangers have landed here, Hellenes;
They seek to avenge Phrixus' blood,
Demand the treasures of the dead man,
And the banner of the god, the Golden Fleece.

MEDEA *(Cries aloud)*

It's happened. Ah, the stroke has fallen, woe!

(Turns to go into the tower)

AEETES *(Detaining her)*

Medea, stop! Stay, crazy girl!

MEDEA

They've come, the avengers, the requiters!

AEETES

Would you desert me when I'm needing you?
Would you behold your father's blood?
Medea, I'm beseeching you, *180*
Speak, counsel, save, help!
Do not yield me to my enemies!
They call themselves Argonauts,
Because they sail on Argo, the swift ship;
Whatever heroes Hellas rears,
Or brave men boasts, they've mustered
For the deathblow upon your father's head.
Help me, Medea! Help, my daughter!

MEDEA

Am *I* to help? You, help yourself!
Give back what you have taken, offering peace. *190*

AEETES

The treasures have been shared with the accomplices;
Will they return what they've received?
Do they posses it still, the foolish spendthrifts,
Lightly consuming what they've lightly won?

Shall I return the glittering Fleece,
The banner of the god, Peronto's own?
Never! Never! And if I did,
Would they spare me and you for that?
All the more surely they would slaughter us,
Avenging their friend's death, 200
Protected by the god's holy pledge.
Ask of your art, give other counsel!

MEDEA

Myself uncounseled, how to counsel you!

AEETES

Very well, stay uncounseled, stubborn girl!
Offer your father's head as sacrifice!
Come, Son, let us go forth
And tender our bare heads to their blows
And fall beneath the strangers' swords.
Come, Son, my only child!

MEDEA

Stay, Father!

AEETES

Then you're willing?

MEDEA

Listen first! 210
I shall attempt to ask the gods
What they ordain, what they permit;
And if they nod, I shall assist you,
Shall help you fight the foe,
Help you forge the deadly arrow
That you will shoot into the dark bushes,
Not knowing, wretched marksman, whom you hit.
So be it! You have ordered, I obey.

AEETES

Medea, my child, my darling child!

MEDEA

Do not rejoice too soon, the end's to come. 220
I'm ready; but first promise me
That, if the deed's accomplished, your land freed,
I hardly dare to hope, yet if it's so,
You'll let me come back to this wilderness
And nevermore disturb me, you, nor others.

AEETES

Why?

MEDEA

Promise this.

AEETES

So be it!

MEDEA

Then agreed!
Enter your servant's house, I'll follow you.

AEETES

This house?

MEDEA

Within, it will be done.

AEETES *(To* ABSYRTUS*)*

Come, Son!

(Exeunt both into the tower)

MEDEA

See where they go, where my blind kinsmen go!
A stupid creature, man, it seems to me. 230
He fares forth on the waves of time,
Endlessly hurled up and down
And should he spy a patch of green,
Fashioned by ooze and stagnant swamp,
And the greenish mold of decay,
He calls out: Land! And rows to it,
And disembarks—and sinks—and sinks—

And nevermore is seen.[6]
Poor, wretched father, wretched man!
Before my vision rise *240*
The dreadful shapes of dismal premonitions,
But veiled and turned away,
I cannot recognize their faces.
Ah, fully show yourselves or disappear
And leave me peace, my dream of peace!
Poor, wretched father, wretched man!
But powerful is the will—and I, I *will,*
Will save him, and will free him
Or with him will die!
O art of darkness that my mother taught me *250*
That thrusts the trunk toward the skies of life
And drives the roots into the secret
Clefts of Hades,
Come at my call! Medea *will!*
To action then!

(To MAIDENS *who appear at the entrance to the tower)*

And you, my faithful servants,
Prepare the cave, prepare the altar!
Medea means to call upon the spirits,
The baleful spirits of horrendous night,
For counsel, and for help, for strength and might.

(Exit into the tower. A pause, then enter JASON *hurriedly)*

JASON

Here I heard voices—here must . . . no one here? *260*

MILO *(Behind the scenes)*

Hullo!

JASON

This way.

[6] Compare the last two lines of Goethe's poem "The Fisher," (lured to his watery doom by a mermaid):

She half pulled him, he half sank in
And nevermore was seen.

MILO *(As before)*

Jason!

JASON

Here, Milo, here!

MILO *(Enters panting)*

Friend, look for someone else to follow you!
Your head and legs are much too fast for me,
They run instead of walking. Most pernicious!
One may excuse legs, spurred on by your age,
But not your head that runs. Then, fare you well!
Find someone else, I say, I've had enough!

(Sits down)

JASON

We've found here, what we looked for—here, there's light.

MILO

Yes, light enough to illuminate us here,
Discover us and kill us, should they wish. *270*

JASON

Milo, afraid?

MILO

(Quickly standing up)

Afraid? My friend, I beg:
Do weigh your words before you speak!

*(*JASON *seizes his hand in propitiation)*

Ah well!
Not only do we run, our words too run
Away with us! But seriously, what are
You seeking here?

JASON

Can you still ask me this?
My friends, who have accompanied me here,

Entrusting to my destiny their welfare,
And making Jason's cause their very own,
Are languishing, just landed from our black ship,
With neither food, nor fresh drink, on this spot,
This craggy and inhospitable shore. *280a*
There is no guide here to direct our path,
No farmer offering us his granary's stores
Or produce of his meadow-nourished herd.
Am I to let my hand fall in my lap
And idly look on, while my good friends languish?
By heaven, they shall have some trusty guide
And food and drink, even if I have to give
My blood as barter!

MILO

Brave and loyal Jason!
Ah, why did you not listen to your friend
And keep away from this unfriendly shore! *290*

JASON

Why should I have? What could I do at home?
My father dead, my uncle on the throne,
Regarding me, his future foe, with envy.
I could not bear it longer, had to leave.
Had he himself, old fox, not ordered me
To voyage to this far-off desert isle[7]
And bring back with me the gods' golden gem,
That's famous through the length and breadth of earth,
And which these dark barbarians once robbed
From heaven-born Phrixus, murdering him as well, *300*
I should myself have set out, willingly,
To get away from his repugnant dealings:
A glorious death for an inglorious life!
Let him who will, blame this, the exchange tempts me!
It is too bad, my friend, I had to drag you
And the others with me, but you wanted this.

[7] Colchis was not, in fact, an island, but part of the Eurasian mainland.

MILO

Indeed I wanted it, and want it still;
For I believe you've drawn me so to you
That I love everything you do and dare.

JASON

My good Milo!

MILO

No, it is wrong, I say. 310
I should be wiser as I am the elder.
If only you had led me anywhere
Except into this godforsaken land!
If, any time a man falls into danger,
Out comes his sword and courage. Ah, but here,
In the damp mists of this depressing land,
Both sword and courage lie encased in rust.
You only hear the waves forever raging,
The dark firs rustling and the tempests roaring,
The sun can scarcely break through the dread cover 320
Of the thick mists and savage forest tops;
No man, no hut, no trace of life around;
Your heart becomes so tense, so drained, so sober,
That you end up by shrinking from yourself.
I, who would listen, when a boy, with wonder
If any spoke of such a thing as *fear,*
Here almost spy a ghost in every bush!
And every withered tree trunk seems an ogre,
And every light a goblin. It's most strange!
What elsewhere goes unnoticed, here seems dreadful, 330
And what elsewhere is dire, is commonplace here.
Just now I saw a big bear in the forest,
Huger perhaps than I have ever seen,
And yet I felt I should be stroking him,
Just as one strokes a pet dog in one's lap,
So small and unimportant seemed the beast
In contrast with his dread environment.
You are not listening?

JASON

JASON *(Who meanwhile has been gazing at the tower)*

Yes, I will go in!

MILO

In, where?

JASON

There, in the tower!

MILO

Man, are you crazy?

(Seizing him)

Listen.

JASON

JASON *(Shaking himself free and drawing his sword)*

I will, who'll stop me? Here's my sword, that guards me *340*
From enemies and from importunate friends.
I find here the first trace of humankind:
I will go in. With drawn sword I shall force
One of the people living in the building
To follow me, and guide our weary host
By a sure way out of this forest's grip,
Where hostile ambushes and hunger more
Assail them, than me any danger here.
Useless your words! I am resolved. Go back!
Hearten our men, I'll bring them succor soon! *350*

MILO

Reflect!

JASON

I have reflected! Who'll be dwelling
In this small house, in ruin and remote?
Some family of barbarians, no one else!
I think you know me well. Who hesitates
Is lost, good sir. Then speak no more, I beg!

MILO

But how will you get in?

JASON

Do you not see
The breach that yawns in the old walls up there?
The sea affords a bridge right up to it
And easily I'll get there swimming.[8]

MILO

Listen!

JASON

Good-bye!

MILO

Let me instead—

JASON

Good-bye for now. *360*

(Dives from a cliff into the sea)

MILO

He takes the plunge! Swims hard, and *makes* it too,
And lets me scold here to my heart's content!
A lionheart, but young, so terribly young!
Here will I stay and wait for his return,
Should anything go wrong, we'll hack our way out.

(He leans against a tree)

[8] Even before he took up the famous theme of Leander's swimming across to Hero's tower, Grillparzer makes Jason do the same, to the tower he has invented for Medea.

SCENE II

A gloomy vaulted room inside the tower. In the left background the image of a god on a high pedestal, in the right foreground a rocky seat.

MAIDENS *with torches carry a small altar and sacrificial vessels, and set them down in an orderly manner. Enter a* MAIDEN, *speaking from the door.*

MAIDEN

Enough! Medea's coming, do not disturb her!

(Exeunt all with the lights. Enter JASON *through a side entrance on the left with his naked sword)*

JASON

A dismal chamber this. But I'm inside!
It seems the house holds more life than I thought.
No matter, so long as I reach my goal! [9]
I'll watch out carefully, till only one *370*
Turns up, then with my sword aimed at his breast
He'll have to come with me, or else face death.

(He looks around with drawn sword)

Is there no exit? Stop. A block of stone.
The pedestal of the image of some god:
Do they revere the gods, yet scorn what's right?
But listen, footsteps! Pale light gliding flows
From arch to arch of the narrow passage.
Someone is coming! Hide me, you dark god!

[9] This line may be taken as the key to Jason's character—as Medea clearly intimates in the last play of the trilogy.

(He hides behind the statue. Enter MEDEA, *a black wand in her right hand and a lamp in her left)*

MEDEA

It is so sultry here, so dull!
Damp smoke chokes the lamp's flame, *380*
It burns without light.

(She puts down the lamp)

Listen! It is my own heart,
Beating strongly against my breast!
How weak, how foolish! On, Medea!
It's your father's cause, the gods' own cause!
What, shall the strangers triumph, Colchis fall?
Never, never.
Then to my work!
Attend, O gracious gods! And hear my voice
And answer all my questions! *390*

(Making signs in the air with the wand)

O you who wander in the robe of night[10]
And voyage on the pinions of the storm,
You dreaded Princes of the deep
Who smile on resolution
And the wingèd deed;
Who hover over corpses
And glut yourselves on the blood of the slain,
Who know men's hearts and guide their wills,
Who count the stalks of the present
And carefully garner the ears of the past *400*
And look into the future's sprouting seed,[11]

[10] Compare Hero's words to the dead Leander in *The Waves of Sea and Love* (Act V, V. 2061):

You who were wandering in the robe of night.

[11] Compare *Macbeth* (Grillparzer's favorite Shakespeare play), Act I, Scene iii, Vs. 58–60, where Banquo, like Medea, addresses the powers of darkness in the shape of the witches:

If you can look into the seeds of time,
And say which grain will grow and which will not,
Speak then to me.

I call on you!
Give me a sign, sure sign
Of what is threatening, what is smiling at us!
By the power given to me,
By the service that I did,
By the word that you know,
On you I call:
Appear! Appear!

(A Pause)

What's that? All's still! *410*
They do not come forth?
Are you angry with me? Or has some foot,
Some criminal foot,
Trodden the sacred spot?
I'm seized with anguish, gripped by horror!

(With rising voice)

Almighty gods! Hearken to my call!
Hear Medea's voice!
It is your friend who calls.
I crave, demand it:
Appear! Appear! *420*

*(*JASON *springs out from behind the statue. She recoils)*

Ha!

JASON

Accursèd witch, you're at your journey's end!
He has appeared, who is to be your doom.[12]

(As he springs out with his drawn sword, he wounds MEDEA *on the arm)*

MEDEA *(Holding her wounded right arm with her left hand)*

Ah woe!

(Hurls herself on the rocky seat, where she moans softly, breathing heavily) [13]

[12] A line pregnant with dramatic irony.
[13] "Breathing heavily," as in Apollonius Rhodius' *Argonautica,*

JASON

You flee? My arm will soon dispatch you!

(Looking around in the dark)

Where has she gone?

(He takes up the lamp and illumines his way)

There! You shall not escape.

(Approaching her)

Accursèd jade!

MEDEA *(Groaning)*

Ah!

JASON

Do you groan? Yes, quake!
My sword shall make short shrift of your dark wiles!

(Illuminating her with the lamp)

But do I see aright? Are you the witch,
Who but now murmured such hoarse curses there?
A feminine creature's lying at my feet,
Defended by the charter of her grace, 430
No magic in her except for her beauty.
Are you the one? Ah, yes! Her white arm's bleeding,
Just wounded by my unrelenting sword,
What were you up to? Are you not aware
I might have killed you, fascinating picture,
With my first stroke in the darkness of the night?
It were indeed a pity with such charm!
Who are you then, equivocal creature,
That seem so beautiful, are yet so evil,
At once so lovable and so abhorrent? 440
What could induce you and your lovely mouth,
That, rose-like, should like roses only breathe

---

which bears a similar relation to Grillparzer's *Golden Fleece* as Musaeus' *Hero and Leander* to his *Waves of Sea and Love.*

The heavenly redolence of honeyed words,
To soil itself with utterance of black horror?
When nature fashioned you, she wrote but: gentle,
With gracious letters on your life's first page,
Who painted magic symbols on the others?
Be gone, I hate your beauty, since it stops me
From duly hating all your wicked tricks!
You're breathing heavily. Your arm is hurting? 450
See, it's the outcome of your evil ways.
It's bleeding! Let me see.

(He takes her hand)

You're trembling, girl!
Your pulse is throbbing, every fiber twitches.
Perhaps you're not as wicked as you seem,
Only infected by this country's wildness,
And in your heart there's shame and sweet remorse.
Come, raise your eyes and look me in the face,
That I might see the enigma of your ways
Illumined in the noonday of your glance.
You're mute? Would you were dumb, and that another 460
Had uttered all those magic syllables
That struck my ear with their accursèd tones,
Some mouth, less worthy to be kissed than yours!
You're sighing! Speak! Come, let your words resound,
Entrust them to the air as messengers,
Else my mouth shall induce them from your lips!

(He bends toward her; the clash of weapons and voices are heard in the distance)

Listen! Voices!

(He lets her go)

Nearer!

(MEDEA stands up)

Your friends are coming,
And I must go. I fancy this will please you?
But I'll see you again, you may be sure!

I have to hear you speaking, speaking gently, *470*
Were it to cost my life! They are approaching.
Do not believe I run from arms and danger,
But even the bravest would not be outnumbered,
And friends await me. Farewell, for the present!

(He goes toward the side entrance, from which he came in. From this, as well as from the main entrance, armed men rush in and ABSYRTUS *with them)*

ABSYRTUS

Back!

JASON

So it's come to fighting! Give way there!

ABSYRTUS

Your sword!

JASON

Yes, in your breast, not in your hands!

ABSYRTUS

Seize him!

JASON *(Taking up his position)*

Come on! The bunch of you cannot daunt me.

ABSYRTUS

Come, let us try!

(Rushes at JASON. MEDEA *wards him off with a gesture. He steps back)*

Why do you stop me, sister?

JASON

You are concerned for me? Sweet creature, thanks!
Not for your help. Your help I do not need, *480*
But thanks for your concern. Maiden, farewell!

(Seizing her by hand and kissing her quickly)

And let this kiss be a sure sign to you
That we shall meet again! Give way!

(He strikes his way through)

ABSYRTUS

At him!

(Exit JASON *through the side door, fighting)*

Quick, after him! He must not escape!

(Hurries with the armed men after JASON*)*

MEDEA *(Who has been standing motionless with her head lowered, now raises her head and eyes)*

Gods!

(Her MAIDENS *stand around her)*

Curtain

ACT II

Vestibule, as at the end of the previous act. It is day.

GORA, PERITTA, MAIDENS

GORA

I tell you, better not talk to Medea.
She's angry at what happened here last night.
And you know how she storms when angry.
Further, she bade you shun her sight.

PERITTA

What shall I do? Who'll help, if not she?
My husband captive, our cottage burnt, *490*
And everything robbed by the strangers.
Who'll hear my pain, who'll save us, if not she?

GORA

Do as you wish, I've warned you,
And it's but right and proper she should listen,
But man not always does what 's right!

PERITTA

Alas!

GORA

Do not lament! What is the use?
Reflect and act, that's what you need!
But where's Medea? Come into her room.

(A MAIDEN *rushes in, breathless)*

MAIDEN

O height of ill luck!

GORA *(Turning back at the door)*

Of folly, I should hope. *500*
What's new amiss?

MAIDEN

The princess' favorite horse—

GORA

The splendid tiger-steed—

MAIDEN

It has escaped!

GORA

What?

MAIDEN

In the commotion last night,
The gates all open, we all in fear,
It bolted from its stable,[14] and was no more seen!
Alas!

GORA

Indeed!

MAIDEN

How shall I flee the princess' anger?
Will she endure this?

GORA

How—is her affair;
But she will have to bear it, since it's so.
Yet I advise you, keep away from her awhile!
But listen: She is coming; Peritta, here! *510*

[14] Perhaps Grillparzer had in mind *Macbeth* (Act II, Scene iv), "And Duncan's horses . . . broke their stalls" (on the night of Duncan's murder). The flight of Medea's horse and her reaction to the news symbolize the disappearance of her proud freedom tamed by the strange new power of love.

(MEDEA *enters from the door on the right, lost in thought. After a pause)*

Medea—

MAIDEN *(Forestalling her and falling at her feet)*

Pardon, O Queen!

MEDEA *(Raising her head)*

What's up?

MAIDEN

Do not crush me in your anger!
Your personal horse, your favorite—it's escaped.

(Pause, during which she scans MEDEA*'s face full of foreboding)*

Not my fault, truly. The terror last night,
The tumult, din—it happened then—
You say nothing! Princess, be angry—

MEDEA

It is well!

(MEDEA *looks at her strangely. The* MAIDEN *stands up)*

GORA *(drawing her aside)*

What did she say?

MAIDEN *(Joyously)*

That it was well.

GORA

That is *not* well!
Does she so lightly bear, what once she'd scarce endure?
That favors our cause, Peritta.
I almost do not like this gentle mood of hers! *520*
I had rejoiced at the thought she would bristle
And have at last to steel herself to do what she should.
Well, come now, come, for you it's better so.
Medea, here is someone else you know.

MEDEA

Who?

GORA

Do you not recognize Peritta, your playmate?
Even if angry—

MEDEA

It is you, Peritta?
My greetings to you, my most cordial greetings!

(Putting her arm around her and leaning on her)

And many happy days we've spent together!
Since then much mischief's happened,
Much mischief since those days, Peritta! *530*
Have you abandoned your herd and house
And come back to me, Peritta?
Be welcome, you are good and gentle,
You shall be nearest to me of my ladies!

PERITTA

No more have I a house, nor herd,
All, all is lost, my husband captive;
Gone is my peace, my blessing and my fortune!

MEDEA

So, he has gone beyond, is dead!
You make me grieve, my poor, poor child!
He was so young, so strong, so splendid, so handsome, *540*
And now cold and dead, you make me grieve!
Ah I could weep, you have so moved me!

(Lays her brow on PERITTA'S *shoulder)*

PERITTA

Not dead, just captive is my husband.
So I came to beg you ask your father
To ransom, save and free him—
Are you listening?

(To GORA*)*

She's silent! What's she thinking?

GORA

She is surprising me not less than you!
This is not Medea's usual manner.

PERITTA

What's this? Can I believe my senses?
I feel your face upon my shoulder, wet; 550
Medea, in tears! O gentle, good Medea!

(Kisses MEDEA'S *hand that hangs down.* MEDEA *pulls herself together, seizes quickly with her right hand her left hand just kissed, and looks fixedly into* PERITTA'S *face. Then she quickly moves away from her and continuing to look fixedly at her, approaches her nurse)*

MEDEA

Gora!

GORA

My lady?

MEDEA

Bid her go!

GORA

So you would—

MEDEA

Bid her go!

*(*GORA *bids* PERITTA *withdraw with a gesture of her hand,* PERITTA *stretches her hands out to her in supplication,* GORA *gestures to her reassuringly to withdraw. Exit* PERITTA, *led off by two* MAIDENS. MEDEA *speaks in the meanwhile)*

Ah! It is hot here—sultry.

(Violently tears asunder her girdle and throws it away)[15]

GORA

She has gone!

[15] One of Medea's many violent, character-revealing gestures in the trilogy.

MEDEA *(Shrinking)*

Gone?

GORA

Peritta's gone.

MEDEA

Gora!

GORA

My mistress!

MEDEA *(Half aloud, taking her aside)*

Were you about last night?

GORA

Where?

(MEDEA *looks at her strangely)*

Here? Why, of course!

MEDEA *(With rapturous glances)*

You mark my words, it was a *god!* [16]

GORA

A god?

MEDEA

I've thought about it a long time,
Long thought and dreamt about it the whole night:
He was a heavenly being, I am sure! *560*
When suddenly he stood there in his rage
Towering in splendor, in his hand a bolt
And two more in his flashing eyes;
My ebbing courage, my annihilation
Convinced me no mere woman bore him.[17]

GORA

What do you mean?

[16] Grillparzer here develops hints in Ovid's *Metamorphoses* (VII), and *Heroides* (XII).
[17] *Macbeth* again?

MEDEA

Yourself, you've told me often
How there appears to those about to die
Heimdar,[18] the terrible god;
Who leads the dead into the terrible depths.
Gora, he was the one, I do believe! *570*
Yes, *Heimdar,* god of death.
He designated his dark sacrifice,
Designated me with his luring kiss;
Medea now must die, and soon descend
Into the shadows of the silent deep.
Believe me, Gora, I am feeling this,
In this my trembling, shriveling of my senses,
In my desire to die now I am feeling
My journey's end's not far!

GORA

Who has so beclouded your senses, *580*
That you see dimly what is plain and clear?
It was a man, an arrogant, insolent man,
Who broke in here.

MEDEA *(Recoiling)*

Ha!

GORA

Yes, who came by night—

MEDEA

Silence!

GORA

Your anguish—

MEDEA

Accursèd woman, silence!

GORA

I may be silent, if you order,

[18] Perhaps Grillparzer culled this name from Scandinavian mythology, where we find the god Heimdallr, the son of Odin.

Once my foster-child and now my mistress;
Yet it is nothing other than I said.

MEDEA

O, how stupid you are and foolish!
How could a stranger come within these walls?
How could a mortal man presume *590*
To thrust himself before Medea's face,
To speak to her, to threaten her, and with his lips—
Be off, wretched woman, off!
Before I kill you,
And avenge your folly
Upon your life.
A man! O shame, disgrace!
Away, you traitress!
Off, else my rage shall smite you!

GORA

I utter what is, not what you would wish. *600*
Am I to go? . . . I'm going.

MEDEA

Gora, stay!
Sweet Gora, have you no kind word for me?
Do you not sense it is, it must be so:
Heimdar it was, the god of stillness,
And now, no further word, no word, O Gora.

(Throws herself around GORA'S *neck and presses her mouth on* GORA'S *lips. After a pause)*

Listen!

GORA

I hear steps.

MEDEA

They're coming! Let's go!

GORA

Stay. It's your brother and your father. Look!

*(*AEETES *and* ABSYRTUS *rush in)*

AEETES

He has escaped, and you must bear the blame!

(To MEDEA*)*

Why did you stay your brother's blow,
When he was poised to kill the criminal? 610

ABSYRTUS

Father, do not scold her for that,
How fearful and distracted was her heart!
Just think! A stranger, alone, at night,
Intruding in her chamber!
Had she no cause for hesitation, Father?
And fear knows never what it does.
Yet the Greek—

MEDEA

Greek?

ABSYRTUS

What else?
It was one of the strangers, the Hellenes,
Landed upon the coast of Colchis,
Argonauts on Argo, their ship 620
Come to lay waste our valleys
And rob our property.

MEDEA *(Seizing* GORA'S *hand)*

Gora!

GORA

You see, it is just as I told you.

ABSYRTUS

They are arrogant and strong,
Yes, by Peronto, strong and bold!
Did I not chase him off, I and my men,
Pressing him hard, back upon his tracks?
But he whirled his sword in circles,
And none of us could near his body.
Then, come upon the sea, he threw himself 630

With a quick dive into the water.
The splash resounded dully through the district,
The foaming water shot aloft,
And he vanished in the cover of the night.

AEETES

Even if he has escaped this time,
He shall not succeed the next!
The bold foreigners, proud and defiant,
Have begged audience of me.
I have assented, hiding my rage,
My deadly hatred in my inmost heart. *640*
But if my secret plan succeeds,
And you're attentive with your arts,
Their dastard temper they'll have cause to rue,
And our dispute be ended scarce begun.
Then come, Medea, and prepare yourself,
To make good where you erred,
And to avenge your own disgrace.
It's now become *your* cause,
They now have outraged even you,
Outraged, through the deed of that bold man. *650*
For if it is true, what Absyrtus told me,
That he has dared, with a dishonest kiss—

MEDEA

Be silent, Father, please!

AEETES

Then it is true?

MEDEA

Do not ask what is true, what false!
Ah, let my blushing cheeks tell it to you,
Let them tell you—what shall I do? Command!
Would you destroy their dastard host,
Just tell me *how,* I'm ready!

AEETES

This is well said, Medea, this I like,
In this I recognize my child in you. *660*

Show that his wanton impudence surprised you,
Let them not think you were a party,
Yourself a party to his dastard deed!

MEDEA

A party? *Who* dare believe that, and of *whom?*

AEETES

Who? Those who saw, who heard it, child!
Who witnessed how Aeetes' royal daughter
Suffered the kiss from the wanton's lips?

MEDEA

Father!

AEETES

Well?

MEDEA

You're killing me!

AEETES

Medea, I do *not* believe it.

MEDEA

Truly not?

Let's go!

AEETES

Where?

MEDEA

Oh, anywhere, *670*
To destroy, to kill, to die!

AEETES

Then you promise me?

MEDEA

I have already said so!

But let us go.

AEETES

First listen!

MEDEA

Not here!
The image of the god is mocking me,
The arches' stones around me seem to turn
To mocking gargoyles and to grinning masks.
Away from the spot of my disgrace!
I'll not again set foot here. Father, come.
Whatever you want, however you want, but let's go!

AEETES

Do listen!

MEDEA

Away!

AEETES

Medea!

MEDEA

Away!

(Rushes off)

AEETES

Medea! 680

(AEETES *and* ABSYRTUS *follow)*

SCENE II

Open space with trees. In the left background the King's tent. Enter eight representatives of the ARGONAUTS *led by a* COLCHIAN CAPTAIN.

CAPTAIN

The king's command is you should tarry here,
He'll soon be here himself.

FIRST ARGONAUT

Command? Worthless barbarian,
For you, maybe, but command for us?

We shall await your king, because we would,
But let him hurry, or we'll seek him out.

SECOND ARGONAUT

Leave him alone, a slave's speech suits a slave!

(Exit the COLCHIAN CAPTAIN*)*

THIRD ARGONAUT

So we are here, our striving's goal attained!
After such dangers, both on land and sea,
Colchis's dismal land of myth enfolds us,
Of which men speak wherever sun may shine. *690*
What no one thought was possible, has happened:
An unknown sea[19] has now at last been crossed
That threatened shipwreck to the first bold sailor;
To new lands and new peoples opened up
Our way and, what was often harder still,
Our way back also opened up inviting;
We are in Colchis, at our journey's end.
Thus far a gracious god has guided us;
But now I fear lest he may turn aside.
We stand upon a hostile shore, surrounded *700*
By death, alien, without advice nor leader—
Jason is missing, who enlisted, led us
Upon this trail, whose own cause we espoused;
He has with Milo left his men behind,
Vanished last night and has no more been seen.
Whether lost in the woods, he's languishing,
Or has been caught in the barbarians' snare,
Or hastened to his death in some foul ambush,
I do not know, but have to fear all these.
Thus broken up, disbanded, isolated, *710*
Each one of us is his own counsel, leader,
And so I ask you, princes of our host,
What shall we do?

(All remain silent with lowered heads)

[19] The Black Sea.

Dumb? Resolution's needed!
Summoned here by the monarch of this land
To audience and to taste his friendliness,[20]
It seemed, now that our leader had been lost,
Dangerous to refuse the proferred call
And to reveal our weakness and distress.
We set out and are here! What shall we do?
Who has good counsel, speak!

SECOND ARGONAUT

You are the oldest, *720*
Speak yourself!

THIRD ARGONAUT

The oldest is not always first,
When it comes to strength and resolution. Ask
Another!

FIRST ARGONAUT

Let us firmly seize our swords
And kill the king and all his faithless people;
Then sail. But first make sure we've shipped the spoils.

THIRD ARGONAUT

And not the land as well, for show at home?
Your counsel's raw, my friend, just like your age.
Let others speak!

SECOND ARGONAUT

You speak, we'll follow you.

THIRD ARGONAUT

My counsel is return! You grumble? Well,
Let some man better speak, I shall agree. *730*
You are all silent, and no one steps forward?
So hear, do not disturb, or else convince me.
We have not reached here through our own endeavors;

[20] Aeetes gave out (Vs. 637–38) that the Greeks had begged audience of him. Whether this was to save face in public, a deft psychological stroke, or only another of the traces of Grillparzer's previous plans, is arguable.

What's Colchis and its mysteries to us?
We followed Jason's courage and good fortune,
Assisting in the task he was commanded.
He did his uncle's bidding, we did his.
Who is the man who'd step in Jason's shoes
If death has taken him, as is too possible?
Who sets his heart on robbing the rare Fleece *740*
That death envelops and most potent perils?
Have you not heard? It lies in deepest caverns,
Watched by a dreadful dragon's poisonous fangs,
Defended by the horrors of black magic,
Protected by all that's accursed and dire.
Which of you dares, who'll lift the golden treasure?
What, no one? Then let no one that *appear,*
Which no one has the strength and will *to be.*
Here I'll lay down my shield and spear
And go to the king as a man of peace. *750*
Let him grant us three days to linger here,
If Jason does not come back, we sail home.
He who thinks like me, let him do the same!
A hero gives his life for something great,
Who squanders it for nothing is a fool!

(Most of them stick their spears into the ground)

Then come to Colchis' king. He will, I fancy,
Gladly exchange his safety for our own.

FIRST ARGONAUT

But stop! There come two Greeks. The first is Milo,
Who went away with Jason, and

(Shouting)

Jason himself!

Jason himself!

SEVERAL

Jason!

ALL *(Tumultuously)*

Jason!

MILO *(Behind the scenes)*

Comrades! 760

Here Jason, Argonauts!

SECOND ARGONAUT *(To the* THIRD*)*

What d'you say now?

THIRD ARGONAUT

That Jason's back, I say, friend, just like you.
Instead of my advice he'll give you action;
I had opinions only in his absence.

(Enter MILO, *leading* JASON *by the hand)*

MILO

Here you have him, have him without a scratch!
Then look your fill at him and shout, rejoice!

(The ARGONAUTS *press around* JASON, *seize his hands and express their joy)*

MIXED VOICES

Friend! Jason! Welcome! Welcome, Jason, brother!

JASON

Have you been anxious for me? Here, I'm back!

(Holding out his hands to the eager throng)

MILO *(Embracing the man next to him)*

Friend, do you see? He's there, quite hale and hearty!
And yet he just escaped alive, by heaven! 770
A hair's breadth, and you'd never more see Jason!
He ventured forth alone—not taking me—
For your sakes, friends, it was, he ventured forth
In the dense woods, alone, into a tower
Stuffed with barbarians to the very top!
Some fighting there!

JASON

Yes, touch and go, indeed!
I would have fallen, if a girl had not—

MILO

A girl? What, some barbarian girl?

JASON

Indeed!

MILO

Why have you told me nothing of this, earlier?
And was she pretty?

JASON

So pretty, beautiful, so— 780
And yet a loathsome, wicked sorceress!
I owe my life to her.

MILO

The splendid girl!

JASON

I cut my way through, and—enough, I'm living,
And am among you . . . But why are you here?

FIRST ARGONAUT

The King of Colchis calls us to an audience,
He wants to know what our intentions are,
And then he will decide.

JASON

Here?

FIRST ARGONAUT

Here's his seat!

JASON

I'll speak to him. If he submits in peace,
Then well and good! Else let the sword decide!

(Pointing to the spears laid aside)

These weapons? Are you here so confident, 790
That you deprive yourselves of their protection?

(They shamefacedly take up once more their discarded spears)

You hold your tongues and lower your eyes, ashamed?
Have you—

(To MILO*)*

Just see how they avoid my glance?
Wretched fellows, I trust it was not fear—
Not *fear,* Hellenes, that cast your spears from you?
It was not fear?

(To MILO*)*

Ah yes, it was! The wretches,
They do not dare accuse me of a lie!
What was it, my poor brothers, that beguiled you?
It was *fear!*

(To one about to speak)

Do not speak, I beg of you,
I can conceive your feelings. Do not speak. *800*
Do not make me ashamed of my own self!
For, O, I cannot witness without tears
The blush of shame in a man's countenance.
I will forget it if I can.

(Enter a COLCHIAN*)*

COLCHIAN

The king is here!

JASON

Then, let's be strong and resolute, my friends.
This barbarous king must not sense what has happened.

(Enter AEETES *with his retinue)*

AEETES

Who is the man, who speaks here for the strangers?

JASON *(Stepping forward)*

I.

AEETES

Begin.

JASON

Arrogant barbarian, do you dare? . . .

AEETES

What do you want?

JASON

Respect.

AEETES

Respect?

JASON

For my arm,

If not my name!

AEETES

Well then, you may proceed. 810

JASON

The ruler of fair Thessaly, Pelias,
My uncle and my lord, sends me to you,
Me, Jason, the commander of these men,
To speak to you just as I now shall speak:
Report has come to us across the sea
That Phrixus, a Hellene of noble blood,
Within your kingdom here, has met his death—

AEETES

I did not kill him.

JASON

Why defend yourself,
Before I even charge you? Hear me first!
Phrixus' ship, that you arrested here, 820
Was laden rich with treasures and with chattels,
When he succumbed to a mysterious death.
His house and mine are very closely kin;
Hence, in my uncle and my lord's name, I
Demand you prompt restore all that was his,
And that has now become mine and my house's.

AEETES

I know nothing of treasures.

JASON

Let me finish.
But the most precious of Phrixus' possessions
Was a most precious and mysterious Fleece
That he, in Delphi's lofty city, took 830
Off from the statue of an unknown god,
Placed there in immemorial far-off days,
They say, by our primeval ancestors,
Who, coming from afar and heaven-born,
Bestrode our land, and, scattering wide the seed
Of fair mankind through the empty wilderness,
Became Hellas' fathers and our forbears.
From them, they say, that emblem's handed down,
A treasured pledge for Hellas' weal and fortune.
Above all I demand this Fleece from you, 840
That it remain a gem of the Hellenes,
And not serve in the hands of rude barbarians
Against them as a mark of victory.
Say, what do you decide?

AEETES

I do not have it.

JASON

Not have the Golden Fleece?

AEETES

I tell you, no.

JASON

Is this your last word?

AEETES

Yes, my last.

JASON

So be it!

(Turns to go)

AEETES

Where are you going?

JASON

To my men,
To summon them to arms, that we might see
If you'll be as untouched by might as right.

AEETES

I scorn your threats!

JASON

For how long, we shall see. 850

AEETES

Madcap! With a pack of adventurers
Would you defy the King of Colchis?

JASON

Yes, I will try.

(About to go)

AEETES

Stop, I believe you're raving.
If the gods' grace is truly attached to that emblem,
If victory and revenge is his who has it,
How can you hope to stand up against me,
In whose hand—

JASON

Ha, quite so, you do have it?

AEETES

I mean, if it were as you think.

JASON

I know enough!
Feeble barbarian, would you base on this
The untenable defiance of your refusal? 860
You hope to win, because you now possess—
The gods give what is neither good nor bad,

And only the recipient shapes the gift.
Like bread bestowed upon us by the earth,
Strengthening the strong, and making worse the sick,
Are all the gracious gifts of the great gods,
Good for the good and fatal for the wicked.
The Fleece, in my hand, leads to victory;
In yours it will assure your dire defeat.
Then speak yourself, how will you dare to touch it, *870*
Bespattered, as it is, with your guest's blood?

AEETES

Silence!

JASON

Say, will you yield it? Yes or no?

AEETES

Do listen.

JASON

Yes or no?

AEETES

Impetuous youth!
Why should we quarrel needlessly?
Let us consider calmly
And then decide what is to happen.

JASON

Then you will give it up?

AEETES

What? Not so fast.
We must first know and understand each other:
One gives up to a friend, not to a foe.[21]
Come, to my place and rest after your voyage. *880*

JASON

I do not trust you.

[21] The word *Fremden* (dative), literally "stranger" or "foreigner," was often used in the sense of *Feind* ("foe"). Here "foe" brings out better the antithesis (and alliteration) with friend (*Freund*).

AEETES

Why not?
Even if my speech be rough, you need not fear.
Be welcome to my country!
Do you love wine? We have all vintages.
The chase? Our forests teem with game.
Do you delight in feminine embraces?
Colchis has—

(Coming nearer to him)

Do you want women?

JASON

Your women? And yet—

AEETES

Do you want women?

JASON

Do you know a tower in the neighboring woods?
But where am I straying? Come to the point, O king! *890*
Will you give me the Fleece?

AEETES *(To a* COLCHIAN*)*

Call Medea and bring wine.

JASON

Once more, will you give me the Fleece?

AEETES

Be calm!

The order is the feast first, then the council.

JASON

I will have none of your gifts.

AEETES

Yes, you shall.
None may depart from my house unrefreshed.
Look, they approach; stranger, be pleased to accept.

(Enter MEDEA, *veiled, with a goblet in her hand, accompanied by* SERVANTS, *who carry drinking cups.)*

Here, drink, my noble guest.

(To MEDEA*)*

Has it been doctored?

MEDEA

Oh, do not ask!

AEETES

Then go and offer it . . .
Refresh yourself, my guest!

JASON

I shall not drink.

*(*MEDEA *winces at the sound of* JASON'S *voice. She looks up, recognizes him, and steps back a few paces)*

AEETES *(To* JASON*)*

Why not?

(To MEDEA*)*

Go to him, go nearer, I say! *900*

JASON

What do I see? These clothes! Maiden, remain!
Your robe brings back to mind a gracious picture
That I a little while—Give me your goblet.
I'll risk it, seeing your exterior! Give.

(He takes the goblet from her hand)

I'll drain it to your health!

MEDEA

Stop!

JASON

What is it?

MEDEA

You're drinking death.

JASON

What?

AEETES

Medea!

JASON *(Throwing away the goblet)*

King,
Your friendship, this? Barbarian, I'll avenge!
But you, who are you, who so strange combine
With cruelty the gentleness of pity?
Let me behold you!

(He tears off her veil)

She! The very same! 910

AEETES

Away, Medea!

JASON

So you are called Medea!
Then speak, Medea.

MEDEA

What do you want?

JASON

What?
Your deeds so soft, and words so hard, Medea?
I've only seen you twice, and both these times
I owe my life to you. Ah, let me thank you!
It seems the gods have destined us to be
Good friends, Medea, and not enemies.
Another glance like this! Turn not away!
Look in my eyes, for honest my intent.

(He seizes her hand and turns her toward himself)

Ah, let me read my fortune in your eyes— 920

(MEDEA tears her hand away)

Do stay!

MEDEA *(Rearing up)*

Bold wretch, you dare? Alas!

(She meets his gaze, shrinks and flees)

JASON

Medea!

(Exit MEDEA. *He hurries after her)*

AEETES

Back!

JASON

You'll have to back, barbarian!—Medea!

(He tries to push his way up into the tent and AEETES *stands, barring his way)*

Curtain

ACT III

The interior of the king's tent. The fold of the tent at the back is of such material that the outlines of the persons outside can be discerned without one's being able to distinguish them precisely.

MEDEA, GORA, MAIDENS *inside the tent.* JASON, AEETES *and characters of the end of the last act outside it.*

MEDEA *stands in the left foreground, upright, her left hand on a table, her eyes turned stark ahead, in the posture of one who is listening to what is going on outside.* GORA, *observing her, stands on the other side of the table.* MAIDENS, *some kneeling, some standing, grouped around her. Some warriors in the background of the tent ranged along the sides.*

JASON *(From outside)*

I will go in!

AEETES *(Outside)*

Back!

JASON

Do you think you'll stop me?
Take your hand from your sword, from sword your hand, I say!
My sword is twitching. I cannot stand being threatened.
I will go in. Give way.

AEETES

Back, saucy fellow!

GORA *(To* MEDEA*)*

The boor is raving.

JASON *(Outside)*

Medea, do you hear me?
Give me a sign if you hear.

GORA

Did you grasp that?

JASON

If you can hear my call, give me a sign!
My bride!

*(*MEDEA, *who has been standing motionless until now, winces and puts her hand on her heaving breast)*

Let me enfold you in my arms. *930*

*(*JASON*'s voice comes ever nearer)*

I've read your heart. You also now read mine.
Medea, come!

AEETES

Back!

GORA

See, he presses in.

*(*MEDEA *tears herself out of the arms of her* MAIDENS *and flees to the other side of the foreground)*

JASON

I'm calling you. I love you, dear Medea.

GORA *(Following* MEDEA*)*

Did you hear that?

*(*MEDEA *hides her eyes with her hand)*

Unhappy girl, so *that* was it?
Hence all your agitation, all your anguish?
O shame, disgrace, could this be true?

MEDEA *(Erect, looking at her haughtily)*

Could what?

JASON *(Tearing apart the folds of the tent)*

I must see her. There she is. Come, Medea!

GORA

He is approaching. Flee.

MEDEA *(To the soldiers in the tent)*

Do you stand idly by?

Use your weapons, help your master.

AEETES *(Who meanwhile has been struggling with* JASON *at the entrance)*

But with my death will you succeed in entering! *940*

(The SOLDIERS *in the tent rush to separate the contestants.* JASON *is pressed back. The folds fall back, shutting him out)*

JASON *(Outside)*

Medea! Well, the sword must now decide.

ABSYRTUS' VOICE

Bare swords! Well, here is mine!

(Clash of weapons outside)

GORA

They're fighting! Gods, strengthen our warriors' arms!

*(*MEDEA *once more stands motionless)*

MILO'S VOICE *(From outside)*

Jason, get back, we're being outnumbered;
Twelve of our host and a hundred of the foe!
Barbarians, do you breach the promised truce?

JASON

Just let them come, they'll have a hot reception!

AEETES

Hack them down if they do not give way!

(The clash of weapons recedes)

GORA

The strangers are being pressed back, our men are winning.
Compose yourself, Medea. Your father's coming. *950*

(Enter AEETES *and* ABSYRTUS*)*

AEETES

Where is she? Here! You traitress!
Dare you sustain your father's glance?

MEDEA *(Approaching him)*

There is no time for words now, only deeds!

AEETES

You dare to tell me that, after what's happened,
Now, when the sword's still naked in my hand?

MEDEA

No further talk of parley or agreement,
Nor vain attempts at sweet accommodation!
Arm your warriors, muster your men,
And straight attack the strangers, attack straight,
Ere they suspect it and compose themselves. *960*
Send them all packing, packing from your land!
Let their swift ship bear them away to safety,
Or death to all of them—to all!

AEETES

Do you fancy you can dupe me, you deceiver?
If you hate them, why throw away the goblet
Delivering them to me, delivering Jason to me—
Yes, Jason—look me in the face! You turn away?

MEDEA

Why do you care to shame me?
You need advice, I'm *giving* you advice.
I say once more: chase away the strangers! *970*
Push them beyond the bounds of your realm;
Let the gray morning, the day that dawns,
See them no more near Colchis' shores.

AEETES

Your conduct puzzles me, Medea.

MEDEA

Was I not puzzled long, myself long puzzled?

AEETES

So you want me to drive away the strangers?

MEDEA

Upon my knees, drive them away, I crave!

AEETES

All of them?

MEDEA

All.

AEETES

All?

MEDEA

Do not question me!

AEETES

Very well then, I'll see my friends are armed.
You'll come with us.

MEDEA

I?

AEETES

Yes, you curious girl! 980
I know your skills: not the arrow from the bow alone,
You also hurl the spear, the mighty lance,
And whirl the sword in your powerful hand.
Come with us, we shall chase our foes away.

MEDEA

Never!

AEETES

You'll not come?

MEDEA

Send me back
Deep in the heart of the country, Father,
Where there are only woods and gloomy gorges,
Fast to all eyes, to all ears, to all voices,
Where only solitude and I may dwell.
There, for you, I will call upon the gods, *990*
For help to you, for power, for victory.
Father, I'll pray for you, not fight.
When the foes have been scattered, no dastard remains,
I shall return and stay with you
And faithfully look after you when old;
Until death comes, the kindly god,
And gently soothing, fingertip on lips,
Upon his dusty, mossy pillow,
Lulls thoughts to sleep and all desires to rest.[22]

AEETES

You'll not come with me, and I am to trust you? *1000*
Tremble, wanton girl! Jason?

MEDEA

Why ask me when you know?
Or must you hear from my own mouth,
What from myself till now I've hidden.
I hid it from me? Why, the gods have screened it!
Do not be troubled by the flaming passion
That spreads—I feel it—hotly on my cheeks!
You want to hear it and I'll tell it you.
I cannot sense and waver in the dark.
Medea must see clearly, all things clearly! *1010*
They say—and I do feel it to be so—
There is a something in the soul of man
That independent of the owner's will,

[22] Compare Schiller's *Maria Stuart:*

> Benevolent and healing, death approaches,
> My solemn comrade, with his darkling wings,
> To cover my disgrace.
>
> (Vs. 3489–91)

With blind violence attracts, repels;
As lightning's drawn to metal, magnet to iron,
So shoots a ray, a most mysterious ray
From man to man, from heart to heart.
It is not charm, nor grace, not right, nor virtue
That ties and unties all the magic threads:
Invisible is attraction's magic bridge, *1020*
However often trodden, none has seen it!
We *must* find pleasing what pleases us;
So far it is compulsion, nature's naked power,
Yet if it is not in us to *force* attraction,
With us it lies to *follow* what attracts,
Here's where begins the bright realm of the will.
And *I* do not *will!*

(With uplifted hand)

Medea does not will!
When I saw him, saw him for the first time,
I felt the blood stand still in all my veins,[23]
Out of his eyes, his hands, his lips, *1030*
There sprayed all over me a thousand sparks
That flared to flame within my heart.
Yet I concealed it even from myself. Only when he uttered it,
Uttered in the fury of his wild deeds,
That he loves—

O sweet name
For an accursèd thing!—
Then it grew clear to me, and *thus* I'll act.
But do not ask me ever more to see him,
Let me flee from him. Man is weak,
Even the strongest, weak! *1040*
When I see him, my senses swim,

[23] This is one of several echoes in *The Golden Fleece* of Racine's *Phèdre,* a play that Schiller had translated. Grillparzer, who had the highest regard for Racine—"as great a poet (*Dichter*) as has ever lived" (Tgb. 3384, 1838) could, of course, savor it in the original. His regard for Schiller as a dramatic poet was less (Tgb. 9, 1808, confirmed when Grillparzer himself was no longer a precocious student, but an acclaimed dramatist in Tgb. 1227, 1822).

With dull fear creeping over head and heart,
And I'm no more the one I am.[24]
Drive him away, pursue him, kill him!
Yes, if he will not fall back, kill him, Father!
I'll gaze upon him dead, with tears I'll gaze,
But not on him alive.

AEETES

Medea!

MEDEA

What have you decided?

AEETES *(Taking her hand)*

You are a splendid girl!

ABSYRTUS *(Taking her other hand)*

My dearest sister!

MEDEA

What have you decided?

AEETES

You are to go back! *1050*

MEDEA

A thousand thanks! And now to work, my father!

AEETES

Absyrtus, pick the bravest in the army
And lead your sister to the rocky cave,
You know . . . where we've preserved it . . . the Golden Fleece!

MEDEA

Not there!

AEETES

Why not?

MEDEA

Never, never!

[24] Compare Peritta in *The Guest* (Vs. 62–63).

There, to the place of our crime?
The glittering Fleece beams but revenge,
Whenever I attempt to read the future,
It flares before me like a blood-red comet.[25]
Should I go there, it menaces misfortune! *1060*

AEETES

You fool! No safer place in all the land!
Also I need you to protect the treasure
With your arts, your incantations.
Go there, or come with me.

MEDEA

So be it, I obey!
But send me by a way where no foe comes on us.

AEETES

There are two ways. One by the enemy's camp,
The other rough and difficult, unfrequented,
Over the bridge it leads to the stream; take that, Absyrtus.
Go now! Here's the key to the portcullis,
Leading to the cavern. Take it, Medea. *1070*

MEDEA

I? Give it to my brother.

AEETES

To you!

MEDEA

Father!

AEETES

Take it, I say, and do not ruffle me;
I've had enough of all your silly whims.

MEDEA

Very well, I'll take it.

[25] Compare Grillparzer's *Ahnfrau,* where Jaromir likens the specter of his ancestress to "a blood-red meteor." (Act III, V. 2114.)

AEETES

Farewell!

MEDEA

Father!

AEETES

Yes?

(Medea throws herself, sobbing loudly, into his arms. More gently)

Silly girl!

(He kisses her)

Farewell, my child!

MEDEA

Father! Till we meet—we meet again!
Till we meet soon, in happiness, again!

AEETES

Of course, in happiness again! Go now!

(Pushing her gently away)

Go now!

MEDEA *(Hiding her eyes with her hands)*

Farewell.

(Exit with ABSYRTUS. AEETES *stays awhile after* MEDEA'*s departure, standing lost in thought with lowered head. Suddenly he springs up, looks swiftly around him a few times and hurries out)*

SCENE II

A wooded landscape on the road leading to the ARGONAUTS' *camp.*

Enter JASON, MILO *and other* ARGONAUTS

MILO

Friends, let us halt here. The barbarians
Pursue us no more. This is the right spot, *1080*
Good for attack as well as for defense.
It's also the one way that leads to the interior
From the king's seat, since the storm last night
Has swept away the bridges on the other;
And if we camp here, we shall cut him off
From any reinforcement he awaits.
One of you go back to the host behind
And lead it here. We shall await you here.

(Exit FIRST ARGONAUT. *To* JASON, *who walks up and down with arms crossed)*

What are you thinking of?

JASON

Of many things.

MILO

Shall I confess? You have astonished me, *1090*
You've shown today a corner of your heart
That's new to me.

JASON

I might as soon have said:
Me too!

MILO

So you're in love with her?

JASON

In love?[26]

MILO

At least you said so loud enough today!

JASON

The moment tore it from me—and confess,
She has now saved my life a second time—

MILO

How? Second?

JASON

First in the tower—

MILO

So that was it,
That made the tower so dear to you?

JASON

Yes, that.

MILO

Indeed!

JASON

Just think what an undoubted claim
On my thanks and—Milo, she's beautiful! *1100*

MILO

Yes, also a barbarian—

JASON

She is good—

MILO

A sorceress as well.

JASON

Yes, that is so.

[26] A good touch depicting straightaway Jason's fecklessness that was to precipitate the terrible catastrophe of *Medea.*

MILO

A fearful woman with her eyes of night!

JASON

A splendid woman with her eyes of night!

MILO

And what do you propose to do?

JASON

To do?

To take the Fleece and so redeem my word,
But leave the other matter to the gods,
Who reign above over both you and me.

MILO

I like that well. By Zeus, you've chosen right!

(Enter an ARGONAUT*)*

ARGONAUT

Left of the stream a cloud of dust is rising *1110*
Signaling enemy approach.

JASON

How many?

ARGONAUT

Forty or fifty, hardly more I think.

JASON

Let us withdraw and hide along the road;
For should they see us, they would not advance.
All hope of an agreement is now gone,
So let the sword now bloodily prevail,
And those approaching start the dance of death.
Withdraw and hold your blows until I tell you.

MILO

Now softly, gently, that they do not spot us.

(Exeunt all, withdrawing. Enter ABSYRTUS *and* COLCHIAN WARRIORS, *with* MEDEA *veiled in their midst)*

ABSYRTUS

Hold all your weapons ready for assault. *1120*
We easily might come upon the foe,
The way here almost passes by their camp.

MEDEA *(Casting aside her veil and stepping forward)*

Their camp? Then why have we come this way?
Why not the other way, my brother?

ABSYRTUS

The storm last night has swept away the bridges;
But now I learnt this. Yet you need not fret.
I shall defend you with my blood.
If you were not here, I should seek them out.

MEDEA

For the gods' sake—

ABSYRTUS

I said: were you not here.
But now you are here, I will not do that. *1130*
Not for the highest prize, for fight and victory
Would I endanger you, my sister!

MEDEA

Then let us quickly pass by.

ABSYRTUS

Come on then.

JASON *(Behind the scenes)*

Now is the time, my friends! Attack!

(Springing forward)

Halt them!

MEDEA *(Crying out)*

He!

(To ABSYRTUS*)*

Let us flee, Brother!

ABSYRTUS

Flee? Fight.

JASON *(To the* ARGONAUTS *pressing forward)*

If they should dare resist, hack them all down;

(To the COLCHIANS*)*

Ground your weapons.

ABSYRTUS

I'll ground you first!
Close your ranks, comrades, and withstand them!

MEDEA

Brother, is this the way you keep your promise?

ABSYRTUS

If I promised to flee, may the gods forgive me, *1140*
Not for breaking my word, but for giving it,

(To his men)

Do not give ground. My father's near, he'll send us aid.

JASON *(Catching sight of* MEDEA*)*

Medea, you? O unexpected fortune!
Come to me!

MEDEA *(To the* COLCHIANS*)*

Guard me.

JASON *(Attacking the* COLCHIANS *opposing him)*

You! Out of the way!
Your blades will not repel but draw the lightning.

(The COLCHIANS *are pressed back, pursued by the Greeks)*

Your men are fleeing. You are in my power.

MEDEA

You lie! In the power of the gods, in mine.
If everything deserts me—I remain.[27]

[27] Grillparzer may have had in mind here Corneille's Medea's

(She snatches weapons from a fleeing COLCHIAN *and advances on* JASON *with shield in front and lowered spear)*

Die or kill!

JASON *(Giving ground to spare her)*

Medea, what are you doing?

MEDEA *(Pressing nearer)*

Kill or die!

JASON *(Smashing her lance with a blow from his sword)*

Enough of this child's play!

(Taking his sword in his left hand, in which he holds his shield)

What now?

MEDEA

Faithless gods![28] *1150*

(Throwing away her broken lance together with her shield, and drawing a dagger)

I still have a weapon.

JASON *(Throwing down his shield and sword and stepping in front of her)*

Kill me, if you can.

---

famous "I," when asked by her companion what remained to her in her desolation (*Médée,* Act I, Scene V). Indeed, Medea's insistence on the power of the will in the first two plays of the trilogy is very Cornelian, although Grillparzer's masterly delineation of her character, culminating in the third play, *Medea,* is much more akin to Racine, whom he greatly preferred, and whose conception of the feminine heart corresponded more nearly with Grillparzer's own.

[28] This scene may be compared with Act III, Scene x of Schiller's *Jungfrau von Orleans,* but where Schiller has introduced a historical deviation of doubtful dramatic validity, with Joan's sudden love for Lionel, ending with the death of his heroine on the field of battle, instead of at the stake at Rouen, Grillparzer here directly illuminates the strength of Medea's love—the beginning and end of her tragedy.

MEDEA *(With averted face and dagger in hand)*

O strength!

JASON *(Gently)*

Kill me, Medea, if you can.

(Medea stands transfixed)

You see? You cannot do it! You are powerless!
Then come to me. Enough of your resistance!
Do you refuse? Just try to, if you can.

(Suddenly seizing her and carrying her up on his arm)

Thus will I seize you, thus hold you aloft
And bear you through the discords of our peoples,
Through hate and death, through battle's bloody waves;
Who'll dare to stop me? Who'll snatch you from me?

MEDEA

Leave me!

JASON

Not until you have spoken gently, *1160*
Until a word, a gesture, or a sound
Betrays, you yield to me, that you surrender.

(Looking up at her and quivering violently)

Medea, please, this sign!

MEDEA *(Softly)*

Jason, leave me.

JASON

Jason!—There, there, you've uttered my name now,
For the first time uttered! O sweetest sound!
Jason! How very beautiful's the name
Now that your lovely lips have spoken it!
My thanks, Medea, my most heartfelt thanks!

(He has put her down on the ground once more)

Medea, Jason! Jason and Medea!
Sweet harmony! Do you not think so too? *1170*
You're trembling? Sit down here, compose yourself.

(He leads MEDEA *to a grassy bank. She follows him and sits, her body bent, her eyes fixed on the ground, her hands, which still hold the dagger, folded in her lap. Standing in front of her)*

What? Ever silent, ever sad and troubled?
O do not fear! You are in friendly hands.
True, I'll not soon return you to your father,
His daughter is a precious pledge to me;
Yet you shall not fare badly now with me,
At least not worse than I shall fare with you.

When I now stand before you, gaze on you,
An almost wondrous feeling creeps in me,
As though I'd crossed the boundary of life *1180*
And were now standing on some unknown star,
Where different are the laws of being, doing;
Where all that happens has no cause nor sequence,
Just being, because it is.
Having come here across a raging sea,
From lands so far away, so quite cut off,
That *wishes* scarce dared form before the voyage,
Bent on a clash and war I reach this shore
And set my eyes upon you, knowing you.
I almost feel at home in this weird land, *1190*
And I, myself adventurous, behold
Without surprise, as though it had to be,
The strange adventures of this wonderland.
Again, if what is strange grows ordinary,
The ordinary in its turn grows strange:[29]

[29] Another of the very numerous examples of antithetic play of words to which Grillparzer was so partial. Here it is dramatically quite apt in Jason's mouth. Occasionally this partiality becomes dramatically inept when, for instance, very sophisticated ideas are thus put into the mouth of the virginal Hero in Act I of *The Waves of Sea and Love,* causing Grillparzer momentarily to deviate into

I have become an *object* to myself,
Some other thinks in me, some other acts.
I often ruminate on my own words,
As though another's, what is meant by them,
And when it comes to deeds, think to myself:[30] *1200*
I am amazed at what he'll do and not do!

One thing alone is clear and that is you!
Yes, you, Medea, however strange it seem!
I, an Hellene, you of barbarous blood,
I, free and frank, you, full of magic wiles,
I, Colchis' foe, you, daughter of her king.
And yet, Medea, ah, and yet and yet!
In my land there's a beautiful belief;
The gods originally had created
Each creature double and then separated; *1210*
Since then each half is searching for the other
Through land and sea, and if they find each other,
Their souls unite and merge and so become
One. Do you feel within you half a heart?
Is it cleft painfully within your breast?
Then come— But no, she sits there dull and dismal,
A rough "no" to my warm interpretation,
The dagger still clenched tight within her hands.
Away with it!

(Seizing her hand and extracting the dagger)

Sweet fingers, let go! Beauteous
Garlands, flowers and jewels you should touch, not *1220*
This blade of steel, made for the hands of men!

MEDEA *(Springing up)*

Away!

JASON *(Holding her back)*

Remain!

---

precisely the fault of which he rightly accused Schiller, namely, of making the character incongruously the author's mouthpiece.

[30] Grillparzer has painted a self-portrait in these lines.

MEDEA

Off, off!

JASON

Remain, I beg!
I say: remain! Do you hear me? You will have to!
Have to! By heaven, even if it costs your life!
What, does a woman dare defy a man?
Remain!

(He seizes her arms with both hands)

MEDEA

Leave me!

JASON

If you obey, else never!

(He wrestles with her resistance)

I long to know the measure of your toughness.

MEDEA *(Falling on her knee)*

Alas!

JASON

You see? Yourself you wanted this.
So recognize your lord and master now!

*(*MEDEA *lies on the ground on one knee, supporting her arm on the other and hiding her face with her hand. He goes up to her)*

Stand up! You've not been hurt? Stand up, I say! *1230*
Sit here and rest, if you know how to rest!

(He raises her from the ground, and she sits on the grassy bank)

In vain I shoot the arrows from my heart,
They ricochet and transfix my own breast!
O how I hate this country, whose rude breath
Has shriveled up the fairest flower of heaven,
That ever bloomed in Nature's fairy garden.
Were you in Hellas, where life's even tenor

Serenely plays, in the bright sunshine there,
Where every eye's alight with smiles like heaven,
Where every word's a greeting, every look *1240*
A genuine harbinger of genuine feeling,
No hate except for lies and cunning, no—[31]
And yet, what am I saying? I know well,
Medea, you are not what you would seem!
In vain you seek to hide yourself, I know you!
You have a true and warm heart in your breast,
Your clouds outside conceal a sun within.
When you saved me, yes, when my kiss on your—
You quake? Look at me—when my kiss on your—
Yes, yes, my eager mouth has touched your lips, *1250*
Before I knew you, almost before I'd seen you,
I had already snatched love's highest gift;
I felt the *life force* welling up to me,
And you would falsely posture now as *stone?*
A true and warm heart's beating in your breast,
You *love,* Medea!

*(*MEDEA *is about to spring up.*
He pulls her down)

Stay, Medea—you love!
I see it in the raging of your breast,
I see it in the flaming of your cheeks,
I feel it in the hot breath you exhale,
And in your trembling I feel it—you love, *1260*
Love *me! Me,* as I *you!* Yes, as I you!

(He kneels before her)

[31] A highly-colored description of ancient Greece, where these vices were no less prevalent than elsewhere. Indeed, it would seem the Greeks positively admired the cunning of Ulysses, not to mention that of Orestes and Iphigenia, who tricked the barbarian King Thoas of his statue of Artemis, in spite of his kindness to the forlorn Iphigenia (see Goethe's *Iphigenie auf Tauris,* based on Euripides). The moral aversion to "lies and cunning" seems rather to spring from the ethics of the Bible, than of ancient Greece. But these rosy sentiments in the mouth of the nostalgic Jason are dramatically not inappropriate here.

O raise your eyes, deny it if you can!
Look at me and say "no" . . . You love, Medea!

(He seizes both her hands and turns the resisting girl toward him, and gazes fixedly at her face)

You're weeping! All in vain, I know no pity! [32]
Look, eye to eye, and say "no." You do love!
I love you, you love me! Say it, Medea!

(He has turned her right against him. Her eye meets his. She looks deep into his eyes)

Your eyes have said so, now your lips must, too.
Say it, Medea, say it: I love you!
Should you find it so hard, I'll teach you, child;
Repeat: I love you!

(He draws her to him; instinctively, she hides her face on his breast) [33]

—And yet not a word! *1270*
Not one word, though I see the savage storm
That's shaking the firm pillars of your soul!
And still no word!

(Springing up)

So be it, stubborn girl!
Go, you are free, I'll not detain you longer.
Return to your own kith and kin once more,
Their human sacrifices, feasts of death,
And to your wilderness, wild girl, return!
Go. You are free, I'll not detain you longer.

AEETES *(From within the scenes)*

Here, Colchians, here!

[32] Contrast Nero, in Racine's *Britannicus,* Act II, Scene ii, V. 402:

I loved the very tears I caused to flow.

[33] Some editions have the reading "in his hair," instead of "on his breast." "Hair" might seem somewhat comic in English!

JASON

Your father is approaching,
Rejoice, I'll not keep you from him. *1280*

(Enter ARGONAUTS *falling back. Behind them* AEETES, ABSYRTUS *and* COLCHIANS *pursuing them)*

AEETES *(As he enters)*

Brave comrades, use your weapons.
Where is my child?

ABSYRTUS

There she is sitting, Father.

AEETES *(To* JASON*)*

Accursèd robber, give me back my child!

JASON

If you request, not if you threaten me.
There is your child. Take her and lead her home;
Not since you want, since she wants and I want.

(Going to MEDEA *and taking hold of her)*

Stand up, Medea. Come. Here is your father.
You longed to go back to him; here he is.
May the great gods forbid that I should hold
You here against your will. *1290*
Why are you trembling? You yourself wished this.

(He leads the tottering girl to her father, and makes her over into his arms)

Here, father, is your child.

AEETES *(Welcoming* MEDEA, *who hides her face on his shoulders)*

Medea!

ABSYRTUS

Sister!

JASON

Now, King, prepare yourself for a fight to the death!

The bonds that stayed my arm are broken now,
And all the flattering fantasies are fled
That slackened my own sinews for the fray;
With her, who now reposes in your arms,
I put our truce aside and breathe but war.
Prepare yourself! Your weal and life are at stake!

(To MEDEA*)*

But you, who lie here quivering and mute, *1300*
Your face turned in hostility away,
Farewell! We're parting now for evermore.
There was a moment when I fondly fancied
That you could feel, that you could more than hate,
When I believed the gods had destined us
For each other, you for me, me for you.
That dream is over now. So go your way!
On two occasions you have saved my life,
I thank you for this, never shall forget it!
In my home, far away, for many years *1310*
I'll tell it in the bosom of my friends,
And when they ask and press: For whom these tears
That glisten strangely in your manly eyes?
Then I shall speak in painful memory:[34]
She was Medea, beautiful and splendid,
But no heart in her breast.

AEETES

Medea, what?
Your face upon my shoulder is all wet.
You're weeping?

JASON

Weeping? Let me see the tears,
Let me believe you know the way to weep!

[34] Compare Medea's great cry in Act IV of *Medea* (V. 1818), when she is meditating the murder of her children:

Nothing alive but memory and pain.

Compare also King Henry's "Saint Crispian" speech in Act IV, Scene iii of Shakespeare's *Henry V*.

Gaze once more on me, ah it is the last time; *1320*
I'll take your gaze far, far away with me!
Remember, it is for the last—last time!

(He holds her hand that hangs down)

AEETES

What, do you dare touch her hand?

JASON *(Letting go of her hand)*

She does not wish it. Well then, so be it!
You'll see me nevermore upon this earth.
Farewell, Medea! Farewell forever!

(He goes off quickly)

MEDEA *(Turning her face and stretching her arms toward him)*

Jason!

JASON *(Turning round)*

At last! Medea! Come to me.

(Rushing to her and taking her hand)

To me!

AEETES *(Holding her by her other hand)*

Off, brazen fellow!

JASON *(Throwing off* AEETES' *hand and snatching* MEDEA *to himself)*

Do you dare, barbarian?
She is my wife!

AEETES

His wife? You're dumb, you reprobate?

JASON *(Leading* MEDEA *to the other side)*

Medea, here, safe from these savages! *1330*
From now on you are mine and no one else's.

AEETES

Medea, you'll not refuse, you'll follow him?

Not thrust your dagger in his criminal heart?
Accursèd drab, was this your handiwork?

(Advancing on JASON*)*

Give me my daughter, my enchanted child!

MEDEA *(Throwing herself between the two men)*
Father, do not kill him! I love him.

JASON

So *he* could tear it from you, but not I!

AEETES

Jade! You confess, yourself confess your shame?
O that I failed to note the blatant ruse,
That made me, myself, thrust her in his arms, *1340*
Trusting her forbears' blood in her veins!

JASON

You dare rail at her?

MEDEA

Listen to me, Father!
It's happened, what I feared. It's happened!
But let's be clear, Father, clear!
A dismal vortex swirls about my senses.[35]
But I will win through, out of the dark night.
There is still time to stop it. Listen to me!

AEETES

What shall I listen to? I've seen it, seen!

MEDEA

Father, do not destroy us all!
Break the spell, allay the storm! *1350*
Bid him remain, this leader of the strangers,
Receive him. Accept him.
Let him reign in Colchis by your side,
Your friend, your son.

[35] Compare Medea to Jason in the last scene of the trilogy (*Medea,* Act V, Vs. 2319–23).

AEETES

My son? My foe!
Death to him, and to you, if you'll not follow!
Will you come with me? Speak, will you, or not?

MEDEA

Listen to me!

AEETES

Will you, or not?

ABSYRTUS

Let her speak, Father.

AEETES

Yes or no?
Let me alone, son! Will you? She will not come! Snake!

(He raises his sword)

JASON *(Putting himself in front of her)*

You shall not harm her!

ABSYRTUS

(At the same time seizing his father's arm)

Father, what are you doing? *1360*

AEETES

You are right. She shall not die, but live,
Live in disgrace and shame, rejected, accursèd,
Fatherless, homeless, godless!

MEDEA

Father!

AEETES

You have deceived, betrayed me;
Stay! You shall no more cross my threshold!
You shall be cast out, like the beast of the wilderness,
Shall die in foreign parts, forsaken and alone.
Follow your paramour back to his homeland,
And share his bed, his wanderings, his disgrace!

Live in a foreign land, a foreigner, *1370*
Disdained, despised, discarded and distraught![36]
Himself, for whom you give up your father and fatherland,
He shall despise you and himself discard you,
When passion is all spent, and all desire stilled:
Then you shall stand and wring your hands,
And stretch them toward your fatherland,
Sundered from it by wide, raging seas,
Whose murmuring waves shall bear to you your father's curse!

MEDEA *(Kneeling)*

Father!

AEETES

Get back! I do not know you.
Come, my son. Her sight's defiling us, *1380*
Her voice in my ear is a dirge of death!
Do not clasp my knees, accursèd whore!
Look at him there, him, you have chosen;
To him I hand you over!
He will avenge me, he will punish you,
He himself, earlier than you think.

MEDEA

Father!

AEETES *(Pushing the kneeling girl away, so that she falls back semiprostrate)*

Away your hand, I do not know you![37]
Let's go, my son, my only child,
Let's go, my son, out of her presence!

(Exit with ABSYRTUS *and* COLCHIANS*)*

[36] Literally: Mocked, despised, scorned, laughed to scorn; but as all four German participles begin with *ver,* it is dramatically more important to keep the alliteration in English with "dis" than to be precisely literal.

[37] The dramatic tension in this scene is exactly paralleled in the last play of the trilogy, when the unfortunate Medea, here rejected by her father, is likewise rejected by her children (*Medea,* end of Act III) having meanwhile been discarded by her husband.

JASON

Barbarian, flee, you'll not escape revenge! *1390*

(To the ARGONAUTS*)*

The moment's come! Friends, have your weapons ready
For the last blow and victory or death!

(Pointing to MEDEA*)*

She knows the Fleece, the place where it is hidden,
With her we'll end our task, then to our ship.

(Going up to MEDEA, *who is still prostrate, supported by one hand, with the other over her brow)*

Stand up, Medea, he has gone—stand up!

(He raises her)

Here you are safe.

MEDEA *(Who has raised herself in his arms, but with a knee still on the ground)*

Jason, was he speaking the truth?

JASON

(Raising her up fully)

Do not think of it!

MEDEA

(Shyly clinging to him)

O Jason, was he speaking the truth?

JASON

Forget what you have heard, what you have seen,
What you have been until this very hour.
Aeetes' child is now the wife of Jason, *1400*
On this breast now depends your right and duty,
And as I tear away this veil from you,
Embroidered with the mystic signs of Hades,
So do I tear you free from all the bonds
That knit you to this land's barbarities.
Here, Greeks, you see a Greek. Salute her thus!

(He pulls away her veil) [38]

MEDEA *(Trying to hold it)*

The adornment of the gods!

JASON

Of Hades, off!
Now your hair, free and frank, waves on your brow;
Thus free and frank you are now Jason's bride.

But one thing more, then on our ship away! *1410*
You know the Fleece, come, show me where it lies.

MEDEA

Ha! Silence!

JASON

Why?

MEDEA

Ah, do not speak of it!

JASON

I've given my word to take it home with me;
I'll not return without the prize of victory.

MEDEA

I tell you, do not speak of it.
An angry god has sent it here;
It brings bad luck, already *has* brought it!
I am your wife. You've snatched it from my lips,
Have torn the trembling word deep from my heart;
I am yours, take me where you will, *1420*
But speak no more about that Fleece.
In the twilight of ominous dreams
The gods have shown it me,
Spread over corpses,

[38] Another of those symbolic gestures to which Grillparzer is partial. Contrast Medea's action in Act II of *Medea,* where she tears her mantle in two to denote the end of their love and bond. (Vs. 1125–28.)

Bespattered with blood,
My blood!
Do not speak of it!

JASON

And yet I must, not only speak of it,
But take it home with me, happen what may.
So leave your fears and guide me to the spot, *1430*
So that I might fulfill my obligations.

MEDEA

I? Never!

JASON

You will not do this?

MEDEA

No.

JASON

If you deny me help, I'll go myself.

MEDEA

Then go.

JASON *(Turning to go)*

I'm going.

MEDEA *(Dully)*

Going—to your death.

JASON

Come, friends, let's reconnoiter for ourselves.

(He goes)

MEDEA

Jason!

JASON *(Turning round)*

What is it?

MEDEA

You're going to your death.

JASON

Did I not come here unafraid of death?

MEDEA *(Hurrying to him and seizing his hand)*

I tell you, you will die!

(Half aloud)

In the cave it lies concealed,
Defended by all the horrors *1440*
Of cunning and of violence.
Labyrinthine passages,
Sense-confusing,
Abysses, treacherously covered,
Daggers beneath each footstep;
Death by inhalation,
Murder in a thousand shapes!
And the Fleece hangs on a tree
Besmeared with poison,
Guarded by the serpent *1450*
That never sleeps,
Unrelenting,
Unapproachable.

JASON

I've given my word and will redeem my promise.

MEDEA

You're going?

JASON

Yes.

MEDEA *(Throwing herself across his path)*

Even if I prostrate fall
And clasp your knees beseeching you to stay,
To stay!

JASON

Nothing could stop me.

MEDEA

Father! Father!
Where are you? Take me with you!

JASON

Why complain?
I fancy I have more cause to complain:
I'm doing what I have to, you may choose. *1460*
Since you refuse to come, I'll go alone.

(He goes)

MEDEA

You're going?

JASON

Yes.

MEDEA

Despite all my entreaties,
You're still going?

JASON

Yes.

MEDEA *(Springing up)*

Then come.

JASON

Where?

MEDEA

To the Fleece,
To death! You shall not die alone,
One house, one body and one ruin—one.[39]

JASON *(Approaching her)*

Medea!

[39] This line is repeated by Medea in Act II of *Medea* (V.1044), but Jason, unlike Medea here, fails to make the emotional response demanded.

MEDEA *(Withdrawing)*

Leave out caresses,
I know what they are worth! O Father, Father!
Then come, let's take what you are seeking:
Riches, honor,
Curses, death! *1470*
In the cave it lies concealed [40]
Woe to you when it's revealed!
Then come.

JASON *(Seizing her hand)*

What's tormenting you?

MEDEA *(Snatching away her hand with a cry)*

Ah! Phrixus! Jason!

JASON

For all the gods' sake!

MEDEA

Then come, come!

(Slips away, with wide-open eyes staring ahead of her. The others follow)

Curtain

[40] Concealed; literally, "preserved" translated "concealed" for the rhyme which is in the original, and which seems dramatically preferable to maintain. For the sake of consistency "concealed" also appears for "preserved" in V.1439.

ACT IV

The interior of a cave. Close set. In the right foreground the bottom of a flight of steps. In the rocky wall of the background a great door shut.

MEDEA *comes down the steps with a goblet in one hand and a torch in the other.*

MEDEA

Do come down. We are there!

JASON *(Above from behind the scenes)*

Let me have light!

MEDEA *(Lighting the descent)*

What is it?

JASON *(Entering, with drawn sword and hastening down the steps)*

Something brushed past me. Halt there!

MEDEA

What?

JASON

By the door it stands, denying entrance.

MEDEA *(Lighting it up)*

See, it is nothing, none denies you entrance.
Unless yourself.

(She puts away the goblet and sets the torch in a ring by the balustrade)

JASON

You are so calm.

MEDEA

And you are not.

JASON

Before it had begun, *1480*
When I but wanted it, you quaked, and now—

MEDEA

I'm horrified you want it, not you do it.
It's the reverse with you.

JASON

My eye is craven,
My heart courageous— Quick to our task—Medea!

MEDEA

What are you staring at?

JASON

Away, away, pale ghost!
Leave the door free, you shall not hold me back!

(Going to the door)

I'll go, despite you, through you to my goal . . . It's gone now!
How does one open the door?

MEDEA

A sword-thrust on the plate
There in the center'll open it.

JASON

Good then!
You wait for me here.

MEDEA

Jason . . .

JASON

What now? *1490*

MEDEA *(Soft and alluring)*

Do not go!

JASON

You're provoking me.

MEDEA

O, Jason, do not go!

JASON

Obstinate woman, can nothing move you
To sacrifice your whim to my resolve?

MEDEA

One honors even the whim of one one loves.

JASON

Enough now, I insist.

MEDEA

Insist?

JASON

Insist.

MEDEA

And all my prayers against it are in vain?

JASON

And all your prayers against it are in vain!

MEDEA

And vain also my death?

(With a quick gesture she snatches his sword)

Look, your own sword,
It's turned against my breast. But one step more
And I shall lie before you cold and dead. 1500

JASON

My sword!

MEDEA

Stand back, you'll take it from my breast!
Will you turn back?

JASON

No.

MEDEA

If I kill myself?

JASON

I may lament you, but cannot turn back.
First comes my word, even if it means your life.

(Advances on her)

Woman, give way, and give my sword!

MEDEA *(Giving him his sword)*

Then take it
Out of my hand, you darling bridegroom!
And kill yourself and me! No more I'll stop you.

JASON *(Going toward the door)*

Ahead!

MEDEA

Stop! One thing more! You want to die at once?
The Fleece on the sacred tree,
A raging dragon guards it, *1510*
Invulnerable his scaly hide,
All-piercing his teeth of steel,
You'll not subdue him.

JASON

I him or he me.

MEDEA

You cruel monster!
Or he you! And still you'll go?

JASON

Why your needless words?

MEDEA

Stop!

Then take this goblet:
In it, from mountain-honey
Brewed, from the dews of night *1520*
And the she-wolf's milk,
A bubbling drink ferments.
Put it down as you enter,
Standing aloof.
And the dragon will come,
Seeking nurture,
To lap up the drink.
Then go to the tree
And take the Fleece—No, do not take it!
Do not take it—stay! *1530*

JASON

Silly woman! Give me the drink.

(He takes the goblet out of her hand)

MEDEA *(Falling round his neck)*

Jason! I kiss you thus, and thus, and thus, and thus!
Go to your grave and leave room too for me!
Stay!

JASON

Leave me, woman! A higher summons calls me.

(Going toward the door)

Were you to hide the terrors of Tartarus,
I will withstand you!

(He strikes the door with his sword)

Open, you gates—ah!

(The doors spring open and disclose an inner, narrower cave, strangely lit. In the background a tree on which hangs resplendent the Golden Fleece. Round the tree and Fleece is coiled a huge serpent, that on the opening of the door juts out its head, hidden

in the foliage, and glares around with forking tongue. JASON *falls back with a cry and returns to the foreground)*

MEDEA *(Laughing wildly)*

Are you quaking? And your bones rattling?
You've wanted it, then why not go?
Strong, daring, violent man!
Bold only against me? [41] *1540*
The serpent makes you quake? You serpent!
Who've coiled 'round me, ensnaring me,
Who's ruined me, and murdered me!
Look, look at it, the monster,
And go and die!

JASON

Last out, my senses, last out!
Why are you quaking, heart? What is it more than dying?

MEDEA

Than dying? Dying? It is certain death!
Go in, my darling bridegroom,
Embrace your hissing bride! *1550*

JASON

Away from me, with all your ravings, woman!
My spirit's drowning in your spirit's waves!

(Speaking toward the door)

Behold me then, you'll find I am your man.
Were you ten times more hideous, here I am!

(He hurries to the attack)

MEDEA

Jason!

JASON

In!

[41] Compare Racine's *Athaliah* (Act III, Scene vii, Vs. 1107–08)
O cowardly people, born for servitude,
Bold only against God!

MEDEA

Jason!

JASON

In!

(He goes in and the doors shut behind him)

MEDEA *(Hurling herself screaming on the closed door)*
He's gone! He's dead!

JASON *(From within)*

Who shut the door?

MEDEA

Not I.

JASON

Open it.

MEDEA

I cannot—for all the gods' sake,
Put down the bowl, do not delay!
You're lost if you delay.
Jason—do you hear me? Put down the bowl! *1560*
He does not hear . . . He's bent upon his task!
His task! Oh help, you gods above!
Look down on us, you heavenly beings!
But no, no, do not look down
On the guilty daughter,
The spouse of the guilty girl!
Ah keep your help and spare me from your vengeance!
Let no divine eye see,
Let dark night cover
Our deeds and us! *1570*
Jason, are you alive? Answer me!
Answer! All silent,
All dead! Ah! He is dead!
He does not speak, is dead—dead!

(She sinks down by the door)

My bridegroom, have you fallen? Leave room,
Room for your bride!

JASON *(Inside, in terror)*

Ah!

MEDEA *(Springing up)*

That was Jason's voice . . . He is alive!
In danger! Let me go to him, door, open!
You think you can resist? I laugh at you!
Open.

(She tears open with a violent pull both sides of the door. JASON *rushes out staggering, bearing the Fleece like a banner on a lance)*

You are alive?

JASON

Alive? Alive? Yes—close that door! *1580*

(He shuts the door in fear)

MEDEA

And have the Fleece?

JASON *(Holding it far from his body)*

Do not touch it! Fire! Fire!

(Holding out his right hand with fingers rigid)

Look at my hand—all burnt—as I touched it!

MEDEA *(Taking his hand)*

Ah! It is bleeding?

JASON

Bleeding?

MEDEA

Also your head.

Are you hurt?

JASON

Do I know? Let's go, let's go!

MEDEA

Did you do what I told you?

JASON

Yes, indeed.
I put the bowl down, with myself apart,
And waited panting. Heard you call my name,
But did not dare reply before the beast.
It raised itself now gleaming and I fancied,
With coils indented, rippling toward me; *1590*
Yet it was but the drink the monster sought,
And stretched out taut it gulped down all the potion
In long and thirsty draughts, ignoring me.
Soon, drunk or dead, it lay there motionless.
I darted from my torturing hiding-place
Up to the tree and Fleece—here it is—Let's away!

MEDEA

Then come and quick.

JASON

As I took it from the tree,
There was a sighing ripple through the leaves
And behind me a groan of "woe." [42]
Ha! . . . who groans?

MEDEA

You yourself!

JASON

I?

MEDEA

Come.

JASON

Where to?

MEDEA

Away.

[42] Compare *Macbeth* (Act II, Scene ii):
Methought I heard a voice cry "Sleep no more" . . .

JASON

Away, yes away. *1600*
You go ahead, I'll follow with the Fleece,
Go quick! Do not delay! Let's out! Ahead!

(Exeunt both up the steps)

SCENE II

Open space in front of the cave. In the background the view of the sea, which is hidden on the right by a hill on the shore, behind which, with only masts and prow visible, lies the ship of the ARGONAUTS.

MILO, ARGONAUTS, *some occupied with preparations for embarkation, some occupied as sentinels or grouped at rest.*

MILO

The ship has come in here. Good. But listen!
Do not cast anchor. Can you hear me? *Not!*
We may be forced to sail at any moment,
And do not know if we'll have time to weigh it.

(Walking up and down)

And still he does not come. To think he trusted her!
I warned him clearly. Would he heed my warning?
Yes, formerly at home he'd heed my words
And also do what my true lips advised, *1610*
Obedient like a child, and yet a man.
But here he is a man completely changed,
Changed, just like all of us, I'd almost said,
By the poisonous air of this enchanted land.
What a woman! I shudder at her thought!
How she was standing there with her dark brows,
Like storm clouds lining her lugubrious forehead,
Her eyelids lowered in gloomy meditation:

Then as she raised them lightning darted forth
From her dark eyes that riveted and struck. *1620*
It struck him! May the gods avert this now!
But what are those two bringing? They are Greeks.
A woman! Tied up! Halt there, boorish cowards!

(Enter two GREEKS. GORA *between them with her hands tied)*

MILO

What's up? Why bind the woman? Set her free.

SOLDIER

The woman, sir, came up to our patrol
And asked about—about the Colchian woman
We took today.

GORA

Colchian woman?
What, slave! She is Medea,
The daughter of the Colchian king,
Where do you hold her? *1630*

SOLDIER

We did not want to let her go, lest she
Informed the enemy of our position,
But, sir, she struggled almost like a man
And so we tied her as she would not yield,
And here she is.

MILO

Untie her bonds at once.

(They do so)

GORA

Where is Medea? Where is my child?

MILO

Your child?

GORA

I've suckled, nursed her
Like a mother, my child. Where do you hold her?

They say of her own free will she remained
With you in the precincts of your camp; *1640*
But it's a lie, I know Medea,
I know my child.
You hold her as a prisoner.
Give her up. Where is she?

MILO

You've come to her as a most fit companion.
She might well feel alone in civilized circles.
Take her to the ship.

GORA

So she is there?

MILO

Do go.
You'll see her all too soon, I fear—go now!

GORA *(Being led away)*

Into the sea, not ship, if you deceive me.

MILO *(Gazing after her)*

If we take all these animals to Greece, *1650*
I fear we shall be crushed to death by crowds
Coming to see the sights! And still he does not come!

(Dull thuds are heard beneath the ground)

What's that? Listen. Does even earth spew portents!
The enemy about?

(To the warriors, drawing his sword)

Ho there! Alert!

(The warriors take up their arms)

The earth is opening—what will happen next?

(A portcullis opens up on the ground. MEDEA *comes out)*

MEDEA

Daylight at last!

(When she comes quite out)

And here are your men.
I've done what I had promised.

*(*JASON *with the banner of the Fleece also comes out.* MEDEA *lets the portcullis drop)*

MILO *(Rushing to him and grabbing his hand)*

Jason, you!
You!

JASON *(Who was standing with lowered head, looks up)*

Jason!—Where? Ah, yes, indeed!

(Extending his left hand to him. In the right hand he holds the banner)

Dear Milo!

MILO *(Coming forward)*

And with the Fleece?

JASON *(Looking round in fear)*

Ha! with the Fleece.

(Holding it up)

Here it is!

(Again looking round)

Ah! What a hideous mantle that—the gray one— *1660*
And the man's wrapped his very nose in it.

(Going up to him)

Lend me your mantle, friend.

(The SOLDIER *hands him the mantle)*

I know you well,
You are Archytes from Corinth, I'm sure.
A gay old dog, a *ghost* with flesh and blood!

(Gripping his shoulder)

With flesh and blood.

(Laughing hideously)

Ha! Ha! I thank you, friend.

MILO

How strange—

JASON *(Putting the mantle round the Fleece)*

Come, let us cover that like this,
And keep it safely here till we require it.

(He leans the Fleece against a rock, on which MEDEA *is sitting, lost in thought)*

What are you dreaming of, Medea? Dreaming now!
Let's save our meditating for diversions
Later, during our long and tedious voyage. *1670*
Come to me now, my wife!—our wedding march
A serpent's hiss beneath the door of death.

MILO *(Turning to* MEDEA*)*

The ship there hides what you'll be pleased to hear—
A woman, claiming to be Medea's nurse
Was brought in—

MEDEA

Gora . . . To her!

JASON *(Roughly)*

Stay, where you are!

*(*MEDEA*, startled, remains standing with her hands on her breast and brow. He says more gently)*

I beg you, stay where you are.

(Leading her back)

Do not go.

(She casts a shy look at him)

Discard the company of those rough folk,

And cultivate instead our company!
We are now one, we have to think as one.

MILO

Come, now, on board!

JASON

Yes, come with me, Medea! 1680
How lukewarm are the foe! I should have loved
To fight, to fight! But they, it seems, are sleeping.

ABSYRTUS *(Behind the scenes)*

This way.

MILO

They are not sleeping.

JASON

All the better.
Close ranks! And make your way back toward our ship.
In our departure let us leave our memory
Forever firm imprinted on their minds.

(He snatches up the veiled Fleece)

Medea, in their midst and do not tremble!

(Enter ABSYRTUS *with* COLCHIANS*)*

ABSYRTUS

Here she is. Come to me, Medea, sister!

MEDEA *(Who at his entrance has involuntarily taken a few steps in his direction, now stops)*

Your sister, true—alas, no more Medea!

JASON

What business have you there? Get back to us! 1690

ABSYRTUS *(Going up to her with pity)*

Could it be true then, what they all are saying,
And I could not believe until this moment,
You wished to go off with the foreign men?

Forsaking our dear country, hearth and home,
Our father, and, Medea, me,
Me too, who loves you so, my poor, dear sister!

MEDEA *(Throwing herself round his neck)*

O, Brother, brother!

(Her voice choked with tears)

Oh, my brother!

ABSYRTUS

No, it is not true! You are weeping.
I too must weep. Yet, what about it!
I'm not ashamed of tears, my faithful comrades; *1700*
I'll show in *battle* what I'm worth.
Do not weep, sister, come with me.

MEDEA *(Hardly audible round his neck)*

Could I but go with you!

JASON *(Going toward her)*

You'd go with him?

MEDEA *(timidly)*

I?

JASON

You said so.

MEDEA

Did I say something, brother?
No, I said nothing!

ABSYRTUS

You did indeed say so, then come, oh come!
I'll take you back to Father, he'll forgive.
My pleas already have half won him over;
He'll certainly forgive. Nothing's yet happened;
The strangers, they have not yet found the Fleece.

MEDEA *(Tearing herself from his arms in terror)*

Not?

(Shuddering)

They have.

JASON *(Tearing the veil from the Fleece and brandishing it aloft)*

Here!

1710

ABSYRTUS

The Fleece!

(To MEDEA*)*

So in the end you have betrayed us.
Then go in misery to your perdition!

(To JASON*)*

Keep her, but give me back the Golden Fleece!

JASON

You dream, my little coxcomb! Get you hence
And tell your father what you here have seen.
I keep his daughter, but return his son.

ABSYRTUS

The Fleece!

JASON

I do not want your blood. In silence go!
My arm is used to fighting against dragons,
And not with fools like you. Go, I say, go!

ABSYRTUS *(Closing in)*

The Fleece!

JASON *(Stepping aside)*

It's dangerous to oppose me, *1720*
For I am raging like the raging lion.

ABSYRTUS

The Fleece!

JASON

Then take it!

(Lifting his arm over his left shoulder, he strikes at ABSYRTUS *with a furious side lunge so that his helmet, shield and sword come rattling down, and he himself, although unwounded, falls down in a daze)*

MEDEA *(Hastily kneels down and hides the head of her fallen brother in her lap)*

Stop!

JASON

I will not kill him.
But he must learn to obey—he *must—obey!*

MEDEA *(Raising* ABSYRTUS*)*

Stand up!

(He stands up and rests his dazed head on her breast)

Are you in pain?

ABSYRTUS *(Faintly)*

My forehead's hurting.

MEDEA *(Pressing her lips on his forehead)*

Dear brother!

MILO *(Who earlier had gone off to keep watch, now returns in haste)*

Up, up, the foe approaches,
In a great number, at their head the King.

MEDEA *(Pressing her brother more closely)*

My father!

ABSYRTUS *(Faintly)*

Our father.

JASON *(To both of them)*

Get back, both of you!

MILO *(Pointing to* ABSYRTUS*)*

Let the son be hostage against his father.
Take him there to the cliff to board the ship!

ABSYRTUS *(Exhausted, wanting to ward off those laying hold of him)*

Dare you touch me?

MEDEA

O brother, let us go. 1730

(They are led to the cliff)

JASON

On board the ship, all, and unfurl the sails.

(Enter AEETES *with armed* COLCHIANS*)*

AEETES *(Rushing in)*

Stop! My children! My son!

ABSYRTUS *(Up on the hill struggling to break free)*

My father!

JASON *(Calling up to those on the hill)*

Hold him!

(To AEETES*)*

He shall stay with me,
And follow me on board, hostage against you.
If but a skiff, or dinghy should pursue us,
Your son shall be consigned to a watery grave.
Only when Colchis' farthest cape is reached,
I'll let him go and send him back to you.
Barbarian, you have taught me how to fight you.

AEETES

Son, will you stay in the hands of these reprobates? 1740

ABSYRTUS *(Fruitlessly trying to extricate himself)*

Leave me!

MEDEA

My brother! Father!

JASON

Hold him.

AEETES

Come, my son.

JASON

In vain!

AEETES

Then I will come to you.
Behind me, Colchians, follow your king!

JASON

Get back!

AEETES *(Pressing on)*

You think you'll frighten me?

JASON

Get back!
You shall not save your son unless you yield.
I promise not to hurt a hair of his!
Bring him on board.

ABSYRTUS *(Struggling)*

Me? Never!

AEETES

My dear son!

ABSYRTUS

Attack them, free your son, O Father!

AEETES

How can I? They will kill you if I do.

ABSYRTUS

Better to die free than to live a slave: *1750*
Then let me fall provided they too fall!

JASON

Take him on board.

AEETES

Come, son.

ABSYRTUS *(Who has wrenched himself free)*

I'm coming, Father!

Free unto death! In death, see I'm avenged!

(He leaps from the cliff into the sea)

MEDEA

My brother! Take me with you!

(She is held back and sinks down)

AEETES

My son!

JASON

He's dead.

I call upon the lofty gods to witness,
You were the one to kill him and not I.

AEETES

My son! Revenge! Revenge!

(Rushing at Jason)

Die!

JASON

Let me be!

Am I to kill you?

AEETES

Murderer, die!

JASON

I, murderer?

Murderer yourself!

(Snatching the Fleece from someone standing near to whom he had earlier given it to hold)

Do you know this?

AEETES *(Staggers back with a cry)*

The Fleece!

JASON *(Flaunting it in his face)*

You know it?
Do you know too the blood bespattering it? 1760
It's Phrixus' blood! There is your son's blood too.
You, Phrixus' murderer, murderer of your son.

AEETES

Earth, swallow me, and open, O you graves!

(Falls to the ground)

JASON

Too late, they cannot hide your dastard deeds.
As instrument of a celestial power
I stand before you. Fear not for your life!
I do not want your death; indeed, die late,
That far-off generations yet may learn
Crimes on this earth must ever vengeance earn.
Now, let us quick on board, unfurl the sails, 1770
And back to Greece!

AEETES *(On the ground)*

Alas! Quite, quite undone!
Place me in the grave beside my son.

(While the COLCHIANS group themselves round the KING, JASON steps on board with the ARGONAUTS)

THE END

III

MEDEA

A Tragedy In Five Acts

CHARACTERS

CREON	*King of Corinth*
CREUSA	*his daughter*
JASON	
MEDEA	
GORA	MEDEA*'s nurse*
HERALD	*of the Amphictyonies*
COUNTRYMAN	
SERVANTS *and* SERVING GIRLS	
CHILDREN *of* MEDEA	

ACT I

Before the walls of Corinth, on the left center, a tent. In the background the sea, along which a part of the town lies on a spit of land. Early morning before dawn. It is still dark.

A SLAVE *stands in the right foreground in a pit, digging with a shovel and throwing out earth.* MEDEA *on the other side. In front of her a black chest strangely inlaid with gold in which she places many articles during the following dialogue.*

MEDEA

Have you not finished?

SLAVE

In a moment, madam.

(GORA *comes out of the tent and remains standing in the distance)*

MEDEA

First veil, then wand, belonging to the goddess,
I will no more have need of you; rest here.
The time for night and magic is now past,
And what befalls, whatever ill or good,
Must still befall in open beam of noon.
This vessel next, that hides mysterious flames
Devouring him who opens unawares;
And then this other, full of sudden death,
Away all, from the joyous touch of life! *10*
You many herbs and stones of baleful power
That sprang from her, I give you back to earth.

(Standing up)

Then rest here, all in concord evermore!
The last is yet to come, the most important.

(The SLAVE, *who meanwhile has climbed out of the pit and placed himself behind* MEDEA, *waiting for her to finish, now in order to assist, lays hold of some covered object fastened to a spear leaning against a tree behind* MEDEA. *The covering falls apart; the Banner with the Fleece blazes forth)*

SLAVE *(Laying hold of the Fleece)*

Is this it?

MEDEA

Stop, do not uncover it!
Let me once more behold you, evil gift!
You witness of the downfall of my kindred,
Drenched with my father's and my brother's blood;
Memorial of Medea's shame and blame.

(She steps on the pole, breaking it in two)

So let me break and cast you back into 20
The lap of night from which you threatening rose.

(She lays the broken banner with the other articles in the chest and shuts the lid)

GORA *(Coming forward)*

What are you doing here?

MEDEA *(Looking around)*

You see, yourself.

GORA

Do you intend to bury all these emblems
Of rarest service that protected you
And may protect still?

MEDEA

That protected me?

Since it protects me no more than it has,
I bury them. I have enough protection.

GORA

Because your husband loves you?

MEDEA *(To the* SLAVE*)*

Are you ready?

SLAVE

Yes, madam.

MEDEA

Come, then!

(She holds the chest by one handle, the slave holds the other and thus they bear it to the pit)

GORA *(Watching from a distance)*

What an occupation
For the right royal daughter of a king!

MEDEA

If you think it so rough, then why not help? *30a*

GORA

I am Jason's servant, not yours,
Since when does one slave serve another slave?

MEDEA *(To the* SLAVE*)*

Now lower it in and cover it with earth!

(The SLAVE *lowers the chest into the pit and shovels earth over it.* MEDEA *kneels alongside)*

GORA *(Standing in the foreground)*

Ah, let me die, O my ancestral gods,
That I may see no more what I now see!
Yet first hurl down the lightning of your vengeance
Upon the traitor who so humbles us!
First let me see him die, then strike me down!

MEDEA

Now it is done. Stamp firmly on the earth,

Then go! I know that you will keep my secret, 40
You are a Colchian and known to me.

(The SLAVE *goes off)*

GORA *(Calling after him in angry scorn)*

Do not inform your lord, else woe to both!
Have you not finished?

MEDEA *(Approaching her)*

Yes, now I'm content.

GORA

You buried even the Fleece?

MEDEA

Yes, even the Fleece.

GORA

So you did not leave it behind in Iolcos,
At Jason's uncle's?

MEDEA

But you've seen it here.

GORA

You had it with you and you buried it;
So everything is buried and forgotten?
The past all blown away,
With but the present, and no future. 50
There was no Colchis and there are no gods.
Your father never lived, nor died your brother!
Since you think it no more, it never happened!
Then also think you are not wretched, think
Your husband, the arch-traitor, loves you still;
Perhaps 'twill turn out so!

MEDEA *(Violently)*

Gora!

GORA

What!

You want me hold my tongue?

Let her who's guilty hold her tongue, not I!
If, from my fatherland, you've dragged me here
To slavery, in your false lover's wake, *60*
Where I, my free arms chained, pour out my sighs
Through all the wretched, wakeful, lonely nights,[1]
And every morning, to the new-born sun,
Curse my gray hair and all my length of days,
A butt to ridicule, a prey to scorn,
Suffering from lack of everything but pain,
Then you shall have to hear me if I speak.

MEDEA

Then speak!

GORA

What I foretold has happened now!
It's scarce a month the waves tossed you on shore,
Unwillingly, seducer and seduced, *70*
And yet you're shunned by all, by loathing followed.
The people find the Colchian woman baleful,
And horrible the priestess of dark powers.
Where you appear they all draw back in terror
And curse you. May they be themselves accursed!
Even your husband, wedded to the stranger,
Is hated for your sake and for his own.
His uncle shut his door upon his face,
His very native city cast him out
When that old uncle died, no one knows how; *80*
He has no house, no resting-place, no home:[2]
What do you now propose?

[1] Compare Goethe's "Harpist's Song" from *Wilhelm Meisters Lehrjahre:*

> Who never ate with tears his bread,
> Who never spent night's wretched hours
> Sitting and weeping on his bed
> He knows you not, you heavenly powers.

[2] Compare Grillparzer's opening lines of a poem composed to be sung at Beethoven's grave (to Beethoven's own trumpet setting) on the occasion of the unveiling of Beethoven's tombstone in November 1827 at Vienna's Central Cemetery:

MEDEA

I am his wife!

GORA

And now intend to do? . . .

MEDEA

To follow him
In need and death.

GORA

In need and death, indeed!
Aeetes' daughter in a beggar's house!

MEDEA

Let us pray to the high gods for a simple heart,
Then we might lightly bear a simple lot!

GORA *(Laughing angrily)*

Ha! Ha! Your husband?

MEDEA

Day breaks, come away!

GORA

You would elude me? Oh, you shan't escape!
The only silver lining in my grief *90*
Is that I see, from our example see,
The gods exist and that requital follows.
Weep your misfortune and I'll comfort you,
Only you must not monstrously pretend,
Denying still the justice of the gods,
When you deny your pain, their punishment.
If you would cure an evil, see it clearly!
Your husband, tell me, is he still the same?

MEDEA

What else?

You who in life had never
Resting-place nor home,

GORA

Ah, do not play with words!
Is he the same, who stormily pursued you, *100*
Who braved a hundred swords to take you off?
The same, who, on the long and lonely voyage,
Conquered the sad reluctance of Medea,
Who wished to die, refusing nourishment,
And all too soon compelled her with his passion?
Is he the same still? What, you tremble? Tremble!
He shrinks and runs from you, he shuns you, hates you;
As you your kindred, so he now betrays!
Bury, you may, the emblems of your deed,
The deed you cannot bury!

MEDEA

Silence!

GORA

No!

MEDEA *(Seizing her arm roughly)*

Silence, I say! *110*
Why must you rave so madly in your rage?
Let us await what's coming, not invite it.
Must what has once been, always so have been
And be forever present? If this moment
Is reckoned still as cradle of a future,
Then why not also grave of what is past?
What never should have happened, ah! has happened,
And I bewail, more bitterly than you think;
But must I then myself destroy myself?
One must be clear, in concord with oneself! *120*
To our undoing has an angry god
Brought us to alien lands, mid alien folk;
What was thought right at home, is here thought wrong,
And what permitted, here pursued with hate.
Then let us, also, change our speech and manners,
And if we may not still be what we would,
Let us at least become what we are able.
What bound me to the land of my forefathers,

I've here entombed in the oblivious earth;
The power my mother had bequeathed to me, *130*
The secret science of mysterious forces,
I have restored to Night that brought it forth,
And now, a helpless woman, weak and weary,
I throw myself into my husband's arms.
He shunned the foreign woman, but his wife
He'll surely welcome as befits a husband.
The day is breaking, a new life with it!
What was, will be no more, what is, shall stay!
But you, I pray you, gentle mother earth,
Preserve in trust what I've entrusted you. *140*

(They go toward the tent, it opens and JASON *emerges with a Corinthian* COUNTRYMAN, *behind him a* SLAVE*)*

JASON

You saw the king himself?

COUNTRYMAN

Indeed, my lord.

JASON

What did you say?

COUNTRYMAN

That someone waited outside
Well known to him, indeed, a former guest,
Who could, however, not set foot inside,
Ringed as he was by foes, by guile encompassed,
Until he had been promised peace and safety.

JASON

What was his answer?

COUNTRYMAN

He will come, my lord.
Here outside they propitiate Poseidon,
Bringing their offerings to the open shore.
The king, with daughter, joins in the procession; *150*
In passing, he will have a word with you.

JASON

Good, that will do, many thanks!

MEDEA *(Coming forward)*

My greetings to you!

JASON

And mine to you!

(To the SLAVE*)*

You and the others go
And cut for me green branches from the trees,
As is the custom here for suppliants;[3]
And mind you keep good order. Do you hear?
Enough!

(The COUNTRYMAN *and the* SLAVE *go)*

MEDEA

I see you're busy.

JASON

Yes.

MEDEA

What, will
You never rest?

JASON

A refugee and rest?
Because he has no rest he seeks a refuge.

MEDEA

You did not sleep last night, you stepped outside *160*
And wandered through the darkness all alone.

JASON

I love the night, the day offends my eyes.

[3] Compare opening lines of Sophocles' *King Oedipus,* see also *The Guest*—Grillparzer's stage directions before the entrance of Phrixus and his Greeks "with green branches in their hands."

MEDEA

Also, you sent a message to the king,
Will he receive us?

JASON

I await his answer.

MEDEA

He is your friend?

JASON

He was.

MEDEA

He will agree.

JASON

Contaminated company is shunned.
You know how everyone's avoiding us;
That even for the death of my false uncle,
Base Pelias, strangled by a god in rage,
The people put the blame on me, your husband, *170*
Who has returned home from the land of magic.
Do you not know?

MEDEA

I know.

JASON

Reason enough
To wander, ever wakeful in the night—
Yet what made you arise before the sun?
What did you seek in darkness? Ah, of course!
Old friends from Colchis conjuring?

MEDEA

No!

JASON

Sure?

MEDEA

I told you: No!

JASON

I must, however, tell you:
You would do well to put all that aside!
Do not brew drugs from herbs, nor potent potions,
Do not address the moon, nor rouse the dead;[4] *180*
They hate that here, and I—I hate it too!
We are no more in Colchis but in Greece,
No more among monstrosities but men!
But I am certain you will no more do this,
You've promised me and you will keep your word.
The blood-red veil you wear around your head
Recalls to me grim pictures of the past!
Why do you not assume our country's dress?
Just as in Colchis I became a Colchian,
So now in Greece become a Greek like me. *190*
Why must you seek remembrance of the past,
When of itself remembrance still pursues us?

(MEDEA *takes off the veil and hands it to* GORA, *in silence)* [5]

GORA *(In a whisper)*

Will you despise your country for his sake?

JASON *(Seeing* GORA*)*

You here? Woman, I hate you most of all!
The moment that I look upon your brow,
The coasts of Colchis rise before my eyes.
Why must you always hang about my wife?
Be off!

GORA *(Sulkily)*

Why?

JASON

Be off!

[4] Calderon's Medea in *Three Greatest Wonders* claimed to practice necromancy.

[5] Compare *Sappho* (Act III, Scene V), where as ordered by Sappho, Melitta "takes off her wreath in silence."

MEDEA

Please, I beg you, go!

GORA *(Gloomily)*

Am I your slave, that you should speak as master?

JASON

I'm itching for my sword; go, while there's time! 200
I've often had a strong desire to test
Whether your brow's as hard as it appears.

(MEDEA firmly but gently leads away GORA, who resists. JASON has thrown himself down on a grassy seat, striking his breast)

Burst from your cage and with that burst be free!
How pleasantly the towers of Corinth lie
Along the seashore in prosperity—
The cradle of my golden days of youth!
The selfsame towers beneath the selfsame sun;
I only, now, a stranger . . . changed within.
O Gods, why was my morn so beautiful,
When you decree to me so dark an evening? 210
Would it were night!

(MEDEA has brought the children from the tent and leads them to him)

MEDEA

Here are two children
Who wish to greet their father,

(To the BOYS)

Give your hand!
Do you hear? Your hand!

(The CHILDREN stand aside timidly)

JASON

(Stretching his hand in sorrow toward the group)

Such was to be the end!
Of savage boors the father and the husband!

MEDEA *(To the* CHILD*)*

Go!

BOY

Father, are you Greek?

JASON

And why?

BOY

Gora abuses you as Greek.

JASON

Abuses?

BOY

They're treacherous and craven folk.

JASON *(To* MEDEA*)*

You hear?

MEDEA

Gora has made them savage. Pardon him!

(She kneels down by the CHILDREN *and whispers alternately to each)*

JASON

Good! Good!

(He has risen)

She kneels there, the unlucky woman
And struggles with her burden and with mine. 220

(Walking to and fro)

The children, leave them now and come to me.

MEDEA

Go, boys, and mind you're good! Do you hear me?

(The CHILDREN *go)*

JASON

Medea, do not think me hard or cruel!

I feel your pain, believe me, deep as mine.
You, faithful, roll away the heavy stone,[6]
That promptly ever rolls back on itself
And bars to us each entrance and each exit.
Are *you* to blame? Am *I?* It just *happened.*

(Taking one of her hands in his and with the other stroking her brow)

You love me, I am not deceived, Medea—
True, in your fashion—yet you do love me, 230
Not only does that glance speak, but your deeds.

(MEDEA *lays her head on his shoulder)*

I know the many griefs that bow your head,
And in my faithful breast compassion stirs.
Then let us carefully and wisely ponder
How best to banish what so closely threatens.
The town below is Corinth. Long ago,
When I was still a raw, unbearded youth,
Escaping from my uncle's savage rage,
The King of Corinth gave me fast asylum,
Remembering his friendship with my fathers, 240
And treated me as a belovèd son.
With him I lived secure for many a year.
Now too—

MEDEA

You hold your tongue?

JASON

Now too, when blind
With rage the world decries, disdains, deserts me,
Now too I hope asylum from this king.
I fear but one thing, not without good cause.

MEDEA

What's that?

JASON

He will receive me, I am sure,

[6] Like the legendary Sisyphus.

The children also, as they are my children,
You only—

MEDEA

If he takes the boys as yours,
He will accept me also as your wife. *250*

JASON

Have you forgotten how it was at home?
In my own native land, my uncle's house,
When first from Colchis' shores I brought you here?
Forgotten all the scorn with which the Greek
Looks down on the barbarian—down on you?
None of the Greeks knows what you are, as I do;
You're not their wife, nor mother of their children;
Not every Greek, as I, was once in Colchis.

MEDEA

Well, what conclusion comes from this harsh talk?

JASON

It is indeed a man's supreme misfortune *260*
That he, indifferent, faces all in life
Until it happens, and no longer once
It has happened. That we must sure avoid!
Then let me to the king, there claim my right
And counter the suspicion cast on us;
But you, meanwhile, stay with the children, hidden
Far from the town until—

MEDEA

Yes, until when?

JASON

Until—why hide your face?

MEDEA

I know enough.
Just that, my father said to me!
To you a torment I, and you to me—

But I'll not yield! Of all I was and all
That I possessed, one thing alone remains,
And unto death I will remain, your wife.

JASON

O how you misinterpret what I said!

MEDEA

Just prove to me I've misinterpreted! *270e* [7]
The king draws near—speak as your heart commands.

JASON

Then let us face the storm until it breaks us.

*(*GORA *comes out of the tent with the* CHILDREN. MEDEA *stands between the boys and remains, at first, watching in the distance. The* KING *enters with his* DAUGHTER, *accompanied by boys and girls carrying sacrificial vessels.*

KING

Where is the stranger? My heart foreboding says:
It is the man they exiled and expelled—
The guilty one, perhaps. Where is the stranger?

JASON

Here I am and respectful bow to you!
No stranger, true, but all too true, estranged:
One seeking help, a suppliant for asylum;
Expelled from hearth and home and quite thrust out,
I beg for my protector's friendly roof. *280*

[7] Medea's five lines after "I know enough" (V.268) have been omitted in the Vienna and Munich editions. I have followed the Berlin Edition, based on the 1822 edition (published in Grillparzer's lifetime, and where presumably he could have suppressed those lines—found in the manuscript—had he really wanted to). The faint pencil deletion in the manuscript on which Reinhold Backmann, the editor of the standard Vienna Edition, relies, seems insufficient evidence to the contrary of the author's ultimate intention. I have numbered 270e, in order not to be too far out with the standard Vienna Edition numbering.

CREUSA

Indeed it's he! See, Father, it is Jason.

(Taking a step toward him)

JASON *(Seizing her hand)*

Yes, I am he, as, Creusa, you are she,
The very same, suffused with radiant sweetness.
Ah, lead me, gracious, to your father's side,
Who stands apart and sternly looks on me,
Withholding welcome; I do not know whether
Angry with Jason or with Jason's blame.

CREUSA *(Leading* JASON *by the hand to her father)*

See, Father, it is Jason!

KING

Greetings to you!

JASON

Your sternness bids the posture that becomes me.
Here, at your feet, come, let me clasp your knees *290*
And stretch my prayerful arms toward your face:
Pray, grant what I besought, give me asylum!

KING

Stand up!

JASON

Ah, not until—

KING

I'm telling you, stand up!

*(*JASON *stands up)*

So with the Argonauts you have returned?

JASON

It barely is a month since I have landed.

KING

The journey's prize, you brought it back with you?

JASON

Yes, to my uncle, who decreed the voyage.

KING

Then why seek refuge from your father's city?

JASON

It drove me out; I am proscribed and helpless.

KING

Tell me the reason why you were proscribed? *300*

JASON

They have accused me of accursèd dealings!

KING

Rightly or wrongly? Firstly, tell me this.

JASON

Wrongly, my lord. I swear it by the Gods!

KING *(Seizing him quickly by the hand and leading him to the foreground)*

Your uncle died?

JASON

He died.

KING

How?

JASON

Not through me!

As true as I am living, not through me!

KING

And yet that is what everyone is saying.

JASON

All I can say, then, everyone is lying.

KING

Can one compel belief against so many?

JASON

Yes, one you know, against so many strangers.

KING

How did the king die?

JASON

His own flesh and blood, *310*
His children, raised their hands against their father!

KING

Most dreadful! Is it true?

JASON

By the high gods!
But let me tell you how it all befell.[8]

KING

Hush, Creusa's here; breathe not a word near her;
I would not see her wincing at such horrors.

(Aloud)

I know enough for now, the rest, anon.
As long as possible, I'll deem you worthy.

CREUSA *(Approaching)*

You've asked him, Father? Then it was not true?

KING

You may now go to him without demur.

CREUSA

You were the one who doubted, never I!
Deep down within my inmost heart I felt *320a*
It was not true, what they all said of him.
He, who was good, how could he act so ill?
Ah, if you knew how they all spoke of you,
So ill, so basely. I shed tears that men
Could be so evil and so slanderous.
You'd hardly left, there swept through all the land

[8] This line too is omitted in the Vienna and Munich editions.

Wild rumors of most cruel crimes committed.
They said you savaged far and wide in Colchis,
They even whispered there you took to wife
A dreadful, poisoning, patricidal woman. *330*
What was she called? Some barbarous name.

MEDEA *(Coming forward with the* CHILDREN*)*

Medea!

I am she!

KING

Is this she?

JASON *(In a dull voice)*

Yes.

CREUSA *(Clinging to her father)*

Most horrible!

MEDEA *(To* CREUSA*)*

You are misled. I did not kill my father.
My brother fell, but ask him if through me?

(Pointing to JASON*)*

On potions, whether carrying cure or death,
I'm expert, and on other matters too.
Be sure, however, I am not a monster,
No murderess either.

CREUSA

Ah, most dreadful!

KING

And she your wife?

JASON

My wife!

KING

The children there—

JASON

They are my children.

KING

Ah, unhappy man! 340

JASON

Yes, most unhappy. Children, bring your branches,
As offerings to the king, and beg protection.

(Leading them by the hand)

Here they are, sire. Then say you will not spurn them!

BOY *(Offering the branch)*

There, take!

KING *(Laying his hands on their heads)*

Poor little fledglings fallen from the nest!

CREUSA *(Kneeling beside the* CHILDREN*)*

Come here to me, you homeless little orphans!
How early does misfortune weigh you down,
So early and alas, so undeserved!
You look like her—you have your father's features.

(Kisses the younger)

Stay here. I'll mother and I'll sister you!

MEDEA

Why do you moan and dare to call them orphans? 350
Here stands their father, who has called them his;
And there's no need for any other mother,
So long as I'm alive.

(To the CHILDREN*)*

Come to me, come!

CREUSA *(Looking up at her father)*

Shall I let them go?

KING

She is their mother.

CREUSA *(To the* CHILDREN*)*

Go to your mother!

MEDEA

You hesitate? [9]

CREUSA *(To the* CHILDREN, *who have clasped her neck)*

Your mother calls. Do go!

(The CHILDREN *go)*

JASON

Then what have you decided?

KING

I have told you.

JASON

You grant me shelter?

KING

Yes.

JASON

Me and my family?

KING

I've promised it *to you*—so follow me!
First to the sacrifice, then to the palace.

JASON *(Turning to go; to* CREUSA*)*

Creusa, will you shake hands as once you did? *360*

CREUSA

You cannot hold it now as once you did.

MEDEA

They go and leave me all alone. Come, children,
Come here to me, embrace me, closer! Closer!

CREUSA *(Turning round and speaking to herself)*

She does not come. Why won't she follow us?

(Returns, but stays at some distance from MEDEA*)*

You'll not come to the sacrifice and palace?

[9] A subtle advance preparation for their rejection of their mother at the end of Act III.

MEDEA

The door is shut upon the uninvited!

CREUSA

My father offered you his hand and roof.

MEDEA

Quite otherwise it sounded, what I heard.

CREUSA *(Coming nearer)*

I have offended you, I know. Forgive me!

MEDEA *(Quickly turning to her)*

How sweet the sound! Who spoke that gentle word? *370*
They often have offended me, mostly deeply;
But no one stayed to ask if I were hurt!
My thanks; and if your heart is ever sore like mine,
May some good soul give you as you've given me
A kindly answer and a gentle glance!

(She would take CREUSA*'s hand, but* CREUSA *withdraws shyly)*

Oh, do not wince! My hand will not defile you!
I was, like you, born daughter of a king,
Like you, I went upon my even way,
Grasping the right thing blindly at first go.
I was, like you, born daughter of a king, *380*
As you stand now, so lovely, bright and radiant,
So also once I stood beside my father,
His idol and the idol of my people.
O Colchis, my belovèd fatherland,
They call you dark. To me you're heaven-bright!

CREUSA *(Taking her hand)*

Poor lady!

MEDEA

You look gentle, kind and good,
And doubtless are. But, please, ah please take care!
The way is slippery, one false step's enough!
Because you've gently floated down the stream,
Along the bank, from flowering branch to branch, *390*

Your boat tossed lightly by the silver waves,
You think you have become a master helmsman?
There, there beyond, the mighty ocean roars,
And if you dare to venture from the shore
The gray wastes of the waves will swallow you.
You stare at me? And shudder now at me?
There was a time I would myself have shuddered,
Had I conceived a creature now like me!

(She hides her face on CREUSA*'s neck)*

CREUSA

She is not savage. Father, see, she's weeping.

MEDEA

Because I'm foreign, from a far-off land 400
And unfamiliar with the manners here,
They all despise me and look down on me
And think I am a wild and barbarous woman,
The lowest and the last of all mankind,
I, who was first in my dear fatherland.
I'll gladly do what you will tell me to;
Only tell me instead of scolding me!
You are, I see, of gentle, winsome ways,
So self-secure, so much at one with self.
To me the Gods denied that happiness, 410
But I will learn from you most willingly.
You know what pleases him, what gives him joy.
O teach me how to please my husband Jason;
I will be grateful to you.

CREUSA

Father, see!

KING

Take her with you.

CREUSA

Medea, come with me.

MEDEA

I shall go willingly where you may lead,

Take me, forlorn, forsaken as I am,
And guard me from that man's unfriendly gaze!

(To the KING*)*

Keep staring at me, you'll not frighten me,
Although I see you're hatching what's not good. *420*
Your child is better than her father.

CREUSA

Come,
He wants your good. You, little ones, come too!

(Leads MEDEA *and her* CHILDREN *away)*

KING

Have you not heard?

JASON

I have.

KING

And she your wife?
We had already heard of it by rumor,
But I could not believe it and still less
Almost, now that I've seen! She—Jason's wife!

JASON

You see the end alone and not the reasons;
Yet only knowing these can you judge right.
I wandered there, in the full bloom of youth,
Through alien seas, to dare the boldest deed *430*
That e'er was done since man has walked the earth.
I had despaired of life and of the world
With nothing left except that glittering Fleece,
That, like a star, shone through the stormy night.
None thought of our returning home; all strove
As though the moment when we won the prize
Would be the final moment of our lives.
And so we wandered, comrades steeled to struggle,
In wantonness of daring and of doing,
Through sea and land, through storm and night and crags, *440*

With death before us and behind us death.
What might have else repelled seemed sweet, attractive,
For Nature there was harsher than the harshest.
In strife with her and savages we met,
The soft heart of the gentlest would turn hard;
The standards of all conduct were forgotten
Of what he saw, each made himself the standard.
What seemed impossible to all took place.
We saw the strange and marveled land of Colchis.
Ah, could you have beheld her misty shores! *450*
The day is night there and the night—sheer terror—
Her men indeed more dreadful than the night.
There I found her who seems so grim to you;
I tell you she appeared like radiant sunshine
That falls into a dungeon through the chink.
If here she's dark, there she seemed light itself,
In contrast with her sinister surroundings.

KING

Never can wrong be right, bad nowhere good.

JASON

Some god above inclined her heart to me;
Through many dangers she stood fast beside me. *460*
I saw her agitated with desire
Which stubbornly she, bridled, kept from me.
Her deeds alone, her words would tell me nothing.
Then madness also whirled within my senses;
Her silence all the more excited me;
Thus put to challenge I strove hard with her
And like a high adventure drove my love.
She lost the struggle. And her father cursed her.
Now she was mine had I not even wished.
Through her I won the enigmatic Fleece. *470*
She led me to that horror-haunted cavern,
Where I victorious won it from the dragon.
Since then, each time I gaze into her eyes,
I see within their depths the serpent gleaming[10]

[10] Just as Grillparzer's Jason saw the dragon (his fatal past) in

And shuddering grant her title of my wife.
We sailed away. Her brother fell—

KING *(Quickly)*

Through her?

JASON

At the hands of the Gods! Her aging father,
Still cursing her and me and all our future,
With bloody nails fell digging his own grave
And died, they say, in raging suicide. *480*

KING

You entered wedlock inauspiciously.

JASON

Ah, even worse was still to follow.

KING

What happened to your uncle? Tell me this.

JASON

Four years a god delayed our slow return,
Driving us crisscross over sea and land,
Cramped in the ship, in close, continuous contact.
My pristine prick of horror was extinguished;
The past was past . . . and she became my wife.

KING

And now at home, in Iolcos, at your uncle's?

JASON

Time blotted out what seemed abominable, *490*
And half barbarian, at her barbarous side,

Medea's eyes, so Heredia's Antony, in the sonnet *Antoine et Cléopâtre,* at the end of the century, was to see his fatal future—the naval disaster at Actium in the eyes of Cleopatra:

> Saw deep within her gold-flecked, starry eyes
> A boundless sea, where fleeing galleys sped.

Jason here identifies with the serpent, the sinister in his and Medea's love, just as Medea had already identified it at its inception in Colchis. (See *The Argonauts,* Act IV, Vs. 1541–45.)

I proudly strode into my native town;
And, mindful of the people's deafening cheers
At my departure, looked for warmer welcome
On home returning as a conquering hero.
But all the streets were silent when I came,
And furtive slipped away the passer-by.
Rumor had whispered in the timid ears
Of my co-citizens all that had happened,
With added horrors, in that dismal land. 500
They fled from me and spat upon my wife—
Mine, mine she was, and *me* they spurned in her!
My uncle cunningly incited them
And, as I asked for my inheritance
That he perversely still withheld from me,
He ordered me to send away my wife,
Whose dark ways, so he said, he found repulsive,
Or else to leave his land, my fathers' land.

KING

And you?

JASON

I? Was she not my wife?
On my protection she had thrown herself, 510
And he, who would pursue her, was my foe.
By the just gods! Even a fair demand
He would not have obtained, then much less this.
I turned it down.

KING

And he?

JASON

Proscribed us both!
I had to leave Iolcos the very day.
But I refused and stayed.
Then suddenly the king took ill. And rumor
Ran through the town with many a strange report:
How he at home sat brooding by the altar
Where hung aloft the dedicated Fleece, 520
Gazing at it with vacant, rolling eyes.

He screamed, his brother stared at him accusing—
My father, whom he wickedly had murdered,
Contending if the Argonauts should sail—
He stared, he screamed, from out the golden glitter
He sent me off to win, the wicked man,
High hoping I would die in the attempt.
And now, pressed by the royal need, his daughters,
My royal cousins, came to me in tears
Beseeching healing from Medea's art. *530*
But I said: No! Was I to save the man
Who'd sought to ruin me and all my kin?
On this, the maidens went away in tears,
But I shut myself in, and did not care;
And though they came repeatedly beseeching,
I held to my resolve and to my "no!"
Thereafter, when that night I lay asleep,
I heard a sudden uproar at my gates;
It was Acastus, son of my bad uncle,
Storming my gate with a rampaging mob, *540*
Calling me murderer, murderer of his father,[11]
Who had just died upon that very night.
I rose and tried to speak, but all in vain.
The raving people drowned my every word
And now began to force their way with stones.
I took my sword and cut my way through them.
Since then I wander through the towns of Greece,
To men a horror, to myself a torment,
And, if you do not take me, quite abandoned.

KING

I've promised you and I will keep my word. *550*
But she—

JASON

Before you finish, hear me first!
Receive us both, my lord, or none receive!
Fresh lease of life I'd have were she away,
But what has been entrusted I protect.

[11] As in Corneille's *Médée* (Act I, Scene I).

KING

The arts she practises, they frighten me;
The power to harm is kindred to the wish,
And she to guile and guilt is not a stranger.

JASON

If she disturbs the peace, then drive her out,
Pursue her, kill her, kill me, kill us all;
But till that happens, grant her just a chance 560
To show that she is fit to dwell with men.
I beg of you, by Zeus, who shields the stranger,
And by the laws of hospitality
That long, long since our ancestors enjoined,
In Corinth and in Iolcos, wise forseeing
Such turns of fortune in some future time.
Pray grant it me, lest, in like misery,
Your own some day may like refusal find.

KING

I bow before the Gods, against my instinct.
Let her remain! But should a single sign 570
Betray her former wildness has returned,
I will without compunction drive her out,
And give her up to those pursuing her.

But here, where for the first time I beheld you,
Come, let a holy altar be erected,
Sacred to Zeus, the guardian God of strangers,
And to your uncle Pelias' bloody shade.
There let us jointly beg the gracious Gods
To bless your entrance once more in my house,
And turn away all evil from our threshold. 580
Come now with me into my royal palace;

(To his followers who now approach)

While you perform what I have just ordained.

(They are about to move off)

Curtain

ACT II

Hall in CREON'*s palace in Corinth.* CREUSA *sitting,* MEDEA *on a low footstool in front of her, with a lyre in her arms; she is dressed in the Greek style.*

CREUSA

Take hold of this string, and of this, like this.

MEDEA

Like this?

CREUSA

No. Keep the fingers more relaxed.

MEDEA

I cannot.

CREUSA

If you put your mind to it.

MEDEA

I put my mind to it but cannot do it.

(She puts aside the lyre and rises)

My hand is only used to javelin-throwing
And the relentless business of the hunt.

(Raising her right hand close before her eyes)

These fingers, I should like to punish them!

CREUSA

How droll you are! I should have greatly liked

To see you giving Jason a surprise
With your song.

MEDEA

Yes, indeed. You are quite right.
I was forgetting. Let us try once more!
You fancy it would please him, really please him?

CREUSA

Of course. He used to sing the song in boyhood,
When he was here and used to live with us.
Each time I heard it, I would spring up happy,
For it meant always he was coming home.

MEDEA

What was the song?

CREUSA

Well, I shall sing it to you.
It is quite short and really not so sweet, *600*
Only he used to sing it with such charm,
So saucily, defiant, almost mocking.

O ye gods,
Ye high gods!
Anoint my head,
Puff out my chest
That I might conquer
Not only men,
But also
Lovely lasses. *610*

MEDEA

Yes, yes, they have accorded it!

CREUSA

What's that?

MEDEA

The content of the little song.

CREUSA

What content?

MEDEA

That he should conquer men
And also lovely lasses.

CREUSA

How strange! I never thought of that before.
I only sang it as I heard him sing.

MEDEA

Thus he stood on the foreign shores of Colchis,
Men falling fast beneath his fatal glance;
And with the same glance threw his fiery brand
Into my wretched breast that sought escape, *620*
Till, smothered long, the flames consuming rose
And fortune, peace, contentment, crackling fell,
Enveloped in the smoke and fiery glow.
Thus he stood, shining in his strength and beauty,
A hero, god, enticing me, enticing,
Till he seduced his victim and destroyed her,
Then cast her off and no one raised her up.

CREUSA

Are you his wife, who speaks so ill of him?

MEDEA

You do not know him, but I know too well!
In all the wide world only he exists, *630*
The rest to him are but his exploits' field.
Quite selfish, less of matter than of mind,
He juggles with his own and others' fate:
If glory beckons, why, he strikes one dead;
If it's a wife he wants, why then, he takes her;
He does but right, yet right is what he wills.
The cost to others irks him not at all!
You do not know him, but I know too well!
And when I call to mind what has befallen,
I think I laughingly could see him die. *640*

CREUSA

Good-bye!

MEDEA

You're going?

CREUSA

Must I hear you longer?
Great gods! Is this how wife should speak of husband?

MEDEA

According as he is; mine acted so!

CREUSA

By the high heavens, if I had a husband,
As mean and wicked as yours never is,
And children whom he gave me as his likeness,
I'd love them all were they to murder me.

MEDEA

That's lightly preached but very hard to practice.

CREUSA

It were less sweet were it easier to practice.
Yet do as you think best, I must go now. *650*
First you beguile me with your gracious words,
Begging me teach you how best you may please him,
And now you vent your hate and scorn against him.
I have observed much that is bad in men,
The worst's a hard and unforgiving heart.
Good-bye, and try to be more kind.

MEDEA

You're angry?

CREUSA

Almost.

MEDEA

Ah, do not, you *too,* cast me off!
Do not desert me, be my shade and shield!

CREUSA

Now you are gentle, yet were full of hate!

MEDEA

The hate for me, for Jason only love! *660*

CREUSA

Then you do love him?

MEDEA

Would I else be here?

CREUSA

The more I think the less I understand.
But since you love him, I'll be kind again
And will impart to you the surest means
To scatter, like the clouds, those brooding humors
I know so well he has. Let us to work!
I saw this morning he was sad and sullen,
Yet sing to him your song and you shall see
How soon he will be merry. Here's the lyre!
I will not let you stop until you know it. *670*

(She sits)

What, still not coming? Must you hesitate?

MEDEA

I gaze at you and must keep gazing still,
And hardly can I take my eyes off you,
Your face as good and beauteous as your soul,
Your heart as bright and girlish as your clothes!
Like some white dove you hover high above us,
With wings outspread, high over this our life,
Your every feather free from all the slime
In which we sink and wallow in our strife.
O cast a ray from your celestial brightness *680*
Into my sore and agonizing breast.
All spite and hate and sorrow, written there,
Blot right out with your hand of innocence,
Replacing them with your clean characters!
The strength, that was my pride from earliest childhood,
Has shown itself as weakness in my struggle:
Oh, teach to me the strength that springs from weakness.

(She sits on the stool at CREUSA'*s feet)*

Here will I wind myself about your feet,
Complaining to you what they've done to me,
And learn what I should not do and what do. 690
I'll follow you, obedient as a handmaid,
And early at the loom begin to weave,
And do all tasks that we despise at home,[12]
Leaving to slaves and to the common herd,
But which the mistress here herself performs,
Forgetting that my sire was King of Colchis,
Forgetting that my ancestors were gods,[13]
Forgetting what has happened and what threatens—

(Starting up and going apart)

No, that I can't forget.

CREUSA *(Following her)*

Why, what's the matter?
Men soon forget, the gods themselves forget 700
The evil that was done in earlier times.

MEDEA *(On her neck)*

You think so? Oh, if I could but believe this!

(Enter JASON*)*

CREUSA *(Turning toward him)*

Here is your husband. Jason, see, we're friends.

JASON

Indeed.

MEDEA

My greetings![14] She is very good.
She wants to be Medea's friend and teacher.

[12] Adversity has matured Medea and curbed the contempt for menial tasks she evinced to Peritta in *The Guest* (Vs. 68–75).

[13] Aeetes, in the legend, was descended from Helios, the sun god.

[14] Medea, thinking to please Jason, salutes him on his entry in the Greek manner.

JASON

Good luck to the attempt!

CREUSA

Why are you gloomy?
Here let us live together happily!
Between my father and the two of you
Dividing my attentions; you and she—

JASON

Medea!

MEDEA

What are your commands, my husband? *710*

JASON

Seen to the children?

MEDEA

I've just seen to them.
They're very merry.

JASON

Go and see once more.

MEDEA

I was with them but now.

JASON

Go, see, I say.

MEDEA

If you insist.

JASON

I wish it.

MEDEA

Well, I'm going.

(Exit)

CREUSA

Why have you sent her off? They are quite happy.

JASON

Ah, now I feel at ease and now can breathe!
My inmost heart constricts at sight of her,
And hidden torments almost throttle me.

CREUSA

What am I hearing? O you righteous gods!
So he speaks now and so spoke she before. 720
Who told me married couples always loved?

JASON

They do! When, after years of well-spent boyhood,
A young man casts his eye upon a maiden
And makes of her the goddess of his dreams,
He searches out her glance that it might meet his,
And when it does he's happy as a king.
He goes then to her father and her mother
To seek her hand and they give their consent.
Then there's a feast and the relations come
And the whole town shares in the celebration. 730
Richly adorned with wreaths and scented flowers,
He leads his bride to temple and to altar.
Blushing and trembling with a gracious awe
At what she yet desires, she moves on.
Her father lays his hands upon her head
And blesses her and children yet to come.
A bridal pair, thus wed, do love each other.
This was to be my lot. It failed to happen!
Just gods! What have I done that you should take
From me what you bestow upon the meanest: 740
A refuge from the world at his own hearth
And in his wife his heart's companion.

CREUSA

You did not woo your wife as others woo?
Her father did not raise his hand in blessing?

JASON

He raised his hand, but with a sword in it,
In place of blessing he bestowed his curse.

However, I have richly paid him back;
His son is dead, himself he's dumb and dead,
His curse alone lives—so it seems at least!

CREUSA

How much a few years' passing changes one! *750*
How gentle you were once and now how harsh!
However, I am as I was before;
What formerly I wanted, I still want,
What then seemed good to me still seems the same,
What then blameworthy, still today I blame.
With you it's otherwise.

JASON

Oh yes, that too!
It is misfortune's ultimate misfortune,
That man can seldom face it undefiled.
Here he must lead, and there, must bow and scrape,
Here take an inch, and there, must take an ell,[15] *760*
And near his journey's end he finds himself
A stranger to him who began the course;
And with the loss of all the world's esteem,
He lacks his single solace, self-esteem.
I have done nothing wicked in itself,
Yet much have willed, sought, wanted and aspired to;
Connived at it while others did the deed;
Not wanting evil, profited by it,
Forgetting still that evil breeds itself.
And now I stand, a sea of misery raging *770*
Around me, and I cannot say: "I have
Not done it." Youth! Why do you not endure
Forever? Fond illusion, blest oblivion,
The moment when one's striving's born and buried!
Ah, how I splashed in high adventure's stream,
My strong breast parting the tempestuous waves!
But manhood comes in all its seriousness,
And dreaming flees. Now stark reality

[15] To maintain the dramatic conciseness of the original, this somewhat free version has been adopted.

Glides softly in and sits with care abrooding.
The present, then, no longer is a fruit tree, 780
Beneath whose shade one may enjoy repose;
It is a seed grain, indestructible,
One buries it and lo, a future sprouts!
What will you do? Where will you be and dwell?
What will become of you? Of wife and children?
That hits us close and keeps tormenting us.

(He sits down)

CREUSA

Why are you worrying? It has been arranged.

JASON

Arranged? Ah yes, just as one, on the threshold,
Extends a bowl of leavings to a beggar.
Is Jason then to need another's care? 790
Must I set feet beneath a stranger's table,
Beg pity with my children from a stranger?
My father was a prince and I am one,
And who is he that can compare with Jason?
And yet—

(He stands up)

I came along the noisy market
And through your city's broadest thoroughfares—
Do you recall how I triumphant strode
Through them, when I came here to take my leave,
The leader of the band of Argonauts?
Then wave on happy wave of thickly thronged 800
Men, chariots, horses, all pressed eager forward;
Spectators on the roofs and on the towers;
Men fought for space as though they sought for treasure,
The air resounded with the clash of cymbals
And with the shouting masses crying "Hail";
They pressed thick all around the noble host,
That, rich adorned in bright, resplendent armor,
The least of them a monarch and a hero,
Surrounded reverently their noble leader;

And it was I who led them, I, their shield, *810*
I, whom the people hailed with shouts of joy—
And now, when I came through those very streets,
No glance, no sign, no word saluted me!
But as I stood and sadly gazed around,
One said: *"It is the height of boorishness*
To stand thus on the road and trouble others."

CREUSA

You will rise up again if you should wish.

JASON

For me all's over. I shall rise no more.

CREUSA

I know the means to make you rise again.

JASON

The means I know myself; could you procure them? *820*
Ordain, I never left my fatherland,
That I remained with you in Corinth here,
That I had never seen the Fleece nor Colchis,
That I had never seen her, now my wife.
Ordain that she return to her accursèd land
And take with her the memory of her there,
Then I will once more be a man midst men.

CREUSA

Is that the only means? I know another:
A heart that's simple and a mind serene.

JASON

If only you could teach me that, dear girl! *830*

CREUSA

The gods grant it to anyone who seeks.
You also had it once and can again.

JASON

Do you still sometimes think of our young days?

CREUSA

Often, and I remember them with pleasure.

JASON

How you and I were one heart and one soul.

CREUSA

I made you gentler and you made me bold.
Remember how I put your helmet on?

JASON

It was too broad; you held it, slightly stooping,
Your little hands upon your golden curls.
Creusa, it was a happy time! *840*

CREUSA

And how delighted Father was at it.
Indeed, he jesting called us bride and bridegroom.

JASON

It did not turn out so.

CREUSA

How much turns out
Quite different from one thinks. Well, never mind!
We will not therefore any less be friends! [16]

(Reenter MEDEA*)*

MEDEA

The children have been cared for.

JASON

Well, that's good.

(Continuing)

The sacred places of our golden youth,
Knitted to memory with silken threads,
All sprang to mind upon arrival here,

[16] Variant for "friends" in Vienna and Munich editions "merry" (*fröhlich*). Another difference in reading with Berlin Edition in V.849.

And I have cooling dipped my breast and lips 850
In the fresh springs of our bright childhood days.
I visited the market where I drove
The chariot-horses dashing to their goal,
Exchanging blow on blow with my opponent,
While you looked on in terror and in anger,
For my sake, foe to all opposing me.
I visited the temple where we knelt
As one, but here forgetting each the other,
And murmuring our prayers unto the Gods,
One heart, one soul, within our double breast. 860

CREUSA

I see you clearly still remember all.

JASON

I take refreshment from it with deep draughts.

MEDEA *(Who has quietly withdrawn and taken up the lyre)*

Jason, I know a song.

JASON

And then the tower!
You know the tower that stands upon the shore,
Where, with your father, you looked out and wept
When I set sail upon my distant voyage?
I had no eye at that time for your tears,
My heart then thirsted only for great deeds.
A puff of wind blew off your pretty veil
And cast it in the sea. I leapt for it 870
And bore it off in memory of you.

CREUSA

Do you have it still?

JASON

Just think how many years
Have passed since then, taking your pledge with them;
With the wind it passed away.

MEDEA

I know a song.

JASON

You called out to me then: Farewell, my brother!

CREUSA

And now I say to you: My brother, hail!

MEDEA

Jason, I know a song.

CREUSA

She knows a song
That you once sang. Listen, she'll sing it to you.

JASON

Indeed! Where was I? All that cleaves to me
From my young days, making a mock of me, *880*
That I should gladly dream and chatter so
Of things that are no more and will not be;
For just as youth lives only in the future,
A man of ripe years lives but in the past;
Neither knows how to live well in the present.
I saw myself a hero rich in exploits
And had a pretty wife and pomp and power
And some place where my children slept secure.

(To MEDEA*)*

What do you want?

CREUSA

To sing a song to you,
Which in your youth you used to sing to us. *890*

JASON

And you will sing it?

MEDEA

As best I can.

JASON

Indeed!
Will you give back to me my youth and all

Its happiness with one poor youthful song?
Enough of that, I say. We'll hold together,
Because it happened thus and turns out so.
But leave aside such songs and foolish things.

CREUSA

Do let her sing it! She has taken pains
To learn it and you now—

JASON

Then sing it, sing!

CREUSA

The second string, remember?

MEDEA *(Stroking her forehead in distress)*

All forgotten!

JASON

You see, I told you so, it is no use! 900
Her hand is used to other kinds of play;
She sang the dragon magically to sleep
With music different from your innocent song.

CREUSA *(Whispering to* MEDEA*)*

O ye gods,
Ye high gods—

MEDEA *(Repeating)*

O ye gods,
Ye high, just, severe gods!

(The lyre falls from her hand. She hides her eyes in her hands)

CREUSA

She's weeping. Oh, how can you be so harsh and savage?

JASON *(Detaining her)*

Leave her, child, you do not understand us.
It is the gods' high hand she is now feeling; 910
Even here it strikes, even here, with bloody grip.
Then do not meddle in the gods' high justice.
Had you but seen her in the dragon's den,

How she rose raging, rivaling the monster,
How from her tongue the poisonous arrows darted
And hate and death blazed from her flaming eyes,[17]
Your bosom would be steeled against her tears.
You take the lyre and sing to me the song
And quell the demon that is choking me!
Perhaps you can, where she cannot.

CREUSA

Most gladly! *920*

(About to take up the lyre)

MEDEA *(Seizing her wrist and restraining her)*

Stop!

(Picks up the lyre with the other hand)

CREUSA

Certainly, you play it yourself.

MEDEA

No.

JASON

You will not give it her?

MEDEA

No.

JASON

Nor me?

MEDEA

No!

JASON *(Stepping up and attempting to seize the lyre)*

But I will take it.

[17] Jason, presumably, is referring to Vs. 1537–52 in Act IV of *The Argonauts,* but, unjust as usual, he represents as "hate and death" what in fact was the outpouring of Medea's fatal love for him.

MEDEA *(Without moving draws back the lyre)*

Useless!

JASON *(Pursuing her hand with his)*

Give it me!

MEDEA *(In withdrawing it, snapping the lyre, which breaks with a crash)*

Here!

In two!

(Throwing the broken lyre in front of CREUSA*)*

In two, the beautiful lyre! [18]

CREUSA *(Withdrawing in terror)*

Dead!

MEDEA *(Looking quickly round)*

Who? *I* live—*live!*

(She stands up to her full height, gazing straight ahead. A blast of trumpets without)

JASON

Ha! What is that? Why do you stand there gloating?
You will, I swear to you, yet rue this moment.

(Another blast of trumpets. The KING *enters quickly through the door.* JASON *approaches him)*

What does this military peal portend?

KING

Unhappy man, you ask?

JASON

I ask, my lord.

KING

The stroke I apprehended has now fallen. *930*
A herald stands outside my palace gates,

[18] Symbolic of Creusa's destruction.

Sent hither from the seat of the Amphictyonies:
He calls for you and for your lady here,
Your ban proclaiming to the air of heaven!

JASON

This too!

KING

So it would seem—but hush, he's here.

(The gates open. A HERALD *enters, followed by two hornblowers. Further back, a larger following)*

HERALD

The Gods and their protection on this house!

KING *(Solemnly)*

Who are you? What is it you want with me?

HERALD

I am the herald of the Gods, dispatched
From the ancient, sacred seat of the Amphictyonies,
That speaks in Delphi's celebrated city. *940*
A sentence of revenge and ban I utter
Against King Pelias' guilty relatives,
Who once in Iolcos reigned but is now dead.

KING

If you the guilty seek, do not seek here,
In his own house, among his children seek them!

HERALD

I found them here and so I speak to them.
Curse on you, Jason! Curse on your wife and you!
You are accused of the accursèd arts,
The guilt of Pelias' mysterious death.

JASON

You lie. I do not know how the king died. *950*

HERALD

Ask her, she probably can tell us more.

JASON

Did she do it?

HERALD

Not through her hands, through arts well known to you,
That you brought hither from her foreign land.
For when the king took ill—already victim,
Perhaps, so strange were his disease's symptoms—
His anxious daughters sought Medea out [19]
And begged her heal their father with her knowledge.
She fell in with their wish and went with them.

JASON

Enough! She did not go. I stopped it and she stayed.

HERALD

The first time, yes. But when the girls again, *960*
Unknown to you, saw her a second time,
She went with them, seeking the Golden Fleece—
Saying it was to her disaster's emblem—
As her reward for her sure medicine.
To this the maidens joyfully agreed
And she went in where the king lay asleep.
She kept on muttering mysterious words,
The king fell into an ever-deeper sleep.
To let bad blood, she told the lord-in-waiting
To slit his veins, and that was also done. *970*
He breathed more easily as he was bandaged.
His daughters thought he was already cured.
Medea then departed, as she said.
His daughters also left while he lay sleeping.
Sudden a cry resounded from his chamber,
The maidens hurry in and—dreadful! horrible!
The old man on the floor in wild distortions,
The bandages around his veins all burst,
In blackish spurts his lifeblood ebbing, ebbing!
By the altar he lay, where the Fleece had hung. *980*
The Fleece had vanished. But she—there—was seen,

[19] As in Ovid's *Metamorphoses* (VII).

Bearing the golden emblem on her shoulders,
At that same moment striding through the night.[20]

MEDEA *(Dully to herself)*

It was my wage.
I shudder when I think of the old man's raving.

HERALD

So that such horrors might no longer be,
Nor poison our fair land with their foul breath,
I here pronounce the high proscription
Of Jason, Aeson's son, the Thessalian,
The consort of a curse, himself accursed, *990*
And drive him out, by virtue of my office,
Out from the god-frequented land of Greece,
And sentence him to exile and to wandering;
With him, his wife, and progeny of their bed.
No portion in his country's soil for him,
No portion for him in his country's Gods,
No portion in the law and haven of Greece!

(Pointing to the four directions)

Proscribed Jason and Medea!
Medea and Jason proscribed!
Proscribed! *1000*
Jason and Medea!
Whoever harbors him or still protects
Him, from hereafter three days and three nights,
Him sentence I to death, if individual,
To war, if city, and to war, if king!
Thus runs the judgment of the Amphictyonies,
And so I lawfully proclaim it wide,
So that each man may know to save himself.
The Gods and their protection on this house!

(He turns to go)

[20] While Ovid definitely depicts his Medea as murdering Pelias, Grillparzer's Medea, a much more sympathetic heroine, may well—as she maintains—have been innocent of his death, provoked by the fatal Fleece. (See Vs. 1455–64.)

JASON

O walls, why are you standing? Fall on me *1010*
And spare the king the pains of killing me!

KING

Stay but a moment, herald, and learn this!

(Turning to JASON*)*

You think I rue already what I promised?
Were you my son and I believed you guilty,
I would deliver you to those who seek you.
But you're not guilty and so I protect you,
Remain with us! Who then will dare to touch
The friend of Creon, for whose innocence
He gives his solemn pledge, who then will dare
To touch my chosen friend, my son-in-law?
Yes, herald, son-in-law, my daughter's husband! *1020a*
What was determined once, in former days,
His happy days, I will now execute,
Now when misfortune's waves are raging round him.
You are betrothed. You stay here with your father.
I will explain it to the Amphictyonies.
And who will still accuse whom I acquitted,
Acquitted through his only daughter's hand?
Tell that to those who have dispatched you here
And be dismissed now with the gods' protection!

(Exit the HERALD*)*

But as to her here, whom the desert spewed, *1030*
To your and to all pious people's ruin,
Her, guilty of the crime you are accused of,
I banish her beyond my country's borders,
And death to her if daybreak find her here!
Depart from the good city of my fathers
And purify the air you have defiled! [21]

[21] Compare Racine's Phèdre's dying words:

> And death, snuffing the luster from my eyes,
> Repurifies the sunlight they defiled.

MEDEA

So this is it? My fault and my fault only?
But I maintain to you I have not done it.

KING

You've done enough, since he set eyes on you;
Out with you from my house and from my city! *1040*

MEDEA *(To* JASON*)*

If I must go, well then, you follow me!
Let punishment be common as the guilt!
You know the saying, "None may die alone"?
One house, one body and one ruin, one!
We swore together in the face of death;
Keep to your promise, come!

JASON

You dare to touch me?
Away from me, my life's abomination!
Who've robbed me of my days and happiness;
Whom I abhorred the moment I beheld you—
Only foolishly calling my inner struggle love! *1050*
Away with you to the wilderness, your cradle,
To the blood-stained folk, your kin whom you resemble!
But first return to me what you have taken:
Give Jason back to me, you criminal!

MEDEA

So you want Jason back? Here! Take him, take him!
But who will give Medea back to me?
Was I the one who sought you in your homeland?
Was I the one who stole you from your father?
Was I the one who thrust—yes, thrust love on you?
Was I the one who tore you from your land, *1060*
Delivering you to alien mock and scorn?
Incited you to outrage and to crime?
You call me criminal? Alas, I am one!
What crimes have I committed and for whom?
Let *these* pursue me with their poisonous hate,
Drive me away and kill me, they have cause,

For I am an abhorrent, abject creature,
My own abyss, my own abomination;
The whole world may abjure me, *you* must not!
You not, the sole cause, root of all the horror, you! [22] *1070*
Remember how I clasped you round the knees,
That time you bade me steal the bloody Fleece?
I dared presume I'd rather kill myself,
And you contemptuously commanded: "Take it!"
Remember how I hugged my dying brother,
Who reeled exhausted from your raging blow,
Till to escape from your continuing spite
He tore himself from me and drowned himself?
Remember? Come forth here, do not withdraw!
Do not retreat from me behind her skirts! *1080*

JASON *(Coming forward)*

I hate, but do not fear you.

MEDEA

Then come forth!

(Half aloud)

Remember—do not view me with such scorn! . . .
How you, the day before your uncle's death,
Just when his daughters took their leave of me,
Whom I dismissed forlorn at your behest;
How in my chamber you came unto me
And with your eyes *thus* gazing into mine—
As though you had a secret plan that sought
To conjure up its fellow from my breast—
How you then said: "If they had come to *me* *1090*
To seek a cure for their base father's illness,
I would have made for him a medicine
That would forever cure both *him* and *me!*"
Remember? Look me in the face, you coward!

[22] A splendid example of Grillparzer's flexible versification, achieving his climax with the unobtrusive addition of two syllables. There are echoes of Seneca's *Medea* in this great speech.

JASON

You reprobate! Why do you rave at me,
Making substantial all my shadowy dreams,
Reflecting myself in your own self's glass
And conjuring my very thoughts against me?
I can remember nothing, I say, nothing
Of all your plottings and your practices.
To me your nature from the first was hateful, *1100a*
And I have cursed the very day I saw you,
And pity only held me to your side:
But now at last forever I renounce you
And curse you as the whole world curses you.

MEDEA

Not so, my spouse, my husband!

JASON

Away!

MEDEA

When my old father threatened me
You promised never to desert me. Keep it.

JASON

You have yourself made forfeit of my promise.
I give you up to your own father's curse!

MEDEA

Come, hateful man, come, husband!

JASON

Back, I say! *1110*

MEDEA

Come to my arms, this was the choice you made!

JASON

Get back! See here my sword! I'll murder you,
Give you not way!

MEDEA *(Drawing ever nearer)*

Then kill me, kill me!

CREUSA *(To* JASON*)*

Stop!
Do not harm her! Let her go in peace!

MEDEA

What! You here, still? You white and silver snake? [23]
Hiss no more, do not lick so lovingly,
You have, at last, the husband you desired!
Was it for this, that so caressingly
You wound your silken coils around my neck?
O for a dagger now to make short shrift *1120*
Of you and of your father, righteous king!
For this you sang that lovely lay?
For this you taught me how to dress and play?

(Tearing off her mantle)

Off with the gifts of the accursed! Away!

(To JASON*)*

Behold! Just as I tear apart this mantle
And press one tattered piece upon my breast
And throw the other piece before your feet,
So also I destroy our love, our bond.
Whatever now ensues is due to you,
Who have outraged misfortune's holy head. *1130*
Give me my children and then let me go!

KING

The children here remain.

MEDEA

Not with their mother?

KING

Not with the criminal!

MEDEA *(To* JASON*)*

Do you say so?

[23] Medea herself was similarly dubbed "Snake" both by Phrixus (*The Guest,* V.433), and by her father (*The Argonauts,* V.1359). Also Melitta by Sappho (*Sappho,* Act III, Scene v. V.1122).

JASON

I do!

MEDEA *(Toward the door)*

My children, do you hear?

KING

Get back.

MEDEA

You bid me go alone? Well, let that be!
But I will say to you: Before the evening falls
My children you shall give. Enough for now!
But as for you who stand there, hypocrite,
Smooth gazing down in falsest purity,
I tell you, you shall wring your lily hands *1140*
And envy my lot when compared with yours.

JASON

You dare!

KING

Away!

MEDEA

I go, but will return,
To fetch what's due to me and bring what's due to you.

KING

What, is she still to threaten to our face?
If words cannot—

(To the GUARDS*)*

You teach her what to do! [24]

MEDEA

Hold back, I say! Who dares to touch Medea?

[24] The Vienna and Munich editions, relying on the manuscript, state, "Let your lances speak!" The Berlin edition, which follows the 1822 edition (the only one published in Grillparzer's lifetime), has been adopted, for experience shows that authors make alterations even at the latest proof stage.

Beware the hour of my departure, King,
You have not seen a gloomier, believe me.
Make room! I go! Revenge, I take with me!

(Exit)

KING

And punishment at least shall follow you! *1150*

(To CREUSA*)*

Sweet, do not tremble, we'll protect you from her!

CREUSA

I wonder only if we're doing right;
For if we do but right, who then can harm us?

Curtain

ACT III

Courtyard of CREON'S *castle. In the background the entrance to the King's palace, on the right, along the side walls, a pillared passage leading to* MEDEA'S *abode.*

MEDEA *standing in the foreground,* GORA *further back, speaking to a* SERVANT *of the King.*

GORA

Go back and tell your king
Medea accepts no messages from slaves.
If he has anything to ask of her,
Let him come himself,
Perhaps she would receive him.

(Exit the SERVANT. *Coming forward)*

They think you would depart,
Taming your hate and your revenge. *1160*
The fools!
Or will you? Will you?
I almost think you will;
For you are now no more Medea,
The royal offspring of the King of Colchis,
The cleverer daughter of a clever mother; [25]
Else would you have so long endured
And suffered, till now?

[25] Compare Horace, *Odes,* I:16:
O lovelier daughter of a lovely mother.

MEDEA

Great gods, do you hear? So long endured
And suffered, till now? *1170*

GORA

I counseled you retreat
When you still wished to linger,
Dazzled, ensnared,
When not yet fallen was the blow
That I foresaw and, warning, pointed out;
But now I say: remain!
They shall not laugh at the Colchian princess,
Nor mock at the blood of my kings:
They *shall* yield the children,
The shoots of the felled royal oak, *1180*
Or else die, fall,
In horror, in night! . . .

Where are your implements?
Or what have you decided?

MEDEA

First I intend to have my children—
The rest hereafter.

GORA

Then you will go?

MEDEA

I do not know.

GORA

They will all laugh at you.

MEDEA

Laugh? Ah no!

GORA

What are you meditating?

MEDEA

I'm trying hard to wish, to think of nothing;
Over the silent abyss *1190*
Let night brood!

GORA

And if you were to flee, where?

MEDEA *(In anguish)*

Where? Where?

GORA

There is no place for us in these parts,
The Greeks, they hate you, they will kill you!

MEDEA

Kill me? They kill me? *I* will kill them, *I!*

GORA

Also back in Colchis danger lowers!

MEDEA

O Colchis, Colchis, O my fatherland!

GORA

You have heard no doubt, as was told to you,
That your father died soon after
You fled from Colchis, when your brother fell?
Died? I fancy it was otherwise, *1200*
That he, seizing his grief like a sword,
Raging against himself, took his own life.

MEDEA

Why do you join in league with my enemies
And kill me?

GORA

You know full well;
I told you and I warned you.
Keep the strangers at arm's length, I said,
Above all him, who leads them,
The smooth-tongued hypocrite, the traitor!

MEDEA

The smooth-tongued hypocrite, the traitor!
Did you say that?

GORA

I did indeed!

MEDEA

And I did not believe you? *1210*

GORA

You did not and you fell in the deathtrap
That now is closing over you.

MEDEA

Smooth-tongued hypocrite! Yes, that's the word!
Had you said this, I would have recognized it:
But enemy you called him, hateful, monstrous;
But he was handsome and kind and I did not hate him.

GORA

So you love him?

MEDEA

I? Him?
I hate him and abhor him,
Like falsehood, treachery,
Like what's most horrible, like myself! [26] *1220*

GORA

Then punish him, strike him!
Avenge your father, your brother,
Our country, our gods,
Our shame, me, you!

MEDEA

First I intend to have my children—
The rest the night still shrouds.

[26] Compare Racine's Phèdre:

I loathe myself much more than you abhor me.
(V. 678)

What do you think of this? If he leads
Her whom I hate
In the solemn bridal procession,
Medea should hurl herself from the rooftops, *1230*
Shivered and shattered at his feet! [27]

GORA

A fine revenge!

MEDEA

Or on the bridal chamber's threshold
She should lie dead in her blood,
With her the children, Jason's children, dead.

GORA

This vengeance falls on you alone, not him.

MEDEA

Would that he did love me,
That I might kill myself to torture him!
Or should I kill her? So false, so pure!

GORA

That's nearer the mark.

MEDEA

Hush! Hush!
Down, whence you came, dark thought, *1240*
Down into silence, down, down into night!

(She muffles herself)

GORA

All the others who accompanied him,
The dastard host of Argonauts,
The all-requiting Gods have struck
Down, avenging, punishing.
All found a shameful death.

[27] It is interesting that the first of the bloody alternatives Grillparzer's Medea contemplates should, like Racine's Phèdre, and unlike Euripides' Medea, be suicide.

He only still escapes—for how long?
Daily I hear, eagerly listening
And greatly refreshing myself, how they fall,
The radiant sons of Greece fall, *1250*
Who returned from ravishing Colchis.
Orpheus[28] was murdered by Thracian women;
Hylas[29] found a watery grave;
Theseus, Peirethous descended
Into Hades' dismal den,
To snatch from the mighty Lord of Shades
His radiant wife Persephone;
But he caught them and holds them imprisoned
In iron chains, in eternal night.[30]

MEDEA *(Quickly drawing her cloak from her face)*

Because they came to snatch the woman, *1260*
Good, good! That *he* did and much more!

GORA

To Hercules, who abandoned his wife,[31]
Enticed by another's love,

[28] Orpheus, the famous singer, and husband of Eurydice, was one of the Argonauts. His murder by Thracian women or Maenads was the subject of Aeschylus' tragedy *Bassarae*.

[29] Hylas, who accompanied the Argonauts as the page of Heracles (Hercules), was dragged into the water at Cios and drowned by the nymphs in love with his beauty.

[30] Theseus, another of the Argonauts, whose father Aegeus was to receive Medea at Athens and wed her, according to another myth (after the end of this tragedy), was the father of Hippolytus and the husband of Phaedra. His descent into Hades is mentioned by both Seneca and Racine.

[31] The death of Hercules by a garment—poisoned with the blood of the centaur Nessus—sent him by his wife Deianira, who had been falsely told by the dying Nessus, slain by Hercules, that his blood was a love charm—is the subject of Sophocles' tragedy *The Trachinian Maidens*. The agonized Hercules was carried dying to his pyre on Mount Oeta. By subtly representing, through Gora, Hercules vindictively murdered by his abandoned wife, instead of, as in Sophocles, the accidental victim of her love, Grillparzer prepares the way for Medea's own wicked revenge in the next act.

She sent in vengeance a garment of linen;
When he put it on, he sank down
In torment and anguish and death-agony,
For she had secretly smeared it
With wicked poison and instant death.
Down he sank and Oeta's wooded slopes
Saw him expire, in flames expire! *1270*

MEDEA

And she herself prepared the garment?
The deadly garment?

GORA

She herself!

MEDEA

She herself!

GORA

For the rough violence of Meleager,[32]
Who slew the boar in Calydon,
Althea killed him, mother killed her son.

MEDEA

Did her husband leave her?

GORA

He killed her brother.

MEDEA

Her husband?

[32] Meleager slew his uncles in the course of a quarrel over the spoils of a boar-hunt. His mother Althea, in revenge, killed her son by burning to ashes a fatal brand which she had previously plucked from the flames and carefully preserved on learning the decree of the Fates that her son would live as long as the brand remained unconsumed. In the legend, Althea committed suicide, but by representing her as living on, Grillparzer prepares his audience for Medea's resolve at the end not to escape by suicide, but to endure and atone.

GORA

Her son!

MEDEA

And after having done it, did she die?

GORA

She lives.

MEDEA

Did that and *lives,* most horrible!
This much I know, this much is clear to me. *1280*
I will not bear injustice go unpunished.
But what's to come I do not, will not know.
He has deserved all, deserved the worst,
But—man is weak,
It were but fair to grant time for repentance!

GORA

Repentance? Ask him yourself if he repents,
For there he comes with hurried steps.

MEDEA

With him the king, my bitter foe,
Who has enticed, seduced him from me.
I will not see him, I could not tame my hate. *1290*

(Goes quickly toward the house)

But if *he* would, if Jason would but see me,
Tell him to come and see me in my chamber;
There I would speak with him, not here,
Beside the man who is my enemy.
They're near. Away!

(Goes into the house)

GORA

She's gone away!
But I must converse with the man
Who's ruined my child, who's forced me

To lay my head on foreign soil
And hide the bitter tears of all my grief
So that no foreign mouth may laugh at them.[33] 1300

(Enter the KING *and* JASON*)*

KING

Why does your lady flee? That will not help.

GORA

Flees, did you say? She left because she hates you.

KING

Call her out.

GORA

She will not come.

KING

Say she must!

GORA

Go in yourself and tell her, if you dare.

KING

Where am I then and *who?* That this old hag
Should in her wildness dare defy me thus?
The maid, in truth, the image of her mistress,
And both the image of their dismal land.
Once more I say, call her!

GORA *(Pointing to* JASON*)*

With him she'll speak.
And let him enter if he has the heart. 1310

JASON

Off, brazen wretch, my bane from the beginning!
And tell her, who resembles you, to come.

[33] Compare Racine's Phèdre:

And masking, with a calm brave front, my fears,
I had to master many a time my tears.
(Act IV, Scene vi, Vs. 1249–50)

GORA

If she resembled me you would not threaten.
But she will yet see clear, then woe to you!

JASON

I will speak with her.

GORA

Enter then.

JASON

I will not!
She must come out, and you go in and tell her!

GORA

Well then, I'll go, so as not to see you longer.
I'll tell her, but she will not come, I know it,
She is too deeply wounded and too proud.

(Goes into the house)

KING

I'll suffer her in Corinth not a day more. *1320*
This one spoke clear what the other darkly brooded.
Such company is all too dangerous!
Even your doubts, I hope, are satisfied.

JASON

Proceed, my lord, in your judicial office!
She can remain no longer at my side,
So let her go; yet light this punishment.
For, true, though I am guilty less than she,
A harder lot, a heavier, weighs me down.
She goes forth to her native wilderness,
And like a filly, freed from all restraint, *1330*
Strains madly back in uncontrollable speed;
But I must dally here in idleness,
Weighed down beneath the mock and scorn of men,
Dull ruminating all the wasted years.[34]

[34] Perhaps the most sickening example of Jason's hypocritical self-pity.

KING

You shall once more arise, believe me, Jason.
Just as a bow that with a quick release
Returns resilient once it speeds the arrow
That bent its back toward the distant target,
So you will tauten once she's far away.

JASON

I feel in me no stir to warrant such a hope. *1340*
I've lost my name, I've lost my fair renown,
I'm only Jason's shadow, not himself.

KING

The world, my son, is less severe than you.
The erring of a man is deemed a crime,
A young man's erring is deemed but an error,
He may retract, make reparation for.
Whatever you, as rash youth, did in Colchis
Will be erased, if now you act the man.

JASON

How happy I, if I could but believe you!

KING

Just let her go away and you shall see. *1350*
Before the judgment seat of the Amphictyonies
I'll go in person and will press your case
And show that it was only she, Medea,
Who perpetrated what you are accused of,
That she's the dark one, she the criminal.
Your ban will be discharged—and if it's not,
Then you shall stand up in your towering strength,
High raising in the air the golden banner,
That you have brought from that most-distant land;
And all the youth of Greece shall stream around you *1360*
Against all adversaries, in their hosts,
Round you the purified, the fresh arisen,
The doughty shield, the Fleece's mighty hero.
You have it still?

JASON

The Fleece?

KING

Of course!

JASON

Not I!

KING

Medea brought it from the house of Pelias?

JASON

Then she has it!

KING

She must surrender it, *must!*
For you it is the pledge of future greatness.
I'll make sure you are once more great and strong,
You, only son of my belovèd friend!
King Creon has great wealth and influence, *1370*
That he will gladly share with his son-in-law.

JASON

Then my inheritance I'll also claim
From the son of my uncle who's withheld it.
I am not poor if I get all my due.

KING

See, our disturber's here. Soon it is over.

(MEDEA comes out of the house with GORA)

MEDEA

What do you want?

KING

The servants, whom I sent,
You sent back to me with ungentle words,
Depending still to hear from me, myself,
What I've ordained and what you are to do.

MEDEA

Then let me hear!

KING

I've nothing fresh to say, *1380*

I but repeat the ban already spoken,
And add you must depart from here today.[35]

MEDEA

And why today?

KING

Because the many threats
You have but now pronounced against my daughter—
Those against me I utterly despise—
The savage temper you have just displayed,
All these proclaim your presence dangerous,
And therefore I insist you go today.

MEDEA

Give me my children and perhaps I shall.

KING

You shall for certain, though the children stay. *1390*

MEDEA

My children stay! But whom am I addressing?
With *him* let me speak, with my husband speak!

KING *(To* JASON*)*

Do not!

MEDEA *(To* JASON*)*

I beg you!

JASON

Well then, let it be!
So that you see I do not fear your words.
Leave us alone, O King, for I will hear her.

[35] A cunning, dramatic stroke, this shortening of Medea's stay, drawing closer the net from which she erupts. In Euripides, on the contrary, Medea prevails upon Creon to grant her an extension.

KING

I go unwillingly. She's crafty, cunning.

(Exit)

MEDEA

He's gone at last! No stranger now disturbs us,
No intervenor between man and wife;
We may speak freely as our hearts command;
And now you tell me what you think?

JASON

You know. *1400*

MEDEA

I know what you would like, not mean, to do.

JASON

The first suffices, for it will decide.

MEDEA

Then I'm to go?

JASON

To go!

MEDEA

Today?

JASON

Today!

MEDEA

You say that and stand calmly facing me?
No shame can lower your eye, nor make your forehead blush?

JASON

I'd have to blush, if I spoke otherwise.

MEDEA

That's fine indeed! And you may still speak thus,
In public, when you wish to make excuses.
But leave this vain show when alone with me!

JASON

To shrink from horrors is to you vain show? *1410*
The world has damned you and the gods have damned you,
And so I give you up to their high judgment;
For it has not, in truth, struck undeserved! [36]

MEDEA

Who is the righteous man with whom I speak?
Is he not Jason? . . . who would be so gentle?
You gentleman! Did you not come to Colchis
And woo with blood the hand of its princess?
You gentleman! Did you not slay my brother,
And fell my father, righteous gentleman?
Are you not casting off the wife you stole? *1420*
You gentleman, you horror, you accursèd! [37]

JASON

You rail. Your words fall jarring on my ears;
You now know what to do and so, farewell!

MEDEA

I do not know yet, stay until I know.
Stay! For I will be calm, as calm as you.
So exile is my portion? And what's yours?
I think the herald held against you too.

JASON

As soon as it is known I'm innocent
Of Pelias' death, the ban will be discharged.

MEDEA

And you'll live happy ever after then? *1430*

JASON

I shall live as befits the unfortunate.

[36] This line is aptly repeated by Medea to Jason at the end of the play (V.2327).

[37] In very different circumstances the frightened Hero similarly upbraids Leander in her terror, in Act III of *The Waves of Sea and Love* (V.1069).

MEDEA

And I?

JASON

You bear the fortune you have drawn yourself.

MEDEA

I drawn myself? You had no part in it?

JASON

No part!

MEDEA

And you did not entreat the death
Of Pelias? . . .

JASON

I did not further it!

MEDEA

And did not tempt me, to see if I'd do it?

JASON

In the first flush of anger much is uttered,
That, on reflection, is never perpetrated.

MEDEA

Once you yourself accused yourself of this.
Now you have found a scapegoat for your guilt. *1440*

JASON

The thought is never punished but the deed.

MEDEA *(Quickly)*

I never did it!

JASON

Who else then?

MEDEA

Not I!
First listen, husband, then you be my judge.

When I came to the door
To fetch the Fleece,
The king lay on his bed;
I heard shrieking; turning to him,
I saw the man leap from his bed
Howling, rearing, turning round and round.
"Do you come, brother," he shrieked, 1450
"To take revenge on me, revenge?
Once more I'll murder you, once more!"
And saying, jumps and seizes me,
In whose hand was the Fleece.
Trembling, I cried
To the gods I know;
I held the Fleece in front, as shield.
Thereupon a mad grin convulsed his features,
Howling, he seized the bandage round his veins
And tore it off, his blood in gushes spurting, 1460
And when I looked around, transfixed with terror,
The king lay at my feet,
Bathed in his very blood,
Cold and dead.

JASON

You tell me this, you infamous enchantress?
Take yourself off from me! Away!
You horrify me! [38] Woe, I ever saw you!

MEDEA

You knew it all along! The very first time
You saw me, you saw me at my arts,
And yet demanded me and fought for me. 1470

JASON

I was a stripling, an audacious fool.
A man rejects what's pleasing to a boy.

[38] Compare Gretchen's famous cry to Faust at the end of Goethe's *Faust,* Part I:

Henry, you horrify me!

MEDEA

O do not scold the golden days of youth!
The head's impetuous, but the heart is good!
O were you what you were, I would be happier!
Take but one pace toward that wondrous time,
When in the verdant freshness of our youth
Our souls met by the flowery banks of Phasis.
How very frank your heart, how very open;
Mine was more overcast and more reserved, *1480*
Yet with your gentle beam you penetrated
And all my darkling senses shone resplendent.
I became yours, you mine. O dearest Jason!
Is it quite gone for you, that wondrous time?
Have all the heavy cares of hearth and home,
Of name and fame, completely killed in you
The lovely blossoms of the tree of youth?
O see! Though I be sunk in misery,
I still think often of our wondrous spring,
And gentle breezes from it warm my spirit! *1490*
If at that time I was most dear, most worthy,
How have I now become repellent, foul?
You knew me fully and yet sought me out;
You took me as I was, then keep me as I am!

JASON

You do not bear in mind all that has since befallen!

MEDEA

It is indeed most dreadful, I admit.
I have done ill to father, ill to brother,
And in my eyes I stand condemned for it;
Let me be punished, gladly I'll atone,
But you may not, not Jason, punish me! *1500*
For what I did was out of love for you.
Come, let us flee, as one, together flee!
Some distant land will harbor us.

JASON

And which?

Where?

MEDEA

Where! [39]

JASON

You keep on raving, scolding me,
I do not rave with you. All's over now.
The gods have laid their curse upon our bond,
As one, engendered but in deeds of horror,
That grew and sought its nourishment in crime.
Let us agree you did not kill the king,
Who witnessed it, who will believe you?

MEDEA

You! *1510*

JASON

And if I did, what influence, power have I?
Then let us yield to Fate and not defy it!
Let each atoning bear his punishment,
In fleeing, you, where you no more may stay,
In staying, I, from where I'd like to flee.

MEDEA

You have not kept the heavier half yourself!

JASON

You think it easy to live as a stranger,
In a stranger's house, at the bounty of a stranger?

MEDEA

If it's so hard, why do you not choose flight?

JASON

Where to and how?

MEDEA

Once you were much less careful, *1520*
When, leaving your own town, you came to Colchis
And marched through far-off lands, seeking vainglorious fame.

[39] In this one word Grillparzer movingly sums up Medea's desolation.

JASON

I am not what I was, my strength is broken
And shriveled lies my courage in my breast.
I must thank you for this; and past remembrance
Weighs down like lead upon my daunted spirit
And I can lift up nor my eyes nor heart.
Also, the boy has since become a man,
And, no more playing childishly with flowers,
He looks for fruit, what's real, permanent. *1530*
I have the children and no place for them;
I must seek wealth for my posterity.
Shall Jason's stock, like some dry, desert weed,
Be trampled in the way by passers-by? [40]
If you have ever loved me, ever prized me,
Prove it by giving back to me, myself,
And granting me a grave on native soil!

MEDEA

And on your native soil a second nuptial bed?
Not true?

JASON

What do you mean?

MEDEA

Have I not heard
How he called you his son and son-in-law? *1540*
Creusa attracts you, that is why you stay?
Is it not true? I have you?

JASON

Never had me,
And neither have me now.

MEDEA

This your atonement?
And must for this Medea go from you?
Did I not stand there, stand there in my tears,

[40] By a fine piece of irony Grillparzer makes Jason himself experience this danger in the last act (Vs. 2300–01).

While you with her once more lived through your youth,
In darling dalliance lingering at each footstep,
Until you dwindled to sweet memory's echo?
But I will not go, never!

JASON

As unjust
And harsh and savage as ever!

MEDEA

As unjust? *1550*
You do not want to wed her? Tell me no!

JASON

I only seek a place to lay my head,
What else may come, I do not know!

MEDEA

I know
And mean to stop it still, with heaven's help.

JASON

You cannot speak more calmly; so farewell!

(Turns to go)

MEDEA

Jason!

JASON *(Turning around)*

What now?

MEDEA

This is perhaps the last time,
The very last time we may see each other.

JASON

Then let us part free from all bitterness.[41]

[41] Compare Grillparzer's later poem "Trennung" ("Separation"), inspired by Marie von Smolenitz, which begins:

Then let us part if we have need to part,
As firm friends still, free from all bitterness.

MEDEA

With love you have seduced me and desert me?

JASON

I must.

MEDEA

My father you have stolen from me *1560*
And steal my husband?

JASON

I am forced to this!

MEDEA

Through you my brother fell, you took him from me,
And desert me?

JASON

As he fell, free from all blame.

MEDEA

My fatherland I left to follow you.

JASON

Your own desire you followed, and not me.
Had you repented, I'd have gladly left you! [42]

MEDEA

The world holds me accursèd for your sake,
And I myself for your sake hate myself,
And you desert me?

JASON

I do not desert you;
A higher judgment cleaves our bonds asunder. *1570*
If you have lost your happiness, where's mine?
Take in exchange my wretchedness for yours!

[42] On two occasions in *The Argonauts,* Medea proved powerless to leave Jason (see Act III, V.1326–27, and Act IV, V.1702–04), as Jason brutally reminds her here.

MEDEA

Jason!

(She falls on her knees)

JASON

What's this, what more d'you want?

MEDEA *(Rising)*

Nothing!

It is all over! Pardon, my forefathers,
O pardon me, proud gods of Colchis,
That I myself have humbled so and you!
I had to try this last prayer. Now I'm yours!

(JASON turns to go)

Jason!

JASON

Don't think you'll soften me!

MEDEA

Don't think I'd want to. Give me my children!

JASON

The children? Never, never!

MEDEA

They are *mine!* *1580*

JASON

They bear their father's name before the world,
And Jason's name shall not adorn barbarians.
Here, in a civilized circle, I shall rear them.

MEDEA

Despised by step-relations. They are mine!

JASON

Beware my pity does not turn to hate!
Be calm, *that* only can relieve your lot.

MEDEA

Well then, I will now set myself to begging!
My husband—no, for that you are no more—
Belovèd—no, for that you never were—
Man—could you be a man and break your word? *1590*
Jason—*pshaw,* for that's a traitor's name!
How must I call you? Cursèd, gentle, good!
Give me my children and then let me go!

JASON

I cannot, I have told you, I cannot!

MEDEA

So hard? You take the husband from his wife,
And still refuse the mother her own child?

JASON

Well then, that you may recognize I'm fair,
One of the boys may go along with you!

MEDEA

One only? Only one?

JASON

Ask not too much,
My duty's near-betrayed now by the little. *1600*

MEDEA

And which one?

JASON

Let them decide themselves, by their own choice!
Whoever wishes, you may take with you.

MEDEA

A thousand thanks, you good and gentle man!
It is a lie indeed to call you traitor.

(Enter the KING*)*

JASON

Approach, O King!

KING

Has all been settled then?

JASON

She's going, and will take one of the boys.

(To one of the KING'*s suite)*

Hasten and bring the children here to us.

KING

What are you doing? Both the boys should stay!

MEDEA

To me what's little seems to you too much?
Fear the just gods, you stony-hearted man! *1610*

KING

To criminals even gods are stony-hearted.

MEDEA

But they perceive what's brought us to the deed.

KING

To evil drives the prick of evil hearts.

MEDEA

Do you discount what else may drive to evil?

KING

I judge myself severely, and so others.

MEDEA

In punishing offenses you commit them.

JASON

I will not let her say I am too harsh.
Therefore I granted her one of the children,
To be his mother's comfort in her sorrow.

(Enter CREUSA *with the* CHILDREN*)*

CREUSA

They told me both the children have been sent for. *1620*

What is intended then and what's to happen?
See how they love me, though just come to me,
As though we had been intimate for years.
My gentle words, to which they're not accustomed,
Won me their love, as their sad fate won mine.

KING

One of the children must go with their mother.

CREUSA

Leave us?

KING

Indeed, it is their father's wish.

(*To* MEDEA, *who is standing sunk in thought)*

The children both are here, now let them choose!

MEDEA

The children! My children! Yes, they are mine!
The only joy I now have in this world. *1630*
O God, whatever wickedness I thought
Obliterate, and leave me both of them!
Then I will go and praise your gracious bounty.
Forgive him—no, not her! . . . Not even him!
Come here, my children, come! Why are you standing
There, nestling at the false breast of my foe?
Oh, if you knew what she has done to me,
You'd arm your tiny hands with murderous weapons,
Contort your tender fingers into claws
And tear her body you are now caressing. *1640*
You dare entice my children? Set them free!

CREUSA

Unhappy woman, I'm not holding them.

MEDEA

Not with your hands, but like their father you
Detain them by your hypocritic glances.
You dare to laugh? I tell you, you shall weep.

CREUSA

Oh, may the Gods destroy me if I laughed!

KING

Do not burst out in spleen, nor anger, woman!
Do what you have to, quietly, or go!

MEDEA

You chide me justly, O my most just king!
But not so kind, it seems to me, as just! *1650*
Or are you also that? Well, both perhaps!
My children, see, they're sending off your mother
Far over land and sea, far, who knows where?
But these dear, good, kindhearted men, your father
And this most just, most righteous, gracious king,
Have granted to her of her children one,
One of the children granted to their mother—
O high gods, do you hear? One, only *one!* . . .
To take with her upon her distant journey.
Whichever one of you loves me the most, *1660*
Let him come to me, for you both may not,
The other must remain here with his father
And with this false man's even falser daughter!
You hear? Why are you wavering?

KING

They're not willing!

MEDEA

That is a lie, you false, unrighteous king!
They want to, but your daughter has enticed them!
Will you not hear? Abominable boys!
Your mother's curse, your father's very image!

JASON

They are not willing.

MEDEA

Let her go away!
The children love me, am I not their mother? *1670*
But she keeps beckoning and enticing them.

CREUSA

I'll step aside, though your suspicion's false.

MEDEA

Now come to me! To me! Adder-brood!

(She steps toward them—they run to CREUSA*)*

They flee me! Flee!

KING

You see, Medea, how
They do not want—and, therefore, you may go!

MEDEA

They do not want? The children not their mother?
It is not true, impossible!
Aeson, my eldest, my darling!
Behold your mother calling, come to me!
I will no more be rough and harsh! *1680*
You shall be my most precious, one possession!
Listen to your mother! Come!—
He turns away! He will not come!
Ungrateful wretch, spit image of his father!
Resembling him in every craven feature
And like him hateful to me;
Keep back, I do not know you!
But you, Absyrtus! Son of my pain,
With the face of the brother I mourn,
Sweet and gentle like him, *1690*
Look, your mother lies here on her knees
Entreating you.
Do not let her plead in vain!
Come to me, my Absyrtus!
Come to your mother . . .
He hesitates! You too will not?
Who will give me a dagger?
A dagger for me and them!

(She leaps up)

JASON

You may but thank yourself, your savage manners
Have turned the children to her gentleness. *1700*
The boys' decision was the gods' pronouncement!
And so depart, but they remain behind.

MEDEA

Children! Listen to me!

JASON

See, they do not listen!

MEDEA

Children!

KING *(To* CREUSA*)*

Take them back to the house.
We must not let them *hate* her, who did bear them!

*(*CREUSA *turns to go with the* CHILDREN*)*

MEDEA

They flee! My children flee from me!

KING *(To* JASON*)*

Come! Useless to complain of what must be!

(Exeunt)

MEDEA

My children! Children!

GORA *(Who has entered)*

Control yourself!
Your foes must not behold their victory!

MEDEA *(Throwing herself on the ground)*

I am defeated, destroyed, trodden to dust! *1710*
They flee me, flee,
My children flee me!

GORA *(Bending over her)*
Do not die! [43]

MEDEA

Let me die!
My children!

Curtain

[43] A gentle touch, proving the "barbarian" Gora to be the sanest, and indeed the humanest character in the trilogy, as further demonstrated by her dignity in the last act.

ACT IV

Courtyard of CREON*'s castle as in the previous act. Twilight.* MEDEA *lies stretched on the steps that lead to her dwelling.*

GORA *(Standing before her)*

Arise, Medea, speak!
Why are you lying dumb, with vacant eyes?
Arise and speak,
Take counsel of our grief!

MEDEA

Children! Children! [44]

GORA

We have to go before night falls. *1720*
The sun has set already,
Prepare yourself for flight!
They'll come, they'll kill us!

MEDEA

Alas, my children!

GORA

Arise, unhappy girl,
And do not kill me with your wail of woe!
Had you but followed, listened to me,

[44] This, carrying on from Medea's cry: "My children!" at the end of Act III, depicts Medea prostrate for hours, as in the prologue of Euripides' play; Grillparzer, however, has skillfully turned Medea's crucial agony, from rejection by Jason to rejection by her children.

We were now home in Colchis,
Alive your kindred and all well.
Arise! What use is it to weep? Arise! *1730*

MEDEA *(Half-raising herself, and kneeling on the steps)*

Thus I knelt, thus I lay,
Thus I stretched out my hands,
Out to my children, and begged
And pleaded: if only one,
One only of my children—
I would have died, had I to lose the other,
But that not even one! Neither came,
They fled from me into my rival's bosom,

(Springing up)

He dared to laugh at it and *she!*

GORA

Alas, the grief, the woe! *1740*

MEDEA

O Gods, is this requital?
I followed as a loving wife her husband;
My father died, but was it *I* who killed him?
My brother fell, but did he fall through *me?*
How I have mourned them, in torment mourned!
How many burning tears I shed [45]
As my libation on their distant graves!
Where there's no measure, that is not requital.

GORA

Your kith abandon you, as you your kindred.

MEDEA

Then I will strike them as the gods struck me! *1750*
Let no crime go unpunished on the earth!
Leave me revenge, just Gods! I'll execute it!

[45] Compare Racine's Phèdre:

I pined, I withered, drowned in burning tears. (V. 690.)

GORA

Think of your welfare, nothing else!

MEDEA

And what has made you then so soft?
You were just snorting rage, and now you whine?

GORA

Pray leave me. When I saw the children flee
From your maternal arms that nourished them,
I recognized in that the gods' own hand;
My heart was broken
And my courage failed. *1760*
I have served and nurtured them,
They were my joy, my happiness,
The pure remains of Colchis, they,
To whom alone I could devote
My whole love for my distant fatherland.
Long have we been estranged, long, you and I!
Once more in them I saw my Colchis,
In them your father and your brother,
Our royal house and *you,*
As once you *were,* not as you *are.* *1770*
I have protected them, nurtured them,
Like the apple of my eye,
And now—

MEDEA

You have their thanks, ingratitude.

GORA

Ah, do not scold the children, they are good!

MEDEA

Good? And flee from their mother?
Good? They are Jason's children!
Like him in feature, in character,
Like him hateful to me.
Had I them here, in the hollow of my hand,
Their life aquiver in my outstretched palm, *1780*

Needing but one snap to annihilate
All that they are and were, that they will be—
See here! . . . They would be now no more!

GORA

Woe to the mother who abhors her children!

MEDEA

What more remains? What more?
If they are left here with their father,
With their faithless shameless father,
What lot is theirs?
Stepchildren will come,
Will spurn them, mock at them *1790*
And at their mother,
The wild woman of Colchis;
While they will either serve as slaves,
Or else frustration, gnawing at their hearts,
Will warp them, a torment to themselves:
If crime is sometimes father of misfortune,
Misfortune far more often fathers crime!
What matters living then?
I would my father had murdered me,
When I was little yet, *1800*
As now had nothing suffered,
Had nothing thought—as now!

GORA

Why are you shuddering? What meditating?

MEDEA

That I must hence, is certain;
But less sure, what else must happen.
When I think of the perfidy I've suffered,
The monstrous crime of which I've been the victim,
My heart flares up in vengeance,
And what's most horrible comes first to mind.
He loves the children, in them sees himself, *1810*
His idol and his inmost being
Reflected in the mirror of their features.

He must not have them, must not!
But *I* will none of them, the hateful breed!

GORA

Come in with me, why linger here?

MEDEA

Then void the entire house—all, all destroyed—
With ruin brooding over barren walls,
Nothing alive but memory and pain!

GORA

Our persecutors soon will come. Let's go!

MEDEA

Did you not say the Argonauts, *1820*
Each one of them, came to a cursèd end,
The penalty of treachery and crime?

GORA

Quite true! And Jason too will end the same.

MEDEA

He shall, I say to you, he shall!
Hylas it was, who found a watery grave,
And Theseus was imprisoned in the Shades;
And that Greek woman, what was her name,
Who, her own blood on her own blood, avenged?
What was her name?

GORA

I know not what you mean.

MEDEA

It was Althea!

GORA

Who struck down her son? *1830*

MEDEA

The very one. Come, tell me all about it.

GORA

Because he killed her brother in the chase.

MEDEA

Her brother only, not her father too?
Had not divorced, disdained, derided her!
And nonetheless she struck him dead,
Her son, the raging Meleager, dead.
Althea was her name, she was a Greek!
When dead he lay? . . .

GORA

Here ends the bloody tale.

MEDEA

It ends! You are quite right; Death makes an end.

GORA

What is the use of words?

MEDEA

You doubt the deed? *1840*
Look, by the high gods! If only he
Had given me *both* children. No, not so!
Could I but take them if he gave me them;
Could I but love them as I now but hate;
Had only something in the world remained
That he had not destroyed for me, not poisoned,
Perhaps I'd go hence, leaving my revenge
To the just gods; but now it cannot be.
They called me wicked when I was not so;
I feel however one may so become. *1850*
Dark deeds of horror rise within my mind,
I shudder—yet take pleasure at the thought! [46]
Now if it's done and over . . .

(In anguish)

Gora!

[46] Compare Hermione in Racine's *Andromaque:*

What pleasure to avenge my wrongs myself,
To draw my arm out dyed in his false blood!
(Act IV, Scene IV, Vs. 1261–62)

GORA

What is it?

MEDEA

Come here.

GORA

Why?

MEDEA

To me!

There lay they, both of them—and the pale bride—
Bleeding—dead—he tears his hair beside her!
Most dreadful, horrible!

GORA

For the gods' sake!

MEDEA

Ha, ha! You're terrified already?
They are but empty words that have escaped me.
My former will now lacks my former strength. *1860*
Yes, were I still Medea, but I'm not!
O Jason, why have you done this to me?
I sheltered you, protected you and loved you.
Whatever I possessed I gave for you.
Why then have you forsaken and forsworn me?
Why do you drive away my nobler self,
Filling my heart with evil thoughts of vengeance?
With thoughts of vengeance without strength to avenge!
The power I inherited from my mother,
From solemn Hecate, Princess of Colchis *1870*
Who bound to me the service of dark gods,
I have interrèd, for your sake interred
In the funereal lap of Mother Earth.
The wand of ebony, the blood-red veil,
Are lying there, while I stand helpless here,
A sport to all my foes, instead of terror!

GORA

Don't speak of this, if you have lost the power.

MEDEA

I know however where it lies.
Out there upon the beach, where beat the waves,
There I have coffin'd it and buried it; *1880*
Throw off a little earth and it is mine!
But deep within my inmost soul I shudder,
When I think on it and the bloody Fleece.
I feel my father and my brother's ghosts
Brood over it and will not let it go.
Do you not know how on the ground he lay,
My gray-haired father, weeping for his son
And cursing me, his daughter? At this, Jason
In hideous triumph, held the Fleece on high;
I then swore vengeance, vengeance on the traitor, *1890*
Who first my kindred killed and now kills me.
Had I my bloody box, I'd execute it,
Only I dare not bring it back;
For were I in the emblem's golden glitter
To see my father's features stare at me,[47]
Believe me, I'd go mad!

GORA

What will you do then?

MEDEA

Let them come,
Let them kill me, I've had enough!
I'll not go hence, but willingly would die.
Perhaps he'll die with me, choked with remorse. *1900*

GORA

The king is here, do take care of yourself!

MEDEA

What can I do else, helpless as I am?
Ah, let him trample on me if he must.

(The KING *enters)*

[47] As Medea depicts Pelias seeing the features of his brother whom he had murdered. (Act II, Vs. 1447–64.)

KING

The evening shadows fall. Your time is up.

MEDEA

I know.

KING

Are you ready to leave?

MEDEA

You're mocking me!
Were I *not* ready, would I leave the less?

KING

I'm glad to find you in so wise a mood.
You thereby take with you less harsh a memory
And you ensure your sons' prosperity.
Now they will be allowed to name their mother. *1910*

MEDEA

Will be allowed? You mean, if they should want to.

KING

That they will want to, you may leave to me.
In the heroic virtues I will train them;
And some day, who knows? . . . their great deeds may
lead them
To distant Colchis, where they'll press their mother,
Grayer no doubt in wisdom as in years,
With filial love upon their filial breasts.

MEDEA

Alas!

KING

Why, what is it?

MEDEA

Ah, but a stab
Of memory, forgetting all that's happened.
Was it to tell me this alone you came here, *1920*
Or are you wanting something more from me?

KING

One thing I overlooked, that now I'll mention.
Your husband brought with him a heap of treasures,
When quitting Iolcos on his uncle's death.

MEDEA

All's safe within. Go in yourself and take them! [48]

KING

Of course the golden gem is also there,
The Fleece, the Argonauts' most-cherished prize?
Why do you turn to go? Come, answer me!
Is it there too?

MEDEA

No!

KING

Tell me where it is.

MEDEA

I do not know.

KING

But you took it away *1930*
From Pelias' house, the herald said as much.

MEDEA

If he said so, it must be true.

KING

Where is it?

MEDEA

I do not know.

KING

Do not think you'll deceive us!

[48] Compare Medea's cold, not to say rude, reply, with her father's similar answer to Phrixus in *The Guest* (Vs. 337–40).

MEDEA

Give it to me and take my life in payment;
If I had it, you'd not stand threatening there!

KING

Did you not bring it out of Iolcos?

MEDEA

Yes.

KING

And now?

MEDEA

I do not have it.

KING

Who else?

MEDEA

The earth.

KING

I think I understand. It must be that.

(To his suite)

Bring here what I commanded. You know what!

(They go out)

You think you'll cheat us with prevarication? *1940*
The earth has it! Well, now I understand.
Don't look away. Turn, look at me and listen!
Upon the seashore where you camped last night,
While working on the building of an altar
To Pelias' shade at my command,
They found—you pale? . . . fresh buried in the ground,
A casket, black, with strange mysterious signs.

(The chest is brought)

Examine, if it's yours.

MEDEA *(Hurling herself on it)*
Yes, mine, it's mine!

KING

The Fleece there?

MEDEA

Yes.

KING

Then give it.

MEDEA

I give it!

KING

I almost grudge the sympathy I showed you, *1950*
Since you deceitfully would deal with us.

MEDEA

Be sure, you will receive what is your due.
Once more I am Medea; Gods be thanked!

KING

Open and give.

MEDEA

Not now.

KING

Then when?

MEDEA

Quite soon!
Too soon!

KING

Then send it off to Creusa.

MEDEA

Off to Creusa! To Creusa?—Yes!

KING

Contains the casket else?

MEDEA

Indeed, much else!

KING

Your property?

MEDEA

But some I'll give as presents!

KING

I do not seek your wealth. Keep what is yours!

MEDEA

Not so; a little present you'll permit; *1960*
Your daughter was so gracious, good to me,
She is to be the mother of my children,
How gladly then would I desire her love!
The Fleece tempts *you,* perhaps she'd like adornments.

KING

Do as you will, but first think of yourself!
Believe me, Creusa looks on you most kindly.
Why, even now she begged me send the children,
That you might see them once before you go,
And say good-bye before your distant journey:
Her plea I turned down, for I thought you raving, *1970*
But now I see you calm, I grant it to you.

MEDEA

A thousand thanks! You good and pious prince!

KING

Stay here and I shall send the children to you.

(Exit the KING*)*

MEDEA

He's gone! He's gone away to meet his ruin!
Infamous knaves, did you not shake and shiver,
When snatching fond from me this latest theft?
Yet all my thanks. You gave me back myself.
Undo the chest.

GORA

I am not able to.

MEDEA

I was forgetting how I locked it fast!
Friends, who are my familiars, hold the key. *1980*

(Turning to the chest)

Up and down,
Within the womb,
Open,
All-concealing tomb!

(The chest springs open)

The lid springs open! Back has come my power!
All there. The wand! The veil! Mine! They are mine!

(Taking them out)

Once more I hold my mother's legacy,
And power wells in my heart and in my arm.
Beloved veil, I cast you around my head!

(Veiling herself)

How warm, how soft, how fresh-enlivening! *1990*
Then come, then come, you hosts of enemies, all,
Banded against me, banded in your fall! [49]

GORA

There underneath it glitters!

MEDEA

Let it glitter!
Soon blood will quench the glow!

[49] Compare Rodrigue's call to his enemies in Corneille's *Le Cid* (Act V, Scene I, Vs. 1561–64):

> Come, rally hither, as one host unite
> And all against me and my passion fight:
> Pit all your might against the bliss I view;
> To bar me from my love, you'd prove too few.

Here they all are, the presents that I offer:
But you I make the bearer of my grace! [50]

GORA

I?

MEDEA

You. Go to the daughter of the king,
Addressing her with gracious flatteries,
And take Medea's greetings with her gifts.

(Taking the articles out of the chest)

This vessel first, that hides most precious unguents, *2000*
The bride will blaze in splendor, should she open it!
Only be careful not to shake it!

GORA

Woe!

(She holds the vessel aslant with the left hand; as she holds up the lid, supporting it with her right hand, a bright flame shoots up)

MEDEA

Did I not tell you not to shake it?
Back to your bower,
Hissing snake;
Soon comes the hour
For you to wake!
Now hold it, and with care, now mind you do!

GORA

I sense what's horrible!

MEDEA

So you begin to note? How wise you are! *2010*

GORA

And I'm to take this?

[50] As in the *Medée* of Corneille and of Cherubini. In Euripides and Seneca, the children, accompanied by Jason, bear the fatal presents.

MEDEA

Yes, obey, you slave!
How dare you argue? Silence! I command you!
Here, on the bowl, thick-lined with burnished gold,
I place the richly decked and stately vessel,
Enwrapping it with what they want so much:
The Fleece . . .

(Throwing it over the objects)

Away and execute your office!
Upon it let this magic garment lie,
A mantle, richly bordered, and right royal,
Mysteriously enshrouding mystery.
Now go and do what I commanded you, *2020*
And bear the gift that foe sends to her foe!

(A SLAVE GIRL *enters with the* CHILDREN*)*

SLAVE GIRL

My royal master sends the children to you.
After an hour or so, I'll fetch them back.

MEDEA

I will return them for the wedding feast.
Take back this nurse with you to the princess.
She goes with greetings and with gifts from me.
Remember, you, what I commanded you!
Silence! I order! Lead her to your mistress.

(Exeunt GORA *and the* SLAVE GIRL*)*

It is begun, but it is not yet ended.
I'm happier now I'm clear what I would do. *2030*

(The CHILDREN, *hand in hand, want to follow the* SLAVE GIRL*)*

Where are you going?

BOY

Home!

MEDEA

Why to your home?

BOY

Our father ordered us to follow her.

MEDEA

Your mother orders you to stay here, stay!
When I consider how my very flesh,
The child whom I have carried in my womb,
Whom I have nurtured on this very breast,
How my own self stands up against myself,
Then fury flashes searing through my soul
And bloody thoughts rear up in rampant terror—
What, tell me, has your mother done to you, *2040*
That you should flee from her and cling to strangers?

BOY

You want to lead us once more to your ship,
Where we feel sick and giddy. We'll stay here.
Right, Brother?

THE YOUNGER

Yes!

MEDEA

You too, Absyrtus, you?
However, better so, better—complete!
Come here to me.

BOY

I feel afraid.

MEDEA

Come here!

BOY

You will not hurt me?

MEDEA

What? Have you deserved it?

BOY

You threw me once upon the ground, because

I am like Father, but he loves me for it.
I'll stay with him and with the gentle lady! 2050

MEDEA

To her you shall go, to your gentle lady!
How much he looks like him, like him, the traitor!
How much he speaks like him. Ah, patience, patience!

THE YOUNGER

I'm sleepy.

THE ELDER

Let us go to sleep. It's late.

MEDEA

You will soon sleep on to your heart's content.
Go there upon the steps and lay you down,
While I take counsel of myself awhile . . .
How carefully he leads his brother up
And takes his own coat off and warmly lays it
Around the shoulders of the little one, 2060
And now, their small and darling arms entwined,
Nestles beside him— He was never bad!
O children, children!

THE ELDER *(Starting up)*

Are you calling?

MEDEA

Sleep!
What would I not give but to sleep like you.

(The ELDER BOY *lies down and sleeps.* MEDEA *seats herself opposite on a bench. It has gradually turned dark)*

The night has fallen. Risen are the stars,
Casting on us their soft and gentle light;
The same today as they were yesterday,
As though all was today like yesterday;
And yet so great a gap between them stands
As firmly parts fair fortune from disaster! 2070
So all-unchanging, absolute, is Nature,

So full of change is man, his puny fate.
When I recount to me the fable of my life,
I feel there speaks an alien voice, me listening
And interrupting: Friend, that cannot be! [51]
Can she, who harbors now these murderous thoughts,
Be she, who wanders in her father's land
Under the pale light of these very stars,
As pure, as meek, from any blame as free
As only babe at mother's breast can be? *2080*
Where is she going? To the poor man's hut,
Whose crops her father's huntsmen trampled down,
To bring him gold and comfort his dejection.
Why is she hastening to the woods? She follows
Her brother, who awaits her in the forest;
And having found each other, like twin stars,
They wander beaming on their wonted way.
Another now approaches, crowned with gold.
It is her father, monarch of the land.
He lays his hand upon her and her brother *2090*
And blesses them, his greatest happiness.
Be welcome, O you gracious, kindly, visions!
Do you come to cheer me in my loneliness? [52]
Come nearer, let me look you in the face!
My dearest brother, do you smile at me?
How strong and handsome you, my soul's delight!
Our father, true, is solemn. Yet he loves me,
Loves me, his own good daughter! What's that, "good"?

(Starting up)

It's all a lie! Old man, she will betray you!
She *has* betrayed, you and herself: *2100*
But you did curse her.
"You shall be driven away
Like a wild beast," you said,
"Shall have no friend, nowhere

[51] Compare Jason in *The Argonauts,* Act III, Vs. 1196–1200.
[52] Hero was to utter almost the identical words in Act III, V. 1062, of *The Waves of Sea and Love.*

To lay your head.
And he, for whom you have betrayed me,
Himself shall be my chief avenger:
He will forswear, forsake you,
Kill you." [53]
O Father, see! Your word is all fulfilled: *2110*
And all-forlorn I stand,
Shunned like a wild beast,
By him forsaken for whom I forsook you:
No resting place. Alas not dead,
With murderous thoughts in my dark mind.
Does your revenge taste sweet?
Are you approaching me? O children, children!

(Hastening to them and shaking them)

Children, do you not hear? Wake up!

BOY *(awaking)*

What do you want?

MEDEA *(Embracing them)*

Ah, put your arms around me!

BOY

I slept so softly!

MEDEA

Slept? How could you sleep? *2120*
Because you think your mother's guarding you?
You never were exposed to greater peril!
How could you think of sleeping here beside me?
Go there within, there inside you may rest!

(The CHILDREN *go to the pillared passage)*

Now they are gone! And now once more I'm well!—
Because they've gone: and what is well with that?
Must I flee less, flee less this very day,
Leaving them here behind with all my foes?

[53] See Aeetes' curse in Act III of *The Argonauts* (Vs. 1364–78).

Their father, is he any less a traitor?
The new bride, will she wed him any less? 2130

Tomorrow, with the rising sun,
I shall stand alone,
The world an empty desert,
Childless and husbandless
On torn and bloody feet
Wandering in misery—where?
But here they'll be rejoicing, mocking me,
My children round the stranger's neck,
Estranged from me and ever distant.
Can you bear that? 2140
Is it not already too late,
Too late to pardon?
Has Creusa not already had the garment,
The cup, the flaming cup?
Listen! . . . Not yet! . . . But soon there shall resound
A cry of lamentation from the castle.
They will come, will kill me,
And spare not even the little ones.
Listen! I heard a cry! . . . The flames are leaping up!
It has befallen! 2150
There can be no return!
Then let it be accomplished to the full! Away!

(GORA *rushes out of the palace)*

O horrible, most horrible!

MEDEA *(Approaching her)*

Has it happened?

GORA

Alas, Creusa dead! In flames the palace.

MEDEA

Are you beyond return, white bride?
Will you entice my children still from me?
Will you entice them? Will you?
Will you still have them, even there?
I send them not to you but to the Gods!

GORA

What have you done? They're coming! *2160*

MEDEA

They're coming? Too late!

(She hastens into the pillared passage)

GORA

Ah woe is me, forced in my old age,
To be unknowing tool of such crimes!
Myself I counseled vengeance, but such vengeance!
But where are the children; I left them here.
Medea, where are you? Your children, where?

(Hastens into the pillared passage. The palace in the background begins to stand out clearly, lit by the swelling flames within)

JASON'S VOICE

Creusa! Creusa!

KING *(From within)*

My daughter!

GORA *(Rushes out of the pillared passage, beside herself, and falls on her knees in the center of the stage, hiding her face in her hands)*

What have I seen? O horror!

*(*MEDEA *steps out of the pillared passage with a dagger in her left hand, and commanding silence* [54] *with her right hand raised aloft)*

Curtain

[54] Similar to the end of the fourth act in Grillparzer's next play, *König Ottokars Glück und Ende,* where the Chancellor commands silence for the sleeping King with his finger on his lips.

ACT V

SCENE I

Courtyard of CREON'S *castle as in the previous act. The* KING'S *dwelling in the background, burnt out and still smoking. Much going to and fro of persons working at the scene of the fire. Dawn.*

The KING *drags* GORA *out of the palace, followed by several female* SERVANTS *of* CREUSA.

KING

Get out, you were the one, who bore my daughter
The bloody gift that brought with it destruction. 2170
O daughter! Creusa, my belovèd child!

(Turning to the SERVANTS*)*

She was the one?

GORA

Yes, I! Unknowing
I brought death into your house.

KING

Unknowing?
Ah, do not think you'll dodge the punishment.

GORA

You think your punishment can frighten me? [55]

[55] Gora here, like Rhamnes in the last act of *Sappho,* and Emilia

Have I not seen with these my very eyes
The children lying dead, in pools of blood,
Snuffed out by her who bore them,
By her whom I brought up . . . Medea?
Since then all other horrors seem but trifles! *2180*

KING

Creusa! My child! Innocent, faithful Creusa!
You monster, did not palsy halt your hand
When you bore death into her precious presence?

GORA

I do not weep for her, she got her due
For coveting misfortune's last possession.
I weep for my dear children, my belovèd,
Whom I have seen slain by maternal hand.
I would you all lay in the grave together,
With the arch-traitor—Jason is his name—
And I were back in Colchis with the daughter *2190*
And children, never setting eyes on you,
Nor on your city, struck with righteous doom.

KING

You would be less defiant if I struck you!
But is it certain that my child is dead?
So many say so, but no one has seen!
Is it not possible to cheat the flames?
Does conflagration rage so soon? No, slowly
It hesitating creeps along the rafters.
This is well known. And yet they say she's dead?
Why, only now she stood before me blooming, *2200*
Then dead? I cannot, no, I daren't believe it!
Involuntarily I turn my eyes,
Believing ever, now and now and now

---

in the last act of Shakespeare's *Othello,* stands up for righteousness. Gora indeed, as a consequence has in this play been awarded by Grillparzer the dignity of the iambic pentameter (already permitted to Medea), in place of the barbarian's free verse, to which Aeetes and Absyrtus had been condemned!

She must appear, all snow-white in her beauty,
A swan come gliding through the darkling ruins.
Who was with her? Who saw it? You? Then speak!
Let not your eyes keep rolling in your head!
Kill me with speech! Is she beyond return?

MAID

Beyond!

KING

You saw it?

MAID

I saw, saw how the flames
Revolving from the golden vessel rose *2210*
Toward her.

KING

Enough! She saw! She is no more!
Creusa! My child! O my belovèd daughter!
One day, when still a child, she burnt her hand
On sacrificial hearth and shrieked in torment.
I rushed to her and clasped her in my arms,
Breathing upon her fingers with my lips;
At that she smiled, despite her bitter tears,
And sobbing gently said: "It's nothing much,
A little pain—but to be *burnt,* no—no!"
And now—

(To GORA*)*

Were I a thousand times to thrust *2220*
My sword into your body, it were nothing!
And as for her, that monster . . . Where is she,
Who's robbed me of my child? Come quick, confess,
Or I shall shake the answer from your mouth
Together with your soul—where has she gone?

GORA

I do not know and do not care to know;
Let her embrace her ruin without me.
Why do you linger? Kill me! I would die!

KING

That will soon happen, first of all confess!

JASON *(Behind the scenes)*

Where is she? Thrust her out to me! Medea! 2230

(Entering with naked sword in his hand)

They told me they had fetched her! Where is she?
What, you here? Where's your mistress?

GORA

Off, away!

JASON

Has she the children?

GORA

No.

JASON

So they are? . . .

GORA

Dead!
Yes, dead, you treacherous hypocrite, both dead!
She wished to save them from the sight of you.
And since to you on earth there's nothing sacred,
She gave them early refuge in the grave.
Just stand and keep on staring at the ground,
You cannot bring the darlings back to life!
They are beyond return—I'm glad of this! 2240
No, not of this, but that it tears your heart,
Of that I'm glad!—You treacherous hypocrite!
Did you not drive them to the grave? And you,
You falsest monarch with your shuffler's face?
Did you not tight beset your noble game
With hunter's nets of shameless treachery,
Till no way out, in rage of desperation,
She sprang beyond your snare, the royal crown,

That ornament of lofty brows, brought low
As implement of unaccustomed murder? 2250
Wring, wring your hands! Yes, wring them for yourselves!

(*To the* KING)

Why did your child covet another's bed?

(*To* JASON)

Why did you steal her, if you did not love?
And if you loved her, why did you forsake?
Let others, nay, let me condemn her deed,
You two have only reaped what was your due!
Now you shall no more mock the Colchian woman.
I do not wish to linger on the earth;
Two children dead, the third now most abhorrent!
Lead me away and kill me if you will: 2260
Some faith in life *beyond* now stirs within,
That I have seen requital follow sin.

(She goes off under guard)

(Pause)

KING

Was I unjust to her? By the great gods,
I did not mean to be! Now to those ruins,
To seek the sad remains of my dear child
And bury them within the lap of earth.

(*To* JASON)

And as for you, go where your footsteps lead;
It's dangerous, I see, to yoke with sin.
Would I had never seen you, never welcomed
You as an honored guest into my house! 2270
My daughter you have taken: get you gone!
Do not take too the solace of my tears!

JASON

You drive me hence?

KING

I cast you out from me.

JASON

What shall I do?

KING

A god must tell you that!

JASON

Who then will guide me? Who will be my aid?
I've hurt my head, wounded by falling splinters! [56]
What, no one speaks? No leader, no sure guide?
Will no one follow me, whom once all followed?
My children's shades, you show to me the way
And lead me to the grave that waits for me! 2280

(Exit)

KING

Now let us set to work! Then mourn forever!

(Exit in the opposite direction)

SCENE II

Wild, lonely region, shut in by woods and rocks, with a hut. The COUNTRYMAN *enters.*[57]

How beautiful the dawn! O gracious Gods,
How beautiful the sun in morning freshness
After the horrors of this stormy night! [58]

(He enters the hut. JASON *staggers in, supported on his sword)*

JASON

I can no further. How my head is burning!
My blood aglow, my tongue to palate cleaving!

[56] This is probably a faint echo of Euripides' *Medea,* where it is foretold that Jason would be killed by a falling spar of Argo timber. Jason is least impressive when whining with self-pity throughout this act.

[57] The same Countryman as in Act I.

[58] As in Shakespeare's *Macbeth,* the murders are capped by raging elements.

Is none there? Must I die of thirst alone?
This is the hut that offered me a refuge,
When I, rich both as man and father, came
To this spot full of new-awakened hope! *2290*

(Knocking)

Only one drink! Only a place to die!

(The COUNTRYMAN *comes out)*

COUNTRYMAN

Who knocks? Who are you, poor exhausted wretch?

JASON

Just water! But one sip! I am that Jason,
The Wonder-Fleece's hero, prince and king!
The leader of the Argonauts, I, Jason!

COUNTRYMAN

What, Jason, you? Then off with you, away!
Do not defile my house by entering it.
You've done to death the daughter of my king,
Demand no shelter at his people's doors!

(He goes in, shutting the door)

JASON

He's gone and leaves me lying in the dust, *2300*
That every passing traveler might tread.
I call thee, Death, come take me to my children!

(He sinks down. MEDEA *comes up behind a rock and stands suddenly before him, bearing the Fleece like a mantle about her shoulders)*

MEDEA

Jason!

JASON *(Half turning)*

Who calls? Do I see right? What, you?
You monster! And you dare to stand before me?
Where is my sword! [59]

[59] One of several parallels with Gotter's melodrama *Medea,* the

(He tries to spring up, but sinks back again)

Alas, my weary limbs
Refuse to serve me more—I'm broken—spent!

MEDEA

Enough. You cannot touch me, for I am
A victim for some other hand than yours.

JASON

Where have you put my children?

MEDEA

They are mine!

JASON

Where have you put them?

MEDEA

They are in a place, *2310*
Where they are better off than you or me.

JASON

They are dead, dead!

MEDEA

To you death seems the worst;
Something far worse I know: stark misery.
Had you not put a higher store on life
Than it deserves, our fate were very different!
We must endure. The children now are free.

JASON

How can you speak so calmly?

MEDEA

Calmly? Calmly!

---

performance of which, together with Cherubini's opera, provided in 1818 the stimulant that led Grillparzer to compose *The Golden Fleece*.

Were you not still a stranger to my breast
As you have ever been, you'd see the pain,
That, seething endless like a surging sea, 2320
Swallows the several ruins of my grief
And drags them, hid in horrid desolation,
Into the vortex of the infinite.
I do not grieve the children are no more,
I only grieve they were and that we are.

JASON

Alas! Alas!

MEDEA

Endure what's stricken you;
For it has not, in truth, struck undeserved!
Just as you lie before me on the ground,
So I once lay in Colchis before you
And begged you spare me; but you did not spare! 2330
With dastard hand you blindly seized the prizes,
Although I warned you, you were seizing death!
So now embrace what you defiant sought:
Yes, death. But now I take my leave of you
For evermore. This is the very last time,
In all eternity the very last time,
That, Husband, I shall speak to you. Farewell!
Now after all the joys of earlier days,
In all the anguish of our present night,
In all the misery that stares before us, 2340
I say to you, my husband, fare you well.
A life of wretchedness now dawns for you,
Yet, whatsoever comes your way, endure,
And be in suffering nobler than in deed!
If in your grief you founder, think of me
And draw some comfort from my greater pain,
That I have done, where you have left undone.
I go my way, bearing my monstrous grief
Around with me through all the gaping world.
One dagger blow were balm, and yet not so! 2350

Medea's hand may not dispatch Medea.
My earlier life has earned a better judge
Than now Medea is. I go to Delphi.
Upon Apollo's altar, whence the Fleece
In former days by Phrixus was removed,
I'll hang it once more, giving back his own
To the dark god, that flames too could not scathe,
And that intact and unconsumed emerged
From the Corinthian princess' bloody blaze.
There I will place myself before the priests *2360*
And ask if they as sacrifice would take me,
Or banish me to some far wilderness,
To find in longer life a longer torment.
Behold the emblem here for which you strove,
That seemed your laurel crown and happiness!
What is earth's happiness? . . . A shadow!
What is earth's laurel crown? . . . A dream!
Poor you, who have of shadows only dreamed!
The dream is spent, only the night not yet.
I now depart, my husband, fare you well! *2370*
We, who for ill-luck came together,
Must now in ill-luck part. Farewell!

JASON

Childless! Alone! Alas, my children!

MEDEA

Bear!

JASON

All lost!

MEDEA

Be patient!

JASON

Oh, to die!

MEDEA

Atone!

I go and never shall you see me more!

(She turns to go)

Curtain

THE END

THE WAVES OF SEA AND LOVE

TRANSLATOR'S NOTE

Grillparzer's *Des Meeres und der Liebe Wellen* has been called the most beautiful love drama in the German language, and this it probably is, ranked by Douglas Yates* with Shakespeare's *Romeo and Juliet:* for though the Gretchen scenes in Part I of Goethe's *Faust* are more shattering in their pathos, yet those love scenes are merely incidental in *Faust,* which cannot conceivably be called a love drama. What is even more certain is that when Grillparzer changed the title of his play from *Hero and Leander* to *The Waves of Sea and Love,* he gave it the aptest and the most beautiful title of any of his plays, interwoven with the theme of love and death, which, like the waves of the sea, forever present in the play, resound through the five acts from beginning to end.

The romance of Hero and Leander, first recorded in Ovid † and Virgil,‡ was nobly sung by the sixth-century poet Musaeus (the Grammarian) in a Greek narrative poem of less than four hundred hexameters, which ends with Hero plunging from her tower to her death at sight of the body of her dead Leander below. This poem of the "divine Musaeus" won the admiration of Christopher Marlowe, whose own fragmentary poem *Hero and Leander* is one of the landmarks of English narrative verse of the sixteenth century, quoted by Shakespeare in *As You Like*

* *Franz Grillparzer* (Vol. I), ed., Douglas Yates (Basil Blackwell, Oxford, 1946), to which English-speaking Grillparzer lovers are greatly indebted.

† *Heroides,* 18 and 19.

‡ *Georgics* 3, 258 *ff.*

It. Marlowe's fragment proved so popular that it was completed after his death by his contemporary George Chapman, whose version of Homer was so to inspire Keats, two centuries later. Of the six "Sestiads" in which Chapman cast the completed poem, Marlowe was the author of the first two and Chapman of the last four. The literary merit may have been in the opposite proportion, but the influence of Chapman, with Hero's death of a broken heart, may have been greater in shaping the end of Grillparzer's play than the many details Grillparzer may have owed Marlowe. Apart from the "Liebestod" at the end, Grillparzer may also have been sufficiently impressed by Chapman's effective reiteration of Leander's name by the grief-stricken Hero, at the end of the poem, to have similarly used it as a dying knell when his heartbroken heroine sinks down to die in Aphrodite's Temple with "Leander! Leander!" on her lips.

Apart from the Greek, Latin and English sources, there was also a Spanish work which Grillparzer with his love of Spanish literature may have known. There was a good deal in Ovid that might have influenced Grillparzer, especially Hero's falling asleep with fatigue in awaiting Leander (Act IV). More recent German sources, in Wieland's *Schach Lolo* and Schiller's *Ballade* "Hero and Leander" must have been familiar to Grillparzer as also the folksong, *Es Waren Zwei Königskinder,* where the false Nun, like the High Priest in the play, puts out the light, which Grillparzer, following Musaeus, makes the symbol of the bond between the lovers.

But whatever these influences and the details that Grillparzer owes to Euripides (*Ion*), Shakespeare (*Romeo and Juliet*), Racine (*Bérénice*), Goethe (*Iphigenie*), Zacharias Werner (*Wanda*), what is striking is how subtly Grillparzer has used his raw materials to create a most impressive and original artistic masterpiece, which, if its insufficient dramatic tension prevents it from being regarded as the greatest of his plays, is certainly the most beautiful, the most popular, and, it would seem—with its intimate recollections of his "ideal" love—perhaps Grillparzer's own favorite.

The cold reception the play received at its first appearance at the Burgtheater on April 5, 1831, merely serves to remind us once more that Vienna, although at that time the undoubted Athens of Europe, despite the rival claims of Weimar, was often mistaken in its initial judgment of the work of Austria's greatest sons, Grillparzer and Mozart, who had to go to Prague for juster appreciation. It is true that the first three acts, as Grillparzer records, were enthusiastically applauded at the first performance, but the last two acts left the audience cold. Now the fourth act, despite its beauties, is fundamentally flawed by the degeneration of the High Priest from a figure worthy to be set beside the Sarastro of the *Magic Flute* into an almost conventional villain; a feature which needlessly persists into the fifth act with the Priest's often inept remarks, in discordant obligato to the beautiful swan-song of the dying Hero. But the fifth act, apart from this minor flaw, is one of the greatest threnodies in dramatic literature and should certainly have moved the audience if at all competently performed. So we are compelled to agree with Heinrich Laube, who triumphantly revived the play in Vienna twenty years later (1851), that the fault must have lain with Frau Rettich who created the rôle of Hero, and who apparently lacked the charm that his Hero, Frau Bayer-Bürck, successfully emanated. In this matter too, Grillparzer's ill luck seemed to have dogged him, for the play was at last ready for the theatre in 1829, at a time when the chief part was destined for the great Sophie Müller who, however, died the following year at the height of her fame before she could create the rôle. Some twenty years after his death, in 1872, Grillparzer's faith in the play was vindicated when it proved the most popular of his plays to be performed during his centenary celebrations in 1891.

The reason for Grillparzer's emotional attachment to this play is not obscure. From his adolescence he was profoundly drawn by the ideal of romantic love—which was to elude him in life. His teenage infatuation for the teenage actress Therese left him physically ill, as he himself records, and as he represents his smitten Leander in Act II. Shortly after this, he came under the highly romantic influence of Shakespeare's *Romeo and Juliet,* to whose Act II Scene ii and Act III his own Act III owes something; though in reality what is remarkable is not the similarity so much as the contrast in tone between the highly charged passion of the Shakespearean lovers—the fourteen year old Juliet invoking her wedding night with:

> Come, civil night,
> Thou sober-suited matron, all in black,
> And learn me how to lose a winning match,
> Play'd for a pair of stainless maidenhoods:
> *(Act III, Sc. ii)*

and the Grillparzer lovers' equally strong passion, no less eloquent for being restrained

Thus, while the young Hero, concerned only for the safety of Leander, who has dangerously erupted into her midnight chamber, urges him to depart:

> Should you reach home,
> Leander, through the dark sea, as you came,
> Take good care of this head, and of this mouth,
> Of these, my eyes, Leander, do you hear?
> Ah, promise me!
> (*Vs. 1230–34*)

and draws back as he is about to embrace her. Leander, begging to be allowed to see her again, bewails the delay conveyed in her reply: "Well then, come at the next full moon" with:

> Till then ten weary days must creep along!
> Can you bear the uncertainty till then? I cannot!
> I shall be fearing we have been observed,
> You in your mind will fancy I am dead,
> And rightly so! For should the sea not gulp me,
> I'll die of care, of anguish and of pain.
> Say: day after tomorrow, say in three days,
> Ah, next week say!

to which Hero, psychologically surrendering, replies:

> Then come again tomorrow.
> (*Vs. 1221–29*)

The first indication that Grillparzer was definitely meditating a work on the theme of Hero and Leander comes in 1820, when, after he had completed *The Golden Fleece* the words "Hero and Leander" appear in his diary (Tgb. 320). In the same year other entries refer to Musaeus' *Hero and Leander* (Tgb. 780), and above all Tgb. 322, where the first sketch of the plot appears:

> Hero and Leander. How no man can touch her, and she becomes priestess of Venus. Then she sees Leander. While fetching water in the grove of the goddess she meets him again. He draws water for her. The third act ends thus: that Leander for the first time swims across to Sestos to Hero's tower, mounts up to her after she has thrown down to him a cloak to muffle himself. Love conversations. Hero hears a noise outside, and as she takes the lamp to investigate what it may be, bids Leander enter her bedroom in the meanwhile. Fourth act. Hero with the feelings of a *woman.* The Priest has noticed that something is afoot, and fishermen have told him about the lamp that was shining all night in the tower. He suspects the significance and determines, once for all, that he will nip the forbidden in the bud. Hero, who has been awake all night, is sleepy. He does not let her have the time to sleep. He keeps her continuously occupied. The evening comes, Hero lights the lamp and wants to keep awake, but yet falls asleep. The Priest puts out the lamp. Act 5. Fishermen find Leander's dead body.

This was the time when Grillparzer was carrying on an affair with Charlotte von Paumgartten, his cousin's wife, who was the prototype of his Medea, and the features of his Hero in this sketch are more in accordance with Charlotte's temperament than with the restrained, essentially innocent, yet determined Hero of the future play of which the young Marie von Smolenitz was to become the prototype. But already in 1821, Grillparzer's interest in Katherina Fröhlich, who became his fiancée and who loved him truly, and was to become his literary heir, although he never married her—or anyone else for that matter—made the original Hero sketch fortunately out of date. In 1822 Grillparzer noted in his diary the existence of Marlowe's poem, but it was not till several years later when Grillparzer was deeply fascinated by the "heavenly beauty" of Marie von Smolenitz, a girl seventeen years his junior to whom he dared not propose—and who on one occasion would not allow him even to kiss her as she considered it would be in some sort "a breach of faith" *—that his virginal Hero of the first three acts, as we finally know her, was conceived.

Work on the tragedy was seriously resumed in 1827, but after getting to Act IV Scene ii, Grillparzer could proceed no further: perhaps because Marie von Smolenitz had accepted the definite proposal for her hand of his friend and rival, the miniature painter, Daffinger, and married him. However, as the marriage proved unhappy and Marie would confide her woes to Grillparzer, he was moved by his love and compassion for her, and speedily completed the play early in 1829, when the so-called "fourth manuscript" was handed over to the copyist on February 26. But, as already indicated, there were delays in production, so that more than two years had to elapse before its first performance at the Burgtheater on April 5, 1831.

Except for the character of the High Priest, all the other characters in the play are splendidly drawn, even though Leander is portrayed more as a lover than as a man, and there are one or two inconsistencies in the character of the heroine herself. The minor characters also, like Ianthe, the Temple Warden, and even Hero's father (the egregious Menander), are very well observed. Naukleros, Leander's friend, in particular, is an excellent creation—loquacious, impudent and loyal. Teasing the stricken Leander, who at her consecration ceremony has fallen hopelessly in love at first sight with the virgin priestess just sworn to chastity, he prattles on:

> But she saw you. I could not fail to note.
> As we knelt there, I behind, you in front,
> By Hymen's statue, by that mighty god,
> And she approached, disseminating incense;
> She stood stone-still, her hand limp in the air;
> Gazing at you, she stood there hesitating,
> One, two, three brief and everlasting moments.
> At last she went on with her sacred task.
> But even in parting her eyes plainly said,
> In harsh breach of the day's cold chastity,

* Breach of faith to Daffinger, with whom she was already involved.

That shuts her out for evermore from love:
"Ah, what a pity, that one is my man!"
(*Vs. 638–649*)

The character of the High Priest is the least satisfactory in the play. In the original sketch of 1820 he appeared rather as a conventional villain, just as Hero and Leander were depicted there as conventional conspiritorial lovers with assignations and cloaks thrown down from the window. All the main characters were recast by Grillparzer after his love for his "ideal" Marie von Smolenitz had at last lighted the lamp of inspiration, leading to composition of the play as we know it. The figure of the Priest, too, was subjected to this ennobling process and in the first three acts Grillparzer represents him as a worthy holder of his high office, fit to be the mentor of his niece Hero, whom he inducts as priestess into the Temple of Aphrodite (Urania) the celestial, not the earthly Aphrodite (Pandemos), as he reminds Hero's mother:

Here is no earthly Aphrodite honored,
Who couples human beings like animals,
But the celestial, risen from the foam,
Uniting sense of spirit, not the senses,
The holy mother of harmonious being,
Sexless because she is herself pure sex.
(*Vs. 363–68*)

He is indeed something of a mystic and is moved, like the psalmist, by the spectacle of the Heavens that "declare the glory of God." Thrilled by the thought that his young niece seeks "composure"—which is "music" to his ear—he promises her a serene future:

Then, child, be of good cheer!
For you shall wander here, a blessèd being,
All dusty wishes withering away;
Just like the man who heavenward looks at evening,
In the dim twilight, seeing only gray,
Drab gray, and neither night nor trace of light,
Yet, vaguely gazing, spots a twinkling star
And then a second, third, a hundred, thousands—

Rich harbingers of a divine-illumined night—
With blessèd tears in his uplifted eyes.
(*Vs.* *955–64*)

It is therefore perfectly understandable that such a man should wish strictly to uphold the priestly code that enjoins chastity on the priestess of Aphrodite and that he should take every legitimate step—even the extreme penalty enjoined by law—to protect her from the amorous attentions of Leander or anyone else. What is not permissible is that to achieve this, he should stoop to subterfuge (to prevent Hero from resting), and even to attempted murder, as he is represented as doing in Act IV—posing the while as an instrument of the gods! Equally deplorable are his conventional and futile attempts to hush up the scandal to his niece, and to keep her on as priestess, despite her broken vows, as he does in Act V—and his insensitivity to the suffering of the dying Hero merely adds insult to injury. Grillparzer seems to have been misled by the example of the envious "false" nun in the German folksong, who likewise "put out the light." That he had this fatal example of envy of others' bliss in mind is suggested by Naukleros' otherwise superfluous dig at the High Priest at the end of Act II, when he upbraids him as:

Self-seeking, arbitrary, harsh old beard!
This is the way you lock up gracious beauty,
Deny the world the warm cheer of her rays,
And deck your deed with sacred subterfuges?

* * *

But you inherited this from the Orient,
This shameful job of jealous Indus slaves,
And veil yourself in outrage and in night.
(*Vs.* *860–71*)

All a trifle hysterical and unjust, since the High Priest shows himself perfectly willing to discharge Hero when her mother states her preference for a "bourgeois" marriage, and it was Hero herself who voluntarily insisted on taking her oath of consecration and chastity.

It was unfortunate that Grillparzer, misled by the folksong, should have set so much store on the extinguishing of the lamp as a prerequisite to Leander's disaster. Musaeus, more dramatically, made Leander's drowning instantaneous with the blowing out of the light by the storm wind, and the "righteous gods," had they wished to punish the lovers, certainly would not have found the rays of any lamp an obstacle to their retribution!

Grillparzer's failure with the High Priest was probably due to a certain moral atrophy in his own otherwise attractive personality, which he himself, many times, most honestly records: his indifference, for instance, on hearing of the account of the death of Marie Piquot, a young girl of his acquaintance who (albeit this was then unknown to him) appears to have literally pined and died of her unrequited love for him (Tgb. 1109, May 5, 1822), and also his apparent selfishness in never marrying Katherina Fröhlich, with whom (together with her sister, Anna) he nonetheless lived for many years till his death. Compare Goethe, who was induced by the pressure of events, after Jena in 1806, to marry Christiane Vulpius, the mother of his son.* This moral insensitivity did definite harm to his genius, for while his women characters escaped its consequences, his heroes, especially those like Phaon, Jason, and to a less extent Leander, in whom he saw himself, were disfigured by it, just like the High Priest. This curious insensitivity was to mar even his last play, *Die Jüdin von Toledo* (*The Jewess of Toledo*), where the supposedly model Spanish king is cured of his love for his murdered Jewish mistress, at sight of her body distorted in death, to the extent that he sacrifices justice, not to say retribution for her murder in the "interests" of the State!

Fortunately, this moral insensitivity is not fatal in the case of Leander, for so attractively has Leander been portrayed (in the first act in his shyness and melancholy he speaks not a word!) that we forgive, in the third act, his intrusion without invitation on the privacy of one vowed to chastity—true, he

* In Grillparzer, it is true, the pressures—the successive suicides of his brother and mother—and the instability of another brother worked the other way, against marriage fraught with the prospect of progeny. But such considerations had no further application after Kathi Frôhlich had past child-bearing age, when her long devotion to him surely deserved public recognition from a great man.

misread the shining of Hero's light across the sea as a direct invitation, and did not thrust his passion on her till she indicated her willingness to receive it; and so elemental is this passion, heedless of danger and death, depicted with the deftest of touches, that we must agree with Naukleros—it would have been useless trying to prevent it:

> I might as well address the roaring sea,
> The raging storm, the wild beast of the desert,
> That follows heedlessly its inborn urge!
> (*Vs. 1606–08*)

Let us examine a little more closely how Grillparzer has succeeded in making Leander the most attractive of the heroes in his Grecian plays. Of course, he was helped by the romance of the legend, hallowed by many poets throughout the centuries, but it is not too much to say that of all the Leanders that have come down to us—of Ovid, of Musaeus, of Marlowe, of Schiller—Grillparzer's Leander is the most appealing.

Taking a hint from Musaeus (not, however, Musaeus' Leander) that many a youth smitten with love for the inaccessible Hero suffered his anguish in silence, a feature Marlowe adopted to some extent—terming his Leander "a novice" in the art of love—Grillparzer expands Musaeus' hint into a full-blown characterization.

His virginal Leander, brought by Naukleros to the Sestos festival to divert him from the melancholy into which his mother's death had cast him, is tongue-tied and abashed throughout Act I, impervious to the feminine beauties from all parts crowding the festival (a feature in Musaeus). The loquacious Naukleros describes them with gusto in Act II:

> From Thrace, as well as prosperous Hellespont,
> The feminine bevy crowded; fairest flowers,
> Carnations, roses, tulips, violets, lilies —
> I fancy here and there a daisy too —
> (*Vs. 610–13*)

But Leander kept his eyes on the ground. It was only on the approach of Hero, who—the height of irony—has just taken her vow of chastity, that Leander, at Naukleros' instance, looked up, and from that moment, was doomed. The hopelessness of his love pained him physically, and he insisted on lingering by the temple, hoping to see Hero again. When she at length approaches to draw water by the spring in the grove, he continues to remain tongue-tied. When Hero, at Naukleros' insistence, speaks to Leander and explains why his love is hopeless, he exclaims dramatically:

> Then drown me in the bottom of the sea!
> (*V. 733*)

When she tries to console him with the thought that he may still happily love elsewhere, Leander leaps up with:

> May the stark cruel earth devour me quite
> And all that's good and lovely shut me out,
> If ever love for any other woman! . . .
> (*Vs. 794–96*)

When shaken by the violence of Leander's passion she indicates (through Naukleros):

> He is so handsome, young, and ah, so good,
> I wish him every joy, all happiness;
> Let him go home—

Leander exclaims:

> I, home? I'll take root here,
> And stand here with these trees all day and night
> And gaze upon that temple's top forever.
> (*Vs. 799–803*)

Convinced now that Hero reciprocates his love, a sudden elation transforms Leander's behavior. No longer is he melancholy and crestfallen. Indeed, he has wrested the leadership from the astonished Naukleros and so swims boldly and single-mindedly across the sea in pursuit of his love, his first venture crowned with satisfaction and his next with death. Most touching, before he sets out on his second venture, is his invocation to Aphrodite:

> And thou, great Aphrodite! Who didst call me,
> In my young ignorance, to teach, while learning,

Thy sweet commandments to my innocent love,
Support me.

(*Vs. 1646–49*)

Grillparzer's finest achievement in this play is in his characterization of Hero, his most fascinating heroine, if Melitta be his sweetest and Medea, dramatically, his greatest. He has woven in her character the innocent and the erotic with such masterly effect that her very eroticism appears innocent, and when she is confronted by her uncle, the Priest, with her breach of faith, she is prepared to refer her own code of behavior to the tribunal of the gods, confident of her acquittal, if not indeed of their approbation! When, in the fourth act, the Priest, reprehending her behavior of the previous night, reminds her of the gods' rights, she replies: "The gods are much too high for our poor rights," and when in the fifth act the Priest endeavors to read her a lesson on the death of Leander with:

The gods have borne aloud their bloody witness;
How great their anger and how grave your wrong,
So let us humbly take our punishment;
What's sacred must be wholly without stain;
May eternal silence bury what has happened.

Hero instinctively senses the hypocrisy of the last line, concerned more with saving the tarnished family honor than in upholding the rights of the gods, and bursts out in splendid naïveté with:

I, bury all my bliss and all my ruin,
And criminally join with criminals?
I'll shout it out aloud through the wide world,
What I have suffered, what possessed, what lost,
What has befallen, how they have pursued me.
I'll loudly curse you, that the winds shall hear,
And bear my curses to the gods' high throne.
You were the one who spread the wicked net
That I pulled tight, and so he was destroyed.

(*Vs. 1928–41*)

Of course, there is an inconsistency in Hero's attitude; she should not have broken her vow of chastity within a few hours of having taken it, unless the fact that the "One, two, three, brief, and everlasting moments" that bound her in all eternity to Leander, having occurred—supreme dramatic irony—within minutes of her having taken the vow, made her vow appear meaningless in her eyes. But in that case, she should clearly have renounced her priestess' office before indulging her passion, and not have sought, as she does in the fourth act, to continue to cling to the rights of the priestess' office at the very moment she was being unfaithful to it both in deed and in spirit. But as she paid dearly for this tragic weakness, we need not be too harsh on her.

Grillparzer has cunningly identified the erotic impulse in Hero with the song of Leda and the Swan, a theme to which he was partial as early as his twentieth year when we see it appear in his fragment *Psyche* (1811), which opens with his heroine Psyche singing a song of seven verses (twenty-eight lines) on the subject, as, like Hero in Act II, she enters carrying a pitcher. Hero, dramatically and more aptly, confines herself to two lines:

> But she is stroking
> The silk-soft down

adding most ingenuously:

> My uncle holds I should not sing the song
> Of Leda and the swan. I wonder where's
> The harm?
>
> (*Vs. 726–30*)

It seems difficult to reconcile with such extreme innocence the initiative of her surrender to Leander that very night, all the more so, as the highly sophisticated sentiments that Grillparzer—in his sometimes excessive partiality for the didactic play of words—in which he unfortunately sought to emulate Goethe and Schiller!—puts in her mouth now and again in the first act, suggest she had considerable education in the affairs of the world. But if we allow her such extreme innocence, then perhaps the initiative of her surrender at the end of Act III becomes dramatically more permissible, inasmuch as we may imagine her as not fully realizing the dangers to which she was exposing herself (and Leander) by embarking on the "waves of love." This first singing of the Leda-and-Swan theme in Act II is a subtle emergence of her subconscious love for Leander, a passion of which perhaps at this stage, only having seen him for "one, two, three, brief and everlasting moments" she was not fully aware. The second time she sings it, undressing alone in her room in Act III, she is fully aware of her inclination for Leander, but as she imagines she may not see him till the next festival, a year hence, if ever again, it has a note of nostalgia in it:

> Th'eternal song! Why does it haunt me so?
> No more do gods assail the wildest towers;
> No swan, no eagle comforts the forlorn;
> (*Vs. 1045–47*)

The next occasion she expresses the theme is when as a "woman" in Act IV, having experienced the ecstasies of love the previous night, she shocks the Priest with the sudden exclamation, at the end of a lilt about a royal princess, cryptically apotheosizing Leander as:

> O radiant swan, winged to the radiant stars!
> (*Vs. 1416*)

The last occasion that the theme occurs is dramatically the most masterly. Hero, worn out by fatigue at the end of the fourth act, is recumbent, with the rising night wind cooling her "eyes and brows and burning cheeks." In a delirium of fatigue and expectant love she apostrophizes the wind caressing her, now turned in her dozing imagination into Leander in the shape of a swan:

> You come across the sea, from him,
> And, oh, your rustling and the whispering leaves
> Sing in my ears: "we are from him, him, him, from him."
> Spread out your wings, enfold them all around
> My brow and head, my neck, my weary arms,
> Embrace me tight, I bare my breast to you—
> And if he comes, call out—Leander—you?
> (*Vs. 1810–16*)

But her Leander now was to come to her only as a corpse, and the sight of his dead body the next morning so breaks her heart that she wishes no more than to be united with him in death.

Grillparzer has composed for her a "Liebestod" that even Wagner could hardly excel; so that we impatiently dismiss the criticism that it is dramatically improbable that her death from grief could have taken place so soon!

To the grieving Naukleros, who arrives to moan over his friend's body, Hero explains in passionate despair the circumstances of his death:

And do you ask, who did it? Look! That man!
(*Pointing to the Priest*)
And I, the maiden-priestess— Are you wondering?

* * *

While he swam on unguarded by a light,
The black clouds hung down low upon the sea,
The waves rose wickedly to meet the clouds,
The stars were blotted out, all round was night.
And he, my prince of swimmers and of love,
Found in the cosmos neither love nor pity.

* * *

Oh, I will weep and weep and cut my veins,
And drown myself in seas of tears and blood
As deep as his, as horrible as his,
As deadly as the sea that's swallowed him!

(*Vs. 1949–74*)

Then as Naukleros continues to mourn, she breaks into an apotheosis of her dead lover, almost worthy of the lamentations of Shakespeare's great Cleopatra over the body of her dead Antony:

Say, he was everything; what now remains
Is but a fleeting shadow, but a void;
His breath was the pure air, his eye the sun,
His limbs the quickening power of burgeoning nature:
His life was life itself: your life, my life,
The life of all the world. When we let it die,
We too all died with him. Come, slothful friend,
Come, let us march in our own funeral:

(*Vs. 1976–83*)

When the Priest orders that Leander's body be borne away for burial across the sea in his native Abydos, Hero mechanically asks for a mantle to accompany the bier and to go and live beside his grave. When the Priest says it is impossible, reminding her she is the Priestess at Sestos, Hero replies in a daze:

> Then see that he is buried on our shore—
> Where he fell dead, and where in death he lay—
> Here at the foot of my tower. And roses
> And white lilies, drenched with dew,
> Shall spring up where he lies.
>
> (*Vs. 2042–46*)

When this too is refused by the Priest, Hero gives up, and before herself falling to join Leander in death, takes her anguished leave of him in accents that intimate why life on earth is impossible for her:

> Never, in all my life, to see you, never!
> You who were wandering in the robe of night
> And cast your bright rays into my dark soul,
> Made blossom everything that's rare and good,
> Will you from here to some dark lonely spot,
> And shall my parched eyes never see you more?
> The day will come and then the quiet night,
> And spring and autumn, and long summer pleasures,
> But never you, do you hear, Leander? . . . never!
> Never, never, never, never!
>
> (*Vs. 2060–69*)

recalling King Lear's five "nevers" over the dead body of Cordelia.

It is therefore with supreme tragic irony that Ianthe takes the wreath from the statue of Hymen to place on Hero's dead body and ends the play, challenging the god of nuptial bliss with:

> You promise much, and do you thus keep faith?
>
> (*V. 2121*)

S.S.

THE WAVES OF SEA & LOVE*

A Tragedy In Five Acts

* This was first performed at the Hofburgtheater in Vienna, on April 5, 1831, and first published in 1840 by J. B. Wallishausser.

CHARACTERS

HERO

HIGH PRIEST, *her uncle*

LEANDER

NAUKLEROS

IANTHE

TEMPLE WARDEN

PARENTS *of* HERO

SERVANTS, FISHERMEN, PEOPLE

ACT I

The scene is in the courtyard in the temple of Aphrodite in Sestos.[1] *Pillars of the peristyle with broad intervals in the center. In the background, the temple to which several steps lead up. In the right foreground the figure of Eros, on the left the statue of Hymen.*

Early morning. HERO, *holding a small basket of flowers on her arm, comes out of the temple, descending the steps.*

HERO

Now, it's been finished and the temple decked,
With myrtle and with roses spread around,
And all awaits the coming festival.

And I'm the cause of this festivity!
I am allowed to consecrate my days,
That roll unnoticed on without a goal,
To the high service of our heavenly goddess,
My lonely days that, like the meadow flowers,
Trampled upon by wandering feet and crushed,
Are now a wreath upon the goddess' head 10
Transfiguring, consecrating her and me.

How happy I that this should be the day,
And such a beautiful and tranquil day!
No cloud disturbs the azure of the sky,

[1] Sestos, on the European side of the Hellespont. There are traces in the play of the influence of Euripides' *Ion,* set at Apollo's Temple in Delphi.

And the great sun bright-rising from the sea,
Shines blessedly above those pinnacles.
Do you view me as one of yours already?
Did they inform you, the light-hearted Hero,
Whom you saw playing on the temple's steps,
That she, pretending to her forbears' right, 20
Who've furnished priests to serve this sanctuary
From dim antiquity—that she pretending
To this rare privilege, is now herself priestess;
Today, today, upon this very day?
The crowd shall see her standing on those steps,
Dispensing sacrifices to the gods,
From every lip shall acclamation burst,
And in the splendor offered to the goddess
The priestess' head shall shine—
But what is this?
Shall I begin my service with delay? 30
I still have flowers, there are still garlands here,
And still those images stand unadorned.

O Hymen, who bind man in holy wedlock,
Accept this wreath from one who's gladly free.
Do you exchange men's souls? O kindly Gods!
I mean to keep mine only to myself,
Who knows, if any man's would profit me?

Let this, my second wreath, be yours, O Eros!
If you're the goddess' son and I her child
We are related; and, as honest siblings, 40
We are at peace and do not harm each other,
So let it be with us: I'll honor you
As one esteems even what one does not know.

Some more flowers for the pavement— But just see,
All the utensils scattered on the ground!
The sprinkling jar and brushes, strands and bands.
It was your task, you slothful temple maidens,
Is this the way you do your duty, girls?
Let it all lie in patent evidence.

And yet, it's torturing my outraged eyes. 50
Enough, I cannot bear untidiness!

(Sets about putting it in order)

Here comes the throng, aglow with vulgar play,
To do now what without them I have finished.

(IANTHE *and several maidens enter)*

IANTHE

What, lovely Hero, so early up at work?

HERO

So early, since, however late, you're not.

(The maidens put the rest in order)

IANTHE

Come now, she's blaming us because the pot
And a few things were not put in their place.

HERO

Many or few, you did not do your work.

IANTHE

We were up early at it, sprinkling, sweeping;
And then we felt like playing in the fields. 60

HERO

So you just went off and—by the high heavens!
When you danced on your merry feet away,
You had no thought left for your goddess' porch,
Nor for your still-unfinished temple work?
Enough, I do not understand you. Silence.

IANTHE

Because you are so cross with all your sulks,
You envy the lighthearted every pleasure.

HERO

I am not cross; gayer, perhaps, than you;
And often had to grumble in the evenings,

When it was time to play, you would not play; 70
Yet I'll not take its savor from what's serious,
To merge it with the savor of the trivial.

IANTHE

Forgive me, we are vulgar, common folk,
While you, of course, spring from the priestly line.

HERO

You've said it.

IANTHE

And are bent on higher things—

HERO

I'm proud to say it's so.

IANTHE

Quite other joys
And nobler pleasures are for you.

HERO

You know
I am no good at jesting, so jest on!

IANTHE

Yet, had you come with us, and seen them both,
The foreign youths, there by the trellised gate— 80

HERO

Be silent!

IANTHE

But I bet you, you yourself
Would have blinked just a little through the bars.

HERO

Silence! I say. I let your jest have play,
And now my ear is shut to idle chatter.
Do stop your talk and fidgets! Else, by heaven!
I shall report it to the Priest, my uncle,
And he will punish you as you deserve,

It irks me to be overcome by anger,
And yet I must, if I'm to hear such talk.
You must not speak, I say, no, not a word! *90*

(The HIGH PRIEST, *accompanied by the* TEMPLE WARDEN, *enters from the right)*

HERO *(Going up to him)*

I'm glad, my noble uncle, you have come.
I was about to lose my temper, now,
The very morning of this festive day,
That will forever— Uncle, pardon me!

PRIEST

What was the cause of all the great commotion?

HERO

The foolish chatter of these frivolous girls,
The wicked mock that lightly disregards
Whatever is beyond its own regard.
Ah, would that wisdom had as many zealous
Apprentices and converts as has scorn! *100*

PRIEST

And who was it, who, bold above the others,
So sinned against the precepts of our house?

HERO *(after a pause)*

On second thoughts, I will not give her name,
Although she does indeed deserve your censure.
Sir, reprimand them all and bid them go;
The guilty girl herself will take her share.

(To the TEMPLE WARDEN*)*

But you, observe the outer trellised gate,
So that no strangers—

PRIEST

What, has? . . .

HERO

Uncle, please.

Then go! . . . And you too! And avoid the anger
That knows its rights and how to take its toll. *110*

(The TEMPLE WARDEN *exits on the left and the* MAIDENS *on the right)*

HERO

Now I am happier! I could pity them,
If on itself their folly would be spent
And not look for companions and approval.

PRIEST

Much as it pleases me you shun the throng
And do not choose a friend from out the crowd,
It irks me yet, indeed I must lament,
No quiet urge has brought you a companion
Of equal stamp in unison of heart.
A lonely life is the priestess' lot,
It's easier far for two to work and bear. *120*

HERO

I do not think companionship will help:
What one must do, is best done by oneself.
How can you call a priestess's life lonely?
When was I ever lonely in this temple?
From early morning clamorous throngs come crowding,
From east and west the people flock inside;
The threshold of this temple never lacked
Gift offerings and sacrificial presents,
Festive processions, hosts of worshipers.
So there is always something to be done: *130*
To clean, adorn, to look to water pitcher,
To sacrificial hearth, to wreath and pillar,
To plinth and pavement and to the high altar.
Where would I find the time to play and chatter,
To gossip with a friend as you propose?

PRIEST

You have not grasped my meaning.

HERO

Maybe so!
What is not grasped arouses no desire.
Leave me just as I am, I'm happy so.

PRIEST

With change of time one's inclinations change.

HERO

We grumble daily, human senselessness *140*
Will still endure however much we rail;
Then why believe the sensible to be
More senseless and more fitful than the fool?
I do not know what I would, and what we chose,
If when there's no choice, you can call it choosing.
A happy accident has brought me, rather,
But half aware to this most hallowed spot,
Where—like the man who, weary in the evening,
Strides from the shore into the summer sea
And, soft enveloped in the tepid flood, *150*
Merges his limbs in the engaging warmth,
So that he scarce distinctly can declare:
Here I feel me, and here an alien substance—
My being gives itself and takes possession.
From the long, dreamy wonderland of childhood
I first, in this place, woke to consciousness.
Here, in the temple, at the goddess' feet,
At last I found myself, my aim in life.
When once exhausted he has reached the shore,
Who would still yearn for the wild, dizzy waves? *160*
These statues and these pillared passages
Are not for me a dead, external show;
My being clings to them as props in growth;
Cut off from them, I would, like them, be dead.

PRIEST

You must beware lest such a narrow aim
May rightly be regarded as self-centered.
A man may justly wish to keep his being

Free from all jars; but to restrict his life,
Apart from all else, only to himself,
Protecting but his own mind's equipoise, *170*
Seems inadmissible, perverse, yes, monstrous,
And at the same time petty, weak and small.
You know, our line, from immemorial time,
Was favored by the gods with priestly honors;
Portents and oracles they took delight
In uttering through our elected mouths:
Are you not tempted then to win this back,
Our splendid privilege; to your great glory
And for the blessèd good of all the people?
I often counseled you to near our goddess' *180*
Most sacred shrine in quiet midnight hours,
And wait intently for the still small voice
With which divinity speaks to our hearts.

HERO

The gods grant different things to different people;
They have not destined me for prophecy.
Moreover, night's for resting, day for working;
I'm happy only in the beam of day.

PRIEST

Today above all should—

HERO

I did go there,
Before the sun had risen, to our temple,
And sat in meditation by her throne; *190*
But no divine voice came to me from high.
Then I took up the flowers that you see,
Entwining garlands for my Holy Lady:
For her, the first, then for that heavenly pair
And was content.

PRIEST

And thought? . . .

HERO

About my work.

PRIEST

And nothing else?

HERO

What else?

PRIEST

About your parents.

HERO

What is the use? They do not think of me.

PRIEST

Indeed, they think of you and yearn for you.

HERO

I know it's different, though you'll not believe.
I always was a burden to them both, *200*
And there were constant quarrels in their house.
My father used to want what none else wanted,
And would oppress and scold me without cause.
My mother used to suffer and be silent.
My brother—of all breathing humankind,
I cannot bear one only—that's my brother.
Since he was older and I but a female,
He looked on me as plaything for his whims;
But I resisted still, in silent fury.

PRIEST

So you're angry with your parents?

HERO

Angry! Oh! *210*
If I forgot them, it was but to love them,
My temper too has been reformed and calm
Since I have been protected by the goddess.

PRIEST

What if they were to come?

HERO

They will not come.

PRIEST

To take you home?

HERO

Away from here? Me? Never.

PRIEST

Your mother with your bridegroom by her side.

HERO *(Turning to go)*

You're jesting, sir, and I, I was not jesting.

PRIEST

Do stay! It *is* a jest. And yet your parents
Are here.

HERO

No. Here?

PRIEST

They came last evening.

HERO

Oh!

And you concealed it from me.

PRIEST

They themselves 220
Did not wish to disturb this festive night,
That will for many a day be your bright morning.
But you are strong and may let them approach.
See who is coming. He approaches—stops—
He takes a deep breath—is upon us.

HERO

Father?

PRIEST

Yes, yes, it's he.

HERO

And he has grown so old?

PRIEST

The woman by his side—

HERO

Ah, Mother! Mother!

PRIEST

Do you grow so pale? And not rush to your loved ones
In happy haste?

HERO

O let me look on them!
I have not seen them once so very long. *230*

(HERO'S PARENTS *enter)*

FATHER

My child! Hero, my child!

HERO *(Hastening to her mother)*

My dearest Mother!

FATHER

Listen, my child, we've come here, all this way—
I am already breathless—far from home,
To witness your divine initiation;
To see you, in the steps of your forefathers,
Assume the right, all others envy us
Throughout the length and breadth of this our land.
And also for the office that our town
Has long invested me with, in full trust.
And the—my wretched chest! . . . What was I saying? *240*
Well, for these reasons we have come here now!
Good morning to you, brother!

HERO

O my Mother!

FATHER

She also! Also she! Though weak and ailing,
She could not bear to stay at home alone;
She wished to take part in your happiness.

The cart has room for two and so she came
Most willingly. And who, however dull,
Would not rejoice in her own daughter's lot,
When she is set on an exalted path?
Who then would listen to dark, little doubts? 250
To—how should I know? As I've said—rejoices.

HERO

But she says nothing.

FATHER

Nothing? Ask her: why?
Her words flow ceaselessly, the whole day long,
At home, even when needless. Ask her: why?
Yet it were better if she held her tongue;
Who cannot utter anything of use
Is wiser to be dumb. Not so, my brother?

HERO

O dearest uncle, bid your brother silence,
So that my mother speak.

PRIEST

Come, let her, Brother!

FATHER

Then speak! But—

HERO

No, no, let her freely speak, 260
Just as she pleases.

MOTHER *(Half aloud)*

O, my dearest child!

HERO

Ah, do you hear? She spoke. Oh, heavenly sound,
That I've not heard so long! My dearest Mother!

PRIEST *(Walking to the background, to a servant)*

Come here!

FATHER

She's all in tears! Great heavens! . . .
What are you doing, Brother?

(He goes to the back, laying his hand on the shoulder of the TEMPLE WARDEN *standing there)*

My good fellow! What are you doing?

PRIEST

A ring-dove flew into this thicket here,
Perhaps to nest. That may not be. Ho, slave!
Look through the foliage and take it out! [2]

FATHER

Whatever for?

PRIEST

Such is the temple's rule.

FATHER

See, they—

PRIEST

Leave them alone!

FATHER

They're talking. *270*

PRIEST

Let them!

HERO *(In the right foreground with her* MOTHER*)*

Come, come, dear Mother, check your tears!
Rather, say clearly what you feel and think.
I'll listen gladly, most attentively!
For I no longer am that restless girl
Whom you once knew within your husband's house:
The goddess has transformed my childish heart,
And I can calmly think and view things now.
Also—

[2] The dove is a symbolic augury of Hero and Leander's fate.

MOTHER

My child!

HERO

Yes?

MOTHER

They are looking at us.

HERO

Great heavens! Within this temple women too
Have rights; and the oppressed may freely speak. 280
Well, since their glances daunt you, I shall stand
Here between them and you—they cannot see you.
Now tell me if I rightly guessed your mind:
You did not come here sharing Father's views,
And, were you free to have your wishes granted,
You'd gladly take your daughter home with you
Far from her haven here, safe from the storms,
Into the mean hut of your dismal cares?
Not so? Is this not true? Deny it, Mother!

MOTHER

My child, I'm old and am alone.

HERO

Alone? 290
You have your husband, true! A prosperous house,
Attentive serving girls to wait on you.
Then—gods! I was forgetting the best stroke
Of fortune—finally, you have my brother!
He'll bring a bride into the house and flourish,
Giving you sons to carry on our line.

MOTHER

Your brother, child—

FATHER *(In the background to the slave)*

Come, keep it up, my man!

MOTHER

Your brother, child, is now no more at home.

HERO

What, not at home?

MOTHER

After much grievous pain,
Still harsher for his parents, he left us 300
And left his bride to dream of him in tears,
And with like-minded men he sallied forth
To dare bold deeds in some far-distant land.
Whether by ship or charger, who can tell?

HERO

So he is there no more? With such good news,
Thrice-willingly I'd go back home with you!
Yet, if he's not, a hundred more are there
Of the same stamp, with headstrong, savage ways;
The iron band of roughness on their brows
With dwarfish thoughts capping their giant wills, 310
Accustomed still to rush with clumsy hands
Into the calm realm of harmonious thought,
Where resolution germs and grows and ripens
In the sweet, gentle rays of heavenly light,
To rush right in and ever to destroy,
Here to uproot, and there to press, pursue,
With purblind minds and base and boorish hands.
And you would like your child to live with these?
Even perhaps—

MOTHER

Why should I hide it from you?
A woman's good is by her husband's side. 320

HERO

Can *you* say that to me and still not blush?
What? Have to look to that man's every glance,
Your lord and master's? Never dare to speak;
Still silent, whispering, even when you're right?
Even when you're wiser, calmer, more efficient?
How can you dare to tell me such a thing!

FATHER *(In the background)*

The mother bird is fluttering!

MOTHER

Alas! Alas!
They have deformed my sweet child's character,
Seduced her heart with vain and selfish teachings,
That obdurate, unmindful of her mother, 330
She spurns the words of her near relatives!

HERO *(Walking away from her)*

But I will wander with my mind serene
Here by my Lady Aphrodite's altar;
Do what is right, not since I am commanded,
But since it is right, and I see it so;
And none shall rob me of this and deprive—

(With strong emphasis)

In sober truth!

THE SLAVE *(Who, standing on a stool in the background is examining the foliage, stumbles)*

Ah!

HERO *(Looking round)*

What?

MOTHER

Do you not know?
They are disturbing innocent, harmless birds,
And tearing out their nest. And so they snatch
The daughter from her mother, heart from heart, 340
And thus they make their sport, alas, alas!

HERO

You're trembling and grow pale.

MOTHER

In this I see
My very fate.

PRIEST *(To the servant, who has placed the nest in a basket, above which the brooding dove is visible)*

Take it away from here.

(The SERVANT *is about to exit)*

HERO

Stop, put it down, if she is grieved by this.
Give, I say!

(She has seized the basket from the SERVANT *as he is exiting)*

Poor creature, why are you trembling?

See, Mother, it's unhurt.

(Stroking the dove)

Have you been frightened?

(She sits down on the steps of the statue in the left foreground, the basket in her hands, while she now invites the dove to fly away by raising it aloft, now is preoccupied with it, examining it closely)

PRIEST *(To the* SERVANT*)*

Did I not order? . . .

(The SERVANT *points in excuse to* HERO. *The* PRIEST *goes up to her)*

Are you still a novice
That you know nothing of our temple's rules?

MOTHER *(Standing in the foreground to the right)*

My heart is failing! Ah, most wretched sight!

PRIEST *(Speaking across to her)*

And now let me tell you, you feeble woman, *350*
Why did you come sowing dissension here?
Why show surprise at what you know's our rule,
The sacred order of our holy temple?
No bird may nest here in the temple's grove,
Nor with impunity may ring-doves coo;

No climbing tendril may embrace the elms,
And all that couples must stay far away,
And she too must submit to the same fate.

HERO *(Stroking the dove)*

Poor creature, how they quarrel over us!

PRIEST

Does this seem hard to you and make you tremble? 360
What do you want? To take her home? Then take her!
The goddess has no need of you nor her.
Here is no earthly Aphrodite[3] honored,
Who couples human beings like animals,
But the celestial,[4] risen from the foam,
Uniting sense of spirit, not the senses,
The holy mother of harmonious being,
Sexless because she is herself pure sex,
And heavenly because she springs from heaven.
The goddess has no need of you, nor her. 370
Then go, find her some undistinguished mate,
Exhausting yourself in the painful process;
Make her the hand-maid of the boor who woos her;
Instead of independent, radiant here,
The only one of her exiguous kin
To be herself, a being, a whole world.
But since you wish it, she is free, then take her!
You are her mother still. You, Hero, follow!
Folly is calling, follow like a woman.

HERO *(Standing up, to the dove)*

You see the worth of words, sweet little thing! 380

(Giving the basket to the SERVANT*)*

Take it away and give it back its freedom,
The freedom every animal desires.

(Exit the SERVANT*)*

[3] Aphrodite Pandemos.
[4] Aphrodite Urania. See Pausanias' discourse in Plato's *Symposium.*

But you, good uncle, do not scold my mother,
For she means well and loves me very dearly.
Yes, dearest mother, let us hold our tongues,
For he is right and only did his duty.
I, go with you? You stay with me! O Mother,
If they at home torment you, come to me.
There is no tumult here, no wounds are opened,
The goddess does not grumble and this temple *390*
Forever looks serenely upon me.
Ah, do you know the bliss of independence?
You've never known it, do not then be envious.
No, follow me, lighthearted to the feast.
Today, proud like a victor, and tomorrow
In even tenor, water jug in hand,
Busy, just as before, upon the altars,
And so, day after day. Come, if you will!
Do come, or else I'll carry you, I'm strong;
Ah, she is softening—smiling—Uncle, see? *400*

(Under her breath)

Give me the signal!
But you follow me,
The time is passing and the feast is ready.

(Dawdling as she goes)

And when you see the ornaments, rich clothes
And all the splendor they prepare for me,
You will yourself—

(Taking a few steps and then turning back)

Do hurry up a little!

(Exeunt both, to the right)

FATHER

Now, Brother, quickly go—

PRIEST

Quickly? Why?

What is to last long must be pondered long;
If I thought she were weak, I would discharge her.

FATHER

But, bear in mind! . . .

PRIEST

Indeed, I bear in mind,
Wholesome and firm constraint is how to settle *410*
All earthly vacillations and confusions.
You'd ever waver mid alternatives,
Were not reality your boundary stone.
Free choice is but the plaything of weak fools;
The wise man sees in every "shall" a "must."
Compulsion, as first duty, is his truth.

(Turning to the SERVANTS*)*

The feast begins.

NAUKLEROS' *voice (Behind the scenes)*

Come here, this way, Leander!

PRIEST

What's that?

TEMPLE WARDEN

Two strangers, weary with long waiting,
Make their own way here, beating back the bushes—
Have you come back? Sir, these are the same men *420*
Who were this morning at the trellised gate—
The people's pressure is growing at the back
And they are grumbling at the long delay.

PRIEST

Keep back those there.

(Exit TEMPLE WARDEN *to the left)*

You others, open now

(To several servants who have gradually come up from the background)

The outer gates that give toward the town.

(To his brother)

Meanwhile, you, give the gods a word of thanks
For your posthumous glory through your child.

(The old man leans on his stick, bowed toward the temple)

Let the crowd enter, do you hear? Keep order,
Lest roughness mar the ceremonial splendor,
And mind your own behaviour today; *430*
Like sun has pleasure its appointed day,
And like the sun its evening: remorse.

TEMPLE WARDEN *(Behind the scenes)*

No, no, I say!

NAUKLEROS *(Behind the scenes)*

Do listen, my good sir.

PRIEST

Keep at your duty; Brother, come with me!

(Exeunt both to the right)

TEMPLE WARDEN *(Entering)*

I take my stand here! Bold boy, will you dare,
And will you further set your foot across me?

NAUKLEROS *(Who likewise has come onstage)*

No, not across you, but, see here, beside you.
So I am here at last. Leander, come!

(Enter LEANDER*)*

TEMPLE WARDEN

The arrogance of youth! Did you not know? . . .

NAUKLEROS

Why, we knew nothing, we are strangers, sir, *440*
And come from Abydos' neighboring shore[5]
To Sestos here, to see your festival.

[5] Abydos, on the Asiatic shore of the Hellespont.

TEMPLE WARDEN

But are you not taught manners too at home?

NAUKLEROS

Indeed we are, and also other maxims,
Such as: "A timid man returns home hungry."

TEMPLE WARDEN

But I—

NAUKLEROS

See, while you here are fussing over
Just two of us, the crowd is flooding in.

TEMPLE WARDEN

Back there! Do you not hear?

(He turns toward the background and regulates the people who, from the left, are pressing in near the temple steps)

NAUKLEROS *(To* LEANDER*)*

Why are you tugging me?
We have at last got here. Who ventures, wins.
This is the best place. Firm upon the plinth *450*
I set my foot, I'll see who drives me off.
And just look at the splendor all around!
The little shrine there, look, the gate, the pillars,
You never see such wonders back at home.
Look, where they set an altar in the center,
For sacrifice I'd say. What are you gazing at?
Stop staring at the floor. Now by the gods!
Has your old melancholy gripped you here?
But I am telling you—

(The people have gradually arranged themselves along the left side up to where the two friends are standing. He looks around)

Now, my good friend,
You press too hard.

(To LEANDER*)*

Listen, I'm telling you *460*

Unless this evening you relate to me
In greatest detail all that happened here
And drink with me a great big jug of wine
In rapturous roar, our friendship's at an end.
Why, all your gloomy mood— But do look there!
The two girls! See, they are the very same
Whom we saw at the trellised gate this morning.
They peer at us. Do you like one? Speak up!

(IANTHE *and another maid-servant have brought a portable altar and put it down in the right foreground by the statue of Eros)*

IANTHE *(Whispering to her companion as they do this)*

There they are. On the right the fairer, taller.
The dark one seems upset. What's troubling him? *470*

NAUKLEROS

Deliberately they're dawdling. How she ogles!

TEMPLE WARDEN *(Coming forward, to the* MAIDS*)*

And now you also! That will do. Be off.

(Exeunt the MAIDS. *To the young men)*

You seem most quick to everything forbidden.

NAUKLEROS

I take what comes. Who hesitates is lost.

(A second altar has been brought and set down on the left by Hymen's statue. A third has already been standing in the center against the steps)

TEMPLE WARDEN

Make room, make room! The altar must go there.

NAUKLEROS

I'll gladly make room, if you give me some.

TEMPLE WARDEN

And mind your manners, do not be presumptuous.

(The music of flutes is heard)

Here's the procession. Back there! Clear the center!

(Regulates the crowd in rows on the left)

NAUKLEROS

They're coming: Look! Now take care, watch it closely!
And stroke the priestess' robe as she goes by, *480*
They say it's sure to cure your melancholy.

(To the music of flutes the procession enters from the right. Sacrificial boys carrying vessels. The leading men of Sestos. Temple maidens, including IANTHE. PRIESTS, HERO *in mantle and headband by her* UNCLE*'s side. Her* PARENTS *follow. They sing)*

O mother of mortals
Who dwellest in Heaven,
Grant us a favorable,
Protective glance!

(The processionists take their place on the right, opposite the serried crowd. The center of the stage is empty)

PRIESTS *(As they take their place)*

All reverence to the gods! [6]

PEOPLE *(Responding)*

May we be blessed!

NAUKLEROS

There comes the priestess. What a lovely woman!
Come, let us kneel. But no, let me first look
Backwards across the pedestal to see
How they perform the rites of consecration. *490*

HERO

(In the background standing where the portable altar has been

[6] Compare Phaon's pregnant plea to Sappho, in Act V of *Sappho,* echoed by her in the very last scene:

To mortals love, and reverence to the gods!
(Act V, scene iii, V. 1782.)

placed. In front of her, two sacrificial boys are kneeling, bearing incense in costly vessels)

Accept this new shoot of thy ancient line,
And favor me, ah, more than I deserve!

(She pours incense into the flame and comes forward, the PRIEST *on her left and her* PARENTS *behind her. The* TEMPLE WARDEN *is some distance away)*

PRIESTS

All reverence to the Gods!

PEOPLE

May we be blessed!

NAUKLEROS

They are approaching. Now, Leander, kneel!

(They kneel, LEANDER *close by the statue of Hymen,* NAUKLEROS *somewhat further back. The rest of the people also kneel)*

HERO

(Comes up to the statue of Eros and pours incense in the flame of the adjacent altar. The PRIEST *is by her side)*

You, who vouchsafe love, take from me all mine.
In greeting you, I take my leave of you.

(She withdraws)

PRIESTS

All reverence to the Gods!

PEOPLE

May we be blessed!

HERO *(Standing by the statue of Hymen)*

Your brother sends me—

NAUKLEROS *(Softly to* LEANDER*)*

Will you not look up?

LEANDER

(Who has been gazing at the ground straight in front of him, now raises his head)

PRIEST

What's up? Why stand stone-still? [7]

HERO

I forgot the tongs.

PRIEST

You have them in your hand.

HERO

You, who vouchsafe— *500*

PRIEST

That was the previous prayer. Enough. The sacrifice!

*(*HERO *pours incense in the fire. A stronger flame shoots up*[8]*)*
Too much! Well, that will do. The temple now.

(They go away. Coming to the center of the stage, HERO *looks back over her right shoulder as if something is wrong with her shoe. Her glance falls on the two young men. Her parents come toward her. The music is heard once more)*

Curtain

[7] Compare Marlowe's *Hero and Leander:*

Stone-still he stood and evermore he gazed (V. 163).

[8] Highly symbolic at the altar of Hymen.

ACT II

The grove of the temple at Sestos. On the left side in the background a seat surrounded by foliage. NAUKLEROS *enters from the left.*

NAUKLEROS

Leander, come! And hurry after me!

LEANDER *(Appearing from the same side)*

Look, here I am!

NAUKLEROS

So quick? Who would have thought it!
Come, tell me how much longer must I lead you,
As punishment for a sin, unknown, undone,
Just like the boy that guides his blind lord's path,
All round the noisy cities where men crowd
From feast to feast, from marketplace to altar, *510*
Seeking some spot to bring you happiness?
And how long must I sit and face you, sick
Of words, scanning your miserable eyes
For the first sign of newly kindled joy,
Only to read your eternal no, no, no!
Can it be helped if your poor mother died? [9]
'Twas right and proper, you, a valiant son,
To humor her in her profound affliction,
Should dwell upon the seashore, far from town
And haunts of men, doing your filial duty. *520*

[9] In Leander, Grillparzer sees himself after his own mother's suicide.

But now that she is dead, what holds you back
From throwing in your lot among your peers,
And sharing with them all their cares and pleasures?
Mourn the good lady, tear your dark brown hair,
But after that return once more to joys
She would you have, you long wished she had had.
Is that not so? Then tell me what you think.
Well?

LEANDER

Ah! I'm tired.

NAUKLEROS

Of course, how very tiresome!
The whole day, in a strange place, crowded out
By strange men and by merry faces, 530
To find one's way through it all, to gape, to listen,
Even to speak. By all the mighty gods,
Who could have stood this?

LEANDER (*Who has sat down*)

I am sick as well.[10]

NAUKLEROS

Sick? Do not worry! That will pass in time.
Just get back home to your old musty hut,
Washed by the sea, amid the dunes and waves
And dismal clouds that ever threaten rain.
Just take your festive clothes off from your shoulders,
And wrapped up in your rough old sailor jerkin,
Sit by the shore, angling the whole day long, 540
Dive in the sea, the envy of the fishes,
With evening, just lie, as once I found you,
Upon your rowboat, with your face turned up,
Your body's burden on reliant shoulders,
The while the vessel rocks upon the waves;
Lie stretched out so and gaze upon the stars

[10] In 1826 Grillparzer records how he too had felt physically ill at the time of his adolescent passion for Theresa, a young actress, some twenty years before.

And think—of your dear mother, who but now
In good time has, in dying, set you free;
Of her; of spirits that dwell high above!
Of—think of Thought; or rather think of nothing! *550*
Only just get there; friend, what is the betting—
You will be well, once more be hale and hearty.
Then let us go, for home is far away,
And time is running out, and friends returning.

LEANDER

It is so shady here. Let's stay awhile!
We'll find a boat with ease. I'll row you back.

NAUKLEROS

Yes, row, you will. See, how his eyes are sparkling!
Beside the helm, his eager hands outstretched,
His taut arms driving ever forwards, backwards,
Now up, now down, away upon the waves! *560*
You feel you are some hero, god, a man;
For other things I must seek some one else.
Yet, my fine friend, it's not a question merely
Of rowing, but of other, weightier matters.
You know, we're standing on forbidden ground,
In the temple grove, prohibited to all
Except on feast days, that today is over;
Watchmen are roaming now through the green bushes
To apprehend intruders they may see,
And take them to the high priest of their temple *570*
For punishment, perhaps the most extreme . . .
Did you say something?

LEANDER

Nothing.

NAUKLEROS

Then let's go!
The freedom of the feast at midday ends,
And the sun's rays are almost at their zenith.
I am not keen, because you wish to dawdle,
To grace the deepest dungeons of this town.

Do you hear? What, still deaf! O gracious gods!
Turn, turn from him just as he turns from you!

There he is leaning, weak, his limbs exhausted.
A handsome youth, and dark, although not tall, 580
His dark brown hair falls on his brow in curls;
His eyes, when not obscured by his eye lashes,
Spark like hot coals when these are newly stirred,
His shoulders broad; his long arms firm and tough,
And both with rounded muscles tautly bulging;
Eros no more, but Hymen's very image.[11]
Girls always stare at him, but he—great gods!
What happened to the soul of this fair body?
He is—how to describe it—timid, dull!
I also am a pretty virile fellow, 590
My yellow hair is rarer than his brown,
Instead of his complexion like an Indian's,
A gleaming white beams over my firm bones,
I'm taller, as is fitting for the leader.
And yet if we both mix in company
With girls, whether at feasts, at games, at dances;
None looks at me, all eyes devour him.
They wink, they nod, they laugh, they ogle, giggle.
All, all for him. They lose their silly heads
Over that dreaming lump, that stupid wretch. 600
But he—why, even then he'll notice nothing.
And should at last he notice, how he'll blush!
Tell me, friend, is this but by accident,
Or do you know you are much more attractive
With strawberry complexion on your cheeks?
This very day in the temple— Good gods! Did it
Not seem as if the earth had drawn all beings
Back in her teeming womb, to fashion girls
From all that rich profusion, only girls?
From Thrace, as well as prosperous Hellespont 610
The feminine bevy crowded; fairest flowers,

[11] Perhaps Grillparzer, when he composed Naukleros' speech, had in mind Marlowe's luscious description of Leander's charms, which fascinated Neptune (Poseidon) himself!

Carnations, roses, tulips, violets, lilies—
I fancy here and there a daisy too—
The lot, a gay, exhilarating sight:
A wandering sea of heads, of snow-white shoulders,
And rounded hips to take the place of waves.
But should you ask him now what he has seen,
If they indeed were girls, or just wild swans;
He'll say he does not know, he walked straight on.
Yet he's the one at whom they all were gazing; *620*
The priestess too. A splendid, radiant woman!
She'd have done better on this festive day
To swear eternal faithfulness to love,
Than give it up, left poor and niggardly;
Fair acolyte of grace and majesty,
With eagle eyes[12] and cooing like a dove,
With noble brow, a fair smile on her lips,
In her appearance, almost like a queen,
Who in her very cradle might well have been crowned.
And then; let me tell you what beauty is. *630*
What do you know of the proud regal neck
Round which the flowing tresses rich entwine;
Of shoulders, that when shyly falling back
Make way for the more richly gifted breasts,
Of dainty ankles and of lightsome foot,
And all the treasures of a favored body?
What do you know? I say, and you saw nothing.
But she saw you. I could not fail to note.
As we knelt there, I behind, you in front,
By Hymen's statue, by that mighty god, *640*
And she approached, disseminating incense;
She stood stone-still, her hand limp in the air;
Gazing at you, she stood there hesitating,
One, two, three brief, and everlasting moments.
At last she went on with her sacred task.
But even in parting her eyes plainly said,

[12] See "Trennung" ("Separation"), in *Tristia ex Ponto,* a cycle of poems, where Grillparzer says of Marie von Smolenitz, his prototype for Hero: *Her eye an eagle's, gazing at the sun.*

In harsh breach of the day's cold chastity,
That shuts her out for evermore from love:
"Ah, what a pity, that one is my man!"
Now don't you smile and lap it up, you wretch! 650
You hide your face? Away with your fat fingers!
No more hypocrisy, just say it's so.

(He takes his hand away from his eyes)

Gods! These are tears. Leander! What? You're crying?

LEANDER *(Who has stood up)*

Leave me alone and do not torture me!
And do not speak, unthinking, of her neck
And figure. Oh, I'm threefold wretched now!

NAUKLEROS

Leander! Wretched? Happy! You're in love.

LEANDER

What did you say? I'm sick. My breast is hurting
Me, not inside me, but here, outside, here;
Just by my bones. Ah, I am sick to death.

NAUKLEROS

You are a fool, but a most fortunate fool! 660a
Great gods, I thank you for afflicting him!
Now rain on him your sharpest, fiercest arrows
Till he calls out to me: "Stop! it's enough,
I will endure what human beings bear."
Come, friend, give me your hand! My friend, at last,
Converted too late by most sweet delights.
You newborn, happy youth! But stay a moment.
I see a nasty stain on our pure joy . . .
Come back into the town; there still assembled
Are all the girls we saw this festive morning. 670
There look around and take your loving pick;
For, friend, the virgin who just made you ripe
Is priestess, and upon this very day
Has sworn forever to abjure all men;

And strict the penalty should she forget,
And also for the man forgetting it.

LEANDER

I knew this. Come, night! Everything is over.

NAUKLEROS

Over? The same old tune, before it has
Even begun? Why? How? You timorous fellow.
Have you no spine to reach the highest delight? *680*
Will you say this to me with quivering cheeks
And rattling bones and think I shall believe it?
You shall remain now. Here! Shall speak to her.
Who knows whether her vow is all that strict,
Or may be quashed, should she recant at once.
Who knows whether your love is all that warm
As now it seems? However that may be,
You shall not hesitate where you must act.
At least know what your fate is, and endure it
And learn to take leave of your boyish years. *690*
We're strangers here. Come! Who shall blame us then,
If, having lost our way, we ask our road?
Eventually we'll reach the house, the temple,
We'll stand before her and hear what she says.
Here comes a maiden with a water pitcher
In each hand. Come, let us enquire of her.
She doubtless knows . . .

(He goes in her direction)

Leander! Fortune's son!
Why are you tugging me? Stay here, it's she,
The virgin—she, the new priestess herself!
She would fetch water from the sacred spring, *700*
As is her duty here. Then seize your moment
And speak out, not too boldly, nor too shyly.
Do you hear? Meanwhile, I'll stand guard round these
bushes
To see all's quiet, no intruder come!

Come here, I tell you; now! Step forward then
And speak— But first be still—come here with me!

(They withdraw)

Enter HERO, *from the left foreground, without her mantle, dressed more or less as at the beginning of the first act, carrying two empty pitchers. She walks straight across the stage.*

HERO *(Sings)*

Then spoke the god;
Come hither to me
In my clouds,
Beside me. 710

*(*LEANDER, *gently pushed by* NAUKLEROS, *has advanced a few paces. He remains standing, his head lowered.* HERO *exits by the right foreground)*

NAUKLEROS *(Coming forward)*

Well, let it be! You have yourself willed this.
If you just cannot seize and win your fortune,
Then learn to do without. It's better so.
Is she not consecrated and thus fatal
To approach? I was indeed half jesting
When I advised you do your uttermost:
And yet it makes me mad to see a man
Who wants and hopes and still has not the courage
To stretch his hand and grasp the crown of victory.
Yet it is better so. Cheer up, my friend! 720
Your timid heart was now a surer guide
Than Nestor's wisdom [13] and Achilles' [14] courage.
Well, let us now go home. Yet, never again
Dare—

[13] Nestor was the wise old man of Greek mythology, immortalized by Homer.

[14] Achilles was perhaps the most famous of the Greek heroes of the Trojan War, celebrated for his victorious duel over Hector. (See Homer's *Iliad.*)

LEANDER

See, she's coming back.

NAUKLEROS

By Jove, she is!

Follow her!

LEANDER

I?

NAUKLEROS

Who else?

LEANDER

I, speak, approach?

(They again draw back. HERO *comes back, carrying a pitcher on her head, and the other hanging down in her right hand.*

HERO *(Sings)*

But she is stroking
The silk-soft down

(Stands still and speaks)

My uncle holds I should not sing the song
Of Leda and the swan.[15]

(Walking on)

I wonder where's
The harm?

(As she reaches the center of the stage, LEANDER *bursts forward and throws himself at her feet with lowered head)*

Great gods! What's that? How shocking, this! *730*
My knees are quaking, and the pitchers slipping.

(She puts down the pitchers)

[15] Leda, wife of Tyndareus, King of Sparta, was approached by Zeus in the shape of a swan, and as a result laid an egg, from which sprang the famous Helen (of Troy).

A man! Why, two! Strangers, what would you have
Of me, the priestess, in the goddess' grove?
I am not unprotected and unwatched;
And should I raise my voice, watchmen will come
And give you cause to rue your insolence.
Then go, while you have time, taking as forfeit
The consciousness of wrong that missed its mark.

NAUKLEROS

Maiden, we did not come to do you harm;
Rather to cure the deep, mysterious ill *740*
That has laid low my friend, him, you see here.
The man is sick.

HERO

Why are you telling me?
Go to the priests in great Apollo's temple:
They cure the sick.

NAUKLEROS

Not sickness of this sort.
For as it gripped him in your festive temple,
It can be cured only in the same place.

HERO

What, at today's feast?

NAUKLEROS

Yes, through your own eyes.

HERO

Is this your meaning? Dare you be so bold?
I thought as much: presumptuous is the mob,
Irreverent, and with no shame nor manners. *750*
I'm going, and shall send servants at hand
To fetch my pitchers, and should you still loiter,
They'll tell you straight how far you are transgressing.

NAUKLEROS

Do not depart thus: look first at the youth,
Whom you so sorely grieve with your hard words.

LEANDER *(Looking up at her)*

Do stay!

HERO

You are, I see, the same young man
Who, at today's feast, knelt by Hymen's altar.
Yet then you seemed to me pious and proper;
It grieves me that I find you otherwise.

LEANDER *(Who has stood up with a protesting gesture)*

Oh no. Not otherwise! Do stay!

HERO *(To* NAUKLEROS*)*

What does he want? *760*

NAUKLEROS

I told you, he is hanging on your glance,
And all your words spell death and life for him.

HERO

Good youth, you have been ill-advised to hope,
And let your heart stray from the rightful path;
For howsoever I explain your meaning,
It seems you think of me with inclination:
But I am Aphrodite's priestess here;
My vows enjoin me to remain unwed.
And therefore it is dangerous to woo me:
Death threatens him who dares embark on this. *770*
So let me have my pitchers and be gone:
I should be sorry were you to be harmed.

(She is about to take hold of the pitchers)

LEANDER

Then drown me in the bottom of the sea! [16]

HERO

You poor young man, how much you make me grieve!

[16] In view of the aftermath this line is pregnant with dramatic irony.

NAUKLEROS

O priestess, do not stop alone at pity!
Be helpful to the youth who loves you so.

HERO

What can I do? You are aware of all.

NAUKLEROS

At least speak a few words to him to cure him.
Come, please! The trees will ward off prying eyes.
I'll put your pitcher in the shade for you; *780*
And so do come and grant us just a word.
Ah, will you not sit here?

HERO

It seems improper.

NAUKLEROS

Do it through pity for the young man's suffering.

HERO *(To* LEANDER*)*

You sit down too.

NAUKLEROS

Yes, here. And you beside him.

*(*LEANDER *sits in the middle, resting his body against the trunk of a tree, hands in lap, looking down straight in front of him.* HERO *and* NAUKLEROS *sit on either side a little forward, so that they can look at each other)*

HERO *(To* NAUKLEROS*)*

I have already told you and repeat this:
No man alive may hope to seek my hand,
For duty bids me live without a husband.
Had you come yesterday, I were still free:
But I have vowed today, and mean to keep it.

(To LEANDER*)*

Ah, do not hide your eyes behind your hands, *790*

Good youth! No, leave this grove with a high heart;
Favor some other woman with your glance
And still enjoy what is denied us here.

LEANDER *(Leaping up)*

May the stark cruel earth devour me quite
And all that's good and lovely shut me out,
If ever love for any other woman—

HERO *(Who has also stood up, to* NAUKLEROS*)*

Tell him, he must not rave. What use to him?
What use to me? Who likes to rack oneself?
He is so handsome, young, and ah, so good,
I wish him every joy, all happiness; *800*
Let him go home—

LEANDER

I, home? I'll take root here,
And stand here with these trees all day and night
And gaze upon that temple's top forever.

HERO

The watchmen of this place will seize and harm him,
Do tell him!

(To LEANDER*)*

And, good youth, should you go home,
Let all the stress and merry tug of life
Efface for you whatever is too much,
The rest preserve and I shall do the same:
And when next year and every following year
This festival returns, then you come back, *810*
Place yourself in the shrine where I may see you;
I shall be glad to find you are at peace.

LEANDER *(Throwing himself at her feet)*

O heavenly woman!

HERO

No, that is not proper.

And look: my uncle's coming. He will scold me,
And justly, for my giving in to you.

NAUKLEROS

Take up your pitcher, let me drink from it.
This is the best way to explain our conduct.

LEANDER *(Pushing him aside)*

Not you, me, me!

HERO *(Holding the pitcher toward him, from which he drinks, kneeling)*

Then drink, and may each drop
Spell comfort, all this water augur bliss.[17]

(Enter the PRIEST*)*

PRIEST

What are you doing here?

HERO

See, he is sick. *820*

PRIEST

The healing of the sick is not your function.
They should go to the temple of Apollo,
Where a host of priests can heal.

HERO

That's what I said.

PRIEST

And more, above all, whether sick or sound:
No man, no stranger, may unpunished enter
The goddess' grove, the priestly precincts here.
If I discharge you, you may thank my grace;
The next time you might fall foul of the law.

NAUKLEROS

Yet I but now saw crowds assembled there,
In temple and in grove, both men and women. *830*

[17] Like the dove of Act I, another symbolic augury, this time of Leander's tragic destiny.

PRIEST

The festival allows for their admission,
They're free to stay from morning until noon.

NAUKLEROS

Well then, the sun has not yet climbed so high,
It burns and blazes, but far from its zenith.

PRIEST

Be glad of that and make use of this span;
For when the sun, upon its journey's peak,
Sucks up the shadows with its thirsty rays,
Here from the temple winding horns shall blare,
At once the feast's end and your pressing peril.
Moreover, I am told you're from Abydos, *840*
Whose citizens are ill-disposed toward us.
Upon the fish trail,[18] elsewhere too at sea,
They clash with Sestos' good citizens.
Think well on this, and that those wronged too often
Take worse revenge, the longer they've postponed it.

NAUKLEROS

But I am thinking: man for man, dear sir.
This is my rule for Sestos' good folk.
Should they lay traps for us upon these shores,
We'll pay them back on our own shores at home.

PRIEST

I'm not disposed to bandy words with you. *850*
I've said all that was needed, speak no more!

(To HERO*)*

You, take your pitchers up and come!

(As the young men are about to assist her)

Leave them!

Maid servants are approaching.

(He beckons to the left in the wings)

[18] Literally "haul."

Follow me.
Much in the temple's waiting to be done.

(Leading HERO *by the hand, exit with her to the left. Enter* IANTHE *meanwhile)*

IANTHE

Now, what have you been up to, handsome strangers?
I saw it all from far. But now make haste.
And who was it who made you press your suit
Upon the priestess, sworn to chastity?
Were I a man, I'd look to find my equal.

(Exit with the pitchers)

NAUKLEROS

(Speaking in the direction of the PRIEST*)*

Self-seeking, arbitrary, harsh old beard! *860*
This is the way you lock up gracious beauty,
Deny the world the warm cheer of her rays,
And deck your deed with sacred subterfuges?
Since when have gods been jealous, warped of mind?
At home, we too revere the heavenly ones;
Yet Zeus' priest serenely walks with us,
Surrounded by his myriad happy kin,
And blesses others, he himself well-blessed.
But you, inherited this from the Orient,
This shameful job of jealous Indus slaves,[19] *870*
And veil yourself in outrage and in night.
But this is how it is. So come, poor wretch!

LEANDER

Poor wretch? Do you mean me?

NAUKLEROS

Whom else? Ah well,
Soon satisfied! Come on!

[19] For "Indus" the Berlin (Deutsche Bibliothek) Edition has the anachronistic "Judas," an even more unfortunate reading!

LEANDER

I'm ready.

NAUKLEROS

What?
Will you not once more gaze upon the place
From which you must forever? . . .

LEANDER

Ever?

NAUKLEROS

No?
Then you would? . . . What is in your mind? Speak up!

LEANDER

Listen! Is not the signal sounding? We must go!

NAUKLEROS

Why so reserved? What are you keeping back?
You do not mean to come back to this place, *880*
Where dungeons, danger, death—

LEANDER

It *is* the signal.
Our friends are going home. Let's go with them.
My life may well be wretched, as you've said:
If it's so poor, for so much why not give it?
What's yet to happen, who can say? Who knows?

(Exit quickly)

NAUKLEROS

Leander! Listen! Keep on fussing, fool,
Over these frigid fellows! Frigid? Ah,
Example teaches. Yet I will protect you.
Should you return, before I've sanctioned this,
We'll have to— Wait for me. Do you hear? Leander! *890*

(Following him with gestures and signs to hold him back)

Curtain

ACT III

Apartment within HERO'*s tower. On the right side of the background, in a broad parapet, the high-constructed bow-window, to which a few wide steps lead up. Beside it a tall lamp-stand. Against the left side of the background the narrow door of the main entrance. A second door, hidden by a curtain on the right side of the center. On the same side in the foreground, a table, beside it a low-backed chair. When the curtain rises a* SERVANT *enters, bearing aloft a lamp which he places on the stand and exits. Directly behind him the* HIGH PRIEST *with* HERO. *She has her cloak over her shoulders, as at the end of Act I.*

PRIEST

The sacred rites have all been duly done,
The night is falling, come into your home,
Yours from today, the priestess' quiet dwelling.

HERO *(Looking round her)*

So it is here!

PRIEST

It is. And as the tower
Within which you behold your vaulted home
Stands on the seashore, separate and alone,
Linked to our dwelling but by passages—
Upon its stout walls it falls sheerly down
To where against its base the ocean roars,
While its tall top rubs shoulders with the clouds, *900*
Peering beyond the sea and air and land—
So shall you live on, separate and at one,

Linked to us mortals as to the immortals,
Mistress of yourself as of others too,
A dual life, a most elect existence,
And shall be happy.

HERO

So it's here!

PRIEST

They have,
I see, assembled for you all the chattels
That usually adorn a priest's abode.
Here there are scrolls, with wise words rich inscribed,
There, board and stylet, for your private thoughts. *910*
Even this lyre here, an ancient heirloom
From your paternal aunt, my own dear sister,
Who once was priestess in this place like you.
There is no dearth of flowers. I see the wreath
You wore today during the consecration.
You'll find here everything to lift the mind.
Not to arouse, yet satisfy desires,
Serving the gods to make you kin to them.

(Pointing to the side door)

This other chamber here conceals your couch,
The same that welcomed the newcomer then, *920*
On your first day, seven creeping years ago,
And since has seen you grow and bloom and ripen,
Becoming wise, serene and chaste and good,
The same, that round your rosy sleeping cheeks
Saw sweet dreams play, dreams of a happiness
Now realized— But you are dreaming still.

HERO

Good Uncle, I am listening.

PRIEST

Shall I own it?
I thought to find you merrier on the evening
Of the auspicious day that crowns our wishes.

What we have striven, hoped for, you *have, are* that, 930
And yet you're cold and dumb and not delighted.

HERO

Uncle, you know, we are not always master
Of every mood that comes and roves and goes,
Just self-creating without consequence.
What's loftiest, fairest, if it does appear,
In so far as it comes as a surprise,
Is almost numbing, as all greatness numbs.
Yet grant me but one night of sweet repose,
Refreshing meditation, and, dear Uncle,
You'll find me just the same as you have known. 940
This place is still, there's scarce a breath of air;
The waves of thought more lightly ebb away,
With all disturbance rippling to the shore,
And, be sure, I shall once more find composure.

PRIEST

Composure? Was this but some slip, my child?
Or did you feel the meaning of the word
You have just uttered, music to my ear?
You've named the mighty leaven of the world
That buoys all greatness a thousandfold aloft
And even bears the trivial toward the stars. 950
The hero's feat, the poet's sacred song,
The prophet's vision, the divinity's trace,
All this, composure quickens and salutes—
While dull distraction but mistakes and mocks.
Do you feel this? Then, child, be of good cheer!
For you shall wander here, a blessèd being,
All dusty wishes withering away;
Just like the man who heavenward looks at evening,
In the dim twilight, seeing only gray,
Drab gray, and neither night nor trace of light, 960
Yet vaguely gazing, spots a twinkling star
And then a second, third, a hundred, thousands—
Rich harbingers of a divine-illumined night—
With blessèd tears in his uplifted eyes.

Beings take shape and faëry mists dissolve,
The background of existence opens up,
And heavenly voices, half from one's own breast
And half from the wide infinite above—

HERO

Uncle, you know, my mind does not presume
To soar to such heights. Do not hope so much! *970*
But be sure I intend to be most faithful
To all my duties and my obligations.

PRIEST

Well, be it so, though hardly right and proper,
When starting on a course, to set your goal
So near, so miserably near, your goal;
Still, let it be for now. Yet mark but this:
In all, the passing of the days may bring you,
Avoid the first cause! He who, bent on action,
Plunges into life's stress, where bold men jostle,
May seek out danger with a naked sword: *980*
The worse the fight, the greater is the glory;
But he who struggles on for self-fulfillment,
Where only wholeness spells mature achievement
Must keep his mind far from the common strife,[20]
For one does not return from this unscathed;
The very scars remain as sharp reminders.
The river, bearing ships and watering meadows,
May force its headlong way through rocks and crags,
And may be sullied by the soil washed down—
It flows on, useful, whether dull or clear; *990*
The source, however, mirroring moon and stars,
That thirsty pilgrims reverently near,
And the priestess, for sprinkling on the altar,
Must undefiled preserve its crystal waves,
The least disturbance leaves its waters sullied.

[20] Grillparzer strikes a profound autobiographical note in this passage, which is nonetheless dramatically apt in the mouth of the not ignoble Priest of the first three acts.

And so sleep soundly! Should you need advice,
Seek it from me, who am your second father;
Yet, should you spurn the counsel of a friend,
You'd also find in me a man who's ready
To shed his own blood from these very veins, 1000

(With outstretched arm)

Should he find but a drop in all the mixture
That hides unrighteousness and harbors taint.

(Exit by the center door)

HERO *(After a pause)*

I clearly see what happened in the grove
With those young men has made him cross with me.
And truly he is right. Could I but own it!
Were I not Hero, not the priestess here,
My service consecrated to the gods,
The younger, shorter one, hair curly brown,
Perhaps would please me— Did I say perhaps?
But by this time I know what's called attraction 1010
Is very real and is to be avoided;
Avoid it then I will. You, kindly gods!
How much one day may teach and ah, how little
A year may give, forget— Well, he is gone,
I'll hardly see him more in all my life,
And so it's over. Ah! Well!

(She takes off her mantle)

Lie there! With what a different mind I took
You up this morning, put you down this evening.
You wrap a whole life in your ample folds!
Keep, what you know, that's put away with you.[21] 1020
Yet, what am I to do, I cannot sleep.

(Seizing the lamp and holding it aloft)

[21] Another symbolic augury charged with dramatic irony. While Hero hopes to put away with her mantle her secret love, she is in fact doffing the symbol of her priesthood.

Shall I look round the place? How wide! How empty!
I'll see you quite enough for many a year;
I'll gladly save your promise, for the future.
Listen! Nothing . . . Alone, alone, alone!

(She has placed the lamp at the side of the window and stands beside it)

How peaceful is the night! The Hellespont
Disports her waves like children at their play;
They hardly murmur, tranced in calm content.
No sound, no gleam around; only my lamp
Casts its pale beams across the darkling air. *1030*
Come, let me shift you here against these bars!
May the late wanderer refresh himself
With the glad thought that someone's still awake,
And to the distant shores on the other side
Be like a star and twinkle through the night.

But if you were observed; come let us sleep,
Pale friend that beckons with your quiet light.

(She carries the lamp)

And as I now put out your gentle ray,
So let me put out too what still glows here,
And never let it shine another evening. *1040*

(She has placed the lamp on the table)

Awake, so late? . . . ah, Mother, Mother, please!
No, children all sleep early! Let that be!

(She takes the jewels out of her hair, singing softly the while)

And Leda's stroking
The silk-soft down.

Th'eternal song! Why does it haunt me so?
No more do gods assail the wildest towers;
No swan, no eagle[22] comforts the forlorn;
Now solitude stays ever solitary.

[22] The feathery disguises in which Zeus prosecuted his illicit loves for Leda and for Aigina.

(She has sat down)

They've also put a lyre in this chamber:
But I have never learnt to play on one; 1050
How much I wish I had! Thoughts, both confused
And merry, flash across my mind;
More easily would they have merged in music.

Yes, yes, you handsome youth, gentle and good,
Of you I'm thinking at this midnight hour;
And with such sweet and comprehensive feelings,
That no transgression lurks beneath their wings.
I wish you well, yet happy you are far;
And if my voice could only reach your ears,
I'd call out to you now: good night!

(LEANDER *in the background appearing at the window from outside)*

LEANDER

Good night! [23] 1060

HERO

Ha! What is that? Is it you, Echo, speaking?
D'you come to cheer me in my solitude?
I greet you, lovely nymph!

LEANDER

O lovely nymph,
I greet you!

HERO

Ah me! That was not an echo!
A head! And arms! A man, there at the window!
He's coming in—he's kneeling on the sill.
Get back! You are a lost man, if I call.

LEANDER

I beg you, grant me but a single moment!

[23] "Good evening" reads better when translating into English, but it is essential to echo Hero's exact words (*vide* next line).

The stones are crumbling under my torn feet.
If you refuse, I shall hurl down to death. *1070*
A breathing space, then I shall climb back down.

(He lets himself into the chamber)

HERO

Stand there and do not move! Unlucky wretch,
What brought you here?

LEANDER *(In the background, remaining standing by the entrance)*

I caught sight of your light
With its bright glimmer twinkling through the night.
Inside me too was night that longed for light;
So I have climbed up here.

HERO

Who's your companion?
Who held your ladder? Offered you his aid?

LEANDER

No ladder led me here, no outside aid.
I placed my foot in the spaces of loose stones,
And clambering up the ivy and the broom *1080*
Came right up here.

HERO

. And had you slipped and crashed?

LEANDER

I had been happy.

HERO

And had you been seen?

LEANDER

I think none has.

HERO

The guardians of the temple,
The watch are at patrol this very hour,

Unlucky wretch! Were you not clearly begged,
Did I myself not beg you to go home?

LEANDER

I did go home, but I could find no peace;
So I plunged in the sea and swam across.

HERO

What? All the way from Abydos' far shore?
Two oarsmen are exhausted by the crossing. *1090*

LEANDER

You see, I've done it. And had I to die,
Drowning a victim to the first wave's onset,
I'd still have been a little nearer you,
And so a sweeter death.

HERO

Your hair is wet,
And wet are all your clothes. You're shivering too.

LEANDER

I'm shivering not with cold, I shake with passion.

(While remaining in the background, about to fall on one knee)

HERO

Now, none of that, but stay, repose a while,
Then quickly you must go. So't was my light,
This lamp that marked your goal and your direction?
You rightly warn me muffle it in future. *1100*

LEANDER

Ah! Do not so! Dear lady, do not so!
I will not come again if you are angry,
But please do not deny me this, your light!

When I rose from my sleepless couch tonight,
And, opening the door of my poor cottage,
From my own dark encounterd a new darkness,
The sea stretched out before me with her shores,
A pitch black carpet, uniform to view,

Muffled as if in mourning and in grief.
I was already drawn by a wild impulse *1110*
When suddenly there flared on the horizon
A little star, that beckoned a last hope.
Its rays threw round the dismal world a net
Spun from a thousand golden faëry threads.
That was your light, the lamp of this your tower.
My heart rose high, pounding in powerful beats
As though it could no longer be contained;
I hurried to the beach, plunged in the sea,
Those rays, my lodestar, ever in my sight.
And so I got here, swimming to this shore. *1120*
I will not come again, if you are angry,
But do not rob me of my starry hope,
Do not cut off the comfort of your light.

HERO

Good youth, ah, do not think I am too cruel
If I return poor answer to your longing;
As I've already said, it cannot be,
I am committed to a rigorous service,
Exacting lovelessness from the priestess:
Had you come one day earlier I were free;
It's now too late. So go, and come no more. *1130*

LEANDER

The manners of your people pass as gentle,
Are they so strict, so full of menaces?

HERO

The Medes and Bactrians in the distant Orient
Would kill Apollo's priestess if she cast
Her eye upon a youthful paramour;
My people, not so murderously inclined,
Spare, it is true, the life of the transgressor,
But still expel her and abominate her,
Together with her whole house, all her kin;
You will agree that must not befall Hero. *1140*
Therefore go now, and shoulder what you must.

LEANDER

Then I must go?

HERO

You must, but not the same way
That brought you here, it's much too dangerous.
Go through that door and follow the long passage
That leads into the open.

(Pausing a moment with agitated attention)

But take care,
For—listen! In the name of all the gods!
I heard some footsteps coming through the passage.
They're coming! Ah! They're here! Unlucky hour!

LEANDER

Is there no place where I may safely hide?
Ha! Inside there!

(Going toward the side door)

HERO

Would you go in my room? *1150*
Stay here! Since you have dared, be caught and die!
I'll go inside myself.

LEANDER

They're coming.

HERO

(Pointing to the side door)

Here!
Go quickly in and take the lamp with you!
Let it be dark here! Do you hear? Quick, quick!
But do not go far in, stay by the door!
Quick, quick, I say!

LEANDER

But you? . . .

HERO

Ah, hush, away!

*(*LEANDER *has taken hold of the lamp and exits through the side door. The room is dark)*

O kindly Gods! I beg you show your mercy!

(She sinks into the chair, half sitting, so that the left knee droops almost down to the ground, hiding her eyes with her hand, her forehead leaning against the table. The TEMPLE WATCHMAN*'s voice from outside)*

WATCHMAN

Is anyone awake?

*(*IANTHE*'s voice likewise)*

IANTHE

You see, all's dark.

(The door is half opened)

WATCHMAN

Still I did see some light.

IANTHE

Imagination.
The priestess lives here, as you know yourself. *1160*

WATCHMAN

But what I did see cannot be gainsaid.

(The door closes)

And when day breaks it shall be proved that I—

(The words die away as the steps recede)

HERO

O shame, disgrace!

*(*LEANDER *enters from the side door)*

LEANDER

So they have gone. Where are you?
Are you still here, sweet lady?

(He touches her shoulder as he gropes)

HERO *(Starting up)*

Where's the light?
The lamp, where is it? Bring the lamp, I say!

(LEANDER goes back)

Oh, all that's evil on my guilty head!

LEANDER *(Who returns with the lamp)*

Here is your light.

(He puts it down)

And with me, thank the Gods! . . .

HERO *(Springing up)*

Thank, did you say? Thank? Why, because you live?
Is that your one joy? You accursèd horror!
Why did you come? Thinking but of yourself,[24] *1170*
Disturbing all my halcyon innocence,
And poisoning the concord in my breast?
Ah, would the roaring sea had swallowed you
When you had merged your body in its waves!
Or that the stones had loosely slipped from you
To which you clung when scaling my lone tower,
And you had—horrible sight—Leander—oh! . . .

LEANDER

What? Why have you stopped scolding?

HERO

Leander, hear me!
Do not return the same way that you came.
That way is dangerous—gruesome, horrible! *1180*
What is it that so blinds a human being,
Making him alien to his own interests
And champion of what's alien? When they came
Just now, three steps away and might have found,

[24] This is very true of Grillparzer's heroes in his Greek plays, all of them a reflection of their author, and we are entitled to detect here a note of self-accusation.

Seen me—I trembled—not for me—what madness!
I trembled all for him!

LEANDER

Dare I believe it?

HERO

None of that! Do not touch me! That bodes no good
That so subverts the essence of one's being,
Puts out the light the Gods have given us,
To lead us as the polar star still guides *1190*
The mariner.

LEANDER

What? Do you call this bad?
And all men deem it highest happiness,

(He kneels before her)

And call it love.

HERO

You most unfortunate youth!
So it has come to you, the pretty word,
And you repeat it, calling yourself happy?

(Touching his head)

And yet must swim on through the cruel sea,
Where every inch is death; once safe on shore
Spies lie in wait for you and cruel murderers—

(*Starts, with a look backwards*)

LEANDER *(Springing up)*

What's wrong?

HERO

Oh, each sound seems to me a watchman's step!
My knees are trembling.

LEANDER

Hero, Hero, Hero! *1200*

HERO

None of that! Do not touch me! You must go.
Myself I'll guide you by a safer way;
For should they come and find you, catch you here—

(Supporting herself on the back of a chair)

LEANDER *(After a short pause)*

And may I, lady, come again?

HERO

What? You!

LEANDER

Do you mean, never? All the future, never?
D'you know this word and all its cruel compass? [25]
Further, you were concerned for me, you know.
I have to go back through the raging sea:
Will you not think I may have drowned and died,
Without news of my crossing?

HERO

Send a message. *1210*

LEANDER

I have no messenger beside myself.

HERO

Then, gracious messenger, do come yourself!
But not here, to this deathtrap. On the shore
A sandy spit juts out into the sea:
Come there, and hide yourself among the bushes,[26]
And as I pass by, I'll hear what you say.

LEANDER

But please be sure this lamp shines on for me,

[25] Compare Racine's *Bérénice* (Act IV, Scene V, Vs. 1110–12):

I'll hear no more; and so farewell forever.
Forever! Ah, my lord, are you aware
How stark these cruel words to lovers are?

[26] The height of dramatic irony, for on Leander's next visit Hero will indeed see him hidden among the bushes—dead.

And marks for me my way to happiness:
When shall I come again? Sweet lady, speak!

HERO

At the next festival.

LEANDER

Why, you are jesting! *1220*
Say when?

HERO

Well then, come at the next full moon.

LEANDER

Till then ten weary days must creep along!
Can you bear the uncertainty till then? I cannot!
I shall be fearing we have been observed,
You in your mind will fancy I am dead,
And rightly so! For should the sea not gulp me,
I'll die of care, of anguish and of pain.
Say: day after tomorrow; say in three days,
Ah, next week say!

HERO

Then come again tomorrow.

LEANDER

What bliss! What happiness!

HERO

Should you reach home, *1230*
Leander, through the dark sea, as you came,
Take good care of this head, and of this mouth,
Of these my eyes,[27] Leander, do you hear?
Ah, promise me!

(Drawing back, as he is about to embrace her)

[27] Leander's magnetic eyes, already praised by Naukleros in Act II, were particularly arresting to Hero. She bewails him dead with the lament, "His breath was the pure air, his eye, the sun." (V. 1978.)

No, no! Just follow me!
I'll show the way.

(She goes to the table to fetch the lamp)

LEANDER *(Following her with his eyes)*
You splendid, heavenly woman! [28]

HERO

You are not coming?

LEANDER

Must I desolate leave
This paradise the very Gods have blessed?
No token of your favor, no poor pledge
To take with me as solace for my longing?

HERO

What do you mean?

LEANDER

Not even kiss your hand? *1240*
And then—they place their lips on lips—
I saw it clearly—whispering to each other
What is too private for the babbling air.
Let my mouth be the mouth, your mouth the ear!
Lend me your ear for my unuttered speech!

HERO

That must not be.

LEANDER

Must I dare all, you nothing?
I, facing death and danger, you denying?

(With childish petulance)

Ah, I shall drown if I return in gloom.

[28] Grillparzer records the "heavenly beauty" of Marie von Smolenitz—the prototype of his Hero—who married his rival, the artist Daffinger.

HERO

You, do not trifle!

LEANDER

Grant a favor, you!

HERO

If then you'll go.

LEANDER *(Falling on one knee)*

Yes! Yes!

HERO

And not scold me *1250*

For having touched your cheek so very lightly;

No, rather if you're thankful and behave.

LEANDER

Still hesitating?

HERO

Fold your arms right back,

Just like a prisoner of love, my prisoner.

LEANDER

Look, it is done.

HERO *(Putting the light on the floor)*

The lamp must not see this.[29]

LEANDER

You are not coming.

HERO

Are you so impatient?

Then I should never—yet, if it makes you happy—

Then take and give!

[29] Grillparzer has recorded (in 1827) how he took this feature from the conduct of Charlotte von Paumgartten, his cousin's wife, the prototype of his Medea, with whom he had a passionate affair. Charlotte, on one occasion, had put the lamp down in order to kiss him before his departure.

(She kisses him quickly)

Now, you must surely go!

LEANDER *(Leaping up)*

Hero!

HERO

No, no!

(Hurrying out of the door)

LEANDER

If I beg you, Hero!
What wretched luck!

(Listening at the door)

But I am hearing footsteps, *1260*
The steps are hers, she's coming to the door,
On tiptoe—she's returning? Gracious gods!

Curtain

ACT IV

An open place. In the background the sea. On the left side at the back, HERO*'s tower, with a window half turned toward the sea and a narrow entrance to which some steps lead up. Beside it on the shore some tall shrubs. In the foreground, on the same side, are arcades and pillars designating dwellings. The right side is clear with trees. Standing across the stage a stone couch.*

SCENE I

After the curtain rises, the TEMPLE WARDEN*'s voice is heard behind the scenes.*

TEMPLE WARDEN

Come here, come here, you servants of this house!

(*Then* HERO *enters from the near foreground on the right.*)

HERO

He's gone across. Thanks be to all the gods!
It seemed as if the cosmos had conspired
To hold him here until the radiant day!
Goings and comings to and fro all night.
And he stood there, crouched in a quiet corner;
At last the favorable moment came—
Now he has gone and I am calm once more. *1270*

(On the same side, further back, the TEMPLE WARDEN *enters, a horn on a band round his body and a spear on his left shoulder, following her each movement)*

TEMPLE WARDEN

I think you saw him.

HERO

Whom?

TEMPLE WARDEN

The foreign fellow
Who dived but now into the sea.

HERO

But now?

TEMPLE WARDEN

Barely three steps from you.

HERO

And did not see him?

(She goes toward the tower)

TEMPLE WARDEN

You did, I think; indeed, you must have seen him.

HERO *(Going on)*

Must I? Am I a watchman then like you?

TEMPLE WARDEN

Not watchman? If a watchman means, who wakes—
You were a long time wakeful by your lamp.

HERO

O how you are all eyes!

TEMPLE WARDEN

I see all clearly!

(The PRIEST *enters from the left)*

PRIEST

Is there some quarrel here?

HERO *(On the steps of the tower)*

The man is mad.

TEMPLE WARDEN

If I would only speak!

HERO

He speaks and speaks. *1280*

I'm going.

PRIEST

Where?

HERO

To the tower.

PRIEST

Why?

HERO

To sleep.

(Exit into the tower)

TEMPLE WARDEN

To sleep, indeed, being awake all night.

PRIEST

What happened here?

TEMPLE WARDEN *(Calling after* HERO*)*

You dare to call me mad,
Because I'm but a servant, you a lady?
You fancy wisdom too is handed down
Like father to the son, like wealth and land?
Ay, wise enough, and sharp enough, and watchful!

(He thrusts the spear into the ground)

PRIEST

Am I to know what's happened? . . .

TEMPLE WARDEN *(Still calling after* HERO*)*

Ay, indeed!

PRIEST *(Turning to go)*

You're keeping yourself company, I see!
I'll not begrudge it and shall leave you free— *1290*

TEMPLE WARDEN

Sir! A man just dived into the sea from here.

PRIEST

So that was it?

TEMPLE WARDEN

And Hero stood nearby.

PRIEST

He would have dived as quickly, stood I near.

TEMPLE WARDEN

And up there in that tower a light was burning
The whole night long.

PRIEST

Indeed, that should not be.
Yet Hero hardly knows that we avoid
Showing the way by means of lights and torches
To foes or evildoers through the crags
That girt the shore protectively around.
So warn her.

TEMPLE WARDEN

Yes, that she might mock me further? *1300*
She knew this well enough, yet burnt her light.
That means she was awake, sir.

PRIEST

Well?

TEMPLE WARDEN

Till morning.
And up there so much noise and yet so secret,
A whispering and a rustling everywhere
The entire area seemed awake, astir:
Mysterious movements in the thickest foliage,

Like puffs of wind where yet no wind was puffing;
The air was alive with sounds the ground reechoed,
And all the sound and fury turned to nothing.
The sea rose roaring higher on the shore, *1310*
The stars were twinkling with their beckoning eyes,
The night appeared a secret half unveiled.
And this tower was the center and the goal
Of all the dull commotion, gentle stirring.
Some twenty times I hurried to its base,
Thinking at last I should resolve the riddle,
And looking up saw nothing but the light
That shone forever on at Hero's window.
On one occasion a man's shadow seemed
To shoot up from the seashore to the tower. *1320*
I followed and found nothing on arrival,
Just rustling and a stirring, as before.

PRIEST

It seems, the kernel of the mystery,
With cause and with effect, lay but in you.

TEMPLE WARDEN

Indeed! Then why, sir, was the light still burning
The whole night till but now, as I've reported?
When the hobgoblin made me almost mad,
I went inside the building, by th'other side,
Where the servants' quarters give on to the tower:
There it was I first caught sight of Ianthe, *1330*
Dressed and adorned as though it were broad day.

PRIEST

The reading of the riddle's pretty clear.
Ask of the girl. Go, call her here: you know
How often she's already caused disturbance.

TEMPLE WARDEN

I thought so too and gave her a good scolding;
And yet the light was at that window, there!
And then: but now when I went to the grove,
A man dives—swish!—into the foaming sea,

And at that very moment Hero walks
Out of the shrubs, barely three steps apart. *1340*

PRIEST

If you would still surmise, seek other props;
Let your suspicions rest but on your equals!

TEMPLE WARDEN

But on my equals? I should have foreseen this!
Of course, a servant has no sense nor judgment.

PRIEST

Call me Ianthe.

TEMPLE WARDEN

But, the light, good sir—

PRIEST

Ianthe, I have told you!

TEMPLE WARDEN

And that man
Who dived into the sea and swam to Abydos?

PRIEST

What did you say? Abydos?

TEMPLE WARDEN

Yes.

PRIEST

Abydos?
Call me Ianthe.

TEMPLE WARDEN

Very well!

PRIEST

Tell Hero! . . .

(Taking a scroll from his breast)

Give her this writing just come from her parents *1350*

And that—rather, let it remain for now—
Tell her I've called her servant-girl.

(Exit the TEMPLE WARDEN *into the tower)*

Abydos!
What causes me to shudder at this name?
Were not the two young strangers from Abydos,
Who in the grove? . . . Madness even to think it!
And yet! Will not the young in years dare all,
And not remain contented with half measures;
Above all, lured by the forbidden? Have
They tried still to pursue the bold adventure
My coming interrupted? And could Hero *1360*
Unknowing bear the guilt of knowing this?
Besides, she's still so young and inexperienced,
So uninstructed to avoid the danger,
Why, even to recognize it . . . But, enough!
A god is stirring in my inmost heart,
Warning me to avert it, ere too late.

(Reenter the TEMPLE WARDEN*)*

Well?

TEMPLE WARDEN

Hero keeps Ianthe still detained,
The priestess is reposing on a couch,
Ianthe kneels by her and talks and dallies,
They told me, pray you—

PRIEST

Why are they delaying? *1370*
Order Ianthe come to me at once.

TEMPLE WARDEN *(Moving back)*

But—

PRIEST

In all else however calm and wise,
When madness once lays hold of a wise woman,
It raves more violently than the wildest folly.

(Enter IANTHE*)*

TEMPLE WARDEN

So you have come at last, you painted lily!
They want to know what kept you up so late.

PRIEST

I find you always privy to all mischiefs
That ever may occur within this house,
Whether by guilt or curiosity.
I am informed suspicious goings-on *1380*
Took place last night here in this very tower;
And this man found you, in the passages,
Still wide awake and dressed up when all slept.
Confront him then and tell us what you know.

(He withdraws)

IANTHE

By all the gods, sir—

PRIEST *(Retorting)*

Leave the gods alone,
And take care first to satisfy us mortals!

IANTHE

But I know nothing! Only heard some movements,
A coming and a going. The night was sultry,
I listened at the door, then went to sleep.

TEMPLE WARDEN

You call that, "at the door," two whole flights up? *1390*
I found you on the way to Hero's chamber.

IANTHE

Alone, I felt afraid; I wished to ask Hero
If she had heard, and felt afraid like me.

PRIEST *(Approaching again)*

But I am telling you: you must confess;
Your hesitations tell me that you know.

(Enter HERO*)*

HERO

What is the matter? Why have we been summoned?

PRIEST

Here is Ianthe whom you know like me.
She is accused that in the depth of night—

HERO

She is unjustly wronged.

PRIEST

Then you know.

HERO

Sir!
I only know how lightly men accuse; *1400*
Above all, this man here has lost his reason.

PRIEST

Yet it is certain; some stranger was at
The tower.

HERO *(After a pause)*

Perhaps, sir, one of the immortals!
Yourself you used to say: in ancient days
A god would often come down to blessed mortals.
To Leda and Admetus,[30] stricken prince,
And strictly guarded Danae[31] came a god;
Why not today? To her? To us? To whom you will?

(She goes to the stone couch to rest)

[30] Apollo, during his banishment from Olympus for killing the Cyclops, served Admetus, King of Pherae, as recounted in the opening lines of Euripides' *Alcestis.*

[31] Zeus once more! . . . this time he descended in a shower of gold on Danae, whom her father, Acrisius, kept imprisoned against an Oracle's prophesying his death at the hands of her son. As a result of this divine contact Danae gave birth to the great hero Perseus, who later accidentally killed his grandfather when throwing the discus.

PRIEST

Could you be mocking? Would you turn the sacred—

(To IANTHE*)*

Now, whether fool or culprit, come, confess! *1410*

IANTHE

Why then, ask Hero. She lives in the tower,
If there were noise, she must have heard it too.

PRIEST *(Approaching* HERO*)*

Do you hear?

HERO *(Who has sat down, half singing, supporting her head on her hand)*

She was so beautiful
A royal princess.

(Speaking)

O radiant swan, winged to the radiant stars!

PRIEST

Hero!

HERO *(Starting up)*

What is it? Who's touching me? What do you want?

PRIEST

Have you so soon forgotten?

HERO

I have not,
I know of what she's groundlessly accused.
Ianthe, do not fear, be of good heart! *1420*
If all of them forsake you, all of them,
In my heart beats for you your warmest champion.

(Kissing her repeatedly)

If they torment you, sweet girl, come to me;
But go now, they are mocking you and me.

PRIEST

Just wait!

(IANTHE *withdraws. To* HERO)

You never loved the girl before;
Why all this sympathy?

HERO *(Who has stood up)*

Why do you ask?
She's wronged. Is not this ground enough?

PRIEST

Who then was cause of all that stir last night?

HERO

Why should it be she?

PRIEST

Who else?

HERO

Ask the winds;
But they are silent too.

PRIEST

Now, as to you; *1430*
A light was burning all night in your tower.
See it does not recur.

HERO

Why, we have oil enough.

PRIEST

But people see it and are prone to gossip.

HERO

Let them.

PRIEST

And yet I counseled you to shun
The least appearance, let alone real grounds.

HERO

What though we shun them, will they likewise shun us?

PRIEST

Do you speak from experience?

HERO

What's the time?
How much longer till evening?

PRIEST

Why this question?

HERO

Shall I confess! I'm tired.

PRIEST

Not having slept?

HERO

Maybe. I think the wind is from the east *1440*
And tranquil is the sea. So then, good night!

PRIEST

In broad daylight? Ah, Hero, Hero, Hero!

HERO

Uncle, what would you?

PRIEST

Have pity on yourself!

HERO

I plainly see around me much is happening
That touches me perhaps most intimately,
I cannot grasp it and my mind is dark.
I'll sleep upon it.

PRIEST

You must firstly *stop!*
You cannot yet withdraw to your apartments!
Much business still is waiting to be done.

HERO

Business?

PRIEST *(Sternly)*

Business.

(More gently)

The cares of your new office. *1450*

Within the temple—yet—was I forgetting? . . .

A letter from your parents came—or rather[32]
I am informed—a messenger from your parents,
On their departure sent by them to us,
Has since arrived on the outer eastern gate
That bars the entrance to our sacred precincts;
But fishermen who dwell beside the sea,
Suspicious of all strangers, and perhaps
Aware already of last night's commotion,
Are stopping him from coming in to us. *1460*
I let you have this pleasure, you go there,
Speak to the man and hear what news he brings.

HERO

Must I myself?

PRIEST

Are you not keen to know?
A message from your parents—then—

HERO

I'm going.

PRIEST

I think you'll find the man beside those huts,
But should you not, should he have wandered off,

[32] This line, along with V. 1707, has been omitted in the Hanser Edition, but seems essential to emphasise the Priest's embarrassed lying, in view of line 1350. It appears in both the other editions, on which I have based my work—see Foreword.

I want you still to follow after him
Till you—

HERO

I'll see to it.

PRIEST

Also look in
At the good steward's of our sacred house;
From there send servants out to look for him: *1470*
And once there, let them show you the provisions
They have collected for the goddess' service.
Why, this last feast has left our temple bare.
We have no incense, sacrificial barley,
Nor linen; if you bring some, I'll be grateful.

HERO

Then I can come home.

PRIEST

Certainly, provided
You have first supervised the pilgrim's lodge,
That stands quite near by on its slender pillars.
Perhaps our man will mostly lie low there.
They also say pilgrims have been assembling, *1480*
Coming from far and wide here to our temple.
Move among them and speak a useful word,
Attend the sacrifices they'll be offering;
And when you have fulfilled your sacred office—
Should there be further time on your way back—

HERO

Enough, good sir! I almost said: "too much."

(Ingratiatingly)

I must confess, I'd rather stay with you.

PRIEST *(Calmly)*

Yet you must go.

HERO

Must I? Well, so be it.

PRIEST

Do take with you Ianthe, your new friend,
Who pleases you so much, to shorten the way. *1490*

HERO

You are quite right, I'll do what you suggest.
Ianthe, come and guide me on my way!
Your merry talk will make our wandering shorter,
And should I weary, offer me your arm.

But you, my peaceful home, now fare you well!
Before the gray of evening I'll be back.

Where are you? Ah!—Today take Hero's role—
And think and speak for me. Another time
I'll gladly play Ianthe—don't be cross!

(Embracing IANTHE*'s neck, exeunt)*

PRIEST

Can I assuage the fury in my breast? *1500*
There's not the least doubt, all the signs concur.
A man around the temple, and she knows it.
And it was one of those two youthful strangers,
One called Leander, Naukleros the other,
Whom, from Abydos, I met in the grove;
But whether for a long time the hypocrite's
Been hiding it from me, or but today—
Naukleros and Leander, who was it?

(With outstretched palms)

In equal scales I'll put your lot in balance.
Both these names are of similar import,[33] *1510*
The count of syllables one and the same,
Each has an equal claim to fortune's favor;
Meantime the one shall be a living soul,
His friend a dead man, dead without delay;

[33] Leander—leader of the people; Naukleros—ship's captain.

For in her absence, I shall set the snares
That will destroy him, should he dare return.
O wretch! Why did you stretch your dastard hand
Upon my child, devoted to my Gods?

(Turning backwards)

What, old man, you still here? Let us go up!
And search out every sign that will disclose *1520*
The dark trace of the deed, still unrevealed.
When night comes and you see the light again—
And yet, who knows, if we are not mistaken?
If faith is blind, suspicion sees too much:
The very least, I order you to doubt
Until I say: "Believe!" Be not afraid!
Just go ahead and open that door there.

(The TEMPLE WARDEN *goes to the tower)*

PRIEST *(About to follow him)*

We will have peace. Let folly's mischief perish!
No more shall morning find it. See, it's spent!

(Exit with the servant into the tower)

SCENE II

Compact landscape. In the right foreground LEANDER'*s hut. Nearby a tree with a votive shrine.*

Enter NAUKLEROS, *who remains standing in front of the hut, stamping his foot on the ground.*

NAUKLEROS

Leander, listen! Open up! Leander! *1530*

He has been sheltered by my care till now.
Last evening I left him in the hut,
Right up till now today, the neighbors say
His door, securely locked, has not been opened.
I must be vigilant to hold him safe.

But why is he delaying? It's so late!
Has his surpassing anguish . . . perhaps even
He has forgotten all his grief and suffering
And is stretched out in dreams? Leander, ho!
You lazybones, without a care! By Apollo,
If you'll not open, I'll burst in the door.

But nonetheless it still seems strange to me—

(He looks through the chinks. Enter LEANDER *in the left background)*

LEANDER

Ho!

(He withdraws again)

NAUKLEROS *(Turning quickly around)*

Who's that? Friend or foe?

LEANDER *(Coming forward)*

Ha! ha! ha! ha!

Frightened?

(He carries a rod in his hand and a veil[34] *under his arm, an end of which he ties in a slip-knot during the following)*

NAUKLEROS

So it is you? And mocking
Your lord and master, too, you jackanapes!
Then—what am I to think? Where have you been?
Did I not leave you in the hut last evening?
And yet today—I know, the neighbors told me—
Your door, securely locked, has not been opened.
From where d'you come and how?

(He puts out his hand to interrupt LEANDER*'s twiddling)*

LEANDER *(Drawing back)*

My rod, my pennon! *1550*

[34] This knotting by Leander of Hero's veil may be regarded as yet another symbol of the bonds of love and of death.

NAUKLEROS

Your hair is wet, your clothes are hanging on you.
You were in the sea.

LEANDER

How clever his conclusion!

(He goes, during the following, to the tree in the background and places rod and veil on a bank beneath the divine image)

NAUKLEROS *(Following his movements)*

Why, in the sea? You did not go? . . . Leander!
Do you not know? They send out spies from Sestos,
They've been already seen upon our shores.
If their suspicion reaches out so far
Across the sea, how much more strictly then
Will they not watch their always-hostile shores?
He'd be a fool, whoever would attempt
To rush into their wide-extended net. *1560*
Then tell me: how?

LEANDER *(Who has again come forward, speaking toward the background)*

Guard it, dear god, for me!

NAUKLEROS

Once more, say how? You know I broke the rudder
Of your own boat and all the neighbors kept
Their skiffs locked up upon my supplication.
If not by boat, then how? Surely not swimming—
Leander, swimming? Do you know the distance[35]
That parts Abydos' shore from Sestos' coast?
No man alive can reach it still alive;
For should his strength endure, the towering cliffs
That run along the whole length of the shore *1570*

[35] About a mile or more. Byron swam the Hellespont in 1810, in confirmation of Leander's feats. Since then, repeated crossings of the English Channel (over twenty miles wide) by swimmers, although accompanied by boats, have somewhat dimmed Leander's exploits as a swimmer, but in no way his romance as a lover.

Afford no lodgment, landing place, nor spot
For safe arrival.

LEANDER

Fancy that! So steep?

NAUKLEROS

True: there is one place between the sheer cliffs;
A fortune's favorite, who does not miss it
In the dark night, may hope to reach it safely.
A tower stands there, built one time for defense,
Where now the virgin priestess lives, whom we
Saw that time in the grove: You've not . . . Leander!
You need not hide your eyes! They have confessed.

Well, you were there last night, not resting here, *1580*
Found luckily the only spot for landing,
Stood with your wet eyes gazing on the tower,
And ogling the dear light inside her chamber;
You saw her fleeting shadows on the walls,
Lucky to wallow in the surfeit of
So much luck, at no greater cost than death.

LEANDER

Poor wretch!

NAUKLEROS

That too! My portrait was too dim.
You saw her, spoke to her, found house and door
Wide open, unwatched, entered—?

LEANDER *(Throwing himself into his arms)*

Naukleros!
Do you not feel the kiss? Not know who gave it? *1590*

NAUKLEROS

Enough! Your kiss means death!

LEANDER

So timorous?
Naukleros, coward?

NAUKLEROS

Yes, yes I see it plainly,
We have changed places, I am timorous now,
You bold; Leander of good heart, Naukleros—
Shall I now have to weep for you so soon?
Then run, run to your death: only one thing,
This one thing, promise me: do not this time,
This one time, seek it, keep away from Sestos!
So that, when you are lying pale and cold
I shall not have to tell myself: *You* were *1600*
The one, who faithlessly betrayed your friend
By showing him the deadly fruits yourself,
Who wove yourself the clinging net that caught him.

(One knee bent to the ground)

Leander!

LEANDER

Are you ill? What's up with you?

NAUKLEROS

Well, you are right and I shall say no more! [36]
I might as well address the roaring sea,
The raging storm, the wild beast of the desert
That follows heedlessly its inborn urge!
So, I shall say no more. But if you still
Hold dear our friendship, that once—

LEANDER

Once? Naukleros! *1610*

NAUKLEROS

Enough! Let deeds speak. If I seem at all
Still worthy of a wretched little service,
Be so good as to open me that door.

LEANDER

Whatever for?

[36] Similarly the kneeling Medea immediately rises when faced with Jason's unresponsiveness (*Medea,* Act III, V.1573).

NAUKLEROS

I beg you.

LEANDER

The key, you know,
Is lying under the stone.

NAUKLEROS

You open it.

LEANDER *(Who has opened the door of the hut)*

Done.

NAUKLEROS

Good! And to let me show my gratitude,
Go inside!

LEANDER

No, not I.

NAUKLEROS

You shall! You must!
I always was the stronger, I'm the elder,
And now my arm is trebly steeled by care.

(Seizing Leander)

I'll seize you, hold you tight and press you firm *1620*
Against the ground. Will you obey me?

LEANDER *(His knee giving way)*

Stop!

NAUKLEROS *(Setting him free)*

Poor wretch, exhausted by the waves and love!
Now, get inside!

LEANDER *(Drawing back)*

Indeed, I will not go!

NAUKLEROS *(Seizing him and pushing him back)*

You will, you shall, you must.

LEANDER

Let me go!

NAUKLEROS

In vain!

(He has pushed LEANDER *through the door, which he now quickly shuts)*

Now, it is shut!

(He turns the key)

And swim again in future!
As jailer, I myself shall bring you food,
But will take good care you do not escape.

LEANDER *(From inside)*

Naukleros!

NAUKLEROS

No!

LEANDER

Just one word!

NAUKLEROS

Not one single!

LEANDER

But if my safety, if my life depended
Upon your hearing me?

NAUKLEROS

What is it then? *1630*

LEANDER

Please, open the door, just a little bit!
My life's in danger if you should refuse.

NAUKLEROS

Well, I shall open it a hand's breadth—

(Recoiling)

What's that?

LEANDER *(Rushes out of the hut, helmet on head, shield on arm and naked sword in hand)* [37]

Come on, come on, why do you not detain me?
I have my father's sword and helmet still,
And death to any man who dare oppose!

Fool, that you are! Do you presume to halt
Whom all the gods protect, their power guides?
I will fulfill what is my destiny:
No man can hold up what the gods dispose. *1640*

Great gods, who saved and sheltered me through all
The watery night *(He kneels),* O powerful Poseidon! [38]
Who putst a bridle on the neighing waves,
And scaredst away death from my dripping mouth,
Almight Zeus! majestic and sublime,
And thou, great Aphrodite! who didst call me,
In my young ignorance, to teach, while learning,
Thy sweet commandments to my innocent love,
Support me, all, and guide me as before!

(Rising and casting aside his shield and sword, but still keeping on his helmet)

No weapons! Your protection is enough. *1650*
And thus secure as in a coat of bronze
I'll boldly plunge into the sea of perils.

(Quickly taking up the rod with the veil and attaching the slip-knot to the top of the rod, while holding the other end of the veil taut in his hand)

And this veil stolen from a sacred place,
I raise as pennon in my daring hand;
Through all the waste of waters it will lead me: [39]

[37] Slightly comic. Grillparzer, more plausibly, had already depicted Jason thus accoutred in *The Argonauts.*

[38] Poseidon was god of the sea, as well as of horses.

[39] Grillparzer is fond of bestowing his heroines with veils, which his heroes seize as emblems of their love; thus Creusa in *Medea* also had her veil which cheered Jason on his voyage to Colchis, while

And should a god vouchsafe I safely land,
Victorious I'll plant it on the shore.
Should I succumb, your will be done! Away!

(Waving the veil like a flag)

Eros and Hymen, go ahead of me,
I'm coming, following, were the third god Death! *1660*

(Exit hurriedly)

NAUKLEROS

Ah, he is mad! Will you not hear? Leander!

(Picking up the weapons)

But I'll not give up yet. I'll muster friends,
And we shall stop him, even if by force.
There slinks a man wrapped in a darkish cloak,
Perhaps some spy already from that temple.
I'll shun him, follow the other. Oh, my friend!

(Exit slowly in the opposite direction)

SCENE III

Place in front of HERO*'s tower, as at the beginning of this act. Enter* HERO, *her hand placed on* IANTHE*'s shoulder, followed by* SERVANTS *with vessels.*

HERO

Do take the vessels to my uncle now;
Tell him—you know already. I'll stay here—

(She sits down)

This man, my parents' messenger, would seem

---

betrayed Medea had to keep her veil—of which Jason did not approve—for her own solace! The symbol of the veil is doubtless inspired by Schiller's ballad, where Hero calls on the sea goddess, Leucothea, to lend Leander in distress the saving grace of her sacred veil, mysteriously woven, like Medea's.

Like hope or fortune: as one seeks, it flees, *1670*
Leaving us all forlorn.

IANTHE

You walked too quickly.

HERO

Well, I have come back here.

IANTHE

Would you not rather
Go up into your room?

HERO

No, only here.
It's not yet evening?

IANTHE

Hardly.

HERO *(Supporting her head on her hand)*

Now, now, now!

(Enter the TEMPLE WARDEN *from the left)*

TEMPLE WARDEN

So you are back? We waited long for you.

HERO

Long? Long indeed! I think you're mocking me!
Did I not promptly go in search of him,
The messenger, that never would appear!
You did this with intention. Heaven knows why!

TEMPLE WARDEN

The messenger came by another way *1680*
When you had hardly left. He's with your uncle.

HERO

And you still kept me in the dark? Great heavens!
Be sure the next time I shall be much wiser.

TEMPLE WARDEN

Your uncle's waiting in the temple.

HERO

Is he?
Then let him wait, for I am staying here.

TEMPLE WARDEN

But he ordered—

HERO

Do what he ordered you;
In future I intend to order myself.
Now go.

(To IANTHE*)*

You too.

IANTHE

But if you wanted something—

HERO

I, nothing. And yet! If you have a mind to.
Please go up and prepare the lamp for me, *1690*
Add some more oil, enough for many hours.
And when night comes—no, I myself will do that.

(Exeunt IANTHE *and the* TEMPLE WARDEN*)*

HERO

And when night comes—It is indeed now falling.
There stands my tower, the gentle waves are murmuring,
And he was here last night, and swore today—
Was it last night? It seems so long ago,
My head is heavy and my mind a blur.
The throbbing day, the cares of that last night,
That was no night, a wakeful day of fear—
Weigh down like lead my melancholy senses, *1700*
With just one bright light shining through the dark:
He's coming. Certainly? Just this once more,
Then he will stay away—Who knows how long!
And only later—I must keep awake!

(Supporting her head on her hand. Enter the PRIEST *with the* TEMPLE WARDEN*)*

PRIEST

Then she will not come?

(The TEMPLE WARDEN *points silently to the resting girl. Walking up to her)*

Hero!

HERO *(Starting up)*

You, my friend? [40]

PRIEST

Yes, I, who am your friend.

HERO *(Standing up)*

Be welcome then!

PRIEST

I'm sorry you have had a wild-goose chase:[41]
Your parents' messenger, you doubtless know—

HERO

I know.

PRIEST

He brought some letters, they are lying
In your room up there—will you not fetch them? *1710*

HERO

Tomorrow I shall read them.

PRIEST

Not today?

HERO

Not now.

PRIEST

You are not keen to know how they may be?

[40] The dozing Hero had Leander in mind.

[41] Omitted in the Vienna and Munich editions. I have followed the Berlin Edition, which makes the already tarnished Priest less uncivil.

HERO

They left here only recently; they're well.

PRIEST

Are you so sure of this?

HERO

I am, good sir,
On testimony of a blessèd feeling
That flows through me, transfiguring all my being,
That all those dear to me are well and happy.

PRIEST

How often feelings err.

HERO

What never erred?
If left a choice, I'll choose the sweeter error.

PRIEST

Where is Ianthe?

HERO

She went in just now. *1720*

PRIEST

After what recently has taken place
She cannot linger longer in our house.

HERO

I told you, you are doing her an injustice.

PRIEST

But can you prove this?

HERO

This is my belief.

PRIEST

Based on a feeling too?

HERO

Yes, on a feeling.

PRIEST

I will have certainty, Ianthe goes.

HERO

Forgive me—but you know I must consent.
The girls are under the priestess' mandate,
I know my rights, just as I know my—
I know my right, sir.

PRIEST

As I know my duties; *1730*
You wanted to say that?

HERO

I wanted to,
And say it now; I know my duties too;
If this means everything a tranquil heart,
In harmony with itself and with the world,
Can set against the rights of other men.

PRIEST

And not against the gods' rights?

HERO

Let's not quibble!
Give yourself and your brother each his portion;
The gods are much too lofty for our poor rights.

PRIEST

You've mellowed.

HERO

Well, sir, though the sun may shine,
The moon too lets the herbs and grasses grow. *1740*

PRIEST

Since you insist so firmly on your rights,
I have to beg you now to pardon me
For having opened your mother's letter.

HERO

What's mine is also yours.

PRIEST

I should much like
You now to read this letter with a warning
It contains.

HERO

Certainly, I shall. Tomorrow.

PRIEST

No, no, today! If it were not too much,
I'd beg you fetch it now.

HERO

You're torturing me,
But that you may see— Is it not yet evening?

PRIEST

Almost.

HERO

I'll fetch the letter. *1750*

(With an expression of obligation)

So that you'll see how much I'm at your service.

(Exit into the tower)

PRIEST

My inmost heart is moved on seeing her!
So calm, so wise, such poise in everything,
And all the time I feel I must tell her:
Beware! Disaster yawns, a chasm by your side!
And yet she is too firm and too assured.
If she is given time and her bright mind
Comes up from the dark flood now swamping it,
If she alights on means of saving him,
Rescuing the culprit from our closing snares, *1760*
Then she is all the more, more surely lost.

Must she be guilty? If a dastard wretch
Boldly embarked on the impermissible—
Even if she, touched, as is the way of youth—

Must she herself, colluding, give the signals,
Herself light him the way to infamy?

(The lamp appears in the window of the tower)

What's that? The lamp is shining. Wretched girl,
It blazes both your punishment and guilt!

(Enter the TEMPLE WARDEN*)*

TEMPLE WARDEN

Do you see the light?

PRIEST

I do. You told the fishermen?

TEMPLE WARDEN

Yes, sir. As you have ordered, they'll not row *1770*
Tonight upon the sea, rough anyhow.

PRIEST

Then all the better! Follow me, she's coming.

(They withdraw to the left. Re-enter HERO *with a scroll)*

HERO

Here is your letter. Won't you take it? Oh!
Where has he disappeared? Well, he'll be back.

(She puts the letter in her girdle)

How sweet your rays, O lamp, my dearest friend!
It's still not night, and yet the only light
Illumining the noisy world around
Shines out from you, from you, sun of my night.
As on their mother's breast all creatures hang
Suckling your rays, in your circumference. *1780*

Here I will sit, and I will guard your light,
So that no envious wind may puff it out.
Here it is cool; warm, drowsy in the tower;
There the dull air weighs down upon my eyes;
But that must not be, I must keep awake.

(She sits)

They have tormented me the whole day long
With coming and with going. With intent!
But why? Why? Why? I do not know their purpose.[42]

(Her head on her hand)

No matter! When my brow will throb no more,
I shall perceive it. Then—shall also—if but— *1790*

(Starting up)

What's that? Who's there, I am alone. Only the wind
Blows gustier from the sea. Then all the better,
You'll bring my darling earlier to the shore.
The lamp's still shining bright. Who wants to dream?
Be up and merry, keeping love's sweet vigil.

(Supporting her head again on her hand)

On second thoughts, I would, he did not come.
Suspicions are aroused, they lurk and spy.
Were they to catch him—O compassionate gods!
Therefore, far better if he did not come.
Only, he wanted it, he begged, entreated. *1800*
Ah, he insists; then come, my sweet youth, come!
I will protect you, like the clucking hen
Guards her young brood, and none shall come near you,
No one but me alone, and not to harm,

[42] Grillparzer records in the manuscript of the play how the passion of love in a woman can make her oblivious to everything but the pursuit of her passion:

> In the fourth act, therefore, there is no trace of anxiety in Hero's mind, although it is fairly obvious to her that suspicions have been aroused. She is already back in the grip of emotion, but of a new emotion, that of a *woman*. Indeed in its grip, but greatly accentuated, sensual, all the demonic power that seizes women, making them totally oblivious, deaf and blind, when a true love has taken hold of their senses . . . Her thoughts are turned wholly on the newly aroused emotion and on its object, with no longer any fear of discovery, or for name or reputation. The Priest makes his suspicions all too clear to her, but she does not notice it. An approaching storm is mentioned; she nonetheless lights the lamp, sensually, as in a dream.

Preserve! Preserve! Ah me! How I am weary!
My foot hurts. Oh, will no one loose my shoe?

(She draws up a foot on the couch)

It pains me here, here. Has some gravel bruised me?

(Drawing up the other foot also in half-prostrate posture)

How pleasant it is! Night wind, come,
And cool my eyes and brow and burning cheeks!
You come across the sea, from him. *1810*
And, oh, your rustling and the whispering leaves
Sing in my ears: "we are from him, him, him, from
him."
Spread out your wings,[43] enfold them all around
My brow and head, my neck, my weary arms,
Embrace me tight, I bare my breast to you—
And if he comes, call out—Leander—you?

(Pause. Enter the TEMPLE WARDEN *on tiptoe, listening, behind him the* PRIEST, *who remains standing at the entrance to the tower)*

TEMPLE WARDEN *(Approaching* HERO*'s couch, with muffled voice)*

Hero! Asleep!

PRIEST

The light beams from the tower,
May the Gods' storm promptly put out your flame!

(Exit into the tower)

TEMPLE WARDEN

What is he hatching? I'm becoming frightened.
Had I said nothing—and yet how could I? *1820*
There, men are walking with their fishing nets.

(Approaching the right side)

What are you doing there? Were you not ordered

[43] She falls asleep dreaming of Leander as Leda's swan.

To stay far from the sea this restless night,
In the securely locked rooms of your huts?

(Coming back)

They think a storm is brewing. Rule, great Gods!

(Looking up at the tower)

The lamp is flickering. Himself! Poor girl,
Is she awaking? No. Does no dream warn you?

(The lamp goes out. HERO *moves as she sighs, and then sinks into a deep sleep. Her head slips from her hand and rests on her upper arm, while her lower arm hangs down loosely. It has become dark)*

I'm shuddering. I would I had my mantle!

(Reenter the PRIEST*)*

PRIEST

Who's speaking? You? Come with me! Night is falling,
And brooding over matters yet unborn. *1830*

(Going up to HERO*)*

Now, heavenly powers, you, execute your office!
The culprits are held down by sea and sleep;
And so your priest's work is accomplished now.[44]
The wood is piled up and the hatchet drawn,
I turn aside. Perform your sacrfice!

(He turns toward the exit)

Curtain

[44] It is precisely because his squalid work in this act cannot be held to be worthy of a true priest, such as Grillparzer seemed to portray in the first three acts, that the character of the Priest has been found wanting by audiences, right from the first performance, and in the considered opinion of Grillparzer himself. The reasons for this dichotomy are discussed in the Translator's Note preceding the play.

ACT V

SCENE I

Place: in front of HERO*'s tower, as at the end of the previous act. It is morning.*

When the curtain rises HERO *stands in the center of the stage, her head supported by her hand, staring straight in front. Enter* IANTHE.

IANTHE

Will you forever stand there, motionless,
Staring at *one* spot? Come into the woods;
The wind has spent itself, the sea grows calm.
But did you hear the roaring all last night?

HERO

Did I hear?

IANTHE

You were outside here, so long. *1840*
Though I at last did hear steps over me;
And yet no light was shining from your room.

HERO

No light! No light!

IANTHE

Some secret's torturing you.
If you confide, it's easier to bear.

HERO

If you've guessed something, must you still ask me?
I should have kept awake but fell asleep,
It was already night, the storm awoke me;
Around me all was black, the lamp extinguished;
I flew inside, my hair all loose and streaming
In the gale. No light! Nor help, nor consolation. *1850*
Dawn found me wailing loudly on my knees—
And yet; and yet! . . .

IANTHE

Poor friend!

HERO

Did you say "poor?"
And yet! Just see! How good the gracious gods!
I'd hardly slept when they put out the light.
At the first streak of daylight, I confirmed it,
With eyes all hot and dry, I checked the lamp:
Not even a hundredth part of oil was burnt,
The wick was scarcely blackened. It was clear,
I'd hardly fallen asleep when it went out.
How good the gracious gods! Had it been later *1860*

(Walking away from IANTHE, *to herself)*

My friend would have been in the raging sea,
And overtaken by the storm, be dead.
And thus he stayed at home, lured by no signal,
And so is safe, alive.

IANTHE

You seem so sure.

HERO

I am, for I'm alive. How good the gracious gods!
And where we erred, in spite of our provision,
They graciously obliterate with their finger,
Denying ruin its malicious pleasure.
But I will also, now and in the future,

Show childlike gratitude to them for this, *1870*
And will improve much that's not right and proper
And may appear displeasing in their sight;
Will be resolved in all things, for the gods
Are gracious to the bold, the resolute;
But now, my girl, go to the landing place!
See, if your eyes can reach the farther shore,
The blest beyond, where—look toward Abydos!
Just now I tried to do so from my tower,
But it was veiled in mist. Now it seems clear.
Would you?

(She sits down)

IANTHE

(Going to the background)

But look! The storm's torn down the shrub *1880*
That grows there at the foot of the tower and
Its scattered branches firmly bar my way.

HERO

Do raise the branches! Must you be so lazy?

IANTHE

But they are wet with rain.

(Brushing the ground with her foot)

There's wrack and seaweed
The sea cast up. Ugh! Mussels and bright baubles!
The storm is used to scattering the ruins
Of its rage here. The remnant of some cloth!
It is so heavy. Some weight from behind
Holds it fast to the ground—ah! it's a veil!
Almost exactly like the one you wear; *1890*
Both ends are fastened up in a slip-knot
Like a flag. Look! Perhaps you recognize it.
Were it not damp I'd roll it up and throw it.

HERO

Do cease your trifling, please, and raise the branches!

IANTHE

They are so heavy. Oh! My festive dress!
I think I can just hold them. Ah, they're slipping!
Do come yourself and help. I'll hold them. Look!

(She has grasped the branches hanging down on the ground and raised them. LEANDER *lies dead on the landing-place)*

HERO *(Standing up)*

I'm coming—what? A man! Leander—woe!

(Rushing back to the foreground)

Deceivers and deceived my wretched eyes!
Can it be really true?

IANTHE *(Who with difficulty looks backwards over the branches)*

Compassionate Gods! *1900*

(Enter the PRIEST *from the right)*

PRIEST

What lamentation breaks the morning calm?

HERO *(To* IANTHE*)*

Let fall the branches, quick!

*(*IANTHE *lets the branches fall; the corpse is covered.* HERO *going towards the* PRIEST *and trying to deny him the view of the background)*

My uncle, you?
About, so early? True, the day is fine.
We both just wanted—gladly, joyously—

(She falls to the ground, supported by IANTHE*)*

PRIEST

What had, has happened?

IANTHE *(Preoccupied with* HERO, *pointing to the shrub)*

O good sir, good sir!

PRIEST

Raise the branches, quick!

(This is done)

O you righteous Gods!
You've taken him. He fell through your own hands!

IANTHE *(Still holding the branches)*

Will none have pity? No assistance, help?

PRIEST

Stop that and come!

(While laying hold of her)

Do you hear? Now hold your tongue!
Should but one word escape of what you've learnt— *1910*

(Withdrawing from her and speaking loudly)

There is an unknown man, a foreigner,
Whose corpse the sea has cast upon our shore!
Our priestess there fell swooning at his body,
Because a man, a human being's dead.

(Enter the TEMPLE WARDEN *and several* SERVANTS *from the right)*

A dead man's lying on the shore. Go, lift him,
So that his friends may come and identify him.

*(*SERVANTS *go to the shrub)*

Not here. Around the tower. By the wharf, right.

(Exeunt SERVANTS *to the left. During the following, signs of their occupation may be perceived through the foliage. Eventually the shrub is raised and made fast, whereafter the place appears empty)*

TEMPLE WARDEN *(Softly)*

So it's—

Be silent!

PRIEST

TEMPLE WARDEN

But to tell you, sir:
The elder of those two young strangers, who
Are known to you, we found him on the shore, *1920*
Disconsolately searching for his friend.
The servants have detained him.

PRIEST

Lead him here.
If more than freedom he has forfeited,
I will restore it, if he takes home that.

(Exit the TEMPLE WARDEN *to the right. To* HERO, *who has got up with* IANTHE*'s help and walked a few steps to the foreground)*

Hero!

HERO

Who's calling?

PRIEST

I. Listen to me!

HERO *(Timidly looking backwards, to* IANTHE*)*

Where is he gone? Ianthe, where?

IANTHE

Ah, me!

PRIEST

Since it has happened—

HERO

Happened? No!

PRIEST

It has!
The Gods have borne aloud their bloody witness,
How great their anger and how grave your wrong,
So let us humbly take our punishment; *1930*
What's sacred must be wholly without stain,
May eternal silence bury what has happened.

HERO

I, bury all my bliss and all my ruin,
And criminally join with criminals?
I'll shout it out aloud through the wide world,
What I have suffered, what possessed, what lost,
What has befallen, how they have pursued me.
I'll loudly curse you, that the winds shall hear
And bear my curses to the gods' high throne.
You were the one who spread the wicked net *1940*
That I pulled tight, and so he was destroyed.
Where have you borne him off? . . . I'll go to him!

(Enter NAUKLEROS *led by the* TEMPLE WARDEN *and several* SERVANTS. *Exit the* WARDEN *immediately to the left)*

You, there, O youth! Do you come to seek your friend?
He lay there, dead! They're taking him away.

NAUKLEROS

Ah woe!

HERO

You wring your hands now it's too late?
You are astounded? Moan? Yes, slothful friend!
He threw himself into the roaring sea,
Protected by no helper, by no god,
And dead I found him lying on the shore.
And do you ask who did it? Look! That man! *1950*
And I, the maiden-priestess—are you wondering?
Menander's Hero,[45] I, we both have done this.
With cunning art he would not let me rest,
Denied me recreation and reflection;
And I, poor fool, became his tool and slept.
The storm arose, extinguishing the lamp,
Making the waters shudder to their depths,
While he swam on, unguided by a light:
The black clouds hung down low upon the sea,
The waves rose wickedly to meet the clouds, *1960*
The stars were blotted out, all round was night.

[45] Hero's father's name was Menander.

And he, my prince of swimmers and of love,
Found in the cosmos neither love nor pity.
He raised his eyes, beseeching, to the gods,
In vain! They did not hear—or were they sleeping? [46]
Then he sank, sank! Once more above the waves,
And then once more, so powerful was his passion,
But much too strong against him proved the league
Of foe and friend, of haters and belovèd:
In chasms yawned the sea and he was dead! *1970*
Oh, I will weep and weep and cut my veins,
And drown myself in seas of tears and blood
As deep as his, as horrible as his,
As deadly as the sea that's swallowed him!

NAUKLEROS

Leander! O my sweet and gentle friend!

HERO

Say he was everything: what now remains,
Is but a fleeting shadow, but a void.
His breath was the pure air, his eye the sun,
His limbs the quickening power of burgeoning nature:
His life was life itself: your life, my life, *1980*
The life of all the world. When we let it die,
We too all died with him. Come, slothful friend,
Come, let us march in our own funeral:
You have two garments, and your friend has none;
Give me your garment; we must bury him.

(NAUKLEROS *takes off his mantle, which* IANTHE *takes)*

But once more let me touch his gentle body,
His noble body, so full of warm life,
Suck wisdom and sweet comfort from his mouth.
Then—yes, what then?—To him!

(To the TEMPLE WARDEN, *who has come back)*

[46] Compare Elijah on Mount Carmel. First Kings, Chapter 18, Vs. 26–27.

Would you deny me?
I will go to my friend! Who'll stop me? You? *1990*

(She makes a violent gesture, then her head and arms sink down listlessly. IANTHE *would support her)*

Leave me! Murder is strong and I have killed him.

(Exit to the left)

PRIEST *(To* IANTHE*)*

Follow her!

(Exit IANTHE. *To* NAUKLEROS*)*

Stay, your life is forfeited.
Yet I'll restore it, if you take his body
Home, and be silent all your life. Did you come alone?

NAUKLEROS

Friends from the other shore have followed me.

PRIEST

Hold them ready— Where did you bear him off?

TEMPLE WARDEN

To the temple, sir.

PRIEST

Why to the temple? Speak!

TEMPLE WARDEN

Such is the custom.

PRIEST

If it's so, it's well!
We should pay heed to customs, they are good.[47]
And now to her! With her disturbance gone, *2000*
Time's healing balsam shall allay her wound.
Yes, this first passion smothered in the bud,

[47] This maxim illustrates one aspect of Grillparzer's own temperament in favor of conservation of the established order, whose tragic dissolution in the Austrian Empire he so clearly apprehended.

Preserves her heart beguiled from any second;
And henceforth sacred— Come with me! You follow.

(Exeunt all)

SCENE II

The inside of the temple.[48] *The center of the stage is veiled by a curtain hanging between pillars. On the right side of the foreground a statue of Eros, on whose arm a wreath hangs. Enter* MAIDENS *who occupy themselves with arranging sacrificial vessels and taking down festoons. Two of them approach the curtain.*

Enter IANTHE

IANTHE

Oh, leave her, do! Grant her a breathing space!
How she must mourn her good, belovèd friend.
She found the place where they had carried him,
Drawn to it by her instinct like the blind,
And fell upon her knees and wept aloud,
Trying in vain to bring him back to life 2010
With her breath's exhalation and her tears.
Then when he paid no heed, since he was dead,
She threw herself upon his pale cold body,
Covering with her breast his belovèd breast,
Her mouth upon his mouth, his hand in hers,
Since then her lamentations have been calmed.
But I am yet afraid, lest she might muster
Fresh strength for further clamor. Well, I'll never
Desire a lover, now or in the future;
True, to possess is sweet, but then to lose! 2020

[48] There are in this scene, as elsewhere in his Grecian plays, traces of the influence on Grillparzer of the last act of Zacharias Werner's *Wanda*.

(Enter from the right the PRIEST *with the* TEMPLE WARDEN *and* NAUKLEROS, *who is followed by several friends)*

PRIEST

Where is she?

IANTHE

There.

PRIEST

Draw up the curtain.

IANTHE

Sir!

PRIEST

Up, I say, up! And hold the people back.

(The curtain is drawn. The cella is seen, to which many broad steps lead up. LEANDER *lies right across on a low bier.* HERO *at some distance on the steps, half prostrate, supported by her right arm, looking intently, as if with curiosity, at the dead man)*

Hero!

HERO

Who's calling me?

PRIEST

I, come here!

HERO

Why?

(She stands up and goes to the foot of the bier, ever gazing at the dead man)

PRIEST

That stranger has been mourned enough already!
What are you doing there?

HERO

I'm thinking.

PRIEST

Thinking?

HERO *(Coming forward)*

What life is all about!
He was so young, so beautiful,
So brimming over with life's radiant fullness;
Now he lies cold and dead. I've tested it,
I laid his hand upon my throbbing breast 2030
And felt the cold stream to my very marrow,
In his stark eyes there was no pupil's sheen.
I'm shuddering. Alas!

PRIEST

My strong, good girl,
Once more my own dear child!

(To NAUKLEROS*)*

You, go up there!
Do you recognize your friend?

NAUKLEROS

It is, it was he.

PRIEST

Now come.

HERO

Why?

PRIEST

They'll be taking him away.

HERO

So soon?

PRIEST

It must be.

HERO

Where?

PRIEST

To his own homeland.

HERO

Give me a mantle.

PRIEST

Why?

HERO

To follow him.
What if he's dead, he still was my dear friend.
I'll dwell upon the shore where he will rest. *2040*

PRIEST

Impossible! Stay here!

HERO

Here?

PRIEST

Priestess, here!

HERO

Then see that he is buried on our shore—
Where he fell dead, and where in death he lay—
Here at the foot of my tower. And roses
And white lilies, drenched with dew,
Shall spring up where he lies.

PRIEST

That must not be.

HERO

What? Not?

PRIEST

It may not be.

HERO

It may not?

PRIEST *(Forcefully)*

No!

HERO

Well, I have learnt to adapt myself to force,
The gods have not willed it, so they've avenged it.
Bear him away! Farewell, my lovely youth! *2050*
How much I now should like to clasp your hand,
But I dare not, you are so icy cold!
As token and as pledge of our last parting,
Take this my wreath, the girdle I unloose
And put into your grave. You, noble image,
All that I was, that I possessed, you have,
Then take this token too, since all is yours.
And so adorned, farewell!

(Some men approach the body)

But halt, I say!
Are you so quick? I say, not yet, not yet!

(Going to the bier)

Never, in all my life, to see you, never! *2060*
You who were wandering in the robe of night
And cast your bright rays into my dark soul,
Made blossom everything that's rare and good,
Will you from here to some dark lonely spot
And shall my parched eyes never see you more?
The day will come and then the quiet night,
And spring and autumn, and long summer pleasures,
But never you, do you hear, Leander? Never!
Never, never, never, never! [49]

(Throwing herself down on the bier and hiding her head in the pillows)

NAUKLEROS

Have pity, sir!

[49] Compare Shakespeare's *King Lear* over the dead body of Cordelia:

> Why should a dog, a horse, a rat have life,
> And thou, no breath at all? Thou'lt come no more,
> Never, never, never, never, never!
>
> (Act V, scene iii)

PRIEST

I do have pity, 2070

Hence I must save her.

(Going up to HERO*)*

It's enough.

HERO *(Standing up with some assistance)*

Enough?

How do you mean, enough! What must I do?

He cannot stay, I must not go with him.

I will take counsel of my noble goddess.

Please, dear Ianthe, lead me to her throne;

Meanwhile, do not touch him.

(To NAUKLEROS*)*

You, promise me!

Give me your hand as pledge—you start? Of course!

Your friend did that to me! You are so warm.

How pleasant this! [50] It is so sweet to live!

But let that go! Now who will warm my hand? 2080

Ianthe, come! But draw the veil away

First from my eyes.

IANTHE

There's no veil on your head.

HERO

True!—Let me go!—And you, beware to touch him!

IANTHE *(Who has been holding* HERO, *to the* PRIEST*)*

Oh, sir! the frost of death is gripping her.

PRIEST

Of death and life, only the doctor knows.

[50] The dying Rudolf II of Hapsburg uses these same terms ("Wie wohl, wie gut!") when looking out of his window to give a farewell benediction to the city of Prague below (*Ein Bruderzwist in Hapsburg,* Act IV, V. 2408).

IANTHE *(Guiding* HERO*)*

Look!—Raise your foot!—You're tottering . . . here,
here!

*(*HERO *mounts the steps, led by* IANTHE. *A number of the* MAIDENS *follow her, placing themselves in a row running down on the right; the rest go on the left so that the bier is hidden by them)*

PRIEST *(Half aloud)*

Remove him in the meanwhile!

NAUKLEROS

Think!

PRIEST

It must be.

When she returns, let every trace be gone.
Your life's at stake.

NAUKLEROS

So be it!

(His companions go around from the back and take hold of the bier)

HERO *(Who, supported by* IANTHE, *has already reached the upper steps, calls out at the same moment, her face still turned toward the cella)*

Leander!

(Quickly turning round, throwing her head and arms aloft)

Leander!

IANTHE *(Enfolding her, to the bearers)*

Stop!

PRIEST

Go on!

IANTHE

She's slipping, falling. *2090*

Put it down quick! Her heart is beating fast.

PRIEST

Heartbeats betoken life, so double heartbeats
Mean double life. You there, take him away!
He, who's browbeaten by the sick, is no doctor.

(The corpse had been carried through the gate in the left background. The PRIEST *follows)*

IANTHE *(Kneeling by* HERO *on the steps)*

Is there no help, no succor here? She's dying!

(Gazing after the bearers)

It is already by the arch. Those who await him
Have come from the other side. Crowds and torches.
The outer gate is opened. Woe, it's shut
With a crack of thunder.[51] All's veiled in the dark.
They have him, hold him. He'll not come again. *2100*

*(*HERO, who until now has been half sitting, leaning against IANTHE*'s knee, slides down and lies on the steps)*

Hero! Alas! Who'll help the wretched girl?

PRIEST *(Reentering)*

They are taking him away, they're rowing fast.
And soon the sea shall part the baleful pair.

IANTHE *(Standing up after a pause and coming down)*

No sea is needed, death has equal power
To part or to unite. Then come and see!
This is how those who die look on this earth.

PRIEST

Is madness speaking? [52]

[51] Compare Goethe's *Iphigenie auf Tauris,* where Orestes says:

I hear the Furies march to Tartarus,
Slamming behind them fast the gates of bronze
With crack of distant thunder.
(Act III, Scene iii)

[52] The High Priest, who had foolishly been making light of Hero's condition with his "double heartbeats mean double life" (Vs. 2092–93), finds incredible Hero's "Liebestod," which Wagner was later to emulate in *Tristan.*

IANTHE

No, no, it is listening.
O wisest fool, behold your wisdom's work!

PRIEST

Were even her life at stake! I'd give mine too
To ward off evil. But it is not true. 2110

(He hurries up the steps, kneeling beside the prostrate HERO*)*

IANTHE

Please bid the men, who bear the youth away,
Outside to wait, their service is still needed.
Two bodies and one grave. Grant this to them!

(To the PRIEST *who is coming down the steps)*

What, man, you're going? You're deserting her?
But stay! One servant-girl demands her freedom;
I'm going home, back to my parents' hearth.

(Exit the PRIEST, *muffling himself)*

You leave in silence? May this silence smite you!

You, maidens, care for her as I did care;
I cannot bear it longer in your house.

*(*IANTHE *takes the wreath from the statue of Eros)*

Here, with her body bear this wreath away. 2120

(Throwing the wreath to the group preoccupied with HERO *and speaking to the statue)*

You promise much, and do you thus keep faith?

Curtain

THE END

About the Translator

SAMUEL SOLOMON was educated at Clifton College, Bristol, and at King's College, Cambridge, where he graduated in the Modern Language Tripos. In 1927 he published *Poems from East and West,* including translations from the French and German. After spending twenty years in the Indian Civil Service, Mr. Solomon returned to England to devote his full time to literary and political activity. He ran for the House of Commons as a Liberal candidate in 1959 and 1964.

Mr. Solomon has also translated Racine's *Théâtre Complet,* which he began in 1949 and finished in 1961. The publication of these plays in English, as well as Racine's prefaces to the plays, was the second translation of all of the plays into English, and the first complete translation of Racine's dramatic works in the twentieth century. These two volumes contain the only English translations of the *Théâtre Complet* with both plays and prefaces.

With his publication of seven of Corneille's plays in 1969 Mr. Solomon confirmed his position as one of the greatest interpreters of French classic theater.